THE WEST
IN THE HISTORY OF THE NATION

A READER

Volume Two: Since 1865

Edited by

William F. Deverell
California Institute of Technology

and

Anne F. Hyde
Colorado College

BEDFORD / ST. MARTIN'S   BOSTON • NEW YORK

For Bedford / St. Martin's

History Editor: Katherine E. Kurzman
Developmental Editor: Heidi L. Hood
Production Editor: Lori Chong Roncka
Production Supervisors: Cheryl Mamaril and Donna Peterson
Marketing Manager: Charles Cavaliere
Editorial Assistants: Gretchen Boger and Molly Kalkstein
Production Assistant: Helaine Denenberg
Copyeditor: Linda Leet Howe
Cover Design: Diana Coe / ko Design Studio
Cover Art: Newsmen Photograph First Atomic Test, 1958. CORBIS / Bettman.
Composition: G & S Typesetters, Inc.
Printing and Binding: Haddon Craftsmen, Inc.

President: Charles H. Christensen
Editorial Director: Joan E. Feinberg
Director of Editing, Design, and Production: Marcia Cohen
Managing Editor: Elizabeth M. Schaaf

Library of Congress Catalog Card Number: 99–65257

Manufactured in the United States of America.

4   3   2   1   0
f   e   d   c   b   a

For information, write: Bedford / St. Martin's, 75 Arlington Street, Boston, MA 02116
(617-399-4000)

ISBN: 0–312–19171–5 (Volume One)
         0–312–19211–8 (Volume Two)

Acknowledgments

[38] "Boulder Canyon Project Fatalities," excerpted from *Building Hoover Dam: An Oral History of the Great Depression* by Andrew J. Dunar and Dennis McBride. © 1993 by Andrew J. Dunar and Dennis McBride. Reprinted with the permission of Twayne Publishers, a Division of Macmillan Reference Library, Simon & Schuster.

PREFACE

*T*he *West in the History of the Nation* is intended for use in the U.S. history survey course, as well as in courses on the history of the American West. Like many survey readers, it is organized according to the topics that most teachers cover, from the earliest encounters between Europeans and Native Americans to the most recent political and social issues of our time. The readings are split into two volumes that overlap at the Reconstruction period.

But this is not a typical American history reader. To help students engage more fully in the study of the nation's past, we provide discussions and documents that make history more familiar and accessible. In every chapter, readings relate to local, regional, and western examples of national themes. Our aim is to show how the same historical forces that propelled such phenomena as the American Revolution, the expansion of slavery, the Civil War, Progressivism, and the Cold War were manifested on the frontier or in the West in unique ways. As the introduction states, we have gathered together a collection of documents that illustrates national events in regional settings but is also sensitive to the important distinctions between the American frontier and the American West. It is this feature that makes these two volumes as well-suited to courses on the West (or, for that matter, the frontier) as they are to courses addressing the whole sweep of American history.

We expect that this reader will be especially interesting to students and instructors at western colleges and universities. But we are also convinced that it will engage teachers and students in any region of the nation who are interested in the voices and topics often neglected in surveys of the American past. Each volume contains an introduction that discusses what we define as "the West" and why, followed by fifteen chapters organized around topics that form the standard fare in survey courses across the nation. Every chapter opens with an image (a photograph, a map, or a drawing) intended to draw students into the discussion that follows. Brief chapter introductions provide a national context for regional documents by connecting the selections to larger themes in American history and (in the "As you read" section) asking students to read the documents with particular questions or themes in mind. Each document is preceded by a brief background discussion on the source and its author, and specific questions invite students to compare the various selections. Finally, each chapter concludes with a brief bibliography of secondary sources, to which students may turn for further information.

The primary sources in *The West in the History of the Nation* are unusual in several ways. Throughout both volumes, we have aimed for a balance between well-known and lesser-known documents. We have also sought to balance the coverage of social and political history, and we are certain that the documents speak from many perspectives and with an array of voices. The West and the frontier have always been places of richly diverse human contact, and we have tried to do justice to that richness in these volumes. Here, students will find the testimony, viewpoints, and ideas of Native Americans and immigrants, the rich and the poor, African Americans and Latinos, men, women, and children. Finally, we have taken care to ensure that the documents are interesting, lively, and exciting. We hope they will form the basis of countless discussions, both in and out of the classroom.

We have deliberately used a broad conception of "the West" in creating this book, one that includes most of the states west of the Mississippi River: Washington, Oregon, California, Idaho, Nevada, Arizona, Utah, Montana, Wyoming, Colorado, New Mexico, North Dakota, South Dakota, Nebraska, Kansas, Oklahoma, and Texas. In Volume One we have also included frontier regions east of the arbitrary dividing line of the Mississippi, areas regarded as the West in earlier periods of the nation's history. Taken together, both volumes faithfully represent the complexity of the West across the whole of American history while reflecting the broader national experience.

Founded on a novel concept — that regional materials can lead to a fundamental understanding of national history — *The West in the History of the Nation* required a great deal of planning and organization, even a few false starts. As editors, we strove to create a new kind of reader, building each volume from the ground up and sometimes discarding what we had already put together. Throughout the process, we class-tested sections on our own students and conferred extensively with the editors at Bedford / St. Martin's. It took time and careful thought to settle on the concepts and presentation strategies that would best fit students and instructors, but we believe that the final arrangement of the reader will prove helpful in teaching American history to the nation's college students.

Acknowledgments

The completion of this book depended on the support, encouragement, and advice of a large group of people. We thank the library staff of the Center for Advanced Study in the Behavioral Sciences at Stanford, California, and especially

Jean Michel and Cynthia Moore, for their cheerful assistance in tracking down documents. At Colorado College, the Tutt Library staff and especially Heather Block, who made heroic efforts as a research assistant and master organizer, deserve our sincere applause.

The editorial staff of Bedford / St. Martin's helped us immeasurably, and without their persistence we would not have been able to produce this book. This project began over a glass of wine with Katherine Kurzman, and we appreciate her guidance and enthusiasm throughout the process. We moved into "high concept" with Chuck Christensen over lunch in Colorado Springs, and his support is gratefully acknowledged here, as is that of Joan Feinberg. Ellen Kuhl shepherded us through the project's early stages with humor and encouragement. At the production and copyediting stages, we were fortunate to be able to work with Lori Chong Roncka and Linda Leet Howe. We are grateful as well to others at B/SM, including Molly Kalkstein, Gretchen Boger, Elizabeth Schaaf, John Amburg, Sandy Schechter, and Helaine Denenberg. Our biggest thanks go to Heidi Hood, who tirelessly championed the project, supported our ideas, and offered countless good ones of her own.

Readers across the nation also helped make this a better book. The opportunity to "test drive" our ideas, our documents, and our organizational strategies was simply invaluable, and we would like to thank the squadron of readers who gave freely of their time and advice in support of the project: David Arnold, Columbia Basin College; Lucy Barber, University of California, Davis; Jolane Culhane, Western New Mexico University; Leonard Dinnerstein, University of Arizona; Lynn Dumenil, Occidental College; Jonathan Earle, University of Kansas; Keith Edgerton, Montana State University–Billings; Richard W. Etulain, University of New Mexico; Paul Harvey, University of Colorado–Colorado Springs; Ronald L. Hatzenbueler, Idaho State University; Jennifer Huntley-Smith, University of Nevada–Reno; Todd M. Kerstetter, Texas Christian University; William L. Lang, Portland State University; Norman D. Love, El Paso Community College; Dean May, University of Utah; C. Jonathan Moses, Flathead Valley Community College; Roger L. Nichols, University of Arizona; Carol O'Connor, Utah State University; J'Nell Pate, Tarrant County College; Kimberly K. Porter, University of North Dakota; Ronald Schultz, University of Wyoming; Michael L. Tate, University of Nebraska at Omaha; Michael Welsh, University of Northern Colorado.

Finally, we want to thank our families for their encouragement and support.

William Deverell, Pasadena, Calif.

Anne Hyde, Colorado Springs, Colo.

CONTENTS

CHAPTER THREE
URBANIZATION
WESTERN CITIES   47

CHAPTER FOUR
POPULISM
POLITICS AND PROTEST   69

CHAPTER THIRTEEN
THE VIETNAM ERA
A Divided West

CHAPTER FOURTEEN
THE 1970s AND 1980s
Environmental Debates in the West

CHAPTER FIFTEEN

CONTEMPORARY AMERICA
IMMIGRATION AND INTEGRATION 283

DEFINING THE WEST AND THE FRONTIER

This book, as its title reveals, is devoted to the West. But the West never has been, and never will be, an unchanging place easily identified by exact boundaries or shared cultures. The West is not an address; talking about "the West" is not like talking about "Manhattan." Definitions of the West have changed over time. In the first years of the European presence on the North American continent, "the West" included both Deerfield, Massachusetts, and Santa Fe, New Mexico. When politicians in the 1790s discussed the problems facing western farmers, they did not mean Kansas or California or Montana; they meant the colonial frontiers of Pennsylvania or Massachusetts or Kentucky. By the 1850s, however, California and Illinois were considered western states, and by 1865, when the Civil War ended, the West had become the region Americans have long since described as western.

Today, most Americans agree on the region that makes up the West. It includes Washington, Oregon, California, Idaho, Nevada, Arizona, Utah, Montana, Wyoming, Colorado, New Mexico, North Dakota, South Dakota, Nebraska, Kansas, Oklahoma, and Texas. The precise borders of this region, however, are often debated. People disagree, for instance, about where the Midwest ends and the West begins and about whether aridity, river systems, and mountains define the region. Is Texas, for example, more a part of the West or of the South? Is the heavily populated and well-watered Pacific Northwest "western"? Despite such interesting problems of definition, there does seem to be some general agreement that most of the states west of the Mississippi River can be considered part of the West.

The regional West is further complicated by the concept of the "frontier." Popular culture and many historians have identified this concept as a crucial component of the West, but in academic circles the frontier remains a hotly debated topic (some historians call it the "f-word"). The historian Frederick Jackson Turner is the most famous scholar to grapple with the concept of the frontier. In an extraordinarily influential essay written in 1893, Turner defined the frontier as a continuous line of national expansion moving ever westward over time, across the Appalachians, the Alleghenies, the Rockies, and then on to the Pacific Coast. And, Turner argued further that this line, where Euro-Americans and Indians met, proved to be the founding place of American democracy and national character. Most historians today fault Turner's vision, powerful though it was, as too simplistic. The frontier did not move in a predictable east-to-west fashion. Cities like Denver and San Francisco emerged and became fully urbanized long before places far to their east had even been settled. Nor did the frontier simply roll over Indian peoples; it changed them, but they continue to play a crucial role in the region as members of powerful tribal nations who own land and resources. In spite of this, Turner's definition of the frontier left an indelible imprint linking the frontier and the West together.

Most historians now see frontiers as zones of encounter that can be found in many different places. These frontier zones, where different groups of people, empires, and societies meet and interact (both peacefully and violently), are often, but not always, found in the West. These frontiers have not moved in straightforward geographic or chronological ways but are a continental phenomenon. This definition of the frontier can just as easily be used to describe the backcountry of colonial New England as it can to describe Indian country on the Great Plains following the Civil War. It can also be argued that a set of new frontiers is emerging today along the Pacific Coast, where Anglo Americans, Mexican Americans, Asian Americans, and an array of new immigrants are negotiating a new culture.

If we were to separate the West from the frontier, this book would not represent a real engagement with the past. Because the West encompasses a now familiar geographic region as well as a collection of places that have been considered the frontier, this collection includes selections from both. We examine the violence that erupted on the "Indian frontier" of the 1860s and 1870s, for instance, where soldiers and settlers clashed with Native Americans attempting to maintain their traditional cultures on lands which Americans coveted. Our journey through the West includes places such as Denver, Salt Lake, and San Francisco, cities which began to grow in the middle of the nineteenth century. As western places, they shared much in common, yet they each had specific identities, as the various documents and images reproduced here show. Throughout the twentieth century, the West continued to face all the national problems and promises faced by other regions in the United States. Westerners grappled with world wars, social upheavals, environmental challenges, and economic downturns. Yet, as this volume's selections illustrate, the West was, and is, more than a subset of the nation. This volume's wide array of sources allow you to see how the West is different from other parts of the nation, in its problems and its problem-solving.

Sometime in the nineteenth century, our modern notion of the West emerged out of the frontier. This volume takes up that transition from the years just following the conclusion of the Civil War. The rich assortment of documents and images in this volume will allow you a unique vantage point from which to examine both the history of the American West and the history of the United States.

THE WEST

IN THE HISTORY OF THE NATION

Ho for Kansas!

Brethren, Friends, & Fellow Citizens:

I feel thankful to inform you that the

REAL ESTATE

AND

Homestead   Association,

Will Leave Here the

15th of April, 1878,

In pursuit of Homes in the Southwestern
Lands of America, at Transportation
Rates, cheaper than ever
was known before.

For full information inquire of

Benj. Singleton, better known as old Pap,

NO. 5 NORTH FRONT STREET.

Beware of Speculators and Adventurers, as it is a dangerous thing
to fall in their hands.

Nashville, Tenn., March 18, 1878.

CHAPTER ONE

RECONSTRUCTION

NEW LIVES IN THE WEST

Robert E. Lee's surrender at Appomattox brought to an end the bloodiest chapter of the Civil War, but it resolved neither the profound tensions in American society between the North and the South nor those between whites and blacks. How could it? Such fault lines went deep into the nation's political, cultural, and economic past. Postwar Reconstruction, the tumultuous period during which the conquered South was reinstated into the Union, revealed just how fractured the country remained after four years of killing. At first the victorious North attempted to rebuild, or reconstruct, the South along new lines of authority and civil rights for recently freed slaves. But after hardly more than a decade, the North abandoned the South, content to let the former states of the Confederacy reconstruct themselves.

As Americans tried to piece their lives together in the aftermath of the Civil War, many turned to the American West for a chance at a new life. New opportunities beckoned, from the Great Plains all the way to the Pacific. European immigrants and Mormon converts, Northerners and Southerners went west in greater and greater numbers. The federal government played a central role in this process by aggressively taking up arms against native peoples; passing legislation that opened public lands to settlement by farmers, ranchers, and town builders; and sponsoring massive public works projects that reshaped the landscape. None

---

African American Migration to Kansas, 1878 (left)

This flyer announces preparations for westward migration at the end of Reconstruction in the late 1870s. As the federal government pulled out of the South, thousands of former slaves looked to the West as an escape from economic obstacles, terrible memories, and constant danger of violence from whites. The West, especially Kansas, began to resemble the Promised Land, at least in the dreams of many of those eager to test their new freedom. How would you sum up the feelings embedded in this flyer? Does it give you any sense of life in the South, the life that so many African Americans wished to escape?

Library of Congress.

of these projects was more important than the first cross-country railroad. Heavily subsidized by federal grants, the transcontinental railroad was completed in the spring of 1869. Soon, additional rail lines created a vast transportation network stretching across the continent.

As the North began to relax its enforcement of the Fourteenth and Fifteenth Amendments, which granted citizenship to freed slaves and the right to vote to all male citizens over twenty-one, in the South, the West began to look increasingly attractive to another group of newcomers: freed slaves. Although the vast majority of the former slaves who left the South after the Civil War went to northern cities, which were undergoing rapid industrialization, some thousands of these new citizens also gazed west. One significant group, comprising as many as twenty thousand people, viewed the West in religious terms, equating it (or parts of it) with the biblical Promised Land. In the late 1870s, former slaves moved almost spontaneously onto the prairies of the nation's heartland and established small farming colonies. They took to calling themselves "Exodusters," because they felt a religious and experiential kinship with the ancient Israelites and their exodus into the Sinai desert.

Despite the religious fervor of these new farming communities, African Americans would discover the West to be far from idyllic. Finding homes where they could live and work free of the shadow of former slaveholders might have been salvation enough. Unfortunately, however, the South did not hold a monopoly on racism; many African Americans found their paths in the West blocked by prejudices that were often as entrenched and as ugly as any they had faced in the South. While black emigrants carved out new lives in the broad fields of the Kansas plains, they faced fresh torment at the hands of white westerners who attacked them and destroyed their property. Some of these attackers were no doubt members of the Ku Klux Klan, the extremist band made up of former Confederate soldiers that continued to wage the Civil War through its violence against African Americans. Ex-slaves who migrated to cities like Denver, San Francisco, and Seattle faced similar obstacles and disappointments.

Other places and jobs also beckoned African Americans. Black cowboys found their labor and their horsemanship skills in demand out west. Black soldiers, many of whom had served with distinction in the Union army at the close of the Civil War, continued to serve in segregated units in the American West throughout the remainder of the century, often posted to Indian territory. Two thousand African American soldiers fought in the U.S. army against native peoples in the West throughout the latter decades of the nineteenth century. The irony of life in the post–Civil War West is that African American soldiers, often denied civil rights because of their race, appeared more patriotic, more American in the eyes of the nation by helping to subdue and destroy the first Americans. "Buffalo soldiers," as they were called by Native Americans who thought their hair resembled the dense coat of the bison, fought in skirmishes and full-scale battles and guarded Native American prisoners over a large area from the eastern Great Plains, west into Utah, and south to the Mexican border.

Reconstruction replaced the struggle of the Civil War with a new kind of struggle. Although the South, with four million freed slaves, felt the impact of the peace more than any other region, the West was also affected. The documents in this chapter offer several views of life in the post–Civil War West. From testimony about the Exodusters and other black emigrants to a journalist's report on the migrations to the autobiographical account of an ex-slave-turned-cowboy, each document reveals the hopes, dreams, and realities of the Reconstruction era.

As you read the selections in this chapter, keep in mind the ways in which, by fostering dreams about freedom or adventure or even great wealth, the West provided hope to people who survived the Civil War. To what extent were their expectations met? How did the region allow the tensions of the Civil War to continue? How did the legacy of the Civil War affect politics and society in the West?

1. ACCOUNTS OF THE EXODUS TO KANSAS

In the political turmoil of Reconstruction, Republicans and Democrats traded charges and countercharges about the treatment of recently freed slaves in the North, South, and West. Democrats claimed that Republicans urged African Americans to migrate out of the South solely to create a Republican majority in the western regions. Republicans responded that freed people moved to places like Kansas only because they had suffered violence and oppression in the former states of the Confederacy. In 1879, Congress initiated an investigation of the causes of African American migration. In hearing after hearing, senators interrogated whites and blacks alike about conditions in places like Louisiana, Indiana, and Kansas. The following document excerpts the testimony of four African American witnesses. Best-known among these witnesses was former slave Benjamin "Pap" Singleton, who had played an instrumental role in urging "Brethren, Friends, & Fellow Citizens" to leave the South for the West since the end of the Civil War (see the flyer reprinted on p. 2). His efforts led to the founding of a number of African American colonies in the years prior to the "Exoduster" movement of the late 1870s. H. Ruby, B. F. Watson, and John Milton Brown offer their thoughts and perspectives on such things as the destitution of Exoduster emigrants, the lure of the West as a land of

freedom, and the failed dreams of emigrants to Texas. How do Reconstruction politics come to light in these testimonies? In what ways were the people of the West
still fighting the Civil War?

BENJAMIN SINGLETON, H. RUBY,
B. F. WATSON, AND JOHN MILTON BROWN
Testimony before the U.S. Senate
1879–1880

[Topeka, Kansas, June 25, 1879]

[BENJAMIN SINGLETON (colored) sworn and examined. . . .]

Q[*uestion*]. Mr. Singleton, you say there is no party spirit in this movement
of emigrants to Kansas? — A[*nswer*]. Well, there was not; I have always been a
Grant man myself.

Q. Among these people out there in Kansas, who are helping it on, are there
any Democrats? — A. In Kansas?

Q. Yes. — A. Let me tell you, as a positive man, I don't know nothing much
about the committee; but let me tell you, right now, one thing, in behalf of my
colonies, that the Democrats are just as good to my people there as anybody else.

Q. O, yes, as kind to you personally; but are any of these people in the societies there that are formed to encourage this emigration of your people and pay
their way and get them out of their Southern homes — are any of these Democrats? — A. Just let me tell you right now that I don't know of any white people
there that is encouraging this emigration. . . .

Q. The Kansas Relief Association that is organized for the purpose of aiding
emigrants to come out there I am referring to; is there anybody connected with
that, either as a member or officer, who is a Democrat? — A. Not that I know, sir;
I don't know, sir, about that.

Q. Well, are any of these branch relief associations there conducted by
Democrats? — A. I don't know, sir, at all; if I knew I would tell you.

Q. As far as you know they are conducted by Republicans? — A. As far as I
know, I suppose they are. You ask me for facts, and I carry them with me to give
to the people.

Q. You carry only the facts with you to give to the people. Well, that is
right. — A. My people that I carried to Kansas ever since 1869 have generally, sir,
come on our own resources, and generally went on our own workings. We have
tried to make people of ourselves. I tell you to-day, sir, this committee is outside

"Report and Testimony of the Select Committee of the United States Senate to Investigate the Causes
of the Removal of the Negroes from the Southern States to the Northern States," 46th Cong., 2nd sess.,
1879, S. Rept. 693, Part II: 338–39, 343, 346, 351, 364; Part III: 389–91, 413–14, 416–18, 425–26.

of me, for I don't know nothing about it hardly; my people depends upon their own resources.

Q. Then you don't know anything about bulldozing[1] in Mississippi and Louisiana? — A. Didn't I tell you I have never been there?

Q. But you talked very hard about them — called them scoundrels, rascals, and so on? — A. I have heard about it, and if the men there bulldozes and wears these false-faces, they ain't nothing else but what I called them; they ain't right, nohow.

Q. Do you believe it? — A. It is the proof of fifty or sixty thousand of them, and it occurs to me that every one of them can't lie about it.

Q. But it is all hearsay with you? — A. I told you I have not seen it myself. You don't think fifty or sixty thousand of them could all tell a lie, do you — you don't think they are all cheating?

Q. O, yes; there are instances where whole nations have lied. — A. Well, mebbe these have lied. I know what I have seen. I have seen women and children in wagons and teams come in, and they said they was run in by the Kuklux[2] into Nashville, and the Democrats have housed them there and given them victuals, and administered to them and cared for them; I have seen that.

Q. Well, that is clever. — A. I am a man of realities; I am a man that will live in a country where I am going to cope with the white man, where the white man will lift himself to the level of justice; but when the white man will think that equal rights under the law to the colored man is a violation of his (the white man's) dignity, then I am going to leave. Suppose now that out in the country there the colored man goes to law to get his contract carried out with a white man; if the Democrats don't say anything, there is a lot of men there that will go around and run that black man out of the country because he took that gentleman up to the law; and suppose he beats that gentleman; why, it is a violation of his dignity, they think, and they won't stand it. . . .

Q. I say, did you never hear the Republican speakers tell the colored people that they would be put back into slavery if the Democrats got into power, and if they did not vote against the Democrats? — A. I have heard something about that.

Q. What have you heard? — A. Well, these threats I have heard myself — I have heard the Democrats stand right up, that is, when the colored man was getting the rights of suffrage, and say, "You damned niggers, we've got you now, and we don't ask you for your suffrage, we don't care for it." Well, that was a chill on them. And there is another thing —

Q. But what was the threat? I don't see what your meaning is. — A. Why, that's threat enough; "You damned niggers, we've got you now."

Q. You called that a threat, did you? — A. Yes; that was enough to scare us.

Q. Did that scare your people? — A. Well, that scared *me*. Then there's another thing. They have got up and looked up in these upper galleries, you know,

---

[1] **bulldozing:** Intimidation of African Americans by whites through violence or other means, particularly to prevent or discourage African Americans from voting.

[2] **Kuklux:** Shorthand reference to the Ku Klux Klan, a secret organization of whites founded after the Civil War to reassert white supremacy. Congress outlawed the Ku Klux Klan in 1871.

where they see these stacks of arms, and they ask, "What are those stacks of arms put up there for?" And they tell them, "They are not for *you*," and they keep wondering what they are there for and that excites us, and makes us want to get away.

Q. Well, you are scared without cause; "The wicked flee when no man pursueth." — A. Mebbe that's it. . . .

[Washington, D.C., April 22, 1880]

H. RUBY (colored) sworn and examined. . . .

Question. Please state where you live, Mr. Ruby. — *Answer.* I am residing in Kansas.

Q. At what point? — A. Oswego, Southern Kansas.

Q. Where has been your home for the past few years? — A. For the last ten years I have lived in Texas.

Q. What part of Texas? — A. From the county of Galveston to as high up as McLennan County.

Q. Where were you born? — A. I was born in New York City.

Q. Did you come from New York to Texas? — A. I went from Central America to Texas.

Q. Did you emigrate from Texas to Kansas? — A. Yes, sir.

Q. Did any others go with you? — A. Yes, sir; ten families went when I did.

Q. You had some reason for going, I suppose; what was it? — A. Well, sir, last July there was a colored man's conference held at Houston, and I was a delegate from my county. The county delegation from my district elected me as a commissioner of emigration; and these colored men that wanted to leave got me to go and pick out locations for them.

Q. You attended the convention at Houston? — A. Yes, sir.

Q. What was the desire among these people to emigrate? — A. The call for the convention was issued the 20th of May, and in the call it was stated that it was a convention for the colored men to take into consideration the religious, political, and educational interests of their race.

Q. Were any complaints made at that convention as to their treatment in Texas? — A. Yes, sir; a majority of the delegates claimed that there were reasons for leaving; and the idea was to impress on the people to get away from there on account of the obnoxious laws of the State.

Q. What features of the laws did they complain of? — A. They complained of this law making qualifications for jurors — that they must be freeholders and know how to read and write.

Q. That is to say, they must own lands? — A. Yes, sir; be a freeholder or householder; then they also complained of the inefficiency of the school law.

Q. Does that jury law apply to whites and blacks alike? — A. Yes, sir; the colored men rent houses and lands but they are not freeholders.

Q. Were there any complaints? — A. Well, they go on to complain that as they did not put the colored man on the juries a good many of them were prosecuted wrongfully and convicted because the white people did not like the blacks. . . .

Q. Do you know anything of the Skull Creek colony?[3] — A. Yes, sir; it is west of Columbus and was established about six years ago. There have been several established in Texas but they have been broken up. The only one I know in operation is at Fort Bend County, in the Senegambian settlements. This Skull Creek colony was composed of some of the best people in these counties. They went there thirty or forty years ago, but last June a crowd of men went down there and killed one of the leading men as he was coming from town with his cotton money and groceries. The people heard the reports of the guns and went out and found him riddled with buckshot and one of his mules gone. They made all kinds of threats against them, and when they could not run them out that way they put up placards telling them to "leave this neck of timber or we will make you."

Q. These placards were addressed to whom? — A. To the colored people of that colony.

Q. What was the result? — A. Some of the young men said they would not go away, but a few weeks afterwards they had to go; their fences were burned and so were their cotton houses and cribs;[4] they were all burned in that colony except two houses, one belonging to a poor white person and another one in which a white man lived.

Q. How many were there in that colony before that? — A. There were twelve families, I think. The only drawback and the fault we find in Texas is that we do not know whether we are safe when we get a homestead. That is what some of them complained of from Lee County.

Q. Tell us what you know about that. — A. In that case even the good people around Giddings say that the outrages were uncalled for. They say that the cowboys went in there and killed these people at that place.

Q. How many people were there living there? — [A.] There were two hundred and fifty or three hundred living there, but they broke up the colony and went back on the farms where they were before. . . .

Q. What about the treatment of colored women down there? — A. That is one of the main grievances of the colored people, and causes of their going out of the South. Another of the main wants of the colored people is education for their children, and in leaving the South they are actuated by the same motives that the colonists were actuated by one hundred years ago. They do not say to the white people, "we will fight you," but they say, "we will leave you." They have to talk up for themselves, or else be like the Indian and be driven from the country. And that which you spoke of is one of the great troubles that is causing them to leave the South. They say that their daughters and mothers and wives are not safe; that they are liable to be insulted at any time, and if a colored man talks up for his family, he is either shot down or taken out at night and bushwhacked or killed. I have talked with them about it, and I have said that if I had any women-folks, and they were insulted, they would have to kill me before I would stand it. But they said to me, "if you lived down there, you have got to take what we give you."

---

[3] **Skull Creek colony:** An African American colony founded in Texas in the early 1870s.
[4] **cribs:** Storage bins or containers for corn and grain.

I lived ten years among them and did take a good deal. The fact is, the colored people must leave there because of their want of education and of protection for their women, and if a man wants to stay, and buys lots, he pays for the lot four times before he owns it.

Q. Is there much political trouble down there on account of your people now? — A. No, sir; not now. They have devices now for keeping the men from voting. It is a kind of bulldozing the same as they have in the North. Sometimes they deceive them by saying that the day of election is changed, or that the next day after the real day is the day of election, and many times the colored people are fooled in that way. . . .

Q. I do not suppose your race expects or wants the Government of the United States to elevate you over the heads of the whites — only to give you a fair chance? — A. That is all we want.

Q. In the matter of schools you say you have a fair chance, the same as the whites? — A. Yes, sir.

Q. Will you get any advantage over the whites, when you go to Kansas? — A. No, sir.

Q. Will you not have some disadvantages there? — A. I do not know.

Q. Do you not know that the constitution of the State of Kansas says that black men shall not vote? — A. Vote how?

Q. At the ballot-box. The word "white" is used in the constitution of Kansas, in describing the qualification of voters. — A. You have asked me a great many questions, now I would like to ask you one: Admitting that the constitution of Kansas does say that, does not the Constitution of these United States say that all men are born free and equal, endowed by —

Q. No, the Constitution of the United States does not say that; that is in the Declaration of Independence; it was Thomas Jefferson, a slaveholder, who said that. — A. Well, notwithstanding that was put in there, has not our race been hewers of wood and drawers of water for the white race for two hundred years, up till the time of the surrender?

Q. Yes; and since then you have been hewers of wood and drawers of water for the Radical party.[5] — A. I don't allow that; I never let the radical party use me for a monkey to pull their chestnuts of [sic] the fire. . . .

[Washington, Friday, March 26, 1880]

B. F. WATSON (colored) sworn and examined.

Question. State your place of residence. — Answer. Kansas City, Mo.

Q. How long have you resided there? — A. Since November, 1878.

Q. Where did you reside prior to that? — A. In Omaha, Nebr.

---

[5] **Radical party:** A reference to the Radical Republicans, a wing of the Republican Party in that era. Radical Republicans designed much of the Reconstruction policies implemented after the Civil War, and they bitterly opposed the more moderate plans of Abraham Lincoln and his successor, Andrew Johnson.

Q. Were you born in Omaha? — A. No, sir; I am a minister by profession, and we receive our appointments at various parts from year to year.

Q. What is your native place? — A. The State of Missouri.

Q. To come to the point itself, what, if anything, have you had to do with assisting the emigrants who have come to Kansas, or to Missouri, from the Southern States? — A. I have been caring for them since last March, in the way of supplying them with food and clothing, and shipping them to Kansas, Nebraska, and Iowa.

Q. From Kansas City? — A. Yes, sir.

Q. In what capacity have you performed that labor? Has it been in connection with any society? — A. We organized a society in Kansas City last spring, but since its first meeting the society has not tried to do anything. Mr. Armor, one of our bankers, raised a fund of $2,000 in Chicago, and requested me to see to its use. There was no committee about it.

Q. Have you seen any considerable number of these emigrants? — A. I have shipped from May to the last of August about 2,500 of them, and have their names.

Q. Where did they come from? — A. From Mississippi and Louisiana. They arrived at Saint Louis and took the boat for Kansas City, and I would meet them there, and send them out to different places.

Q. Was there any money raised to help them except the amount that you speak of? — A. No, sir; not by me.

Q. How was that raised? — A. On hearing of the suffering of those parties who were arriving there at Wyandotte, Mrs. Armor went there, and her brother, who has a packing-house in Chicago, on her solicitation, went out and raised $2,000 for them. They seemed to be so destitute that Mr. Armor thought they had better try to relieve their suffering.

Q. Do you know whether any number of these people have found places? — A. Generally they have; the most of them that we sent to Topeka. More than two hundred were sent to Nebraska, and I have letters from Nebraska and Colorado and as far east as Illinois.

Q. From whom were those letters? — A. They were from people who desired this kind of labor.

Q. How many applications have you of that kind? — A. Four or five hundred still pending.

Q. Not supplied? — A. Not supplied.

Q. Have you had any before, that you have supplied? — A. Yes, sir; a great number.

Q. From all you know, is there a great demand for this kind of labor? — A. Yes, sir; throughout Missouri they want a good many, but they don't desire to stop there.

Q. Why not? — A. Because it has been a slave State, and they want to get to Kansas.

Q. What do you know of any political burdens that are moving them in their coming there? — A. I have conversed with a good many of them, but some of them give that as a reason. . . .

Q. What stories did they tell? — A. Various stories; generally, that their lives were insecure; that they had no chance for making a living; that no protection was given them in the South, and that many of them had to run away, the same as they did before the war, when they would slip out at night and make for the free States. A man by the name of George Washington, from Louisiana, told me that when he started from home he had to leave at twelve o'clock at night and carry his budget[6] on his head to the river, and that then they were followed, but having met up with their crowd of friends they managed to protect themselves. A good many of them stopped on the banks of the river for many weeks before they could get a boat to take them up the river. Many of those from Mississippi stated that they had no trouble in their section, but that they were having it all around them and they did not know when it would come to them. Last summer I assisted an excursion from Kansas City to Topeka, made up of bulldozers[7] and colored people who came from Canton to Topeka. I saw a man by the name of Matthews, from Copiah County, and a man by the name of Bunch, from Yazoo; they were white men. They had heard that the bones of these colored people were bleaching on the fields out there, and they brought some of the colored people to see the sight and go back home and tell the news.

Q. What do you say was the object of that excursion? — A. It was to disgust these representative colored men, and to show them how badly they were treated in Kansas. They had been told that they were doing well out there, and they wanted to show them the bones of their fellow men who had come ahead. They came back and told me that if I saw any of these colored people who wanted to go back to Mississippi they could come free of charge. There was an agent in Kansas City all last summer to furnish transportation and provisions to those who wanted to go back. . . .

Q. These colored people have heard of John Brown and Kansas before? — A. Yes, sir; and they know more about Kansas than any other State. They know that it is the land of freedom.

Q. And it is a land of freedom they are looking for? — A. Yes, sir; and it is not only from the South that they are coming but from counties in Missouri also. . . .

Q. You spoke also of a man named George Washington, from Louisiana, who had to run away in order to get to Kansas. — A. Yes, sir.

Q. What part of Louisiana did he come from? — A. I cannot tell without my book here. I put down the names of persons, but I remember him because I nicknamed him "President," and he told me how he would have to go through swamps twenty-five miles to get to the river and the boat in order to get away.

Q. Do you think that these people were being killed down there for coming away? — A. Yes, sir.

Q. Do you think that the white people loved them so much that rather than see them go away they preferred to kill them? — A. Yes, sir; rather than for them to leave there.

---

[6]**budget:** Leather pouch.
[7]**bulldozers:** See footnote 1 on p. 7.

Q. You say they all told you that their lives were insecure and their political privileges denied them, and that they were leaving the South on that account? — A. Yes, sir.

Q. And you gave an opinion that the exodus would not stop until the people wiped out their miserable laws down there? — A. Yes, sir. I understand they are trying to pass a law in Mississippi — whether they did or not I do not know, but they had in other States — that no meeting of the colored people for the purpose of emigration shall be held, and that the leaders of them should be punished. . . .

[Washington, Friday, March 26, 1880]

JOHN MILTON BROWN (colored) sworn and examined. . . .

Q. Then the cold weather of Kansas, their exposure to storms, their sufferings from destitution, and all that, they prefer to endure rather than what they left behind them in the South? — A. Yes, sir; they love the Southern soil; they enjoy its climate; but it is the greatest horror of their lives to mention the idea of their going back there to suffer what they have suffered in the past. They will not go back. They will die first.

Q. What is your idea, from the communication and intercourse that you have had with these colored men, who have come into Kansas since this exodus commenced, of the probable future of the movement? — A. I think it will increase rapidly all the time, unless speedy action is taken on the part of the white people of the South. If the Southern white people would give the colored people there the same rights and the same treatment which they receive in Kansas, they could stop the whole thing inside of six months.

Q. Other things being equal, that is, if given the same rights and privileges and protection in the one place as in the other, where would the colored people prefer to live, in Kansas or in the South? — A. I never yet met a colored man or woman but what said they would rather live in the South, two to one, than in Kansas, if they could have the same rights there that they have in Kansas.

Q. In your opinion, then, the only remedy for the exodus is different treatment of the colored people by the white people of the South? — A. It rests in the hands of the Southern white people altogether.

Q. What, in your belief, will be the extent of the exodus if that treatment is not changed? — A. It will continue to go on for the next twenty years, and until all, or a very large majority, of the colored people get out of the South. They will go to the Indian Territory,[8] which from present appearances will before long be opened up to white immigration; they will go to other Western States besides Kansas, and to the Western Territories; they will be scattered all over the Northern States. . . .

[8] **Indian Territory:** Territory set aside by the U.S. government in the early nineteenth century as home for the so-called Five Civilized Tribes — Choctaw, Creek, Seminole, Cherokee, and Chickasaw — who were moved there in the period 1820–1840. Following the Civil War, the western portion of the Indian Territory was given over to other tribes moved there. Indian Territory was eventually absorbed into Oklahoma. Brown's discussion here is ironic, since the Five Civilized Tribes adopted slavery and joined the Confederacy during the Civil War.

2. A NATIONAL MAGAZINE'S REPORT OF AFRICAN AMERICAN MIGRATION

African American migration from the postwar South to the North and the West intrigued the nation's press. This article, published in the well-known popular magazine Scribner's Monthly, *is an apt example of the nation's interest in the Exoduster campaign, which, given its religious overtones, was all the more intriguing. Henry King's essay tempers descriptions of the Exodusters and their arrival in Kansas with his own opinions about the movement, the place of African Americans in the West, and the health of the nation after the long years of war. How does the author describe the conditions of the Exoduster emigrants on their arrival in Kansas? How do these descriptions compare with those in the congressional testimony in the previous selections? What observations does King make about the reception these emigrants received?*

HENRY KING
"A Year of the Exodus in Kansas"
1880

One morning in April, 1879, a Missouri River Steamboat arrived at Wyandotte, Kansas, and discharged a load of colored men, women and children, with divers[1] barrels, boxes and bundles of household effects. It was a novel, picturesque, pathetic sight. They were of all ages and sizes, and every modulation of duskiness, these new comers; their garments were incredibly patched and tattered, stretched and uncertain; their "plunder," as they called it, resembled the litter of a neglected back-yard; and there was not probably a dollar in money in the pockets of the entire party. The wind was eager, and they stood upon the wharf shivering; and when the boat backed away, a sort of dumb awe seemed to settle upon and possess them. They looked like persons coming out of a dream. And, indeed, such they were, in more than casual fancy; for this was the advance-guard of the Exodus.

Soon other and similar parties came by the same route, and still others, until, within a fortnight, a thousand or more of them were gathered there at the gateway of Kansas — all poor, some sick, and none with a plan of future action beyond the abstract, indefinite purpose somehow to find new homes. There was an element of wonder in the matter, which the hungry and undecided creatures themselves could not explain; they appeared to be as much surprised at being there as others were at seeing them there. They had not quitted the South because they

---

[1] **divers:** Various.

Scribner's Monthly (June 1880): 211–14, 216.

wished to do so, they were mainly prompt to say; when questioned for the specific causes of their coming, they were evasive and reticent. But they were not going back. That much they declared with one voice, and a resolute and convincing emphasis; and as for what lay ahead of them, well, "de good Lord" could be trusted.

The case was one to appeal with force to popular sympathy, even in its surface aspect alone; and when there was added the reflection that these patient and simple people, steeped in poverty, had left the clime of their nativity and choice, to search, however blindly, for a chance to better their condition, the heart of the observer had to own a special pity for the poor wanderers. And pity in the West is practical. So temporary shelter was speedily provided for them; food and the facilities for cooking it were furnished them in ample measure; and local philanthropists hastened to devise measures that should secure them homes and employment. Then came more of them. The tide swelled daily. Protests began to go up from the border towns, and that aroused public feeling throughout all Kansas, and brought meetings and speeches, committees and contributions. The sentimental view of the question quickly took precedence, as it could hardly fail to do under the circumstances. In a certain, effective sense, the very raggedness and misery of the immigration was accepted as its best excuse for being. The peculiar history of Kansas — a history crowded with opportune and feverish memories — was invoked, like a piece of holy writ, to vindicate and exalt the movement; there were not wanting, as there are never wanting at such times, those who saw in it the hand of Providence; and the Governor himself, speaking from the capital, welcomed the thickening freedmen, in impulsive and glittering rhetoric, to "the State made immortal by Old John Brown."[2] . . .

All through the summer months they continued to come, not from any one State or section in particular, but from nearly all parts of the South. Perhaps the welcome and assistance extended to such as had already reached Kansas operated to hurry others northward, and to take them to that friendly locality. Certain it is that designing agents of transportation lines, anxious only to secure passenger traffic and pausing at no deception, used this feature of the case to stimulate a general colored hegira[3] to what was thus made to seem a new Canaan.[4] All the Missouri River boats left St. Louis packed with them. Every train brought squads, companies, battalions of them. Not a few came through on foot, all the way from Alabama. The barracks were over-run, the resources of the Relief Association taxed to the utmost. Public sentiment grew critical and apprehensive; the emotional view of the matter gave way to considerations involving serious fears and

[2] **John Brown:** Antislavery warrior active in the border wars of Kansas in the mid-1850s. Following the opening of Kansas to slavery in 1854, the territory became a battleground for pro- and antislavery forces. Guerrilla warfare broke out sporadically in the years prior to the Civil War. The territory became known as "bleeding Kansas." Brown and his followers killed five proslavery men in 1856; three years later, Brown attempted to seize a federal arsenal at Harper's Ferry, West Virginia, in an attempt to start an antislavery revolution, an action for which he was hanged.
[3] **hegira:** A flight or escape from danger.
[4] **Canaan:** The Promised Land.

perplexities. Six months had sufficed to stamp the movement — the problem, as it was now seen to be — with national importance. The Exodus was no longer a mere random interlude; it had become a profound and baffling study. . . .

There are, at this writing (April 1, 1880), from 15,000 to 20,000 colored people in Kansas who have settled there during the last twelve months — 30 per cent. of them from Mississippi, 20 per cent. from Texas, 15 per cent. from Tennessee, 10 per cent. from Louisiana, 5 per cent. each from Alabama and Georgia, and the remainder from the other Southern States. Of this number, about one-third are supplied with teams and farming tools, and may be expected to become self-sustaining in another year; one-third are in the towns, employed as house-servants and day-laborers, and can take care of themselves so long as the market for their labor is not over-crowded; the other one-third are at work in a desultory fashion for white farmers and herders, and doing the best they can, but powerless to "get ahead" and achieve homes and an assured support without considerable assistance. The poverty of these people cannot be too strongly dwelt upon; for that has been their stumbling-block from the start and is to-day the one paramount consideration of the Exodus. . . .

And they are still coming. The influx continued, more or less, through all the winter months, mainly from Texas. Probably three or four thousand arrived between November and March; and since the first of March, an average of three hundred per week have reached Topeka. The flight increases instead of diminishing. Those in the best position to judge, say that it is not unlikely that as many as fifty thousand may come during the approaching summer. A year's experience has demonstrated that there is method, agreement, determination, in the movement. It is now an open secret that the question of a general removal to the North has been thought and talked of for several years by the freedmen in all the old slave-holding States. The first year's outcome has encouraged them, so reports allege; the infection is stronger and more pervasive than it was twelve months ago; and the shrewdest observer dare not venture to name the possible limit of the strange, risk-beset and problematic undertaking.

It is not within the writer's purpose to attempt an analysis of the causes of the Exodus — least of all, to touch its political bearings or suggestions. Any survey of the subject would be incomplete, however, which omitted to set forth, candidly and inquiringly, the statements most commonly made by the freedmen in Kansas regarding their abandonment of the South. They assert that there is no security for their lives and property in their old homes; that the laws and courts are studiedly inimical to them and their interests; that their exercise of the electoral franchise is obstructed and made a personal danger; that no facilities are afforded or permitted them for educating their children; that their family rights and honor are scoffed at and outraged, as in slave days; and finally, — and this is the most frequent complaint, — that they are so unjustly and unfairly dealt with by white land-owners, employers and traders, that it is impossible to make a living. The facts they offer in support of these statements are not conclusive, to be sure, since they relate chiefly to special instances, and we cannot know how far such instances reflect the general sentiment in a given county or State. Isolated and individual acts of fraud and outrage are not alone sufficient, of course, to condemn a whole community, particularly without opportunity for explanation and defense; but truth requires the admission that these charges are too numerous, and the worst of them too well substantiated, to be disposed of as mere accidental grievances; they raise a valid presumption, to say the least, that there must be something radically wrong in the society where such things are permitted. . . .

3. AN AFRICAN AMERICAN COWBOY'S LIFE

Exoduster emigrants to Kansas began African American colonies, and they mostly lived and worked together side by side. Some black emigrants to the West lived more solitary lives. One of these was Nat Love. Born into slavery, Love certainly led, as he put it, an "unusually adventurous life." Not long after the Civil War, Love went west, where he soon found work, like hundreds of other African American men, as a cowboy. In later years, Love worked as a Pullman porter, riding in a railcar across the western spaces he once covered on horseback. In this passage drawn from his autobiography, Love discusses how he came to know about the West and how he ended up working on the range. It should be pointed out that scholars have expressed skepticism about the reliability of parts of Love's account. Do Nat Love's tales match the traditional image of the "cowboy and Indian" West? What factors motivated Love to move to the American West? How do his reasons for migrating compare with those of the Exodusters? How might you compare the West of the Exodusters to the West of Nat Love?

NAT LOVE
From *The Life and Adventures of Nat Love*
1907

The World Is before Me. I Join the Texas Cowboys. Red River Dick. My First Outfit. My First Indian Fight. I Learn to Use My Gun.

It was on the tenth day of February, 1869, that I left the old home, near Nashville, Tennessee. I was at that time about fifteen years old, and though while young in years the hard work and farm life had made me strong and hearty, much

Nat Love, *The Life and Adventures of Nat Love* (New York: Arno Press, 1968), 40–45.

beyond my years, and I had full confidence in myself as being able to take care
of myself and making my way.

I at once struck out for Kansas of which I had heard something. And believing it was a good place in which to seek employment. It was in the west, and it
was the great west I wanted to see, and so by walking and occasional lifts from
farmers going my way and taking advantage of every thing that promised to assist
me on my way, I eventually brought up at Dodge City, Kansas, which at that time
was a typical frontier city, with a great many saloons, dance halls, and gambling
houses, and very little of anything else. When I arrived the town was full of cow
boys from the surrounding ranches, and from Texas and other parts of the west.
As Kansas was a great cattle center and market, the wild cow boy, prancing horses
of which I was very fond, and the wild life generally, all had their attractions for
me, and I decided to try for a place with them. Although it seemed to me I had
met with a bad outfit, at least some of them, going around among them I watched
my chances to get to speak with them, as I wanted to find some one whom I
thought would give me a civil answer to the questions I wanted to ask, but they
all seemed too wild around town, so the next day I went out where they were
in camp.

Approaching a party who were eating their breakfast, I got to speak with
them. They asked me to have some breakfast with them, which invitation I gladly
accepted. During the meal I got a chance to ask them many questions. They
proved to be a Texas outfit, who had just come up with a herd of cattle and having delivered them they were preparing to return. There were several colored
cow boys among them, and good ones too. After breakfast I asked the camp boss
for a job as cow boy. He asked me if I could ride a wild horse. I said "yes sir." He
said if you can I will give you a job. So he spoke to one of the colored cow boys
called Bronko Jim, and told him to go out and rope old Good Eye, saddle him
and put me on his back. Bronko Jim gave me a few pointers and told me to look
out for the horse was especially bad on pitching. I told Jim I was a good rider and
not afraid of him. I thought I had rode pitching horses before, but from the time
I mounted old Good Eye I knew I had not learned what pitching was. This proved
the worst horse to ride I had ever mounted in my life, but I stayed with him and
the cow boys were the most surprised outfit you ever saw, as they had taken me
for a tenderfoot, pure and simple. After the horse got tired and I dismounted the
boss said he would give me a job and pay me $30.00 per month and more later
on. He asked what my name was and I answered Nat Love, he said to the boys we
will call him Red River Dick. I went by this name for a long time.

The boss took me to the city and got my outfit, which consisted of a new
saddle, bridle and spurs, chaps, a pair of blankets and a fine 45 Colt revolver. Now
that the business which brought them to Dodge City was concluded, preparations were made to start out for the Pan Handle country in Texas to the home
ranch. The outfit of which I was now a member was called the Duval outfit, and
their brand was known as the Pig Pen brand. I worked with this outfit for over
three years. On this trip there were only about fifteen of us riders, all excepting
myself were hardy, experienced men, always ready for anything that might turn

up, but they were as jolly a set of fellows as on [sic] could find in a long journey. There now being nothing to keep us longer in Dodge City, we prepared for the return journey, and left the next day over the old Dodge and Sun City lonesome trail, on a journey which was to prove the most eventful of my life up to now.

A few miles out we encountered some of the hardest hail storms I ever saw, causing discomfort to man and beast, but I had no notion of getting discouraged but I resolved to be always ready for any call that might be made on me, of whatever nature it might be, and those with whom I have lived and worked will tell you I have kept that resolve. Not far from Dodge City on our way home we encountered a band of the old Victoria tribe of Indians and had a sharp fight.

These Indians were nearly always harassing travelers and traders and the stock men of that part of the country, and were very troublesome. In this band we encountered there were about a hundred painted bucks all well mounted. When we saw the Indians they were coming after us yelling like demons. As we were not expecting Indians at this particular time, we were taken somewhat by surprise.

We only had fifteen men in our outfit, but nothing daunted we stood our ground and fought the Indians to a stand. One of the boys was shot off his horse and killed near me. The Indians got his horse, bridle and saddle. During this fight we lost all but six of our horses, our entire packing outfit and our extra saddle horses, which the Indians stampeded, then rounded them up after the fight and drove them off. And as we only had six horses left us, we were unable to follow them, although we had the satisfaction of knowing we had made several good Indians out of bad ones.

This was my first Indian fight and likewise the first Indians I had ever seen. When I saw them coming after us and heard their blood curdling yell, I lost all courage and thought my time had come to die. I was too badly scared to run, some of the boys told me to use my gun and shoot for all I was worth. Now I had just got my outfit and had never shot off a gun in my life, but their words brought me back to earth and seeing they were all using their guns in a way that showed they were used to it, I unlimbered my artillery and after the first shot I lost all fear and fought like a veteran.

We soon routed the Indians and they left, taking with them nearly all we had, and we were powerless to pursue them. We were compelled to finish our journey home almost on foot, as there were only six horses left to fourteen of us. Our friend and companion who was shot in the fight, we buried on the plains, wrapped in his blanket with stones piled over his grave. After this engagement with the Indians I seemed to lose all sense as to what fear was and thereafter during my whole life on the range I never experienced the least feeling of fear, no matter how trying the ordeal or how desperate my position.

The home ranch was located on the Palo Duro river in the western part of the Pan Handle, Texas, which we reached in the latter part of May, it taking us considerably over a month to make the return journey home from Dodge City. I remained in the employ of the Duval outfit for three years, making regular trips to Dodge City every season and to many other places in the surrounding states with herds of horses and cattle for market and to be delivered to other ranch owners all over Texas, Wyoming and the Dakotas. By strict attention to business, born of a genuine love of the free and wild life of the range, and absolute fearlessness, I became known throughout the country as a good all around cow boy and a splendid hand in a stampede.

After returning from one of our trips north with a bunch of cattle in the fall of 1872, I received and accepted a better position with the Pete Gallinger company, whose immense range was located on the Gila River in southern Arizona. So after drawing the balance of my pay from the Duval company and bidding good bye to the true and tried companions of the past three years, who had learned me the business and been with me in many a trying situation, it was with genuine regret that I left them for my new position, one that meant more to me in pay and experience. I stayed with Pete Gallinger company for several years and soon became one of their most trusted men, taking an important part in all the big round-ups and cuttings throughout western Texas, Arizona and other states where the company had interests to be looked after, sometimes riding eighty miles a day for days at a time over the trails of Texas and the surrounding country and naturally I soon became well known among the cowboys, rangers, scouts and guides it was my pleasure to meet in my wanderings over the country, in the wake of immense herds of the long horned Texas cattle and large bands of range horses. Many of these men who were my companions on the trail and in camp, have since become famous in story and history, and a braver, truer set of men never lived than these wild sons of the plains whose home was in the saddle and their couch, mother earth, with the sky for a covering. They were always ready to share their blanket and their last ration with a less fortunate fellow companion and always assisted each other in the many trying situations that were continually coming up in a cowboy's life.

When we were not on the trail taking large herds of cattle or horses to market or to be delivered to other ranches we were engaged in range riding, moving large numbers of cattle from one grazing range to another, keeping them together, and hunting up strays which, despite the most earnest efforts of the range riders would get away from the main herd and wander for miles over the plains before they could be found, overtaken and returned to the main herd.

Then the Indians and the white outlaws who infested the country gave us no end of trouble, as they lost no opportunity to cut out and run off the choicest part of a herd of long horns, or the best of a band of horses, causing the cowboys a ride of many a long mile over the dusty plains in pursuit, and many are the fierce engagements we had, when after a long chase of perhaps hundreds of miles over the ranges we overtook the thieves. It then became a case of "to the victor belongs the spoils," as there was no law respected in this wild country, except the law of might and the persuasive qualities of the 45 Colt pistol.

Accordingly it became absolutely necessary for a cowboy to understand his gun and know how to place its contents where it would do the most good, therefore I in common with my other companions never lost an opportunity to practice with my 45 Colts and the opportunities were not lacking by any means and so in time I became fairly proficient and able in most cases to hit a barn door providing the door was not too far away, and was steadily improving in this as I was in experience and knowledge of the other branches of the business which I had chosen as my life's work and which I had begun to like so well, because while the life was hard and in some ways exacting, yet it was free and wild and contained the elements of danger which my nature craved and which began to manifest itself when I was a pugnacious youngster on the old plantation in our rock battles and the breaking of the wild horses. I gloried in the danger, and the wild and free life of the plains, the new country I was continually traversing, and the many new scenes and incidents continually arising in the life of a rough rider.

Suggestions for Further Reading

Athearn, Robert G. *In Search of Canaan: Black Migration to Kansas, 1879–80.* Lawrence: Regents Press of Kansas, 1978.

Crockett, Norman L. *The Black Towns.* Lawrence: Regents Press of Kansas, 1979.

Foner, Eric. *Nothing but Freedom: Emancipation and Its Legacy.* Baton Rouge: Louisiana State University Press, 1983.

——. *Reconstruction: America's Unfinished Revolution, 1863–1877.* New York: Harper and Row, 1988.

Gordon, Jacob U. *Narratives of African Americans in Kansas, 1870–1992.* Lewiston, N.Y.: Edwin Mellen Press, 1993.

Painter, Nell I. *Exodusters: Black Migration to Kansas after Reconstruction.* New York: W. W. Norton, 1976.

Stewart, Paul W., and Wallace Yvonne Ponce. *Black Cowboys.* Broomfield, Colo.: Phillips Publishing, 1986.

Taylor, Quintard. *In Search of the Racial Frontier: African Americans in the American West, 1528–1990.* New York: Norton, 1998.

Wohaw's Self-Portrait, 1878

This drawing was made by the Kiowa warrior Wohaw ("Spotted Cow") while he was a prisoner at Fort Marion, in St. Augustine, Florida. Captured along with other Kiowa, Cheyenne, and Comanche Indians following the 1874 Red River War in the Texas Panhandle, Wohaw produced many drawings during his imprisonment, some depicting the life he once knew on the Southern Plains, some picturing his new life of confinement. Here, Wohaw, who has written his name above the self-portrait, pictures himself caught between two worlds and offering a peace pipe to each. Such was the fate of thousands of Native Americans in the years following the Civil War, as the relentless invasion of their former lands continued. What are some of the symbols of Wohaw's dilemma of identity? Who is Wohaw's intended audience?

Missouri Historical Society, St. Louis.

CHAPTER TWO

WESTERN CONQUEST

WAR AGAINST NATIVE AMERICA

Although American migration to what we now know as the American West had begun well before the Civil War, the end of that conflict accelerated the process, as the selections in Chapter One illustrate. Traveling over the ever-widening transportation networks provided by new railroads and better roads, and lured by the expectation of a better life (or at least an adventurous trip), tens of thousands of native-born Americans and foreign immigrants alike sought new opportunities on western farms and in western cities and towns.

But whose West was it? The federal government claimed (or at least coveted) the area and through such legislative tools as the Homestead Act of 1862 actively encouraged settlement and growth. Legions of settlers responded. All across the West, from the Canadian border down through the Rocky Mountains to the Pacific, homesteaders took up federal parcels of land in one land rush after another. Eastern politicians and newspaper editors trumpeted the democratic promise of the West, a place they saw as vast and empty. But the West was not uninhabited, nor was it unclaimed. A large number of Indians, from diverse tribes, cultures, and nations, lived there, either as a result of ancient patterns of migration and settlement or through the actions of the U.S. government, which forced them to move from areas east of the Mississippi River.

The history of the West's Indian wars has been greatly distorted in popular culture. Cowboys and Indians did not clash in great numbers, nor did Indians massacre huge numbers of settlers as they plodded west in covered wagons. In reality, Indian-settler conflict was both more mundane and more complicated. Cattle, for instance, played an important role: the relentless beef markets that demanded more range cattle helped drive the bison, a critical resource for Plains Indians, to the edge of extinction. This process in turn helped to weaken and drive native people from places like Kansas, Wyoming, and Nebraska as the once huge bison herds thinned.

By the mid-nineteenth century, Europeans and Americans had been fighting the continent's native peoples for hundreds of years. But in the decades after the Civil War, national leaders believed that the end of the conflict was in sight. In their minds, Native Americans must move aside to reservations, where they could adapt to "American" and Christian customs, or be rendered extinct. This was a far cry from earlier, pre–Civil War efforts to push Indians farther west, where they could be left alone in what earlier maps called "Indian Territory," a chunk of the American Southwest now largely contained within the state of Oklahoma. By the latter third of the nineteenth century, however, it had become clear that a separate "Indian Territory" could not possibly survive the advancing westward expansion.

Circumstances and institutions all conspired against Native Americans. U.S. military leaders and civilian politicians often differed over what to do about "the Indian problem," thus making it certain that government policy would be confused and even contradictory. Missionary and reform groups demanded access to Indians to bring Christian salvation and Americanization. Miners and farmers demanded access to native reservation lands. Newly arrived railroad tourists and settlers expected the Indians they saw to be peaceful, exotic attractions.

Native Americans responded to these crises in a variety of ways. Some tribes adopted "white" ways, attempting with greater or lesser success to integrate into the surrounding farm, town, or city society. Others retreated to the isolation of the reservation, adopting some aspects of the dominant culture and resisting others. Reservations, which would come to dominate the federal government's Indian policy, were, in the words of historian Richard White, "paradoxical places where Indians were to be temporarily segregated in order to prepare them for ultimate integration into the larger society."

Other tribes, particularly those on the Plains and in the Southwest, fought back (often against traditional tribal enemies allied with the U.S. army as scouts and combatants). Often they had no choice. In 1865, one army general ordered his Montana command to accept no "overtures of peace or submission from Indians" but to "attack and kill every male Indian over twelve years of age." Several treaties signed in 1865, which deeded huge chunks of Montana's Powder River country to natives, fell apart when gold miners refused to honor them. Sioux bands, in league with Cheyenne and Arapaho allies, lashed back at whites. One famous action was the Fetterman Massacre, in which Captain William J. Fetterman and eighty of his men, riding out from Fort Phil Kearny in the Dakota Territory on a winter's day in 1866, got wiped out to a man. This humiliating defeat, which foreshadowed George Armstrong Custer's destruction at the Little Bighorn River in Montana Territory ten years later, gave the military an excuse to adopt even harsher measures against Indian enemies.

Brutal warfare erupted elsewhere as well. Cheyenne and Arapaho warriors attacked white settlements in Kansas. Apaches on the Mexican border carried on a running battle with U.S. and Mexican troops until they were finally surrounded in the late 1880s and sent across the nation to military prisons in Florida. In Colorado, Arapahos and Utes fought sporadic engagements against farmers, settlers, and mining caravans. In the Black Hills of Dakota Territory, gold miners trampled on another treaty that had set aside land sacred to the Lakota Sioux on their reservation. But the federal government's refusal to enforce the treaty set off renewed warfare. In the summer of 1876, Custer and several hundred of his men were annihilated at the Battle of the Little Bighorn. This Indian victory was short-lived. Custer's bloody defeat made him a martyr, and public opinion demanded retribution. Within a year, those bands of Indians who had fought at the Little Bighorn were captured, along with others who had resisted exile to reservations.

By the late 1880s, significant Native American opposition to westward expansion had all but ended. The vast majority of the West's Indians had been killed or shunted off to reservations or boarding schools run by Protestant or Catholic missionaries. The Dawes Act of 1887, a mixture of reform and coercion, tried to make farmers — and hence "good Americans" — of Native Americans living on reservations. The measure attempted to address a complicated issue through a simplistic solution: chopping reservation lands up into individual parcels. Indians would farm their own land, grow food, earn money, and in the process learn what were considered the appropriate traits of citizenship. The provisions of the Dawes Act required that Indians give up tribal life and all claims to their ancestral lands. The clumsiness of this wrongheaded effort, despite some good intentions, made it but the latest of any number of approaches to the "Indian Problem."

Sporadic conflict continued to break out, even into the early twentieth century. In 1890, at the Wounded Knee Reservation in South Dakota, federal troops massacred nearly one hundred and fifty Sioux men, women, and children who had gathered in hopeful expectation of the coming of a new world. Periodic clashes with the federal government continued, in fact, throughout the twentieth century.

The documents reproduced in this chapter illustrate the complexities of the war against Native America in the second half of the nineteenth century. Colonel John Chivington of the Colorado militia attempts in a message to the people of Colorado to justify his role in a notorious massacre. Colonel Henry Carrington tries to do the impossible: keep white miners, settlers, and traders from menacing Native Americans in Montana. In what could have been an answer to Carrington, Lieutenant Colonel Richard Dodge suggests that white settlers deserved greater access to Indian lands, regardless of Indian opposition. The Sioux warrior Wooden Leg describes his role in the Battle of the Little Bighorn, and Chief Joseph, the political leader of Oregon's Wallowa Valley Nez Percé Indians, describes why he and his people fled toward Canada in the late 1870s.

As you read through the documents for this chapter, consider the ways in which they contradict one another. How do the political statements of Colonel John Chivington, for example, relate to the orders issued by Colonel Henry

Carrington? What would Chief Joseph of the Nez Percés say in opposition to Chivington's views? How would Wooden Leg likely have summed up the state of Indian affairs in the 1870s or 1880s?

---

4. A MILITARY OFFICER JUSTIFIES THE SAND CREEK MASSACRE

During the Civil War, Governor John Evans of Colorado Territory embarked on his own war against the Cheyenne Indians in order to gain political prestige. The governor's ally in this war was Colonel John Milton Chivington, a former Methodist minister seeking fame as an Indian fighter and the head of the Colorado militia. The Cheyenne Chief Black Kettle, however, desired peace. He did not get it. While camped peacefully alongside Sand Creek in the flatlands of eastern Colorado — beneath an American flag — Black Kettle's band of over one hundred Cheyenne women and children (most of the men were absent) were massacred by Chivington and the Colorado militia in the winter of 1864. The Sand Creek Massacre shocked even those accustomed to the horrors of warfare between Native Americans and American settlers and soldiers. "It is difficult to believe," a government investigative panel later stated, "that beings in the form of men could commit or countenance the commission of such acts of cruelty and barbarity." Chivington was subsequently removed from his command. In this statement, designed to justify his actions, Chivington addresses the events that led up to the massacre and proclaims that, under the circumstances, his attack upon the Cheyennes was appropriate and legitimate. What claims does Chivington make about his innocence? Are they credible? What other sources would you wish to examine before you made up your mind? What is Chivington's attitude toward the Cheyennes?

JOHN MILTON CHIVINGTON
"To the People of Colorado"
·1865

When I arrived at Fort Lyon on an expedition against the Indians in November, 1864, I was informed that the Indians on Sand Creek were hostile. Ma-

John Milton Chivington, "To the People of Colorado." Synopsis of the Sand Creek investigation. Denver, Colorado, June 1865: 5–8.

jor Anthony, commanding the post, whom I thought was better acquainted than any one else with the relations that existed between the Government and the Indians as regarded peace or war, informed me, on different occasions, that the Indians were hostile, that he had repeatedly fired upon them; that the Indians had sent him word that if he wanted a fight to come out to Sand Creek and they would give him as big a fight as he wanted; that every man of his command would go gladly, and urged an immediate departure. Anthony after the battle of Sand Creek, exulted over the fight, and thought it was the biggest thing on record, and witnesses say they never heard him speak of it except exultingly.

Have I not shown all these facts by witnesses under oath, and can the people of Colorado, or the world, say, that though I had been governed by the most rigid rules of civilized warfare, that with such statements from the commanding officer of a fort made to me, that my conduct could be adjudged anything but honorable. I am but human, and the same means of knowledge by which the public have been informed of the "Chivington massacre," I was informed of the hostility of the Indians on Sand Creek. If Major Anthony, in representing the relations that existed between the troops and the Indians, wilfully lied, then Major Anthony is the responsible party, and the world cannot consistently punish me for the crimes of others, for certainly, from all accounts, I will have enough to answer for without them.

The morning of the 29th day of November 1864 finds us before the village of the Indian foe. The first shot is fired by them. The first man who falls is white. No white flag is raised. None of the Indians show signs of peace, but flying to rifle pits already prepared, they fight with a desperation unequalled, showing their perfect understanding of the relations that existed as regards peace or war, as forty-nine killed and wounded soldiers too plainly testified. Our command consisted of nearly six hundred men. The fight continued till nearly three o'clock in the afternoon. Stephen Decatur swears that being detailed as clerk, in company with Lieut. Col. Bowen, he rode over the field where the fight had occurred and counted four hundred and fifty dead warriors, and that no more women and children were killed than would have been killed in a white village under like circumstances; that the women and children that were killed could not have been saved if the troops had tried; that they were in the rifle pits with the warriors; that there were very few women and children killed; that after he returned to the village he saw things that made him desire to kill more Indians; that he saw great numbers of white scalps, daguerreotypes, part of a ladies toilet, and children's wearing apparel. Would not such sights make any person feel as Stephen Decatur did? Stephen Decatur is a husband and a father, and how many harrowing thoughts of murder and suffering would a spectacle like this call up, and how many endearing reminiscences would be swept into the gulf of horror on an occasion like this. Stephen Decatur has spent seven years among the Indians and is acquainted with them. He had been a soldier before, and speaks of this fight as being the hardest he ever saw, on both sides. He had seen the Lipan or Camanche Indians scalp their own dead. Husbands and fathers, under similar circumstances what would you have done? *Coaxed* the chiefs to have taken their warriors away, or like white men and true soldiers accepted their wager of battle and whipped them if you could. Yet this is all that was done at Sand Creek. Though hundreds of Colorado soldiers are to-day branded as murderers, and that in many instances by men without knowing or caring whether the charge be false or true. It is sufficient if he be a soldier, in the eyes of these malignant cowards. He must as a natural consequence be a murderer, while others wearing the uniform of officers, without the courage to perform a brave deed themselves, are the loudest to condemn the conduct of a brother soldier who wins a single laurel that they cannot steal. Such men are more to be feared than the crawling viper. Perjury, larceny or robbery are no obstacles in their road to vengeance, venomous as reptiles and cowardly as curs. But what is the cause of all this trouble — whence the source of this cry of holy horror that has been rung with such startling effect upon the minds of the unsophisticated people of New England, the people generally of the States, and especially the billious old maids in the United States Senate and the House of Representatives? Why it originates in the fertile minds of two Government employees conspiring together to swindle the Government, as one of them states, out of $25,000. Through the influence of friends he has in Washington, and by whom he expects to get his claims allowed, probably some high official who is desirous of making an honest dollar by advocating the cause of the honest old men of the wilderness, the veracious John Smith, Indian interpreter and that reliable, respectable old gentleman, Major Colley, Indian Agent.[1] But under the solemn and binding obligations of an oath, what does Major Talbott say? Simply that Major Colley and John Smith stated to him that they would do anything to ruin Col. Chivington; that they were even equally interested in their trade with the Indians — one an Indian Agent, the other Indian Interpreter; that they had lost one hundred and five buffalo robes and two white ponies by Col. Chivington's attack on the Indian village at Sand Creek; that they would collect $25,000 for it of the Government, and eventually damn Col. Chivington; that John Smith boastingly stated that the eastern papers would be filled with accounts of Sand Creek, as a massacre; that they would go to Washington and represent to the committee on the Conduct of the War that Sand Creek was a massacre. What did they mean when they said they would do *anything* to ruin Col. Chivington? The word has a broad signification, and did they not include *perjury?* It appears to us without any stretch of the imagination, they did take the expression we will go to Washington and represent Sand Creek as a massacre; the eastern papers will be filled with accounts of Sand Creek as a massacre, by letters from Fort Lyon, and we will do *anything* to ruin Col. Chivington," and draw your own conclusions. If it appears to you as it does to me, perjury would be no obstacle to these worthies in their road to vengeance. If they would deliberately conspire to rob the Government out of $25,000, through the influence of their friends would they not also be guilty of *perjury*, to ruin their enemies? Then what conclusions are we compelled to arrive at? That perjury has been perpetrated by these worthies, abetted by their friends and the honorable gentlemen who com-

---

[1] **Indian Agent:** An official representative of the U.S. government.

pose the Committee on the Conduct of the War,—they whose piercing criticism has been a terror to evil doers in the States,—they who, from their high order of intelligence have been supposed to be able to draw aside the thick curtain that concealed the dark deeds of the adepts in crime and allow the sunlight of truth and justice to shine in upon it, are made the *innocent tools* of two ignorant old Indian trappers and traders, to wreak disgrace and ruin upon Col. Chivington and Colorado soldiers generally. Truly these two old gentlemen, Colley and Smith, must have read the Scriptures, for they appear to have been, in Washington, "as innocent as lambs and as wary as foxes."[2]

Now, fellow citizens, what do you think of the Chivington massacre, whose horrors have filled so many columns of the papers in the States and called down upon Colorado so many disgraceful epithets, while at the same time our enterprising freighters, emigrants and settlers, with their wives and children, have been murdered, scalped and their bodies horribly mutilated by these much abused sons of the plains. . . .

Lo, the poor Indian, in thy untutored greatness, you have proved yourself, with the assistance of high officials, your friends, a good diplomat. You have long been a bone of contention and many a villainous swindle has been perpetrated upon the Government in thy name and humanity, which would put to blush the unparalelled commander of the sons of sin, His Satanic Majesty, the Devil.

J. M. CHIVINGTON,
Late Col. 1st Cavalry of Colorado,
Com'd'g Dist. of Colorado

---

[2] **"Innocent as lambs and as wary as foxes"**: A biblical reference, perhaps to Matthew 10:16.

5. Instructions to Whites in Indian Country

Emigrant wagon trains and miners fanned out across the wide spaces of the American West once the Civil War had ended. Army commanders at various frontier forts and outposts issued orders to wagon masters and leaders of other settler and miner parties not to interfere with the local Native American populations in hopes that contact between groups might remain peaceful. In this selection, Colonel Henry B. Carrington, who had charge of a vast chunk of the northern Great Plains, tries to get settlers, miners, and other emigrant parties to behave peaceably when they cut through Indian country. Yet, although the document stated that peace could be maintained, it was a hopeless cause. Settlers, miners, and adventurers commonly disregarded such orders, and their stubborn insistence on going where they should not go and doing what they should not do only exacerbated tensions between Indians and whites. Within months of issuing these orders, Colonel Carrington would have to explain how the Fetterman Massacre could have taken place on his watch. According to Carrington, what are the important reasons why trouble breaks out between Indians and whites? How do you think he planned to enforce these rules? Do you think any other methods of addressing the "Indian Problem" would have worked in the second half of the nineteenth century?

HENRY B. CARRINGTON
Orders to Civilian Wagon Trains in Montana
1866

1. All trains, whether large or small, must stop at Reno Station, formerly Fort Reno,[1] on Powder River, and report to the post commander.

2. Thirty armed men constitute a party which, upon selection of its commander or conductor, will be allowed to proceed. The reduction of this number will depend upon the general conduct of trains and the conditions and safety of the route, of which due notice will be given.

3. When a train shall have organized, the conductor will present to the post commander a list of the men accompanying the said train, upon which list, if satisfactory, he will endorse, "Permission given to pass to Fort Reno." Upon arrival of a train at Fort Reno, the conductor will report with his list, indorsed[2] as above mentioned, to the post commander to receive the same indorsed approval as in the first instance to pass to the next post. This examination and approval must be had at each post, so that the last post commander on the Upper Yellowstone will have the evidence that the train has passed all posts.

4. The constant separation and scattering of trains pretending to act in concert must be stopped; and for the information of emigrants and well-disposed citizens the following reasons are given: viz:

> First, nearly all danger from Indians lies in the recklessness of travelers. A small party when separated, either sell whisky to or fire upon scattering Indians, or get in dispute with them, and somebody is hurt. An insult to an Indian is resented by the Indians against the first white men they meet, and innocent travelers suffer.
>
> Again, the new route is short and will be made perfectly secure. The cooperation of citizens is therefore essential for their own personal comfort as well as for the interests of the public at large; and if citizens ask, as they will of course

---

[1]**Fort Reno:** Older name for Fort Phil Kearny.
[2]**indorsed:** Endorsed.

Dee Brown, *The Fetterman Massacre: An American Saga* (London: Barrie and Jenkins, 1972), 60–61.

rightly expect, the protection and aid from Government troops, they must themselves be equally diligent in avoiding difficulties with Indians, or among themselves, and the consideration paid to any complaint will be measured by the apparent good faith with which citizens regard the regulations for the management of the route.

5. When trains scatter and upon reporting at any post there shall be found a substantial variation from the list furnished, all of the remaining teams will be stopped until the residue of the train arrives, or is accounted for; and until this is done they will not be permitted to unite with other trains to complete numbers, which their insubordination or haste has lost or scattered.

6. The main object being perfect security to travel, all citizens are cautioned against any unnecessary dealings with Indians, against giving or selling ardent spirits, against personal quarrels with them, or any acts having a tendency to irritate them, or develop hostile acts or plans. A faithful and wise regard for these instructions will, with the aid of the Government troops, insure peace, which is all important and can be made certain.

7. A copy of these instructions will be properly and publicly posted at the office of each post or station commandant, and all conductors of trains will have their attention called thereto, with instructions to notify all who travel in their charge.

6. A MILITARY OFFICER'S VIEW OF THE BLACK HILLS

Lieutenant Colonel Richard Dodge's book The Black Hills: A Minute Description of the Routes, Scenery, Soil, Climate, Timber, Gold, Geology, Zoology, Etc., *published in 1876, was a virtual tourists' and miners' guide to a region supposedly off-limits to non-Indians. Dodge's claims—that Indians had not established permanent settlement rights in the region and that the "Indian problem" had not been dealt with effectively by the U.S. government—were commonly held assumptions. On the heels of publications such as these and the Black Hills gold rush of 1874, more and more adventurous, greedy, and often foolhardy miners penetrated the Black Hills, crossing treaty lines in the process. Sentiments from supposed authorities like Dodge, whose perspective on the territory ("a true oasis," he called it) is reproduced here, did little to lessen tensions or the likelihood of violence. In what ways does Dodge hint at his own solution to the "Indian problem"? What reasons does Dodge offer for why the Black Hills ought to be thrown open to settlement, mining, and growth? What counterarguments could have been made by Native Americans in the Black Hills?*

RICHARD I. DODGE
"Indians and the Indian Question"
1876

It is believed by some persons that the Crow Indians, the former owners, actually occupied and lived in the Black Hills before being driven out by the Sioux. I do not think so, for two reasons: First, If this country had been used as a residence, even thirty years ago, some marks of its occupation would still be visible. Second, The mountain Crows are known to be determined fighters, in their own fastnesses.[1] Had even a small band occupied and defended the Hills, they could have held it until now against the whole Sioux nation, who, though excellent horseback fighters, are worth nothing on foot; and though most dangerous, aggressive enemies on the plains, are timid as hares in woods and mountains.

My opinion is, that the Black Hills have never been a permanent home for any Indians. Even now small parties go a little way into the Hills to cut spruce lodge-poles, but all the signs indicate that these are mere sojourns of the most temporary character.

The "teepe," or lodge, may be regarded as the Indian's house, the wickyup[2] as his tent. One is his permanent residence, the other the make-shift shelter for a night. Except in one single spot, near the head of Castle Creek, I saw nowhere any evidence whatever of a lodge having been set up, while old wickyups were not unfrequent in the edge of the Hills. There is not one single teepe or lodge-pole trail, from side to side of the Hills, in any direction, and these poles, when dragged in the usual way by ponies, soon make a trail as difficult to obliterate as a wagon road, visible for many years, even though not used.

Several small parties of Indians, overcome by curiosity, and reassured by the presence of the "soldiers,"[3] came into the Hills this summer. The most intelligent of these, an Indian named Robe Raiser, was quite communicative, and informed the interpreter that, though fifty years old, and though he had been around the Hills almost every year of his life, he had never before ventured inside; that when passing north or south in the fall, the squaws come in sometimes to cut lodge-poles, the bucks venturing to hunt a little, but that these stops are very short. His reasons for the Indians not coming in were: First, That the Hills are "bad medicine," and the abode of spirits. Second, That there is nothing to come for except lodge-poles, the game being scarce and more difficult to kill than that on the plains. Third, That the thickets are so dense that their ponies are soon lost if

---

[1] **fastnesses:** Secure places or fortifications.
[2] **wickyup:** A framed structure, often very mobile, with a covering of bark or brush.
[3] **"soldiers":** It is unclear what Dodge means by the quotation marks. He may be referring to Indian warriors accompanying other Indians into the Black Hills.

Richard Irving Dodge, *The Black Hills: A Minute Description of the Routes, Scenery, Soil, Climate, Timber, Gold, Geology, Zoology, Etc.* (New York: James Miller, Publisher, 1876), 136–41, 149–51.

turned loose, and the flies are so bad that they are tormented and worried out, if kept tied up. Fourth, That it rains very frequently, and that the Indian does not like rain. Fifth, That it thunders and lightens with terrible force, tearing trees to pieces and setting fire to the woods. He said, moreover, that the Indians had never lived here, and did not and would not live here now; that they did not want the country, and would have sold or given it away long ago to the whites, but for the "squaw men" about the reservations, who urged them to make a "big fuss" and they would be sure to get a "big price" for the country.

These statements are borne out by those of every Indian communicated with, and by the observation of every man of our party. The Indians do not live in, occupy, or use the country in any way (except for lodge-poles, as stated); they do not want it; the large majority would willingly give it to the whites, but for the exertions and influence of as rascally a set of white men as curse the earth. It appears probable that there will be a war on this question. Some homes will be ruined, some good men and valuable citizens will be murdered, some women ravished, some babies brained against burning door-posts, and all because a few miscreants want to make money.

The Black Hills are closed to settlers by virtue of a treaty with the Indians, which treaty, the settlers claim, has been violated by the Indians time and again. By it the Indians agreed to abstain from robbery and murder of the whites. Within a very short time after it was made, the very Indians making it murdered an officer of the army, and though (I am told) the individual Indians who committed the crime are well known, though the jewelry and other articles of the murdered man are worn openly by the murderers, not only is nothing said about it, but the murderers and their families are "good Indians," living at the reservation and drawing their rations with excellent regularity. . . .

It may appear very singular to most persons that a question so easy of solution as this Indian problem should have been allowed to disturb and agitate the country for so many years.

It must appear strange, the facts being known to almost every intelligent person of the land, that agents of the Government have been permitted to starve and swindle the Indian year after year with impunity.

The murder of a family by white ruffians, with the accompaniment of rape and arson, would send a thrill of horror through every breast. No stone would be left unturned to capture the villains and bring them to the gallows. Yet every year murders, arsons, rapes are permitted to the Indian as pastimes, the murderers, though known, not only remaining unmolested, but being fed and petted by the agents of a Government which owes protection to all its citizens.

The impunity which surrounds all these abuses is, however, easily accounted for, when we reflect on the enormous power of money, and the desperate passion with which some men pursue gain.

There is more money in this Indian question than in any other which agitates the country, and where money is, there power is also.

Some of the greatest fortunes of this country have been founded on Indian contracts, Indian agencies, Indian trade.

Some of our wealthiest and most powerful citizens are, at this moment, pecuniarily interested in having this matter remain just as it is, and the Indian Ring[4] is the wealthiest and most powerful in the land. . . .

Conclusion

The "Black Hills" country is a true oasis in a wide and dreary desert. The approaches from every direction are through long stretches of inhospitable plains, treeless and broken, in which the supply of water is so saturated with bitter and nauseous alkalies as to be unfit for the continuous use of the white man. . . .

I but express my fair and candid opinion when I pronounce the Black Hills, in many respects, the finest country I have ever seen.

The beauty and variety of the scenery, the excellence of the soil, the magnificence of the climate, the abundance of timber and building-stone, make it a most desirable residence for men who want good homes.

As a grazing country it cannot be surpassed; and small stock-farms of fine cattle and sheep cannot, I think, fail of success.

In a few years, when this wilderness shall have been made to "blossom as the rose," with cozy farms and comfortable residences, when rocky crags shall have been crowned with palatial hotels, the tourist will find an ample reward in climbing the rugged heights, or exploring the dark defiles of this wonderful land.

Gold there is, everywhere in the granitic areas; gold enough to make many fortunes, and tempt to the loss of many more. The very uncertainty has a fascination for many men. It is a grand lottery! Only a few draw prizes, but each may be the favorite of the "fickle goddess."

This hope, this barest chance, will draw thousands of men from comfortable homes and sorrowing friends.

In a few weeks or months the eager thirst for "pot-holes"[5] will have deserted the better class, and they will settle down into valuable citizens of a country destined in a few years to be an important and wealthy portion of the great American Republic.

---

[4]**Indian Ring:** Dodge is charging that a syndicate of U.S. officials, Indian agents, and commercial vendors have gotten wealthy through illegal or questionable activity in filling the contracts that supplied food and other goods to Indians on reservations.
[5]**"pot-holes":** Mining strikes.

7. A CHEYENNE VIEW OF BATTLE

In 1874, troops under the command of George Armstrong Custer found gold in the Black Hills. Miners soon began to stream into the area, in stark violation of the Laramie Treaty of 1868. Sioux Indians and their allies retaliated, and Custer and other military officers and units were sent out to push the Indians onto reservations. But things did not work out as the U.S. army planned. On June 25, 1876, Custer, along with several hundred of his men, died in a brief but fierce battle near the banks of the Little Big Horn River in Montana. The humiliating defeat galvanized the army, which quickly conquered the Native Americans of the Northern Plains.

Nearly sixty years after the battle, the Cheyenne warrior Wooden Leg recalled the event and his role in it, in conversation. In this excerpt from the transcription of Wooden Leg's reminiscences, the aged Cheyenne remembers the tumult and excitement of that fateful day when Custer and his few hundred men blundered into a gathering of four thousand Indians, the largest congregation of Native American warriors ever assembled in North America. As you read Wooden Leg's account, think of the sights and sounds of the battle he is describing. How would his viewpoint affect the portrayal of this battle in a film? Do Wooden Leg's memories of the battle and the behavior of the Indians fit what Chivington believed about Native Americans? What does this reminiscence reveal about codes of conduct among Indian warriors?

WOODEN LEG
Account of the Battle of the Little Bighorn
1931

In my sleep I dreamed that a great crowd of people were making lots of noise. Something in the noise startled me. I found myself wide awake, sitting up and listening. My brother too awakened, and we both jumped to our feet. A great commotion was going on among the camps. We heard shooting. We hurried out from the trees so we might see as well as hear. The shooting was somewhere at the upper part of the camp circles. It looked as if all of the Indians there were running away toward the hills to the westward or down toward our end of the village. Women were screaming and men were letting out war cries. Through it all we could hear old men calling:

"Soldiers are here! Young men, go out and fight them."

We ran to our camp and to our home lodge. Everybody there was excited. Women were hurriedly making up little packs for flight. Some were going off northward or across the river without any packs. Children were hunting for their mothers. Mothers were anxiously trying to find their children. I got my lariat and my six shooter. I hastened on down toward where had been our horse herd. . . .

Thomas Marquis, ed., *Wooden Leg: A Warrior Who Fought Custer* (Lincoln: University of Nebraska Press, 1962), 217–28, 231, 236–37, 240, 247–48, 256.

My father had caught my favorite horse from the herd brought in by the boys and Bald Eagle. I quickly emptied out my war bag and set myself at getting ready to go into battle. I jerked off my ordinary clothing. I jerked on a pair of new breeches that had been given to me by an Uncpapa Sioux. I had a good cloth shirt, and I put it on. My old moccasins were kicked off and a pair of beaded moccasins substituted for them. My father strapped a blanket upon my horse and arranged the rawhide lariat into a bridle. He stood holding my mount.

. "Hurry," he urged me. . . .

The air was so full of dust I could not see where to go. But it was not needful that I see that far. I kept my horse headed in the direction of movement by the crowd of Indians on horseback. I was led out around and far beyond the Uncpapa camp circle. Many hundreds of Indians on horseback were dashing to and fro in front of a body of soldiers. The soldiers were on the level valley ground and were shooting with rifles. Not many bullets were being sent back at them, but thousands of arrows were falling among them. I went on with a throng of Sioux until we got beyond and behind the white men. By this time, though, they had mounted their horses and were hiding themselves in the timber. A band of Indians were with the soldiers. It appeared they were Crows or Shoshones. Most of these Indians had fled back up the valley. Some were across east of the river and were riding away over the hills beyond.

Our Indians crowded down toward the timber where were the soldiers. More and more of our people kept coming. Almost all of them were Sioux. There were only a few Cheyennes. Arrows were showered into the timber. Bullets whistled out toward the Sioux and Cheyennes. But we stayed far back while we extended our curved line farther and farther around the big grove of trees. Some dead soldiers had been left among the grass and sagebrush where first they had fought us. It seemed to me the remainder of them would not live many hours longer. Sioux were creeping forward to set fire to the timber.

Suddenly the hidden soldiers came tearing out on horseback, from the woods. I was around on that side where they came out. I whirled my horse and lashed it into a dash to escape from them. All others of my companions did the same. But soon we discovered they were not following us. They were running away from us. They were going as fast their tired horses could carry them across an open valley space and toward the river. We stopped, looked a moment, and then we whipped our ponies into swift pursuit. A great throng of Sioux also were coming after them. My distant position put me among the leaders in the chase. The soldier horses moved slowly, as if they were very tired. Ours were lively. We gained rapidly on them.

I fired four shots with my six shooter. I do not know whether or not any of my bullets did harm. I saw a Sioux put an arrow into the back of a soldier's head. Another arrow went into his shoulder. He tumbled from his horse to the ground. Others fell dead either from arrows or from stabbings or jabbings or from blows by the stone war clubs of the Sioux. Horses limped or staggered or sprawled out dead or dying. Our war cries and war songs were mingled with many jeering calls, such as:

"You are only boys. You ought not to be fighting. We whipped you on the Rosebud. You should have brought more Crows or Shoshones with you to do your fighting."

Little Bird and I were after one certain soldier. Little Bird was wearing a trailing warbonnet. He was at the right and I was at the left of the fleeing man. We were lashing him and his horse with our pony whips. It seemed not brave to shoot him. Besides, I did not want to waste my bullets. He pointed back his revolver, though, and sent a bullet into Little Bird's thigh. Immediately I whacked the white man fighter on his head with the heavy elk-horn handle of my pony whip. The blow dazed him. I seized the rifle strapped on his back. I wrenched it and dragged the looping strap over his head. As I was getting possession of this weapon he fell to the ground. I did not harm him further. I do not know what became of him. . . .

Indians mobbed the soldiers floundering afoot and on horseback in crossing the river. I do not know how many of our enemies might have been killed there. With my captured rifle as a club I knocked two of them from their horses into the flood waters. Most of the pursuing warriors stopped at the river, but many kept on after the men with the blue clothing. I remained in the pursuit and crossed the river. . . .

Another enemy Indian was behind a little sagebrush knoll and shooting at us. His shots were returned. I and some others went around and got behind him. We dismounted and crept toward him. As we came close up to him he fell. A bullet had hit him. He raised himself up, though, and swung his rifle around toward us. We rushed upon him. I crashed a blow of my rifle barrel upon his head. Others beat and stabbed him to death. I got also his gun. . . .

I returned to the west side of the river. Lots of Indians were hunting around there for dead soldiers or for wounded ones to kill. I joined in this search. I got some tobacco from the pockets of one dead man. I got also a belt having in it a few cartridges. All of the weapons and clothing and all other possessions were being taken from the bodies. The warriors were doing this. No old people nor women were there. They all had run away to the hill benches to the westward. I went to a dead horse, to see what might be found there. Leather bags were on them, behind the saddles. I rummaged into one of these bags. I found there two pasteboard boxes. I broke open one of them.

"Oh, cartridges!" . . .

Now I need not be so careful in expending ammunition. Now I felt very brave. I jumped upon my horse and went again to fight whatever soldiers I might find on the east side of the river. . . .

From our hilltop position I fired a few shots from my newly-obtained rifle. I aimed not at any particular ones, but only in the direction of all of them. I think I was too far away to do much harm to them. I had been there only a short time when somebody said to me:

"Look! Yonder are other soldiers!"

I saw them on distant hills down the river and on our same side of it. The news of them spread quickly among us. Indians began to ride in that direction. . . .

Not many people were in the lodges of our camp. . . .

More and more Indians were flocking from the camps to that direction. Some were yet coming along the hills from where the first soldiers had stopped. The soldiers now in view were spreading themselves into lines along a ridge. The Indians were on lower ridges in front of them, between them and the river, and were moving on around up a long coulee to get behind the white men. . . .

The slow long-distance fighting was kept up for about an hour and a half, I believe. The Indians all the time could see where were the soldiers. . . .

After the long time of the slow fighting, about forty of the soldiers came galloping from the east part of the ridge down toward the river, toward where most of the Cheyennes and many Ogallalas were hidden. The Indians ran back to a deep gulch. The soldiers stopped and got off their horses when they arrived at a low ridge where the Indians had been. Lame White Man, the Southern Cheyenne chief, came on his horse and called us to come back and fight. In a few minutes the warriors were all around these soldiers. Then Lame White Man called out:

"Come. We can kill all of them." . . .

A Sioux wearing a warbonnet was lying down behind a clump of sagebrush on the hillside only a short distance north of where now is the big stone having the iron fence around it. He was about half the length of my lariat rope up ahead of me. Many other Indians were near him. Some boys were mingled among them, to get in quickly for making coup blows [1] on any dead soldiers they might find. A Cheyenne boy was lying down right behind the warbonnet Sioux. The Sioux was peeping up and firing a rifle from time to time. At one of these times a soldier bullet hit him exactly in the middle of the forehead. His arms and legs jumped in spasms for a few moments, then he died. The boy quickly slid back down into a gully, jumped to his feet and ran away. . . .

The shots quit coming from the soldiers. Warriors who had crept close to them began to call out that all of the white men were dead. All of the Indians then jumped up and rushed forward. All of the boys and old men on their horses came tearing into the crowd. The air was full of dust and smoke. Everybody was greatly excited. It looked like thousands of dogs might look if all of them were mixed together in a fight. . . .

Seven of these last soldiers broke away and went running down the coulee sloping toward the river from the west end of the ridge. I was on the side opposite from them, and there was much smoke and dust, and many Indians were in front of me, so I did not see these men running, but I learned of them from the talk afterward. They did not get far, because many Indians were all around them. . . .

---

[1] **making coup blows:** Delivering final blows to the dead or wounded enemy.

I took one scalp. As I went walking and leading my horse among the dead I observed one face that interested me. The dead man had a long beard growing from both sides of his face and extending several inches below the chin. He had also a full mustache. All of the beard hair was of a light yellow color, as I now recall it. Most of the soldiers had beard growing, in different lengths, but this was the longest one I saw among them. I think the dead man may have been thirty or more years old. "Here is a new kind of scalp," I said to a companion. I skinned one side of the face and half of the chin, so as to keep the long beard yet on the part removed. . . .

I rode away from the battle hill in the middle of the afternoon. Many warriors had gone back across the hills to the southward, there to fight again the first soldiers. But I went to the camps across on the west side of the river. I had on a soldier coat and breeches I had taken. I took with me the two metal bottles of whisky. At the end of the arrow shaft I carried the beard scalp.

I waved my scalp as I rode among our people. The first person I met who took special interest in me was my mother's mother. She was living in a little willow dome lodge of her own. "What is that?" she asked me when I flourished the scalp stick toward her. I told her. "I give it to you," I said, and I held it out to her. She screamed and shrank away. "Take it," I urged. "It will be good medicine for you." Then I went on to tell her about my having killed the Crow or Shoshone at the first fight up the river, about my getting the two guns, about my knocking in the head two soldiers in the river, about what I had done in the next fight on the hill where all of the soldiers had been killed. We talked about my soldier clothing. She said I looked good dressed that way. I had thought so too, but neither the coat nor the breeches fit me well. The arms and legs were too short for me. . . .

There was no dancing nor celebrating of any kind in any of the camps that night. Too many people were in mourning, among all of the Sioux as well as among the Cheyennes. Too many Cheyenne and Sioux women had gashed their arms and legs, in token of their grief. The people generally were praying, not cheering. . . .

8. A Nez Percé's Call for Peace

A year after Custer's humiliating defeat, the army went after a band of the Nez Percé Indians of eastern Oregon. Led by Hin-mah-too-yah-lat-kekht (Thunder traveling over the mountains), or "Young Joseph" (as whites called him to distinguish him from his father), the Wallowa Valley band of the Nez Percés wanted nothing to do with reservation life. Following a series of clashes with white settlers, Joseph's band begin a remarkable sprint eastward, first toward the countryside surrounding Yellowstone (which had been made the nation's first National Park in 1872) and then north to Canada. Just forty miles short of the border, the majority of the band, exhausted, cold, and hungry, surrendered to General Nelson Miles. From there, the Nez Percés were shuttled off to imprisonment in interior camps, forts, and reservations in the West. Only in 1885 were they allowed to move to the Nez Percé reservation in Idaho.

In this document, published in the pages of a leading magazine not long after his capture, Young Joseph discusses his views of Indian affairs, especially as they relate to the dramatic story of the Nez Percés. "An Indian's View" was originally delivered as a speech in Washington, D.C. Though Chief Joseph's remarks called for an ambitious rethinking of the government's Indian policies, the speech, in the end, accomplished little other than to make him a well-known, well-respected tribal leader. In this excerpt he relates how his band of Wallowa Nez Percés felt forced into flight. Given his remarks in this speech, what decisions do you think Chief Joseph would have made if he were able to influence U.S. Indian policy? How would Lieutenant Colonel Richard Dodge have responded to this speech? What would Colonel Chivington propose? How does religion influence Joseph's perspective?

CHIEF JOSEPH
"An Indian's View of Indian Affairs"
1879

My friends, I have been asked to show you my heart. I am glad to have a chance to do so. I want the white people to understand my people. Some of you think an Indian is like a wild animal. This is a great mistake. I will tell you all about our people, and then you can judge whether an Indian is a man or not. I believe much trouble and blood would be saved if we opened our hearts more. I will tell you in my way how the Indian sees things. The white man has more words to tell you how they look to him, but it does not require many words to speak the truth. What I have to say will come from my heart, and I will speak with a straight tongue. . . .

We did not know there were other people besides the Indian until about one hundred winters ago, when some men with white faces came to our country.

Young Joseph, "An Indian's View of Indian Affairs," *North American Review* 269 (April 1879): 415–16, 419–25, 432–33.

They brought many things with them to trade for furs and skins. They brought to-bacco, which was new to us. They brought guns with flint stones on them, which frightened our women and children. Our people could not talk with these white-faced men, but they used signs which all people understand. These men were Frenchmen, and they called our people "Nez Percés," because they wore rings in their noses for ornaments. Although very few of our people wear them now, we are still called by the same name. These French trappers said a great many things to our fathers which have been planted in our hearts. Some were good for us, but some were bad. Our people were divided in opinion about these men. Some thought they taught more bad than good. An Indian respects a brave man, but he despises a coward. He loves a straight tongue, but he hates a forked tongue. . . .

For a short time we lived quietly. But this could not last. White men had found gold in the mountains around the land of winding water. They stole a great many horses from us, and we could not get them back because we were In-dians. The white men told lies for each other. They drove off a great many of our cattle. Some white men branded our young cattle so they could claim them. We had no friend who would plead our cause before the law councils. It seemed to me that some of the white men in Wallowa were doing these things on purpose to get up a war. They knew that we were not strong enough to fight them. I la-bored hard to avoid trouble and bloodshed. We gave up some of our country to the white men, thinking that then we could have peace. We were mistaken. The white man would not let us alone. We could have avenged our wrongs many times, but we did not. Whenever the Government has asked us to help them against other Indians, we have never refused. When the white men were few and we were strong we could have killed them all off, but the Nez Percés wished to live at peace. . . .

On account of the treaty made by the other bands of the Nez Percés, the white men claimed my lands. We were troubled greatly by white men crowding over the line. Some of these were good men, and we lived on peaceful terms with them, but they were not all good.

Nearly every year the agent came over from Lapwai[1] and ordered us on to the reservation. We always replied that we were satisfied to live in Wallowa. We were careful to refuse the presents or annuities which he offered.

Through all the years since the white men came to Wallowa we have been threatened and taunted by them and the treaty Nez Percés. They have given us no rest. We have had a few good friends among white men, and they have always advised my people to bear these taunts without fighting. Our young men were quick-tempered, and I have had great trouble in keeping them from doing rash things. I have carried a heavy load on my back ever since I was a boy. I learned then that we were but few, while the white men were many, and that we could

---

[1] **Lapwai:** The Lapwai Reservation in Idaho, where the Nez Percés had been ordered to move. Some Nez Percé bands had signed an earlier treaty agreeing to go to the reservation; Joseph's Wallowa Val-ley Nez Percés had not signed the treaty.

not hold our own with them. We were like deer. They were like grizzly bears. We had a small country. Their country was large. We were contented to let things remain as the Great Spirit Chief made them. They were not; and would change the rivers and mountains if they did not suit them.

Year after year we have been threatened, but no war was made upon my people until General Howard[2] came to our country two years ago and told us that he was the white war-chief of all that country. He said: "I have a great many soldiers at my back. I am going to bring them up here, and then I will talk to you again. I will not let white men laugh at me the next time I come. The country belongs to the Government, and I intend to make you go upon the reservation."

I remonstrated with him against bringing more soldiers to the Nez Percés country. He had one house full of troops all the time at Fort Lapwai.

The next spring the agent at Umatilla agency sent an Indian runner to tell me to meet General Howard at Walla Walla. I could not go myself, but I sent my brother and five other head men to meet him, and they had a long talk.

General Howard said: "You have talked straight, and it is all right. You can stay in Wallowa." He insisted that my brother and his company should go with him to Fort Lapwai. When the party arrived there General Howard sent out runners and called all the Indians in to a grand council. I was in that council. I said to General Howard, "We are ready to listen." He answered that he would not talk then, but would hold a council next day, when he would talk plainly. I said to General Howard: "I am ready to talk to-day. I have been in a great many councils, but I am no wiser. We are all sprung from a woman, although we are unlike in many things. We can not be made over again. You are as you were made, and as you were made you can remain. We are just as we were made by the Great Spirit, and you can not change us; then why should children of one mother and one father quarrel—why should one try to cheat the other? I do not believe that the Great Spirit Chief gave one kind of men the right to tell another kind of men what they must do."

General Howard replied: "You deny my authority, do you? You want to dictate to me, do you?"

Then one of my chiefs—Too-hool-hool-suit—rose in the council and said to General Howard: "The Great Spirit Chief made the world as it is, and as he wanted it, and he made a part of it for us to live upon. I do not see where you get authority to say that we shall not live where he placed us."

General Howard lost his temper and said: "Shut up! I don't want to hear any more of such talk. The law says you shall go upon the reservation to live, and I want you to do so, but you persist in disobeying the law" (meaning the treaty). "If you do not move, I will take the matter into my own hand, and make you suffer for your disobedience."

---

[2] **General Howard:** O. O. Howard, an army officer and one-armed Civil War veteran who had earlier headed up the Freedman's Bureau in the South.

Too-hool-hool-suit answered: "Who are you, that you ask us to talk, and then tell me I sha'n't talk? Are you the Great Spirit? Did you make the world? Did you make the sun? Did you make the rivers to run for us to drink? Did you make the grass to grow? Did you make all these things, that you talk to us as though we were boys? If you did, then you have the right to talk as you do."

I said: "War can be avoided, and it ought to be avoided. I want no war. My people have always been the friends of the white man. Why are you in such a hurry? I can not get ready to move in thirty days. Our stock is scattered, and Snake River is very high. Let us wait until fall, then the river will be low. We want time to hunt up our stock and gather supplies for winter."

General Howard replied, "If you let the time run over one day, the soldiers will be there to drive you on to the reservation, and all your cattle and horses outside of the reservation at that time will fall into the hands of the white men."

I knew I had never sold my country, and that I had no land in Lapwai; but I did not want bloodshed. I did not want my people killed. I did not want anybody killed. Some of my people had been murdered by white men, and the white murderers were never punished for it. I told General Howard about this, and again said I wanted no war. I wanted the people who lived upon the lands I was to occupy at Lapwai to have time to gather their harvest.

I said in my heart that, rather than have war, I would give up my country. I would give up my father's grave. I would give up everything rather than have the blood of white men upon the hands of my people.

General Howard refused to allow me more than thirty days to move my people and their stock. I am sure that he began to prepare for war at once. . . .

There were bad men among my people who had quarreled with white men, and they talked of their wrongs until they roused all the bad hearts in the council. Still I could not believe that they would begin the war. I know that my young men did a great wrong, but I ask, Who was first to blame ? They had been insulted a thousand times; their fathers and brothers had been killed; their mothers and wives had been disgraced; they had been driven to madness by whisky sold to them by white men; they had been told by General Howard that all their horses and cattle which they had been unable to drive out of Wallowa were to fall into the hands of white men; and, added to all this, they were homeless and desperate.

I would have given my own life if I could have undone the killing of white men by my people. I blame my young men and I blame the white men. I blame General Howard for not giving my people time to get their stock away from Wallowa. I do not acknowledge that he had the right to order me to leave Wallowa at any time. I deny that either my father or myself ever sold that land. It is still our land. It may never again be our home, but my father sleeps there, and I love it as I love my mother. I left there, hoping to avoid bloodshed. . . .

My friends among white men have blamed me for the war. I am not to blame. When my young men began the killing, my heart was hurt. Although I did not justify them, I remembered all the insults I had endured, and my blood was on fire. Still I would have taken my people to the buffalo country without fighting if possible. . . .

When I think of our condition my heart is heavy. I see men of my race treated as outlaws and driven from country to country, or shot down like animals.

I know that my race must change. We can not hold our own with the white men as we are. We only ask an even chance to live as other men live. We ask to be recognized as men. We ask that the same law shall work alike on all men. If the Indian breaks the law, punish him by the law. If the white man breaks the law, punish him also.

Let me be a free man — free to travel, free to stop, free to work, free to trade where I choose, free to choose my own teachers, free to follow the religion of my fathers, free to think and talk and act for myself — and I will obey every law, or submit to the penalty.

Whenever the white man treats the Indian as they treat each other, then we will have no more wars. . . .

For this time the Indian race are waiting and praying. I hope that no more groans of wounded men and women will ever go to the ear of the Great Spirit Chief above, and that all people may be one people.

[Hin-mah-too-yah-lat-keht] has spoken for his people.

[Young Joseph.]

Washington City, D.C.

Suggestions for Further Reading

Brown, Dee. *The Fetterman Massacre: An American Saga.* London: Barrie and Jenkins, 1972.

Calloway, Colin G., ed. *Our Hearts Fell to the Ground: Plains Indian Views of How the West Was Lost.* Boston: Bedford Books, 1996.

Hutton, Paul. *Phil Sheridan and His Army.* Lincoln: University of Nebraska Press, 1985.

Josephy, Alvin. *The Nez Percé and the Opening of the Northwest.* New Haven: Yale University Press, 1965.

Paul, Rodman. *The Far West and the Great Plains in Transition, 1850–1900.* New York: Harper and Row, 1988.

Schultz, Duane P. *Month of the Freezing Moon: The Sand Creek Massacre.* New York: St. Martin's Press, 1991.

Utley, Robert. *The Indian Frontier of the American West, 1846–1890.* Albuquerque: University of New Mexico Press, 1984.

West, Elliott. *The Contested Plains: Indians, Goldseekers, and the Rush to Colorado.* Lawrence: University Press of Kansas, 1998.

Wooster, Robert. *The Military and United States Indian Policy, 1865–1903.* New Haven: Yale University Press, 1988.

San Francisco, c. 1890

At the time of this photograph, San Francisco held nearly three hundred thousand people, making it the eighth largest city in America. Like its urban counterparts in the East, San Francisco owed its growth to immigration and industrial expansion. In 1890, with more than a third of its populace born outside the United States, the city was one of the most ethnically diverse places in the country, if not the world. These identical side-by-side images are mounted on a card and were meant to be viewed through a device called a stereopticon, which produced a three-dimensional effect. Stereographic photography, all the rage in the latter part of the nineteenth century, offered people the illusion of visiting new places. This street scene would convey to viewers in other parts of the country a vivid sense of bustling prosperity. No longer a rough-and-ready gold rush town, San Francisco boasted tall buildings, paved sidewalks, and fashionably dressed people. Miners' dungarees, the uniform of the forty-niners, are conspicuously absent. Why do you think a photograph like this might be interesting to someone in the East or the South? Does this look like a city in the West?

Bancroft Library, University of California at Berkeley.

CHAPTER THREE

URBANIZATION

WESTERN CITIES

In the decades following the Civil War, America reinvented itself as an urban nation. Once centers of commerce and trade, cities became centers of
industrial expansion. Fueled by important innovations in technology and
transportation — railroads, better factory machinery, and more-efficient trolley
systems, for instance — American cities expanded outward. New York, already
huge in 1870 with nearly a million people, boasted a population five times larger
by 1910. In Chicago, the brash young city of the Midwest, the population increased tenfold during the same period. Cities farther west also witnessed rapid
growth.

Many factors combined to propel urbanization forward, but the most important were the twin phenomena of industrialization and immigration. American cities operated like magnets, attracting millions of people from all over the
world. Eastern and Southern Europeans, Irish, Germans, Russians, Jews, Chinese, and others saw in American cities the possibility of a better life and seized
on the chance. Many found factory jobs in the cities, but life for these urban immigrants was difficult. Not only did they have to contend with poor conditions in
city slums, but they also met hostility in a variety of forms from protest in the press
to direct violence.

Industrial growth and city growth went hand in hand. Chicago expanded, for
example, because its massive stockyards, where immigrants found steady work,
used a sophisticated web of railroad networks to ship beef all over the country.
San Francisco, already a center of industry, built upon advances in machinery
to become an even bigger center of industrial activity. The pattern recurred
across the nation and throughout the West: industrial enterprises supplied factory
jobs, luring new immigrants and thus contributing to urban growth. Native-born
Americans also headed for the cities in large numbers by the 1870s and 1880s, in
response to falling farm prices and depleted soil. Workers from rural areas also

found employment in factories and in the countless small businesses and shops that had sprung up to serve the growing population.

America's urban growth from 1870 to 1910 affected western cities much as it did other urban areas. By century's end the West had been transformed. It was no longer that earlier wilderness of Lewis and Clark, traditional Native American life, and Spanish missions. Western urbanization was the next step in a process that had begun before the Civil War. Westerners gradually congregated into hamlets, which became villages and then towns. But city growth in the West was markedly different, both in terms of proportion and rate of change. By the 1870s, railroads crisscrossed the West in an iron web of communication and transportation. This new industrial force on the landscape — and in the economy — played a powerful role in urbanization, especially in the West, where distances between places were vast. A railroad rolling through a small town might mean that the town would grow into a city, provided that the railroad's presence fostered nearby industries or promoted the local real-estate market. But if the railroad's managers and owners opted to bypass the town, the results could be disastrous. Without the railroad, tourist access, publicity, and links to markets for buying and selling goods were limited. The railroad was a key to western urban expansion.

Aiding the growth of cities were the "boosters," the untiring individuals and companies that "boosted" or championed the fine points and attractions of particular cities. They papered the nation with maps, photographs, advertisements, and circulars extolling the "delights" of Denver, the "charms" of Seattle, or the "promise" of Boise. Every western city (or town wanting to be a city) had its own promoters. These boosters had a stake in the game: land to sell or businesses to promote. The railroads, especially the giant corporations like the Southern Pacific and the Atchison, Topeka & Santa Fe, were among the most important boosters of all, controlling the lifelines of trade and travel.

There is little doubt that people answered the call. Denver, with a population of over 30,000 in 1880, was already a good-sized American city and large by western standards. Within ten years, however, its population would reach nearly 100,000. Further to the west, San Francisco, the nation's tenth largest city in 1870, had by 1890 become a major manufacturing center. More remarkable still was the growth of Los Angeles, a village of only a few thousand residents when California became a state in 1850. Within twenty-five years, Los Angeles had a transcontinental rail connection and a regional population of more than 30,000 people. Farming, ranching, real estate, orange growing, and an additional cross-country rail line provided the city's boosters with a lot more to boast about: by 1890, the Los Angeles basin held a population of over 100,000 people, and by 1920, ten times that many.

Along with growth came typical urban concerns, such as the spread of disease, overcrowding, water and sewage problems, labor disputes, and crime. Racial intolerance and violence also plagued western cities. As African American emigrants to the West discovered, they did better in isolated, all-black communities, away from the discriminatory actions of white neighbors. Anti-immigrant activities, directed particularly at the Chinese, became commonplace. In California, Chinese laborers migrated to cities like San Francisco following the completion of the transcontinental railroad in 1869, which they had helped to build. Once there, however, they faced vicious attacks and condemnation at the hands of rival workers and politicians out to stop further Chinese immigration to the United States.

The selections in this chapter examine the process of city-building in the West after the Civil War. Late-nineteenth-century travelers' descriptions of Salt Lake City and Denver convey some sense of each city's look and feel in these years of concerted growth. A description of San Francisco in the 1880s focuses on "the Chinese question," replaying some of the era's uglier stereotypes but at the same time wondering whether Americans ought to treat immigrant populations with greater humanity. A cartoon from the period offers further perspective on this issue. Booker T. Washington's description of Boley, an all-black colony in Oklahoma, suggests why African Americans felt that separation from white America was preferable to integration, even in the supposedly more egalitarian American West. Finally, official census figures measure the rapid urbanization and diversity of the West at the end of the nineteenth century.

As you read the following selections, consider how urbanization changed the way people lived. What examples of change can you identify in the documents reproduced here? How do the commentators compare cities in the West to those in the East? What connections do you see between industry, immigration, and urbanization in the West?

---

9. A Tourist's View
of the Utah Territory

An eastern writer who was extremely fond of the West, Samuel Bowles wrote numerous books and articles extolling the virtues of the region. In this document, Bowles writes of time he spent in Salt Lake City, the capital of the Utah Territory. Founded in the late 1840s by Mormons fleeing persecution in other parts of the nation, Salt Lake City grew with the faith of those who settled it. Like many travelers before and after him, Bowles is fascinated by the Mormon capital. For him, the city is at once exotic and mundane. Bowles is bemused by Mormon practices and the city's mixture of civil and religious government, but he is also clearly appreciative of Salt Lake City's neatness and its tidy urban plan. In what ways does Bowles compare Salt Lake City to other American cities of the period? How does he describe the city's diversity of population and opinion?

SAMUEL BOWLES
A Week in Salt Lake
1869

The city has, indeed, a most charming location, and is happily laid out and improved. Coming out of the mountains on the east and north, we enter upon a high plateau or "bench" of land, commanding the valley for forty or fifty miles to the south, and west to Salt Lake and the mountains that seem to rise from out of the water, and, stretching southward, guard the valley in that direction. The city lies directly below, . . . under the highest mountains, on what seems almost a level plain, but holding a grade that keeps the irrigating streams in quick motion, and promotes dryness and health, — with wide sweep of fertile valley before it, Salt Lake shimmering with the sunlight in the far distance, and the delaying Jordan ribboning the gardens of grain and grass below, — with mountains behind white-capped in snow even under the summer's sun, and hills in front that often rival them in hight and garniture, — Salt Lake City spreads itself with luxuriance of space, and with luxuriance of garden and orchard growth, that almost hides its buildings.

The streets are broad and regular, — one hundred feet from curb to curb, — dividing the town into squares of just ten acres, and these again are divided into eighths, which leaves an acre and a quarter for each home. Only in the business streets and in the lower and poorer quarters are these home lots subdivided. The houses were originally altogether of adobe, or mud bricks dried in the sun; now, stone and red brick are introduced for the larger buildings and stores, and lumber varies with the earlier material in dwellings and second-rate business establishments. The houses are mostly small, and a story or a story and a half in height; they often suggest the peculiar institution of the country by a long frontage with numerous distinct entrances. The number of wives a man has is frequently indicated by the number of front doors to his house.

A full square of ten acres in the center of the city is devoted to the central

Samuel Bowles, *Our New West: Records of Travel between the Mississippi River and the Pacific Ocean* (Hartford, Conn.: Hartford Publishing, 1869), 219–25.

church edifices. Here is the old Tabernacle, a large, low, barn-like structure, holding several thousand people; also the new Tabernacle, which will contain from ten to fifteen thousand, is two hundred and fifty feet long, one hundred and fifty feet wide, and ninety high, built of stone, covered by a grand arched dome, and looks in the distance like a huge deep platter turned bottom up. In the most conspicuous location of the same square lie the foundations of the Grand Temple, begun many years ago, and to be finished when the church has leisure and money enough. The plan proposes a structure that rivals the cathedrals of Europe, and is grander than any church edifice in America. This square is surrounded by a strong, high wall of adobe brick and plaster.

Similarly guarded from cunning eyes or profane entrance by a high, strong wall, is Brigham Young's[1] entire square, opposite. Within this are the "tithing-house," where are gathered in the tenth part of every man's yearly productions or profits, the other offices and store-houses of the church, two large houses for Young and his extensive family and his private offices, a school-house with cupola for his children, immense barns and sheds for his animals, and far in the rear his grand model flouring-mill. Fine gardens and orchards fill up the vacant places. Here is the central life and authority of the State. The telegraph of the church, extending all over the Territory, centers here, and here is the office of the special church newspaper organ.

The principal business street is long and well built. There are a few stores of the very first character, both in size, amount and variety of goods, and extent of business done. There are several firms, some Mormon, others not, that do a business of a million and over each every year. The great Mormon establishments often connect manufacturing of some kind with their business, and frequently have branch stores all over the territory; but they are all in the hands of close allies, relatives, or subservient instruments of Brigham Young, and are under his sharp surveillance. The hotels, two of which are large and well managed, are all kept by Mormons; and so far as possible, all the avenues to money-making, all the instrumentalities of life in the city, are in the hands of creatures of the head of this Church and State organization. If a Mormon is suspected of unsoundness, or is getting too rich and powerful, he is persecuted out of the way, or "called of God" to go as missionary somewhere, and leave his business in somebody else's hands, or the "tithings" are applied so sharply as to keep his fortune within reasonable bounds. Many cases are given in illustration of these and other ways of enriching the church and preventing the growth of individual power.

Within the last few months, a new plan has been devised for extending and compacting the business affiliations of the church. It is that of putting all extensive trade and manufacturing operations into coöperative associations, and inviting all the Mormon population to take shares in them. The great Mormon stores

---

[1] **Brigham Young's:** Young succeeded Joseph Smith as the spiritual and political leader of the Mormon Church and led the Mormons to Salt Lake City in the 1840s.

in Salt Lake City have been thus converted, and the principle is rapidly extending to all business enterprises in every part of the Territory. It has two advantages, — that of extending the common interests of the grand organization, and ensuring the enforcement of the rule that Mormons shall buy only of Mormons, and that of distributing the losses of any revulsions in business, or any break-down of the Mormon rule, growing out of the revolutionary influences of the Railroad. It strengthens the power of the leaders, and it enables them to change their investments, or, as they say in Wall Street, to "unload."

The long dry summers of all our New West render irrigation a necessity to all diversified culture of the soil. . . . The streams that come out from the mountains are diverted and divided through the streets of the town, and among the farms of the valley above the River Jordan. Thus lively brooks course down the gutters of the streets, keeping the shade trees alive and growing, supplying drink for animals and water for household purposes, and delightfully cooling the summer air; besides being drawn off in right proportion for the use of each garden. . . . Under this regular stimulus, with a strong soil, made up of the wash of the mountains, the finest of crops are obtained; the vegetable bottom lands of the New England rivers or of the interior prairies cannot vie with the products of the best gardens and farms of these western valleys and plains under this system of irrigation. There needs to be enough rain in the spring or winter moisture remaining to start the seeds, and there generally is; after that, the regular supply of water keeps the plants in a steady and rapid growth. . . .

The soil of this and the smaller neighboring valleys is especially favorable to the small grains. Fifty and sixty bushels is a very common crop of wheat, oats and barley; and over ninety have been raised. President Young once raised ninety-three and a half bushels of wheat on a single acre. I should say the same soil located in the East, and taking its chances without irrigation, would not produce half what it does here with irrigation. Laborious and expensive as the process must be, the large crops and high prices obtained for them have made it a very profitable recourse.

But a singular change seems to be creeping over all our Western regions under settlement, in this matter of climate and of rain. Summer rains are palpably on the increase, and the necessity of irrigation is lessening, especially for the grains and slow-growing vegetables. When the Mormons first came here, there was no rain from April to November; but now summer showers are of frequent occurrence. . . . Connected with this change, it is observed here that Salt Lake is growing in size and freshness, and the Jordan increasing in width and sluggishness of movement. In broader phrase, the whole basin, once evidently filled with water, is slowly returning to its old condition. The Lake is rising at the rate of a foot a year. General Connor's little steamboat, that has been carrying ties for the Railroad across the Lake during the last year, certainly rode for a mile over what was good grazing-ground five years before. Does Providence propose to drown the Mormons out, and with water solve the problem that is puzzling our moral philosophers and statesmen? . . .

10. A Day in Denver

The British lawyer W. R. Russell traveled throughout the United States and parts of Canada in 1881 and 1882 as a member of a small company of wealthy tourists. Like thousands of others who could afford to do so, Russell and his companions toured the country by railroad. Such tourist excursions became extremely popular once the transcontinental railroad was completed, and an entire tourist economy developed around them: travel agencies made bookings and other arrangements for the entire trip, luxury hotels sprang up in formerly out-of-the-way places, and the railroad companies published guidebooks and brochures listing and describing various journeys and sights. Tourists expected to see the West's natural grandeur, but they were also surprised by the size and appearance of its cities. In this selection, Russell describes a day he spent in the capital of Colorado. What surprises Russell about Denver? What comparisons does he make between Denver and cities elsewhere in the world? Are these comparisons meaningful or simply descriptive flourishes? What do you think Russell expected the city to look like?

W. R. RUSSELL
"Denver City"
1882

. . . The evidences of a bustling city were not wanting in the approaches to the capital of Colorado. There were tall chimneys vomiting out smoke in the distance, and near at hand trains of wagons were toiling over the dusty plain — still 5000 feet above the sea-level — fast trotters and people on horseback, beer-gardens, factories of all kinds, brick-kilns, and then a fringe of log houses and wooden shanties, before the train stopped at the imposing and substantial depot.

It was a quarter-past eight, nearly dark, when we reached Denver, and glad were we to get into the hall of the Windsor Hotel, which was crowded with a mixed multitude — miners, and speculators, and traders, and some travellers like ourselves — a very busy scene indeed. In the hotel were all human comforts nearly; hot and cold baths, and good rooms, and more appliances of civilised existence, for those who could pay for them, than could be found in many hostelries of approved reputation in venerable towns at home. . . . [A]s we peered out of our windows over the roofs of the wide-spread houses of the town, we could see the snow on the lofty ranges of hills, watered by the South Platte River and Cherry Creek, which surround the cup in which Denver has been built in

W. R. Russell, *Hesperothen; Notes from the West: A Record of a Ramble in the United States and Canada in the Spring and Summer of 1881*, vol. 2 (London: Sampson Low, Marston, Searle and Rivington, 1882), 91–97.

obedience to the impulses of the increasing population, which now numbers, I believe, 38,000 souls. There was a bright glare from the gas-lighted streets, sounds of music, and a tumult of life in the town which would have been creditable to an ancient metropolis. In the morning from the hotel windows appeared a beautiful and wide-spread panorama of the hills we had seen the evening before, peak above peak, . . . all capped with snow, now bathed in a flood of fervent sunshine, the snow lighted up by the peculiar crimson tints common in Alpine regions. . . . There were, perhaps, at that moment some hundreds, if not thousands, out of the population of 37,000 or 38,000 of the city, who belonged to the adventurous classes — sporting-men, betting-men, ring-men, bar-keepers, hell-proprietors,[1] and their satellites, and the scum of the saloons attracted from the great cities of the States for hundreds of miles, by the prey which miners with belts full of gold, half mad with drink, and always fond of excitement, frequently are; and if to these be added the dissolute loafers and broken-down mining speculators, the strength of the army arrayed against the law may be estimated; and the wonder is that among a population armed to the teeth there are not more cases of such violent deeds as we were reading of at breakfast. To the stranger there was no evidence of the existence of these disturbing elements, unless the bearded and booted men with speculation in their eyes, in the hotel passages and halls, belonged to the dangerous, as they certainly did to the mining, classes. As to the resources of the city, . . . [there] is everything that any one can want to be had for money in the place, and much more than most people need. Paris fashions and millinery are in vogue. There are fine shops, handsome churches, a theatre, breweries, factories, banks, insurance offices.

The principal street exhibits pretty young people, who would have no occasion to fear comparison with the *beau monde* in Eastern or European capitals. The thoroughfares are crowded with vehicles, and spruce carriages and well turned-out horses may be seen in the favourite drive, that has been made over an indifferent road to the base of the Rocky Mountains, which appear to be close at hand, though they are thirteen miles away. But here and there in the well-dressed crowd may be seen a Bohemian *pur sang*,[2] or a miner in his every day clothes, bent on a rig out and a good time of it. The streets, unpaved, dusty, and rugged, are very wide, and bordered with trees, and the houses generally are built of good red brick instead of wood; and there are runnels of water like those one sees in Pretoria and other Dutch towns in South Africa. . . .

There are many ready-made clothing establishments in the main streets, and there is a heavy trade in tinned provisions. Through the Western States, as in South Africa, the débris of provision-tins constitutes a certain and considerable addition to the objects to be seen in the vicinity of every house, and to the mounds of rubbish in the street of every village. How indeed could the first-comers in such regions keep body and soul together without the supplies in such

[1] **hell-proprietors:** Gambling-house owners.
[2] *pur sang:* Pure blood.

a portable form of the first necessaries of life? Having once run up a town in these remote wastes, the inhabitants are still compelled to make a liberal use of the same sort of food, and mines of tinned iron gradually accumulate around them.

Our first excursion was to the Argo Works. . . . The works are at some distance outside the town, but the lofty chimneys vomit out quite sufficient vaporous fumes and smoke to blight the vegetation and to give the people near at hand a taste of their quality. . . . The Argo Works simply assay and reduce ores on commission, but the business is on a very large scale. Immense piles, in fact small mountains, of brown, cinnamon and earth coloured dust and rock were heaped up in the sheds, to be brought to the furnaces and turned, when divested of the lead, iron, copper, and gold, out in ingots of silver. . . .

The business of assaying here must be profitable, and if the reputation of any firm be once established there is a secure fortune for its members. The miners flock to them, and they can dictate terms. . . . As a specimen of what Messrs. Bush and Tabor of our hotel give their guests for dinner, let me offer you this *menu* of the 5.30 ordinary to-day (June 16). Soup, beef à l'Anglaise; fish, boiled trout, anchovy sauce; corned beef, leg of mutton, sirloin beef, chickens with giblet sauce, fricassee à la Toulouse, veal, kidneys sautés aux croûtons, rice, croquettes, baked pork and beans, saddle of antelope, currant jelly, lamb, tongue, chicken salad, spiced salmon; innumerable "relishes" and vegetables, baked rice pudding, strawberry pie, apricot pie, jelly, blancmange, vanilla ice cream, macaroons, pound cake, fruit, Swiss cheese, nuts, coffee, &c. The wines were not cheap. . . . Orders for "drinks" at the bar after dinner were much more general[3] than orders for wine at dinner.

Denver, in spite of its mineral wealth, is very poor, however, in that of which the want would make life, even in America, intolerable. The supply of drinking-water is scanty and bad, and last year there was nearly a water famine. The *cartes* in the hotel announced "Water used in this room is boiled and filtered." But great efforts have been made to furnish the inhabitants with a store, constant and adequate, of the precious fluid, and we saw very considerable works, the property of an Irish gentleman, erected before the town attained its present dimensions, which were to be supplemented by a new enterprise respecting which we heard much. Perhaps no town of equal size in an equal length of time has ever had so much money and money's worth flowing in and through it as Denver since the Colorado mines were worked. It is asserted that the trade of the town for 1881 will exceed 8,000,000*l.* Colorado in 1879 yielded ores to the value of more than 3,750,000*l.* The output in the present year will exceed that of 1880. In that year $35,417,517 worth of gold and $20,183,889 of silver (more than 11,000,000*l.*) was deposited in the United States Mint and Assay Office. There is, besides, vast wealth in flocks and herds, and Denver is the place where the people resort from Colorado for purposes of trade and pleasure; altogether an astounding place, with a future quite dazzling to think of, . . .

[3] **general**: Common.

11. THE CHINESE QUESTION IN A CALIFORNIA CITY

Willard Glazier, a writer and military officer who claimed to have lived in more than one hundred cities in the United States, wrote Peculiarities of American Cities *in the early 1880s, when agitation over "the Chinese question" had reached a fever pitch in western cities. The Pacific coast was a hotbed of anti-Chinese feeling, and San Francisco the capital of racial intolerance. Although it was home to as much as a third of California's Chinese population, the city relegated the Chinese to poorly paid work in laundries and factories. Yet many white workers feared Chinese competition and charged the Chinese with driving down the cost of labor. Anti-Chinese sentiments prompted the formation of political parties whose platform and slogan was "The Chinese Must Go!" Other western cities displayed attitudes that were little better and sometimes much worse. Both Rock Springs, Wyoming, and Los Angeles witnessed race riots in which mobs invaded local Chinatowns and killed dozens of people. In large measure in response to such vehemence, Congress passed the Chinese Exclusion Act in 1882, which barred further Chinese immigration to the United States.*

In this selection, Glazier describes his impressions of San Francisco and the city's Chinese population. Although he falls into conventional racial stereotypes, he also recognizes the ironies in the anti-Chinese movement. How would you characterize Glazier's view of the Chinese? How does he connect "the Chinese question" to the growth of San Francisco?

WILLARD GLAZIER
"San Francisco"
1883

. . . The Chinese problem is one which is agitating the country and giving a coloring to its politics. The Pacific States seem, by a large majority of their population, to regard the presence of the Mongolian among them as an unmitigated evil, to be no longer tolerated. Eastern capitalists have hailed their coming as inaugurating the era of cheap labor and increased fortunes for themselves. Hence the discussion and the disturbances. A lady who had made her home in San Francisco for several years past, says, in a letter to the writer of this article, "A person not living in California can form no conception of the curse which the Chinese are to this section of the world."

Captain Willard Glazier, *Peculiarities of American Cities* (Philadelphia, 1886), 469–71.

Yet without them some of the great enterprises of the Pacific coast, notably the Central Pacific Railroad, would have remained long unfinished; and they came also to furnish manual labor at a time when it was scarce and difficult to obtain at any price. The Chinaman is a strange compound of virtue and vice, cleanliness and filth, frugality and recklessness, simplicity and cunning. He is scrupulously clean as to his person, indulging in frequent baths; yet he will live contentedly with the most wretched surroundings, and inhale an air vitiated by an aggregation of breaths and stenches of all kinds. He is a faithful worker and a wonderful imitator. He cannot do the full work of a white man, but he labors steadily and unceasingly. He takes no time for drunken sprees, but he is an inveterate opium smoker, and sometimes deliberately sacrifices his life in the enjoyment of the drug. He is frugal to the last degree, but will waste his daily earnings in the gambling hell and policy shop. Scrupulously honest, he is yet the victim of the vilest vices which are engrafting themselves upon our western coast. Living upon one-third of what will keep a white man, and working for one-half the wages the latter demands, he is destroying the labor market of that quarter of our country, reducing its working classes to his own level, in which in the future the latter, too, will be forced to be contented on a diet of "rice and rats," and to forego all educational advantages for their children, becoming, like the Chinese themselves, mere working machines; or else enter into a conflict of labor against labor, race against race.

The latter alternative seems inevitable, and it has already begun. China, with her crowded population, could easily spare a hundred million people and be the better for it. Those one hundred million Chinamen, if welcomed to our shores, would speedily swamp our western civilization. They might not become the controlling power — the Anglo-Saxon is always sure to remain that — but as hewers of wood and drawers of water, as builders of our railroads, hands upon our farms, workers in our factories, and cooks and chambermaids in our houses, a like number of American men and women would be displaced, and wages quickly reduced to an Asiatic level; and such a time of distress as this country never saw would dawn upon us.

There seems to be no assimilation between the Caucasian and the Mongolian on the Pacific slope. In the East an Irish girl recently married a Chinaman; but in San Francisco, though every other race under the sun has united in marriage, the Chinaman is avoided as a pariah. White and yellow races may meet and fraternize in business, in pleasure, and even in crime; but in marriage never. Chinamen rank among the most respected merchants of San Francisco, and these receive exceptional respect as individuals; but between the two races as races a great gulf is fixed. The Chinese immigrant takes no interest in American affairs. His world is on the other side of the Pacific. And the American people return the compliment by taking no interest in him. It is undeniable that, by a certain class of San Francisco citizens, popularly known as Hoodlums, the treatment of the Chinese population has been shameful in the extreme. A Chinaman has no rights which a white man is bound to respect. Insult, contumely, abuse, cruelty and injustice he has been forced to bear at the hands of the rougher classes, without hope of redress. He has been kicked, and cheated, and plundered, and not a voice has been raised in his behalf; but if he has been guilty of the slightest peccadillo, how quickly has he been made to feel the heavy hand of justice!

It seems a pity that before the cry was raised with such overwhelming force, "The Chinese must go!"[1] some little effort had not been made to adapt them to Western civilization. They are quick to take ideas concerning their labor; why not in other things? We have received and adopted the ignorant, vicious hordes from foreign lands to the east of us, and are fast metamorphosing them into intelligent, useful citizens. We are even trying our hand upon the negro, as a late atonement for all the wrong we have done him. But the Indian and the Chinaman seem to be without the pale of our mercy and our Christianity. It might not have been possible, but still the experiment was worth the trying, of attempting to lift them up industrially, educationally and morally, to a level with our own better classes, instead of permitting them to drag us down. Returning to their own country, and carrying back with them our Western civilization, as a little leaven, they might have leavened the whole lump. It is too late for that now, and the mandate has gone forth: "The Chinese must go!" Considering all things as they are, rather than as they might have been, it is undoubtedly better so, and the only salvation of our Pacific States. . . .

[1] **"The Chinese must go!"**: A racial and political rallying cry of the 1870s, used most effectively by white working-class politicians and activists in San Francisco worried about competition from Chinese labor. Sentiments such as these led to the 1882 Chinese Exclusion Act.

12. THE CHINESE QUESTION IN CARTOON

The controversy over the presence of the Chinese in the cities and towns of the West played itself out in innumerable newspaper columns, editorials, pamphlets, and posters during the 1870s and early 1880s. The question also prompted cartoonists to weigh in on one side or the other. Most often, the Chinese found themselves viciously lampooned in racist cartoons that derided everything about them: their physical appearance, their social practices, their living conditions, even their eating habits. This cartoon (right) is an exception to the general trend of racial antagonism, in that it emphasizes an economic basis for the West's virulent anti-Chinese feeling. In view of Glazier's comments and this cartoon, how do you think economic incentives influenced the anti-Chinese movement in the West? What other period sources might tell you more about the situation? How does the tone of the cartoon's caption compare with the way the cartoonist has depicted the Chinese immigrant?

"UNCLE SAM'S HOSPITALITY"

1882 — economic threat

UNCLE SAM'S HOSPITALITY.

Keep off! You are so industrious and economical that our boys
can't compete with you.

George Augustus Sala, *America Revisited: From the Bay of New York to the Gulf of Mexico* (London:
Vizetelly and Co., 1882), 237.

13. AN AFRICAN AMERICAN COMMUNITY

Booker T. Washington, the head of the African American Tuskegee Institute in Ala-
bama, visited Oklahoma shortly before it became a state in 1907. There he saw first-
hand the racial and ethnic diversity of the former Indian Territory. In this essay he

describes his impressions of Oklahoma, its inhabitants, and the all-black colony of Boley. Washington briefly discusses the history of African American migration to the West and writes of the ways in which the young state's Indian, African American, and white populations treat one another. Boley, a growing colony of several thousand people, was of particular interest to the famed educator. Though Washington refers to the colony as a town, the U.S. Census Bureau, with an urbanization scale of 2,500 people, would have considered Boley — and any other western community of its size — a city. What ingredients of western city-building does Boley have? What is Washington's impression of the levels of western racial tolerance? In Washington's eyes, what makes Boley "western"?

BOOKER T. WASHINGTON
"Boley, a Negro Town in the West"
1908

Boley, Indian Territory, is the youngest, the most enterprising, and in many ways the most interesting of the negro towns in the United States. A rude, bustling, Western town, it is a characteristic product of the negro immigration from the South and Middle West into the new lands of what is now the State of Oklahoma.

The large proportions of the northward and westward movement of the negro population recall the Kansas Exodus of thirty years ago, when within a few months more than forty thousand helpless and destitute negroes from the country districts of Arkansas and Mississippi poured into eastern Kansas in search of "better homes, larger opportunities, and kindlier treatment."

It is a striking evidence of the progress made in thirty years that the present northward and westward movement of the negro people has brought into these new lands, not a helpless and ignorant horde of black people, but land-seekers and home-builders, men who have come prepared to build up the country. In the thirty years since the Kansas Exodus the Southern negroes have learned to build schools, to establish banks and conduct newspapers. They have recovered something of the knack for trade that their foreparents in Africa were famous for. They have learned through their churches and their secret orders the art of corporate and united action. This experience has enabled them to set up and maintain in a raw Western community numbering 2,500, an orderly and self-respecting government.

In the fall of 1905 I spent a week in the Territories of Oklahoma and Indian Territory.[1] During the course of my visit I had an opportunity for the first time to

[1] **Territories of Oklahoma and Indian Territory:** Oklahoma Territory had been carved out of the western part of Indian Territory in 1890. The two merged to become the state of Oklahoma in 1907.

Outlook (4 January 1908): 28–31.

see the three races — the Negro, the Indian, and the white man — living side by side, each in sufficient numbers to make their influence felt in the communities of which they were a part, and in the Territory as a whole. It was not my first acquaintance with the Indian. During the last years of my stay at Hampton Institute I had charge of the Indian students there, and had come to have a high respect both for their character and intelligence, so that I was particularly interested to see them in their own country, where they still preserve to some extent their native institutions. I was all the more impressed, on that account, with the fact that in the cities that I visited I rarely caught sight of a genuine native Indian. When I inquired, as I frequently did, for the "natives," it almost invariably happened that I was introduced, not to an Indian, but to a Negro. During my visit to the city of Muskogee I stopped at the home of one of the prominent "natives" of the Creek Nation, the Hon. C. W. Sango, Superintendent of the Tullahasse Mission. But he is a negro. The negroes who are known in that locality as "natives" are the descendants of slaves that the Indians brought with them from Alabama and Mississippi, when they migrated to this Territory, about the middle of the last century. I was introduced later to one or two other "natives" who were not negroes, but neither were they, as far as my observation went, Indians. They were, on the contrary, white men. "But where," I asked at length, "are the Indians?"

"Oh! the Indians," was the reply, "they have gone," with a wave of the hand in the direction of the horizon, "they have gone back!"

I repeated this question in a number of different places, and invariably received the same reply, "Oh, they have gone back!" I remembered the expression because it seemed to me that it condensed into a phrase a great deal of local history.

One cannot escape the impression, in traveling through Indian Territory, that the Indians, who own practically all the lands, and until recently had the local government largely in their own hands, are to a very large extent regarded by the white settlers, who are rapidly filling up the country, as almost a negligible quantity. To such an extent is this true that the Constitution of Oklahoma, as I understand it, takes no account of the Indians in drawing its distinctions among the races. For the Constitution there exist only the negro and the white man. The reason seems to be that the Indians have either receded — "gone back," as the saying in that region is — on the advance of the white race, or they have intermarried with and become absorbed with it. Indeed, so rapidly has this intermarriage of the two races gone on, and so great has been the demand for Indian wives, that in some of the Nations, I was informed, the price of marriage licenses has gone as high as $1,000.

The negroes, immigrants to Indian Territory, have not, however, "gone back." One sees them everywhere, working side by side with white men. They have their banks, business enterprises, schools, and churches. There are still, I am told, among the "natives" some negroes who cannot speak the English language, and who have been so thoroughly bred in the customs of the Indians that they have remained among the hills with the tribes by whom they were adopted. But, as a rule, the negro natives do not shun the white man and his civilization, but, on the contrary, rather seek it, and enter, with the negro immigrants, into competition with the white man for its benefits.

This fact was illustrated by another familiar local expression. In reply to my inquiries in regard to the little towns through which we passed, I often had occasion to notice the expression, "Yes, so and so? Well, that is a 'white town.'" Or, again, "So and so, that's colored."

I learned upon inquiry that there were a considerable number of communities throughout the Territory where an effort had been made to exclude negro settlers. To this the negroes had replied by starting other communities in which no white man was allowed to live. For instance, the thriving little city of Wilitka, I was informed, was a white man's town until it got the oil mills. Then they needed laborers, and brought in the negroes. There are a number of other little communities — Clairview, Wildcat, Grayson, and Taft — which were sometimes referred to as "colored towns," but I learned that in their cases the expression meant merely that these towns had started as negro communities or that there were large numbers of negroes there, and that negro immigrants were wanted. But among these various communities there was one of which I heard more than the others. This was the town of Boley, where, it is said, no white man has ever let the sun go down upon him.

In 1905, when I visited Indian Territory, Boley was little more than a name. It was started in 1903. At the present time it is a thriving town of two thousand five hundred inhabitants, with two banks, two cotton gins, a newspaper, a hotel, and a "college," the Creek-Seminole College and Agricultural Institute.

There is a story told in regard to the way in which the town of Boley was started, which, even if it is not wholly true as to the details, is at least characteristic, and illustrates the temper of the people in that region.

One spring day, four years ago, a number of gentlemen were discussing, at Wilitka, the race question. The point at issue was the capability of the negro for self-government. One of the gentlemen, who happened to be connected with the Fort Smith Railway, maintained that if the negroes were given a fair chance they would prove themselves as capable of self-government as any other people of the same degree of culture and education. He asserted that they had never had a fair chance. The other gentlemen naturally asserted the contrary. The result of the argument was Boley. Just at that time a number of other town sites were being laid out along the railway which connects Guthrie, Oklahoma, with Fort Smith, Arkansas. It was, it is said, to put the capability of the negro for self-government to the test that in August, 1903, seventy-two miles east of Guthrie, the site of the new negro town was established. It was called Boley, after the man who built that section of the railway. A negro town-site agent, T. M. Haynes, who is at present connected with the Farmers' and Merchants' Bank, was made Town-site Agent, and the purpose to establish a town which should be exclusively controlled by negroes was widely advertised all over the Southwest.

Boley, although built on the railway, is still on the edge of civilization. You can still hear on summer nights, I am told, the wild notes of the Indian drums and the shrill cries of the Indian dancers among the hills beyond the settlement. The outlaws that formerly infested the country have not wholly disappeared. Dick

Shafer, the first Town Marshal of Boley, was killed in a duel with a horse thief, whom he in turn shot and killed, after falling, mortally wounded, from his horse. The horse thief was a white man.

There is no liquor sold in Boley, or any part of the Territory, but the "natives" go down to Prague, across the Oklahoma border, ten miles away, and then come back and occasionally "shoot up" the town. That was a favorite pastime, a few years ago, among the "natives" around Boley. The first case that came up before the Mayor for trial was that of a young "native" charged with "shooting up" a meeting in a church. But, on the whole, order in the community has been maintained. It is said that during the past two years not a single arrest has been made among the citizens. The reason is that the majority of these negro settlers have come here with the definite intention of getting a home and building up a community where they can, as they say, be "free." What this expression means is pretty well shown by the case of C. W. Perry, who came from Marshall, Texas. Perry had learned the trade of a machinist and had worked in the railway machine shops until the white machinists struck and made it so uncomfortable that the negro machinists went out. Then he went on the railway as brakeman, where he worked for fifteen years. He owned his own home and was well respected, so much so that when it became known that he intended to leave, several of the County Commissioners called on him. "Why are you going away?" they asked; "you have your home here among us. We know you and you know us. We are behind you and will protect you."

"Well," he replied, "I have always had an ambition to do something for myself. I don't want always to be led. I want to do a little leading." . . .

A large proportion of the settlers of Boley are farmers from Texas, Arkansas, and Mississippi. But the desire for Western lands has drawn into the community not only farmers, but doctors, lawyers, and craftsmen of all kinds. The fame of the town has also brought, no doubt, a certain proportion of the drifting population. But behind all other attractions of the new colony is the belief that here negroes would find greater opportunities and more freedom of action than they have been able to find in the older communities North or South.

Boley, like the other negro towns that have sprung up in other parts of the country, represents a dawning race consciousness, a wholesome desire to do something to make the race respected; something which shall demonstrate the right of the negro, not merely as an individual, but as a race, to have a worthy and permanent place in the civilization that the American people are creating. . . .

14. Demography in the West

The following two documents, one a brief excerpt from the 1890 census and the other an excerpt of a table from the 1900 census, reflect both the growth and the diversity of the West at the close of the nineteenth century. According to the 1890 census, an unbroken line of frontier no longer existed in the nation. Although census officials could once define a border in the American West between settlement and wilderness, now they could no longer find it. The concept was itself muddled, for with it came all kinds of preconceived notions about what constituted settlement, civilization, wilderness, and progress. It also assumed that American history was a one-way movement from the East to the West in which "civilization" pushed aside what the nineteenth century called "savagery." This description of a frontierless America prompted the historian Frederick Jackson Turner to ponder the origins of American democratic institutions and the role the West had played in their development. The 1900 census document (right), a table of demography statistics from the West, shows population growth and diversity. It is important to note this diversity; European and other immigrants arrived in the cities of the East but many went West, either directly or within a short time. There, they most often ended up in the expanding cities. How would you describe the tone of the 1890 assessment of the nation's progress? What does it imply about western urban growth? What can you determine from the 1900 population figures?

U.S. Census Bureau
Statistics Measuring Progress and Birthrates
1890 and 1900

1890

This census completes the history of a century; a century of progress and achievement unequaled in the world's history. A hundred years ago there were groups of feeble settlements sparsely covering an area of 239,935 square miles, and numbering less than 4,000,000. The century has witnessed our development into a great and powerful nation; it has witnessed the spread of settlement across the continent until not less than 1,947,290 square miles have been redeemed from the wilderness and brought into the service of man, while the population has increased and multiplied by its own increase and by additions from abroad until it numbers 62,622,250.

During the decade just past a trifling change has been made in the boundary between Nebraska and Dakota by which the area of Nebraska has been slightly increased. Dakota territory has been cut in two and the states of North Dakota and South Dakota admitted. Montana, Wyoming, Idaho, and Washington have also been added to the sisterhood of states. The territory of Oklahoma

Eleventh Census of the United States, 1890, Population, Part I, xxvii–xxviii.

Native and Foreign Born Population, by States and Territories Arranged Geographically, in 1880, 1890, and 1900, with Increase since 1890.

STATES AND TERRITORIES	NATIVE BORN			FOREIGN BORN			INCREASE FROM 1890 TO 1900			
							Native born		Foreign born	
	1900	1890	1880	1900	1890	1880	Number	Percent	Number	Percent
Western division	3,245,028	2,331,359	1,267,635	846,321	770,910	500,062	913,669	39.2	75,411	9.8
Montana	176,262	99,828	27,638	67,067	43,096	11,521	76,434	76.6	23,971	55.6
Wyoming	75,116	47,642	14,939	17,415	14,913	5,850	27,474	57.7	2,502	16.8
Colorado	448,545	329,259	154,537	91,155	83,990	39,790	119,286	36.2	7,165	8.5
New Mexico	181,685	149,023	111,514	13,625	11,259	8,051	82,662	21.9	2,366	21.0
Arizona	98,698	69,448	24,391	24,233	18,795	16,049	29,250	42.1	5,488	28.9
Utah	222,972	157,715	99,969	53,777	53,064	43,994	65,257	41.4	713	1.3
Nevada	32,242	32,649	36,613	10,093	14,706	25,653	[2]407	[2]1.2	[2]4,613	[2]31.4
Idaho	137,168	71,092	22,636	24,604	17,456	9,974	66,076	92.9	7,148	40.9
Washington	406,739	267,227	59,313	111,364	90,005	15,803	139,512	52.2	21,359	23.7
Oregon	347,788	260,387	144,265	65,748	57,317	30,503	87,401	33.6	8,431	14.7
California	1,117,813	847,089	571,820	367,240	366,309	292,874	270,724	32.0	931	0.3
Alaska	50,931	15,381	—	12,661	16,671	—	35,550	231.1	[2]4,010	[2]224.1
Hawaii	63,221	48,117	—	90,780	41,873	—	15,104	31.4	48,907	116.8

[1] Includes persons in the military and naval service of the United States (including civilian employees, etc.) stationed abroad, not credited to any state or territory.
[2] Decrease.

Twelfth Census of the United States, 1900, Population, Part I, xcix.

has been created out of the western half of the Indian territory, and to it has been added the strip of public land lying north of the panhandle of Texas.

The most striking fact connected with the extension of settlement during the past decade is the numerous additions which have been made to the settled area within the Cordilleran region. Settlements have spread westward up the slope of the plains until they have joined the bodies formerly isolated in Colorado, forming a continuous body of settlement from the east to the Rocky mountains. Practically the whole of Kansas has become a settled region, and the unsettled area of Nebraska has been reduced in dimensions to a third of what it was ten years ago. What was a sparsely settled region in Texas in 1880 is now the most populous part of the state, while settlements have spread westward to the escarpment of the Staked Plains. The unsettled regions of North Dakota and South Dakota have been reduced to half their former dimensions. Settlements in Montana have spread until they now occupy one-third of the state. In New Mexico, Idaho, and Wyoming considerable extensions of area are to be noted. In Colorado, in spite of the decline of the mining industry and the depopulation of its mining regions, settlement has spread, and two-thirds of the state are now under the dominion of man. Oregon and Washington show equally rapid progress, and California, although its mining regions have suffered, has made great inroads upon its unsettled regions, especially in the south. Of all the western states and territories Nevada alone is at a standstill in this respect, its settled area remaining practically the same as in 1880. When it is remembered that the state has lost one-third of its population during the past ten years, the fact that it has held its own in settled area is surprising until it is understood that the state has undergone a material change in occupations during the decade, and that the inhabitants, instead of being closely grouped and engaged in mining pursuits, have become scattered along its streams and have engaged in agriculture. . . .

Suggestions for Further Reading

Abbott, Carl. *Portland: Planning, Politics, and Growth in a Twentieth-Century City.* Lincoln: University of Nebraska Press, 1983.

Barth, Gunther. *Instant Cities: Urbanization and the Rise of San Francisco and Denver.* New York: Oxford University Press, 1975.

Larson, Lawrence H. *The Urban West at the End of the Frontier.* Lawrence: Regents Press of Kansas, 1978.

MacDonald, Norbert. *Distant Neighbors: A Comparative History of Seattle and Vancouver.* Lincoln: University of Nebraska Press, 1987.

Miller, Zane L., and Patricia M. Melvin. *The Urbanization of Modern America: A Brief History.* 2nd ed. San Diego: Harcourt, Brace, Jovanovich, 1987.

Monkkonen, Eric. *America Becomes Urban: The Development of U.S. Cities and Towns.* Berkeley: University of California Press, 1988.

Reps, John W. *Cities of the American West: A History of Frontier Urban Planning.* Princeton: Princeton University Press, 1979.

Starr, Kevin. *Americans and the California Dream.* New York: Oxford University Press, 1973.

CHAPTER FOUR

POPULISM

POLITICS AND PROTEST

The magnitude and speed of urban growth in the 1890s left its mark on the countryside. So, too, did the coming of the depression of 1893. In the spring of that year, the stock market collapsed. As crop prices fell, rural families saw their sons and daughters migrate to the cities in search of work, discontent boiled over into radicalism, and the American farm belt, especially in the South and the West, became a hotbed of political and cultural protest.

Rural dissent, often in the form of organized criticism of the political economy of industrializing and urbanizing America, had been rising steadily since the end of the Civil War. Farmers were losing ground, culturally as well as economically, as a result of the powerful social forces remaking America. A farmers movement, organized around a loose confederation of clubs called the Grange, had spread across the Midwest and Far West in the 1860s and 1870s. Members were interested in cooperatives, price controls, and firmer economic footing for independent growers; they hoped that by combining forces, they might exercise more political power in an increasingly industrialized America.

The Granger movement lost steam in the 1880s, in part because of costly attempts to manufacture farm equipment for its members (and thus bypass the big manufacturers). But the Grange helped encourage other efforts at change in rural areas. Out of the dust of the Granger movement arose a number of farmers' alliances in the South and West. By the early 1890s the alliance movement

---

William Jennings Bryan Campaign Poster, 1900 (left)

William Jennings Bryan ran for president for a second time in 1900, four years after losing in the 1896 campaign that saw the Populists and the Democrats unite on a "fusion" ticket. This poster from the 1900 campaign, displaying symbolic references to such things as the railroad "octopus" and the Liberty Bell, is an example of the ways in which Bryan tried to appeal to voters across a wide geographical, occupational, and regional perspective during both attempts to win the presidency. What other symbols can you find in this poster?

Library of Congress.

had mounted a viable third-party challenge to the two-party dominance of Republicans and Democrats by electing independent candidates to state seats. In 1892, encouraged by these successes, the alliance movement spawned a national political party called the People's Party, also known as the Populist Party, and launched a campaign for the White House.

Populists were a mix of many things: conservative one moment, radical the next; open-minded, closed-minded; racially egalitarian, racially exclusive. Historians have disagreed, and continue to disagree, about what Populism meant and what its political programs signified, but a few things are certain. Like Grangers, Populists were angry — sometimes to the point of violent action — about the declining centrality of rural life in America and joined together to do something about it.

As part of their national campaign, Populists tried to link city and country, looking for ways to bond together for a common cause with urban or factory workers who were also disenchanted with the new urban and industrial order. In campaigns attacking the centralized banking authority, corporate (especially railroad) hierarchies, and the political structures tied to them, Populists and their allies in the cities tried to remake America. This explicit class-based appeal gave Populism its radical tinge: workers and farmers ought to band together so the American political economy could be reformed to benefit the laborers, who were the producers of wealth, rather than the corporations and monopolies that hoarded profits. And they did band together, whether on the front lines of railroad strikes in California, in the midst of mining strife in the Rockies, or elsewhere in the West.

This campaign to unite workers and farmers for electoral strength was no flash in the pan. The Populist presidential candidate James B. Weaver lost the 1892 election, but he won several western states outright (Kansas, Colorado, Idaho, and Nevada) and polled a million votes. Some states elected Populist governors, and some cities Populist mayors. Through this remarkable showing, Populists posed a challenge to the status quo that frightened the Republican and Democratic parties. The Populists did not limit their influence to politics. Industrial violence throughout the 1890s — and there was a lot of it — often involved farmers. For instance, the 1894 Pullman Strike, which paralyzed rail traffic in California and elsewhere, saw farmers in active support of striking railroad workers. Both believed that railroad corporations had grown too powerful: workers resented corporate labor practices, and farmers thought railroads charged unfair prices to transport produce to market. The same story of solidarity was repeated in countless other such alliances throughout the West.

Just as significant was the Populist stance on gender. Populism offered women, many of them farming women, their first chance at active, and often very public, political participation. In this regard, the movement echoed the West's more fully developed appreciation of the involvement of women in public affairs. Across the West, beginning in the states of Wyoming, Colorado, Idaho, and Utah, women gained the right to vote years in advance of eastern and southern women. In fact, it would be a full generation before the Constitution would grant all American women the right to vote, yet Populism's progressive legislation in the West offered many women a chance to play important public roles as speakers and political organizers.

Populism eventually faded as a political movement. After Weaver's defeat in 1892, the Populists endorsed a Nebraskan Democrat, William Jennings Bryan, in the 1896 presidential election. Bryan stridently opposed the gold standard, which tied the U.S. money supply to federal gold reserves. This had become too critical for the Populists to ignore. Like Bryan, Populists, especially those in the mining states of the West, favored "free silver," or the unlimited coinage of silver by the federal government, which the gold standard would prevent. The worsening depression of the 1890s raised this issue above all other Populist goals. Populists hoped that federal purchases of western silver would drive up farm prices by increasing the money supply.

Despite pleas by some Populists to, in the words of one leader from Texas, "stand by the demands of the industrial people!," the free-silver issue siphoned off farmer votes and undercut the rest of the Populist platform. By supporting Bryan, the Populists yanked the heart out of their third-party challenge. Urban industrial workers did not find enough compelling reasons to support the free-silver campaign with their votes, especially since they expected that free silver would encourage inflation. Their counterparts in the mines deserted the movement in disgust once powerful silver-mine industrialists, also obvious free-silver advocates, began waving "Bryan for President" banners. A star of American politics at thirty-six, Bryan give one of the most compelling and dramatic of all American political speeches, his "Cross of Gold" address, at the convention. But it was not enough. Populists could not bring the Democrats enough votes. Republican William McKinley, an easterner tied to conservative eastern and urban interests, trounced Bryan on election day and, with him, the movement itself.

The documents in this chapter introduce a number of Populists and Populist perspectives. Some sense of the appeal of Populism to women can be gleaned from Annie Diggs's description of women in the alliance movement. William Jennings Bryan's famous speech before the 1896 Democratic Convention illustrates how fervently people felt on the issues of the gold standard and free silver. Daniel Zercher lists many reasons why he chose to become a Kansas Populist, and the newspaper journalist William Allen White offers his opposition to Populism in a famous essay. The final selection is drawn from the opening pages of a best-selling novel of 1901 that seeks to describe, according to Populist sensibilities, an immensely powerful railroad corporation.

As you read these selections, think about regional differences in the Populist movement. Why did Populism take hold in a state like Kansas? What would

Populists in Kansas have in common with Populists in California? How would William Allen White respond to the issues raised by Annie Diggs or Daniel Zercher? How would either of these two Populist supporters answer White's criticisms? Do you see any parallels in the speech of William Jennings Bryan and the fiction of Frank Norris?

---

15. WOMEN IN THE POPULIST MOVEMENT

The alliance movement, which grew out of the Grange, would become the Populist movement with the formation of the People's Party in 1892. The following magazine article, published the same year Populism "went national," describes the role of women in the movement and the ways in which Populism responded to women's political interests. According to Annie Diggs, women were drawn to the alliance for a number of reasons: political commitment, boredom, loneliness, the desire to associate with other women, and the sheer excitement of the cause. A prominent orator and politician in her own right, Annie Diggs had been active in Kansas temperance and suffrage reform for more than a decade when she wrote this essay. By the mid-1890s, she would become one of the best-known women in the Populist movement and the state librarian of Kansas. What indication, if any, does Diggs give about the possible appeal of Populism among urban or industrial workers, men or women? How does she describe the reaction of opponents to alliance women?

ANNIE L. DIGGS
"The Women in the Alliance Movement"
1892

The women prominent in the great farmer manifesto[1] of this present time were long preparing for their part; not consciously, not by any manner of means even divining that there would be a part to play. In the many thousands of isolated farm homes the early morning, the noonday, and the evening-time work went on with a dreary monotony which resulted in that startling report of the physicians that American farms were recruiting stations from whence more women went to insane asylums than from any other walk in life.

---

[1] **manifesto:** A declaration of principles, usually, as in this case, political.

The Arena 31 (June 1892): 161–63, 165, 179.

Farm life for women is a treadmill. The eternal climb must be kept up though the altitude never heightens. For more than a quarter of a century these churning, washing, ironing, baking, darning, sewing, cooking, scrubbing, drudging women, whose toilsome, dreary lives were unrelieved by the slight incident or by-play of town life, felt that their treadmills slipped cogs. Climb as they would, they slipped down two steps while they climbed one. They were not keeping pace with the women of the towns and cities. The industry which once led in the march toward independence and prosperity, was steadily falling behind as to remuneration. Something was wrong.

The Grange came on — a most noble order, of untold service and solace to erstwhile cheerless lives. Pathetic the heart-hunger for the beauty side of life. The Grange blossomed forth in "Floras" and "Pomonas." There was a season of sociability, with much good cookery, enchanting jellies, ethereal angel cakes, and flower-decked tables. There was much burnishing of bright-witted women — not always listeners, often essayists. Sometimes, indeed, leaders of discussion and earnest talk about middlemen, the home market, the railroad problem, and such other matters as would have shed light on the cause of the farmer's declining prosperity had not wary politicians sniffed danger, and, under specious pretense of "keeping out politics lest it kill the Grange," tabooed free speech and thus adroitly injected the fatalest of policies. The Grange is dead. Long live the Grange born again — the Alliance! this time not to be frightened out of politics or choked of utterance; born this time to do far more than talk — to vote.

The Granger sisters through the intervening years, climbing laboriously, patiently, felt their treadmill cogs a slipping three steps down to one step up. Reincarnate in the Alliance the whilom[2] Floras and Pomonas became secretaries and lecturers. The worn and weary treadmillers are anxious, troubled. They have no heart for poetry or play. Life is work unremitting. There is no time for ransacking of heathen mythologies for fashions with which to trig out modern goddesses. Instead of mythologic lore, they read "Seven Financial Conspiracies," "Looking Backward," "Progress and Poverty." Alas! of this last word they know much and fear more — fear for their children's future. These once frolicking Floras and playful Pomonas turn with all the fierceness of the primal mother-nature to protect their younglings from devouring, devastating plutocracy.

Politics for the farmer had been recreation, relaxation, or even exhilaration, according to the varying degree of his interest, or of honor flatteringly bestowed by town committeemen upon a "solid yeoman" at caucus or convention. The flush of pride over being selected to make a nominating speech, or the sense of importance consequent upon being placed on a resolution committee to acquiesce in the prepared document conveniently at hand — these high honors lightened much muddy plowing and hot harvest work.

But the farmers' wives participated in no such ecstacies. Hence for them no blinding party ties. And therefore when investigation turned on the light, the women spoke right out in meeting, demanding explanation for the non-

---

[2] **whilom:** Formerly or, in this usage, former.

appearance of the home market for the farm products, which their good husbands had been prophesying and promising would follow the upbuilding of protected industries. These women in the Alliance, grown apt in keeping close accounts from long economy, cast eyes over the long account of promises of officials managing public business, and said, "Promise and performance do not balance." "Of what value are convention honors, or even elected eloquence in national Capitol, if homelessness must be our children's heritage?"

Carlyle's Menads,[3] hungrier than American women are *as yet*, penetrated the French Assembly "to the shamefulest interruption of public speaking" with cries of, "*Du pain! pas tant de longs discours!*" Our Alliance women spake the same in English: "Bread! not so much discoursing!" "Less eloquence and more justice!" . . .

In several states, notably Texas, Georgia, Michigan, California, Colorado, and Nebraska, women have been useful and prominent in the farmer movement, which indeed is now widened and blended with the cause of labor other than that of the farm.

Kansas, however, furnished by far the largest quota of active, aggressive women, inasmuch as Kansas was the theatre where the initial act of the great labor drama was played. . . .

The great political victory of the people of Kansas would not have been won without the help of the women of the Alliance. Women who never dreamed of becoming public speakers, grew eloquent in their zeal and fervor. Farmers' wives and daughters rose earlier and worked later to gain time to cook the picnic dinners, to paint the mottoes on the banners, to practice with the glee clubs, to march in procession. Josh Billings' saying that "wimmin is everywhere," was literally true in that wonderful picnicking, speech-making Alliance summer of 1890.

Kansas politics was no longer a "dirty pool."[4] That marvellous campaign was a great thrilling crusade. It was religious to the core. Instinctively the women knew that the salvation of their homes, and more even, the salvation of the republic, depended upon the outcome of that test struggle. Every word, every thought, every act, was a prayer for victory, and for the triumph of right. Victory was compelled to come.

Narrow ignoramuses long ago stumbled upon the truth, "The home is woman's sphere." Ignoramus said, "Women should cook and gossip, and rock cradles, and darn socks" — merely these and nothing more. Whereas the whole truth is, women should watch and work in all things which shape and mould the home, whether "money," "land" or "transportation." So now Alliance women look at politics and trace the swift relation to the home — their special sphere. They say, "Our homes are threatened by the dirty pool. The pool must go."

Before this question of the salvation of the imperilled homes of the nation, all other questions, whether of "prohibition" or "suffrage," pale into relative in-

---

[3] **Carlyle's Menads:** A reference to the British historian Thomas Carlyle and his history of the French Revolution.
[4] **"dirty pool":** A general reference to undemocratic combinations of economic and political power.

consequence. For where shall temperance or high thought of franchise be taught the children, by whose breath the world is saved, if sacred hearth fires shall go out? The overtopping, all-embracing moral question of the age is this for which the Alliance came. Upon such great ethical foundation is the labor movement of to-day building itself. How could women do otherwise than be in and of it? . . .

Consider this Kansas record, oh supercilious sneerer at "strong-minded" women. Most of these women have opened their mouths and spake before many people; they have sat in counsel with bodies of men, among whom were their husbands and sons. And oh, Ultima Thule of "unwomanliness," they have voted — actually cast ballot, thereby saying in quietest of human way that virtue shall dethrone vice in municipal government. All these heretical things have they done, and yet are womanliest, gentlest of women, the best of homekeepers, the loyalest of wives, the carefulest of mothers.

What answer to this, oh, most bombastic cavillers — you who would shield woman from the demoralizing ballot? What answer, most ridiculous of theorists, who tremble lest any sort of man-made laws be mightier than nature's laws, who writhe lest statutes should change the loving, loyal mother-nature of woman? Let not such preposterous theorist come into the presence of the six stalwart sons of halofaced Mrs. Davis and suggest that their most revered mother is "unsexed" because of ballot box and politics.

Thus splendidly do the *facts* about women in politics refute the frivolous *theories* of timorous or hostile objectors. The women prominent as active, responsible factors in the political arena are those who are characterized by strong common sense, high ideals, and lofty patriotism. . . .

16. DEFENDING POPULISM

Daniel Zercher's laundry list of the reasons he supported the Populist Party was part of the 1894 "Manifesto" of the People's Party of Kansas but mixed national issues with local conditions. This is not surprising: Populism, like any even moderately successful national political movement, was elastic enough to incorporate the local with the national, the regional with the federal. Pronouncements like Zercher's, which appeared in a book heralding Populism, were not uncommon to the movement, which depended on the voices of everyday Americans to make the case for its principles. Which reasons seem directed solely at issues in Kansas? in the West? Which seem truly national in scope? How would you compare Populism's regional dimensions to the challenge it posed nationally? Which reasons would William Allen White (see Document 17 on p. 79) find particularly objectionable? What phrases or words are now obscure?

DANIEL ZERCHER
"75 Reasons Why I Am a Populist"
1894

1. Because I am in favor of an increase in the volume of money.

2. Because I am in favor of less taxes.

3. Because I am in favor of the remonetization of silver.

4. Because the Populists in congress vote as a unit on the questions that interest the masses — the gold power being unable to divide them.

5. Because I am in favor of paper, silver and gold comprising the money of this country.

6. Because I am in favor of a graduated income and property tax.

7. Because I am opposed to the issuing of bonds in time of peace for the running expenses of the government or for any other purpose.

8. Because I am opposed to the secretary of the treasury having power to issue bonds, except in times of war.

9. Because I am opposed to the exception clause on the greenback.[1]

10. Because I am in favor of the free coinage of silver.

11. Because I am in favor of the poor man having an equal show with the rich.

12. Because I am opposed to the governmental policy of loaning money to banks at 1 per cent. per annum, and refusing to loan it on farms or other good security at any price.

13. Because I am opposed to the granting of subsidies and land grants to railroads or other corporations.

14. Because I am opposed to alien ownership of land in America.

15. Because I am in favor of special privileges to none.

16. Because I am in favor of equal justice to all.

17. Because I am opposed to trusts and combines, the result of the legislation for the past 30 years.

18. Because I am opposed to selling our products in a free-trade market and buying our necessities in a protected market.

19. Because I am opposed to the immigration of pauper labor, without proper restrictions.

20. Because I believe there are several questions which more concern the American people than the tariff.

21. Because I believe that the general government should issue and coin all the money.

---

[1] **greenback:** Paper money. Greenbacks could be used for nearly all transactions, but they were not honored for certain debts of the U.S. government. Supporters of the Greenback movement, or the Greenback Party, many of whom became Populists, wished the government to honor and issue greenbacks more freely and were opposed to the gold standard.

Kansas State Central Committee, People's Party of the United States, *Stubborn Facts in a Nutshell: Manifesto by the State Central Committee of the People's Party* (Topeka: The Advocate Publishing Company, 1894), 55–59.

22. Because I am opposed to national banks as banks of issue.

23. Because I am in favor of the government establishing postal savings banks in lieu of national banks.

24. Because I am in favor of a service pension to all soldiers or sailors of the union army in addition to a pension for disabilities received.

25. Because I am in favor of our government keeping its credit, honor and promises by paying the soldiers of the union army the $16 per month agreed upon for their services, instead of about $6.84 per month, which the depreciated currency amounted to.

26. Because of Republican extravagance on statehouse contracts.

27. Because I believe in rigid economy in governmental affairs.

28. Because the People's Party of Kansas saved the taxpayers over a million dollars during its administration.

29. Because the People's Party keeps its pledges.

30. Because the Populist board of railroad assessors equalized the assessment of railroad property of the state with other property.

31. Because corporations and the wealthy classes should not be granted favors by courts and relieved in the payment of their taxes when the same are denied to the common people.

32. Because no political party is worthy of support that promises bimetalism[2] in its platform and votes single gold standard in congress.

33. Because I am in favor of government ownership of the means of transportation and communication.

34. Because I am in favor of the municipal ownership of electric street railways, electric-light plants, water works, and other public utilities.

35. Because I believe that, with government ownership of the means of transportation and communication, their employés will receive at least $2.25 per day where they now receive $1.10 per day.

36. Because many Populists in Kansas had courage enough to leave a party that had 82,000 majority for the sake of principle.

37. Because Geo[rge]. L. Douglass, a Republican, battered down the doors of representative hall with a sledge hammer.

38. Because every overt act that caused legislative disturbance and trouble in Kansas was committed by the Republicans.

39. Because the Populist senate and Dunsmore house passed the maximum-freight-rate bill.

40. Because I love the People's Party for the abuse it has received, on the principle that Republicans do not usually "throw clubs into a tree unless there are some good apples growing there."

41. Because a Populist superintendent of insurance is collecting reciprocal taxes due the state from insurance companies to the amount of thousands of dollars.

42. Because the Republican house compelled the payment of a board bill

---

[2] **bimetalism:** A Populist political plank that urged the government to use both gold and silver as currency; the gold standard would prevent this.

for Republican members and officers of the Douglass house to the amount of $1,460.20.

43. Because the Republican majority of the supreme court usurped the constitutional authority of the house of representatives.

44. Because Populists favor liberal public improvements.

45. Because I am in favor of the government erecting a post-office building in every city of over 5,000 inhabitants in the United States, and increasing the volume of currency sufficient to pay for them, thus giving employment to our starving millions. This would also save rent.

46. Because Populists will enact and enforce good, wholesome laws if given an opportunity.

47. Because under old party rule the prices of silver, wheat and cotton have constantly declined.

48. Because Republicans always lack just a few votes when it comes to enacting legislation in the interest of the common people.

49. Because the Republicans demonetized silver in 1873.

50. Because the Democrats demonetized silver in 1893.

51. Because Republicans had at least 15,000 illegal voters return to Kansas on passes and vote the Republican ticket.

52. Because Republican loan agents refused to renew farm loans for Populists without first extorting from them a pledge to vote the Republican ticket.

53. Because the Republican canvassing boards counted in Republican legislators when Populists were elected.

54. Because I believe that the person receiving the highest number of legal votes cast for him is elected.

55. Because I believe that a citizen of Oklahoma should not sit as a member in a Kansas legislature.

56. Because a Republican county clerk transposed the figures of a Democratic candidate, who was elected, to the Republican candidate.

57. Because I do not think that a certificate of election is sufficient without a majority of legal ballots back of it.

58. Because Republicans printed and sent out, at public expense, documents for campaign purposes in Swede, German, and English.

59. Because the Populist board of railroad commissioners have reduced freight rates on agricultural implements, coal, and other merchandise, to various points.

60. Because Higgins, Humphrey, Hovey & Co., held a secret lottery drawing behind closed doors, contrary to the statute.

61. Because the Populists proposed to arbitrate the points at issue in the legislature of 1893, and proposed as an arbitrating committee nine judges, as follows: Five Republicans, two Democrats, and two Populists, which proposition was rejected by the Republicans.

62. Because the Populists afterwards offered to refer their claims to an arbitrating board consisting of two Republican judges and one Populist judge, which was also rejected by the Republicans.

63. Because a third proposition was made by the Populists, proposing Chief

Justice Horton (Rep.) and Associate Justice Allen (Pop.), and they two should select a third man, the same to compose an arbitrating committee, whose decision should be final. This was also rejected by the Republicans.

64. Because Sheriff Wilkerson refused to protect state property when called on to do so by Governor Lewelling.

65. Because a Populist law and a Populist state printer have saved the state over $80,000 on state printing in two years.

66. Because a Populist secretary of state has conducted his office without any *extra* clerk hire and, besides, turned into the state treasury, the first year, $1,894.40.

67. Because a Populist bank commissioner turns into the state treasury more than $1,500 per annum, in fees, more than his Republican predecessor.

68. Because of secret rebates to purchasers and contractors of supplies for our state institutions under Republican rule.

69. Because I am opposed to watered stocks of corporations.

70. Because I am opposed to the waving of the bloody shirt[3] or sectional strife.

71. Because the Populist board of equalization made the lowest state tax levy ever made in Kansas.

72. Because Republican newspapers have injured the credit of Kansas in the East, and driven capital out of the state.

73. Because there are but two great political parties, the People's Party and Wall Street.

74. Because the Republicans and Democrats of New Jersey are driving Western capital out of the state.

75. Because I believe in the principles enunciated in the Omaha platform.

[3] **bloody shirt:** Keeping the sectional crisis alive after the Civil War, especially through the actions of the Democratic Party in the South, was known as "waving the bloody shirt."

17. A Newspaperman Opposes Populism

Not everyone in the West supported Populism's demands or its description of economic and political distress. One fierce opponent was the young journalist William Allen White of the Kansas newspaper Emporia Gazette. *His editorial "What's the Matter with Kansas?" attacked Populists and their movement as so much bluster, hot air, and wild ideas. White called the Populists "gibbering idiots" who saw conspiracy lurking around every corner, who feared the things they could not understand, and who had no reasonable plan to address the problems they shouted about. White's editorial, which helped make him famous, reveals the class antagonisms that colored much of the opposition to the Populist campaign. What are White's major points? How would one determine whether he was correct in his assumptions about the "who" and "what" of Kansas Populism? How do you think Daniel Zercher (see Document 16 on p. 75) would respond to White's criticisms? How would Annie Diggs (see Document 15 on p. 72) answer White?*

WILLIAM ALLEN WHITE
"What's the Matter with Kansas?"
1896

Today the Kansas Department of Agriculture sent out a statement which indicates that Kansas has gained less than two thousand people in the past year.
There are about two hundred and twenty-five thousand families in this state, and
there were ten thousand babies born in Kansas, and yet so many people have left
the state that the natural increase is cut down to less than two thousand net.

This has been going on for eight years.

If there had been a high brick wall around the state eight years ago, and not
a soul had been admitted or permitted to leave, Kansas would be a half million
souls better off than she is today. And yet the nation has increased in population.
In five years ten million people have been added to the national population, yet
instead of gaining a share of this — say, half a million — Kansas has apparently
been a plague spot and, in the very garden of the world, has lost population by
ten thousands every year.

Not only has she lost population, but she has lost money. Every moneyed
man in the state who could get out without loss has gone. Every month in every
community sees someone who has a little money pack up and leave the state.
This has been going on for eight years. Money has been drained out all the
time. In towns where ten years ago there were three or four or half a dozen
money-lending concerns, stimulating industry by furnishing capital, there is
now none, or one or two that are looking after the interest and principal already
outstanding.

No one brings any money into Kansas any more. What community knows
over one or two men who have moved in with more than $5,000 in the past three
years? And what community cannot count half a score of men in that time who
have left, taking all the money they could scrape together?

Yet the nation has grown rich; other states have increased in population and
wealth — other neighboring states. Missouri has gained over two million, while
Kansas has been losing half a million. Nebraska has gained in wealth and population while Kansas has gone downhill. Colorado has gained every way, while
Kansas has lost every way since 1888.

What's the matter with Kansas?

There is no substantial city in the state. Every big town save one has lost
in population. Yet Kansas City, Omaha, Lincoln, St. Louis, Denver, Colorado
Springs, Sedalia, the cities of the Dakotas, St. Paul and Minneapolis and Des
Moines — all cities and towns in the West — have steadily grown.

Take up the government blue book[1] and you will see that Kansas is virtually
off the map. Two or three little scrubby consular places in yellow-fever-stricken

---

[1] **government blue book:** A listing of those people holding federal office.

Irwin Ungar, ed., *Populism: Nostalgic or Progressive?* (Chicago: Rand McNally, 1964), 50–53.

communities that do not aggregate ten thousand dollars a year is all the recognition that Kansas has. Nebraska draws about one hundred thousand dollars; little old North Dakota draws about fifty thousand dollars; Oklahoma doubles Kansas; Missouri leaves her a thousand miles behind; Colorado is almost seven times greater than Kansas — the whole west is ahead of Kansas.

Take it by any standard you please, Kansas is not in it.

Go east and you hear them laugh at Kansas; go west and they sneer at her; go south and they "cuss" her; go north and they have forgotten her. Go into any crowd of intelligent people gathered anywhere on the globe, and you will find the Kansas man on the defensive. The newspaper columns and magazines once devoted to praise of her, to boastful acts and startling figures concerning her resources, are now filled with cartoons, jibes and Pefferian speeches. Kansas just naturally isn't in it. She has traded places with Arkansas and Timbuctoo.

What's the matter with Kansas?

We all know; yet here we are at it again. We have an old mossback Jacksonian who snorts and howls because there is a bathtub in the State House; we are running that old jay for Governor. We have another shabby, wild-eyed, rattle-brained fanatic who has said openly in a dozen speeches that "the rights of the user are paramount to the rights of the owner"; we are running him for Chief Justice, so that capital will come tumbling over itself to get into the state. We have raked the old ash heap of failure in the state and found an old human hoop skirt who has failed as a businessman, who has failed as an editor, who has failed as a preacher, and we are going to run him for Congressman-at-Large. He will help the looks of the Kansas delegation at Washington. Then we have discovered a kid without a law practice and have decided to run him for Attorney General. Then, for fear some hint that the state had become respectable might percolate through the civilized portions of the nation, we have decided to send three or four harpies out lecturing, telling the people that Kansas is raising hell and letting the corn go to weed.

Oh, this is a state to be proud of! We are a people who can hold up our heads! What we need is not more money, but less capital, fewer white shirts and brains, fewer men with business judgment, and more of those fellows who boast that they are "just ordinary clodhoppers, but they know more in a minute about finance than John Sherman";[2] we need more men who are "posted," who can bellow about the crime of '73, who hate prosperity, and who think, because a man believes in national honor, he is a tool of Wall Street. We have had a few of them — some hundred fifty thousand — but we need more.

We need several thousand gibbering idiots to scream about the "Great Red Dragon" of Lombard Street.[3] We don't need population, we don't need wealth, we don't need well-dressed men on the streets, we don't need cities on the fertile prairies; you bet we don't! What we are after is the money power. Because we have become poorer and ornerier and meaner than a spavined, distempered mule, we, the people of Kansas, propose to kick; we don't care to build up, we wish to tear down.

---

[2] **John Sherman:** U.S. senator from Ohio and author of the Sherman Anti-Trust Act of 1890, which outlawed trusts or associations that restrained trade.
[3] **Lombard Street:** A term for London's financial district.

"There are two ideas of government," said our noble Bryan[4] at Chicago. "There are those who believe that if you legislate to make the well-to-do prosperous, this prosperity will leak through on those below. The Democratic idea has been that if you legislate to make the masses prosperous their prosperity will find its way up and through every class and rest upon them."

That's the stuff! Give the prosperous man the dickens! Legislate the thriftless man into ease, whack the stuffing out of the creditors and tell the debtors who borrowed the money five years ago when money "per capita" was greater than it is now, that the contraction of currency gives him a right to repudiate.

Whoop it up for the ragged trousers; put the lazy, greasy fizzle, who can't pay his debts on the altar, and bow down and worship him. Let the state ideal be high. What we need is not the respect of our fellow men, but the chance to get something for nothing.

Oh, yes, Kansas is a great state. Here are people fleeing from it by the score every day, capital going out of the state by the hundreds of dollars; and every industry but farming paralyzed, and that crippled, because its products have to go across the ocean before they can find a laboring man at work who can afford to buy them. Let's don't stop this year. Let's drive all the decent, self-respecting men out of the state. Let's keep the old clodhoppers who know it all. Let's encourage the man who is "posted." He can talk, and what we need is not mill hands to eat our meat, nor factory hands to eat our wheat, nor cities to oppress the farmer by consuming his butter and eggs and chickens and produce. What Kansas needs is men who can talk, who have large leisure to argue the currency question while their wives wait at home for a nickel's worth of bluing.

What's the matter with Kansas?

Nothing under the shining sun. She is losing her wealth, population and standing. She has got her statesmen, and the money power is afraid of her. Kansas is all right. She has started in to raise hell as Mrs. Lease[5] advised, and she seems to have an over-production. But that doesn't matter. Kansas never did believe in diversified crops. Kansas is all right. There is absolutely nothing wrong with Kansas. "Every prospect pleases and only man is vile."

[4]**Bryan:** William Jennings Bryan, Populist and Democratic candidate for president in 1896.
[5]**Mrs. Lease:** Mary Elizabeth Lease, Kansas Populist leader and speaker.

18. SILVER POPULISM
AND THE "CROSS OF GOLD"

This speech ranks as one of the greatest in American history. Bryan, whose youth and vigor captivated the nation, stormed into the national political limelight off the flat farmlands of Nebraska. As the Democratic nominee for president in 1896,

Bryan agreed with the Populists only on the silver issue; he championed a plan for the government to go forward with the unlimited production of silver money, which farmers hoped would drive up inflation and raise fallen crop prices. Western mine owners were eager to supply the silver. This speech, given at the Democratic convention in Chicago, electrified listeners and made it clear that the Democrats and Populists would win or lose the presidency on the silver issue. They lost. William McKinley, the Republican nominee, got the votes where they mattered most — in the East. The East did not care about silver, or Populism, the way the West did. Bryan made a remarkable speech, blasting the moneyed, urban East for ignoring the rural West and South. But the speech succeeded far more as oratory than as policy and, ironically, its sheer success helped sink the Populist cause as Bryan became identified with the silver issue and not broader Populist issues. What makes this such a successful speech? What points does Bryan drive home the hardest? In what ways does Bryan appeal to westerners?

WILLIAM JENNINGS BRYAN
Speech to the Democratic National Convention
1896

. . . Never before in the history of this country has there been witnessed such a contest as that through which we have just passed. Never before in the history of American politics has a great issue been fought out as this issue has been, by the voters of a great party. On the fourth of March, 1895, a few Democrats, most of them members of Congress, issued an address to the Democrats of the nation, asserting that the money question was the paramount issue of the hour; declaring that a majority of the Democratic party had the right to control the action of the party on this paramount issue; and concluding with the request that the believers in the free coinage of silver in the Democratic party should organize, take charge of, and control the policy of the Democratic party. Three months later, at Memphis, an organization was perfected, and the silver Democrats went forth openly and courageously proclaiming their belief, and declaring that, if successful, they would crystallize into a platform the declaration which they had made. Then began the conflict. With a zeal approaching the zeal which inspired the crusaders who followed Peter the Hermit,[1] our silver Democrats went forth from victory unto victory until they are now assembled, not to discuss, not to debate, but to enter up the judgment already rendered by the plain people of this country. In this contest brother has been arrayed against brother, father against son. The warmest ties of love, acquaintance and association have been disregarded;

---

[1] **Peter the Hermit**: Christian evangelist of the Crusades.

Donald K. Springen, *William Jennings Bryan, Orator of Small-Town America* (New York: Greenwood Press, 1991), 133–39.

old leaders have been cast aside when they have refused to give expression to the sentiments of those whom they would lead, and new leaders have sprung up to give direction to this cause of truth. Thus has the contest been waged, and we have assembled here under as binding and solemn instructions as were ever imposed upon representatives of the people. . . .

We say to you that you have made the definition of a business man too limited in its application. The man who is employed for wages is as much a business man as his employer, the attorney in a country town is as much a business man as the corporation counsel in a great metropolis; the merchant at the cross-roads store is as much a business man as the merchant of New York; the farmer who goes forth in the morning and toils all day — who begins in the spring and toils all summer — and who by the application of brain and muscle to the natural resources of the country creates wealth, is as much a business man as the man who goes upon the board of trade and bets upon the price of grain; the miners who go down a thousand feet into the earth, or climb two thousand feet upon the cliffs, and bring forth from their hiding places the precious metals to be poured into the channels of trade are as much business men as the few financial magnates who, in a back room, corner the money of the world. We come to speak for this broader class of business men.

Ah, my friends, we say not one word against those who live upon the Atlantic coast, but the hardy pioneers who have braved all the dangers of the wilderness, who have made the desert to blossom as the rose — the pioneers away out there [pointing to the West], who rear their children near to Nature's heart, where they can mingle their voices with the voices of the birds — out there where they have erected schoolhouses for the education of their young, churches where they praise their Creator, and cemeteries where rest the ashes of their dead — these people, we say, are as deserving of the consideration of our party as any people in this country. It is for these that we speak. We do not come as aggressors. Our war is not a war of conquest; we are fighting in the defense of our homes, our families, and posterity. We have petitioned, and our petitions have been scorned; we have entreated, and our entreaties have been disregarded; we have begged, and they have mocked when our calamity came. We beg no longer; we entreat no more; we petition no more. We defy them.

The gentleman from Wisconsin has said that he fears a Robespierre.[2] My friends, in this land of the free you need not fear that a tyrant will spring up from among the people. What we need is an Andrew Jackson to stand, as Jackson stood, against the encroachments of organized wealth.

They tell us that this platform was made to catch votes. We reply to them that changing conditions make new issues; that the principles upon which Democracy rests are as everlasting as the hills, but that they must be applied to new conditions as they arise. Conditions have arisen, and we are here to meet these conditions. They tell us that the income tax ought not to be brought in here; that it is a new idea. They criticize us for our criticisms of the Supreme Court of the United States. My friends, we have not criticized; we have simply called attention

[2] **Robespierre:** French revolutionary executed in 1794.

to what you already know. If you want criticism, read the dissenting opinions of
the court. There you will find criticisms. They say that we passed an unconstitutional law; we deny it. The income tax law was not unconstitutional when it was
passed; it was not unconstitutional when it went before the Supreme Court for
the first time; it did not become unconstitutional until one of the judges changed
his mind, and we cannot be expected to know when a judge will change his
mind. The income tax is just. It simply intends to put the burdens of government
justly upon the backs of the people. I am in favor of an income tax. When I find
a man who is not willing to bear his share of the burdens of the government
which protects him, I find a man who is unworthy to enjoy the blessings of a government like ours.

They say that we are opposing national bank currency; it is true. If you will
read what Thomas Benton said, you will find he said that, in searching history, he
could find but one parallel to Andrew Jackson, that was Cicero, who destroyed
the conspiracy of Cataline and saved Rome. Benton said that Cicero only did for
Rome what Jackson did for us when he destroyed the bank conspiracy and saved
America. We say in our platform that we believe that the right to coin and issue
money is a function of government. We believe it. We believe that it is a part of
sovereignty, and can no more with safety be delegated to private individuals than
we could afford to delegate to private individuals the power to make penal statutes
or levy taxes. Mr. Jefferson, who was once regarded as good Democratic authority, seems to have differed in opinion from the gentleman who has addrest us
on the part of the minority. Those who are opposed to this proposition tell us
that the issue of paper money is a function of the bank, and that the Government
ought to go out of the banking business. I stand with Jefferson rather than with
them, and tell them, as he did, that the issue of money is a function of government, and that the banks ought to go out of the governing business. . . .

And now, my friends, let me come to the paramount issue. If they ask us why
it is that we say more on the money question than we say upon the tariff question,
I reply that, if protection has slain its thousands, the gold standard has slain its tens
of thousands. If they ask us why we do not embody in our platform all the things
that we believe in, we reply that when we have restored the money of the constitution all other necessary reforms will be possible; but that until this is done there
is no other reform that can be accomplished.

Why is it that within three months such a change has come over the country? Three months ago, when it was confidently asserted that those who believe
in the gold standard would frame our platform and nominate our candidates,
even the advocates of the gold standard did not think that we could elect a President. And they had good reason for their doubt, because there is scarcely a State
here to-day asking for the gold standard which is not in the absolute control of
the Republican party. But note the change. Mr. McKinley was nominated at
St. Louis upon a platform which declared for the maintenance of the gold
standard until it can be changed into bimetallism by international agreement.
Mr. McKinley was the most popular man among the Republicans, and three
months ago everybody in the Republican party prophesied his election. How
is it to-day? Why, the man who was once pleased to think that he looked like

Napoleon — that man shudders to-day when he remembers that he was nominated on the anniversary of the battle of Waterloo. Not only that, but as he listens he can hear with ever-increasing distinctness the sound of the waves as they beat upon the lonely shores of St. Helena.

Why this change? Ah, my friends, is not the reason for the change evident to any one who will look at the matter? No private character, however pure, no personal popularity, however great, can protect from the avenging wrath of an indignant people a man who will declare that he is in favor of fastening the gold standard upon this country, or who is willing to surrender the right of self-government and place the legislative control of our affairs in the hands of foreign potentates and powers.

We go forth confident that we shall win. Why? Because upon the paramount issue of this campaign there is not a spot of ground upon which the enemy will dare to challenge battle. If they tell us that the gold standard is a good thing, we shall point to their platform and tell them that their platform pledges the party to get rid of the gold standard and substitute bimetallism. If the gold standard is a good thing, why try to get rid of it? I call your attention to the fact that some of the very people who are in this convention to-day and who tell us that we ought to declare in favor of international bimetallism — thereby declaring that the gold standard is wrong and that the principle of bimetallism is better — these very people four months ago were open and avowed advocates of the gold standard, and were then telling us that we could not legislate two metals together, even with the aid of all the world. If the gold standard is a good thing, we ought to declare in favor of its retention and not in favor of abandoning it; and if the gold standard is a bad thing why should we wait until other nations are willing to help us to let go? Here is the line of battle, and we care not upon which issue they force the fight; we are prepared to meet them on either issue or on both. If they tell us that the gold standard is the standard of civilization, we reply to them that this, the most enlightened of all the nations of the earth, has never declared for a gold standard and that both the great parties this year are declaring against it. If the gold standard is the standard of civilization, why, my friends, should we not have it? If they come to meet us on that issue we can present the history of our nation. More than that; we can tell them that they will search the pages of history in vain to find a single instance where the common people of any land have ever declared themselves in favor of the gold standard. They can find where the holders of fixt investments have declared for a gold standard, but not where the masses have. . . .

You come to us and tell us that the great cities are in favor of the gold standard; we reply that the great cities rest upon our broad and fertile prairies. Burn down your cities and leave our farms, and your cities will spring up again as if by magic; but destroy our farms and the grass will grow in the streets of every city in the country.

My friends, we declare that this nation is able to legislate for its own people on every question, without waiting for the aid or consent of any other nation on earth; and upon that issue we expect to carry every State in the Union. I shall not slander the inhabitants of the fair State of Massachusetts nor the inhabitants of the State of New York by saying that, when they are confronted with the proposition, they will declare that this nation is not able to attend to its own business. It is the issue of 1776 over again. Our ancestors, when but three millions in number had the courage to declare their political independence of every other nation; shall we, their descendants, when we have grown to seventy millions, declare that we are less independent than our forefathers? No, my friends, that will never be the verdict of our people. Therefore, we care not upon what lines the battle is fought. If they say bimetallism is good, but that we cannot have it until other nations help us, we reply that, instead of having a gold standard because England has, we will restore bimetallism, and then let England have bimetallism because the United States has it. If they dare to come out in the open field and defend the gold standard as a good thing, we will fight them to the uttermost. Having behind us the producing masses of this nation and the world, supported by the commercial interests, the laboring interests, and the toilers everywhere, we will answer their demand for a gold standard by saying to them: You shall not press down upon the brow of labor this crown of thorns, you shall not crucify mankind upon a cross of gold.

19. THE LONG REACH OF THE RAILROAD

California novelist Frank Norris wrote his best-selling novel The Octopus *at the turn of the century, after the Populist movement had faded. But his description of the corporate and political behemoth (in this case, California's Southern Pacific Railroad) that wrapped its tentacles around everything in its way represented the view of many Populists who believed that the power of the railroad was out to crush them financially and politically. Although this passage is not a factual description of the railroad's power, it is a view of the railroad that many Populists would have appreciated. As this chapter's opening image (p. 68) shows, William Jennings Bryan included the grasping octopus on his 1900 Presidential campaign poster, implicitly arguing that he alone could slay the corporate beast. What kinds of power — corporate, technological, or otherwise — does the novelist grant the railroad in this passage? How do you think a railroad official would answer these "charges"?*

FRANK NORRIS
From *The Octopus*
1901

. . . By now, however, it was dark. Presley hurried forward. He came to the line fence of the Quien Sabe ranch. Everything was very still. The stars were all

Frank Norris, *The Octopus: A Story of California* (New York: Doubleday, 1948), 46–48.

out. There was not a sound other than the *de Profundis*, still sounding from very far away. At long intervals the great earth sighed dreamily in its sleep. All about, the feeling of absolute peace and quiet and security and untroubled happiness and content seemed descending from the stars like a benediction. The beauty of his poem, its idyl, came to him like a caress; that alone had been lacking. It was that, perhaps, which had left it hitherto incomplete. At last he was to grasp his song in all its entity.

But suddenly there was an interruption. Presley had climbed the fence at the limit of the Quien Sabe ranch. Beyond was Los Muertos, but between the two ran the railroad. He had only time to jump back upon the embankment when, with a quivering of all the earth, a locomotive, single, unattached, shot by him with a roar, filling the air with the reek of hot oil, vomiting smoke and sparks; its enormous eye, Cyclopean, red, throwing a glare far in advance, shooting by in a sudden crash of confused thunder; filling the night with the terrific clamour of its iron hoofs.

Abruptly Presley remembered. This must be the crack passenger engine of which Dyke had told him, the one delayed by the accident on the Bakersfield division and for whose passage the track had been opened all the way to Fresno.

Before Presley could recover from the shock of the irruption, while the earth was still vibrating, the rails still humming, the engine was far away, flinging the echo of its frantic gallop over all the valley. For a brief instant it roared with a hollow diapason[1] on the Long Trestle over Broderson Creek, then plunged into a cutting farther on, the quivering glare of its fires losing itself in the night, its thunder abruptly diminishing to a subdued and distant humming. All at once this ceased. The engine was gone.

But the moment the noise of the engine lapsed, Presley — about to start forward again — was conscious of a confusion of lamentable sounds that rose into the night from out the engine's wake. Prolonged cries of agony, sobbing wails of infinite pain, heart-rending, pitiful.

The noises came from á little distance. He ran down the track, crossing the culvert, over the irrigating ditch, and at the head of the long reach of track — between the culvert and the Long Trestle — paused abruptly, held immovable at the sight of the ground and rails all about him.

In some way, the herd of sheep — Vanamee's herd — had found a breach in the wire fence by the right of way and had wandered out upon the tracks. A band had been crossing just at the moment of the engine's passage. The pathos of it was beyond expression. It was a slaughter, a massacre of innocents. The iron monster had charged full into the midst, merciless, inexorable. To the right and left, all the width of the right of way, the little bodies had been flung; backs were snapped against the fence posts; brains knocked out. Caught in the barbs of the wire, wedged in, the bodies hung suspended. Under foot it was terrible. The black blood, winking in the starlight, seeped down into the clinkers between the ties with a prolonged sucking murmur.

[1] **diapason:** With the full range of an instrument or voice.

Presley turned away, horror-struck, sick at heart, overwhelmed with a quick burst of irresistible compassion for this brute agony he could not relieve. The sweetness was gone from the evening, the sense of peace, of security, and placid contentment was stricken from the landscape. The hideous ruin in the engine's path drove all thought of his poem from his mind. The inspiration vanished like a mist. The *de Profundis* had ceased to ring. . . .

Then, faint and prolonged, across the levels of the ranch, he heard the engine whistling for Bonneville. Again and again, at rapid intervals in its flying course, it whistled for road crossings, for sharp curves, for trestles; ominous notes, hoarse, bellowing, ringing with the accents of menace and defiance; and abruptly Presley saw again, in his imagination, the galloping monster, the terror of steel and steam, with its single eye, Cyclopean, red, shooting from horizon to horizon; but saw it now as the symbol of a vast power, huge, terrible, flinging the echo of its thunder over all the reaches of the valley, leaving blood and destruction in its path; the leviathan, with tentacles of steel clutching into the soil, the soulless Force, the iron-hearted Power, the monster, the Colossus, the Octopus.

Suggestions for Further Reading

Argersinger, Peter H. *The Limits of Agrarian Radicalism: Western Populism and American Politics.* Lawrence: University Press of Kansas, 1995.

Goodwyn, Lawrence. *Democratic Promise: The Populist Moment in America.* New York: Oxford University Press, 1976.

Larson, Robert W. *New Mexico Populism: A Study of Radical Protest in a Western Territory.* Boulder: Colorado Associated University Press, 1974.

McMath, Robert C. *American Populism: A Social History, 1877–1898.* New York: Hill and Wang, 1993.

Nugent, Walter. *The Tolerant Populists: Kansas, Populism and Nativism.* Chicago, University of Chicago Press, 1963.

Ostler, Jeffrey. *Prairie Populism: The Fate of Agrarian Radicalism in Kansas, Nebraska, and Iowa, 1880–1892.* Lawrence: University Press of Kansas, 1993.

Pollack, Norman. *The Populist Response to Industrial America.* Cambridge: Harvard University Press, 1962.

Wright, James Edward. *The Politics of Populism: Dissent in Colorado.* New Haven: Yale University Press, 1974.

Detail from a Union Broadside, c. 1907

Industrial expansion all across America came at a price: social upheaval and strife. No region of the nation expressed these tensions more glaringly than the mining communities of the American West, as striking miners faced off against their employers and, often, state and federal soldiers. This graphic image, designed in 1907 by William "Big Bill" Haywood, the founder of the Western Federation of Miners, expressed the radical union's opposition to martial law imposed in the mining camps of some Rocky Mountain towns. In questioning the legality of certain acts by authorities — including the chaining of strikers to trees and their imprisonment in corrals (or "bull-pens") — the Western Federation asked, "Is Colorado in America?" How might this image have been used in the battle for public opinion?

Courtesy of the Idaho State Historical Society.

CHAPTER FIVE

THE AGE OF INDUSTRIALIZATION

Labor Unrest in the Mining West

I ndustrialization in the post–Civil War era forever changed the physical and social landscape of the American nation. But industrial growth did not proceed smoothly. As labor unions swelled in size and number, tremendous friction developed between laborers and their employers. Perhaps more than any other area of the country, the mining regions of the Rocky Mountains and Far West, which saw bitter and protracted strife, epitomized the contested progress of industrialization. This is not to suggest, however, that such struggles were limited to the West. Every part of the nation experienced similar difficulties during the painful shift to industrialization. The rise of Populism throughout the South and the West can be viewed as a sign of working people's discontent with the way industrialism was taking control of the economy. Mill towns in the South, rail yards in Chicago, and steel mills in Pennsylvania reverberated with tension as much as the mining and industrial communities of Colorado, New Mexico, and Arizona.

But the West seemed to encounter particular difficulty. Indeed, if one were to look for outbreaks of violence, one would find it in the western mines and deadly clashes between workers and employers, not in the six-gun showdown on Main Street. With the advantage of hindsight, it is even possible to argue that the West underwent a protracted labor war from the 1870s well into the first decades of the twentieth century. From Bisbee, Arizona, to Cripple Creek, Colorado, from Boise, Idaho, to California's capital in Sacramento, labor troubles seemed as much a part of the landscape as the coal or silver, lead, copper, and gold buried below the surface. No western region was left untouched.

The fights that erupted in mines and mining towns, grim and often extremely violent, defy simple generalizations. Mining itself took many forms, depending on the natural resources being mined and the power of the corporate interests that hired and fired. A western mine could be small, worked by an individual miner or two, but by the 1870s and 1880s, it was more likely that a miner in the West worked for wages. This was also true for the thousands who comprised the rest of the industrial workforce in the post–Civil War West. Railroad workers entered the wage system and worked in conditions nearly as dangerous as the mines, as did the swelling ranks of workers who built the West's booming cities.

Workers organized, or they tried to. Trade unions were tolerated in many industries, but they scrambled to gain a political or economic foothold. Matters grew especially tense in the 1890s as the effects of the national depression worsened labor relations in the mines. Cripple Creek miners, like striking rail workers in California, found themselves facing U.S. troops sent out to enforce order. In Idaho's panhandle region of Coeur d'Alene, one violent episode followed another. Strikers surged through the streets of mining towns, men were murdered for their pro-worker or pro-owner beliefs, and striking miners were even forcibly corralled in fenced enclosures called "bull-pens." In 1905, former Idaho governor Frank Steunenberg, a supporter of the mine owners, was killed by a bomb wired to the front gate of his house in Caldwell. In 1917, the authorities in Bisbee, Arizona, working in league with heavily armed vigilantes, rounded up radicals and suspected radicals, as many as twelve hundred people, and put them on railcars headed out of the state.

This chapter focuses on the Western Federation of Miners (WFM). Founded during the labor struggle in Montana and Idaho, the WFM was an organization of miners dedicated to radical reform of the American industrial system. Led by the charismatic and ambitious William "Big Bill" Haywood (later instrumental in organizing the Industrial Workers of the World), the WFM was a powerful force of socialist opposition to mine owners throughout the West and south into Mexico. The WFM's concerted and violent critique not only of mining corporations but of the whole fabric of American capitalism, set it apart from less radical unions. Vehemently opposed to the WFM, mine owners banded together and looked to the federal government for legal and military support. Victories for radical labor, in contrast, were few and far between — a dynamited mine here and there, some protracted strikes, and most prominently, Haywood's acquittal in the conspiracy trial that tried to link him to Steunenberg's assassination.

The documents in this chapter present these conflicts from a variety of perspectives. The novelist Jack London offers a prolabor, proworker viewpoint. The WFM voices its concerns in a document submitted to Congress. The journalist Ray Stannard Baker proffers a middle-of-the-road approach, hoping, it would seem, to prevent further bloodshed and violence. "Mother Jones," a famed radical and, like London, a friend of the miners, questions the legality of various measures in her letter from Colorado. Finally, John D. Rockefeller, a mine owner, offers a somewhat conciliatory if defensive position in a speech delivered in Colorado.

As you read these selections, think about the point of view of each of these commentators. What audience do they write for? What additional sources would help you see all sides of the Colorado labor strife? Why would people living in mining towns choose one side over the other? What other options were open to them?

---

20. UNREST IN IDAHO

In addition to short stories and novels such as The Call of the Wild *and* White Fang, *Jack London wrote newspaper articles and essays for the socialist press, which had a large readership, especially in the nation's cities. Many of London's writings, fictional as well as journalistic, have strong prolabor and proworker perspectives; his political positions and his outspokenness helped make London an unpopular figure in the eyes of mine owners and big business interests. This brief piece, published in the* Chicago Daily Socialist, *pertains to the trial of "Big Bill" Haywood and other WFM officials, who were charged with assassinating Frank Steunenberg, the former governor of Idaho. What evidence does London use to bolster his argument that there is "something rotten" in the justice system in Idaho? How does this essay compare with the point-by-point argument put forward by the Western Federation of Miners (see Document 21 on p. 96)? Would London's essay be convincing to union opponents?*

JACK LONDON
"Something Rotten in Idaho"
1906

Up in the State of Idaho, at the present moment, are three men lying in jail. Their names are Moyer, Haywood and Pettibone.[1] They are charged with the murder of Governor Steunenberg. Incidentally they are charged with thirty, sixty or seventy other atrocious murders. Not alone are they labor leaders and murderers, but they are anarchists. They are guilty, and they should be swiftly and immediately executed. It is to be regretted that no severer and more painful punishment than hanging awaits them. At any rate there is consolation in the knowledge that these men will surely be hanged.

[1] **Moyer, Haywood and Pettibone:** Along with William Haywood, Charles Moyer and George Pettibone, also officials of the Western Federation of Miners, were charged with complicity in the murder of former governor Steunenberg of Idaho. All were acquitted.

Philip S. Foner, ed., *Jack London, American Rebel* (New York: Citadel Press, 1947), 407–10.

The foregoing epitomises the information and beliefs possessed by the average farmer, lawyer, professor, clergyman and businessman in the United States. His belief is based upon the information he has gained by reading the newspapers. Did he possess different information, he might possibly believe differently. It is the purpose of this article to try to furnish information such as is not furnished by 99 percent of the newspapers of the United States.

In the first place, Moyer, Haywood and Pettibone were not even in the State of Idaho at the time the crime with which they are charged was committed. In the second place, they are at present in jail in the State of Idaho because of the perpetration of lawless acts by officers of the law, from the chief of the state executives down to the petty deputy chiefs — and this in collusion with mine owners' associations and railroad companies.

Here is conspiracy self-confessed and openly flaunted. And it is conspiracy and violation of law on the part of the very men who claim that they are trying to bring punishment for conspiracy and violation of law. This is inconsistency, to say the least. It may be added that it is criminal inconsistency. . . .

The evidence against these labor leaders is contained in the confession of one Harry Orchard. It looks bad, in the face of it, when a man confesses that at the instigation of another, and for money received from that other, he had committed murder. . . .

But this is not the first time that these same labor leaders have been charged with murder; and this is not the first confession implicating them. Colorado is a fertile soil for confessions. Moyer, in particular, has been in jail many times charged with other murders. At least five men have solemnly sworn that at his instigation they have committed murder. Now it is a matter of history that when the tool confesses, the principal swings.

Moyer gives the lie to history. In spite of the many confessions he has never been convicted. This would make it look bad for the confessions. Not only does it make the confession look rotten, but the confessions, in turn, cast a doubt on the sweetness and purity of the present confession of Harry Orchard. In a region noted for the rottenness of its confession-fruit, it would be indeed remarkable to find this latest sample clean and wholesome.

When a man comes into court to give testimony, it is well to know what his character is, what his previous acts are, and whether or not self-interest enters into the case. Comes the mine owners' association of Colorado and Idaho to testify against Moyer, Haywood and Pettibone. Well, then, what sort of men are the mine owners? What have they done in the past?

That the mine owners have violated the laws countless times, there is no discussion. That they have robbed thousands of voters of their suffrage is common knowledge. That they have legalized lawlessness is history. But these things have only a general bearing on the matter at issue.

In particular, during and since the labor war that began in Colorado in 1903, the mine owners have charged the members of the Western Federation of Miners with all manner of crimes. There have been many trials, and in every trial the verdict has been acquittal. The testimony in these trials has been given by hired Pinkertons[2] and spies. Yet the Pinkertons and spies, masters in the art of gathering evidence, have always failed to convict in the courts. This looks bad for the sort of evidence that grows in the fertile Colorado soil.

But it is worse than that. While the Pinkertons and spies have proved poor evidence-farmers, they have demonstrated they are good criminals. Many of them have been convicted by the courts and sent to jail for the commission of crimes ranging from theft to manslaughter.

Are the mine owners law abiding citizens? Do they believe in law? Do they uphold the law? "To hell with the Constitution" was their clearly enunciated statement in Colorado in 1903. Their military agent, General Sherman Bell said: "To hell with habeas corpus! We will give them post-mortems instead!" Governor Gooding, the present governor of Idaho, has recently said: "To hell with the people."

Now it is but natural to question the good citizenship of an organization of men that continuously and consistently consigns to hell the process of habeas corpus, the people and the Constitution. In Chicago a few years ago some men were hanged for uttering incendiary language not half so violent as this. But they were workingmen. The mine owners of Colorado and Idaho are the chief executives, or capitalists. They will not be hanged. On the contrary, they have their full liberty, such liberty they are exercising in an effort to hang some other men whom they do not like.

Why do some mine owners dislike Moyer, Haywood and Pettibone? Because these men stand between the mine owners and a pot of money. These men are leaders of organized labor. They plan and direct the efforts of the workingmen to get better wages and shorter hours. The operation of their mines will be more expensive. The higher the running expenses, the smaller the profits. If the mine owners could disrupt the Western Federation of Miners, they would increase the hours of labor, lower wages, and thereby gain millions of dollars. . . .

. . . Judas betrayed Christ to crucifixion for thirty pieces of silver. Human nature has not changed since that day, and it is conceivable that Moyer, Haywood and Pettibone may be hanged for the sake of a few millions of dollars. . . .

In brief, the situation at present in Idaho is as follows: following a long struggle between capital and labor, the capitalist organization has jailed the leaders of the labor organization. The capitalist organization is trying to hang the labor leaders. It has tried to do this before, but its evidence and its "confessions" were always too rotten and corrupt. Its hired spies and Pinkertons have themselves been sent to prison for the commission of all manner of crimes, while they have never succeeded in sending one labor leader to prison.

The capitalist organization has been incendiary in speech, and by unlawful acts has lived up to its speech. It will profit by exterminating the labor organization. The capitalist organization has a bad character. It has never hesitated at

---

[2]**Pinkertons:** Private detectives of the Pinkerton Detective Agency.

anything to attain its ends. By sentiment and act it has behaved unlawfully, as have its agents whom it hired. The situation in Idaho? There can be but one conclusion — THERE IS SOMETHING ROTTEN IN IDAHO!

21. The Miners Reply

The WFM answered some of the charges made against it by Colorado mine owners and property owners in this statement, printed as an official document of the U.S. Senate. The WFM outlines the goals and principles established at the organization's founding in 1893. In language rooted in the American Revolution, the WFM casts itself as the protector of the rights of the American worker. According to the WFM, the owners of western mines, many of whom were foreign-born, are guilty of operating their companies and their mines under outrageously dangerous conditions. They are the true criminals in the mining districts of the West. How does this WFM statement compare with Ray Stannard Baker's views in Document 22 (p. 101)? What are the WFM's major points defending the activities it has been involved in? How would John D. Rockefeller Jr. (see Document 24 on p. 107) have viewed these political expressions?

Western Federation of Miners
Statement in Answer and Rebuttal
1904

Statement

In support of the resolution introduced by Senator Patterson, of Colorado, the Western Federation of Miners desires to submit a reply to the lengthy statement introduced by Senator Scott, of West Virginia, in rebuttal of the fabricated and unsupported assertions contained in said statement. The document introduced by Senator Scott to the United States Senate brands the Western Federation of Miners as a criminal organization and has been introduced for the sole purpose of poisoning the public mind. In order that the honorable body which compose the Senate of the United States may have a clear conception of the objects and aims of the Western Federation of Miners we hereby present the preamble of our organization:

"Statement of the Western Federation of Miners," 58th Cong., 2d sess., 1904, S. Doc. 163: 1–6, 39–41.

Preamble

We hold that all men are created to be free and should have equal access and opportunity to the enjoyment of all benefits to be derived from their exertions in dealing with the natural resources of the earth, and that free access and equal opportunity thereto are absolutely necessary to man's existence and the upward progress of the human race. Since it is self-evident that civilization has, during centuries, made progress in proportion to the production and utilization of minerals and metals, both precious and base, and that most of the material prosperity and comforts enjoyed by mankind are due to this progress, it is highly fitting and proper that the men who are engaged in the hazardous and unhealthy occupation of mining, milling, smelting, and the reduction of ores should receive a just compensation for their labors, which shall be proportionate to the dangers connected therewith, and such protection from law as will remove needless risk to life or health, and for the purpose of bringing about and promoting these and other proper and lawful ends, and for the general welfare of ourselves, families, and dependent ones we deem it necessary to organize and maintain the Western Federation of Miners, and, among our lawful purposes, we declare more especially our objects to be:

First.   To secure compensation fully commensurate with the dangers of our employment and the right to use our earnings free from the dictation of any person whomsoever.

Second.   To establish as speedily as possible, and so that it may be enduring, our right to receive pay for labor performed, in lawful money, and to rid ourselves of the iniquitous and unfair system of spending our earnings where and how our employers or their agent or officers may designate.

Third.   To strive to procure the introduction and use of any and all suitable, efficient appliances for the preservation of life, limb, and health of all employees, and thereby preserve to society the lives and usefulness of a large number of wealth producers.

Fourth.   To labor for the enactment of suitable laws and the proper enforcement thereof.

Fifth.   To provide for the education of our children and to prohibit the employment of all children until they shall have reached at least the age of sixteen years.

Sixth.   To prevent by law any mine owner, mining company, or corporation, or the agents thereof, from employing detectives, or armed forces, and to provide that only the lawfully elected or appointed officers of the county, State, or province, who shall be bona fide citizens thereof, shall act in any capacity in the enforcement of the law.

Seventh.   To use all honorable means to maintain and promote friendly relations between ourselves and our employers, and endeavor by arbitration and conciliation, or other pacific means, to settle any difficulties which may arise between us, and thus strive to make contention and strikes unnecessary.

Eighth.   To use all lawful and honorable means to abolish and prevent the system of convict labor from coming into competition with free labor and to demand the enforcement of the foreign contract-labor law against the importation of pauper labor from any foreign country, and also to use our efforts to make it unlawful to bring persons from another State, Territory or province to take the places of workingmen on a strike, or who may be locked out, by means of false representation, advertisements, or other misleading means.

Ninth.   To demand the repeal of conspiracy laws that in any way abridge the right of labor organizations to promote the general welfare of their membership, and also to use our influence to bring about legislation which will prevent government by injunction by either Federal, State, or provincial courts. To procure employment for our members in preference to non-union men, and in all lawful ways cooperate with one another for the purpose of procuring a just share of the product of our toil and mutual advancement in order that the general welfare of the membership and their families may be steadily advanced and promoted.

Tenth.   To use our united efforts to discourage the contract-labor system, and, as soon as practicable, to abolish the same, believing the said system to be detrimental to the best interests of organized labor.

For the further enlightenment of the members of the United States Senate, and in order to show that our organization is a legitimate body, we quote the following from the constitution:

> SEC. 2. The objects of this organization shall be to unite the various persons working in and around the mines, mills, and smelters into one central body, to practice those virtues that adorn society, and remind man of his duty to his fellow man, the elevation of his position, and the maintenance of the rights of the workers.

Previous to an applicant being initiated to membership in the Western Federation of Miners or taking the obligation, the following assurance is made:

> This body exacts no pledge or obligation which in any way conflicts with the duty you owe to your God, your country, or your fellow-man.

The Western Federation of Miners was organized in Butte, Montana, on May 15, 1893, and for ten years the organization has kept inviolate the principles enunciated in the preamble and constitution.

Because of the success, growth, and strength of the organization, and because of its progressive spirit in defending the humblest of its members from the tyranny of corporate oppression, the Federation has been assailed, not only by the federated might of the smelting trust and the various mine-owners' associations, but corporation journals owned and controlled by magnates in the mining and smelting industries have loaded their editorial columns with slander and vituperation in obedience to the mandates of the moneyed fraternity that molded the convictions of mortgaged editors. The Western Federation of Miners has never waged a battle except in self-defense. All strikes that have arisen can be traced to the encroachments of corporations, whose managers received their orders and instructions from a foreign source.[1] . . .

Permit us to call the attention of the United States Senate to the reckless slaughter of human life that may be laid at the door of the mine operators.

In Scofield, Utah, some three or four years ago, nearly three hundred miners were killed by an explosion, which resulted on account of the failure of the mine owners to comply with the law governing ventilation. In May, 1901, a disaster occurred in Fernie, British Columbia, where 137 men lost their lives and a coroner's jury brought in a verdict of culpable negligence against the company, and this "criminal" organization, the Western Federation of Miners, immediately sent a representative with $3,000 for the relief of the widows and orphans. Before all of the bodies were removed from the mine, Manager Tonkin reduced the wages of those who survived this blood-curdling disaster.

It should be fresh to the memory of the members of the United States Senate concerning the appalling disasters which have taken place in Tennessee, Wyoming, and Pennsylvania, and all of which could have been averted if the mine operators had placed a higher value upon human life than dividends and complied with the laws of the respective States. . . .

In Park City, Utah, at the Daly-West mine, thirty-five miners were killed by an explosion of giant powder that was stored in the mine by the company contrary to every safeguard which common sense should suggest.

In November, 1901, twenty-two miners lost their lives by being suffocated on account of a fire which destroyed a boarding house that was connected with the tunnel of the Smuggler Union mine, a property that was then under the management of Arthur L. Collins. The law had not been complied with, for the doors of the tunnel were not so adjusted as to prevent the flames and smoke from entering the mine. The mine operators shed no tears for the sacrifice of these twenty-two miners who were smothered to death, but when some unknown assassin pulled the trigger and ended the life of one man, Arthur L. Collins, a mighty wail went up and the finger of suspicion was pointed at the Western Federation of Miners.

It is only but a few days ago when fifteen men were hurled into eternity at the Independence mine, in the Cripple Creek district, through defective machinery and an incompetent engineer who was imported by the Mine Owners' Association as a strike breaker, and in whose ignorant keeping, for mercenary reasons, was placed the lives of all the men in the mine. . . .

[1] **from a foreign source:** A reference to non-American, often English, ownership of many western mining operations.

The people of this nation for a century and a quarter have celebrated the anniversary of that great epoch in American history, and dedicated with parade and speech the memorable 4th day of July in commemoration of the notes of liberty that rang from the old casting suspended in the tower of Faneuil Hall, signalizing the birth of a Republic whose people had groaned beneath the yoke of king rule. Each succeeding year the people have gathered in city, town, and hamlet and boasted of the justice and freedom contained in the Declaration of Independence. The eloquent tongue and the poetic pen have paid tributes to our liberty and made us feel that here in this land where Columbus planted the Cross — the emblem of Christianity — men were kings and women were queens, armored and shielded with a panoply of sovereignty that proclaimed defiance to every species of despotism. . . .

Upon the industrial battlefield for a quarter of a century in this nation has been heard the dying wails and groans of labor's victim. The pistol of the hired corporate murderer and the rifle of the uniformed soldier have poured their missiles of death into the ranks of labor, and moneyed nobility has applauded with cheers the wanton slaughter. The soil of every State of our Union has been wet with the blood of labor's martyrs to appease the thirst of soulless greed. The commandment "Thou shalt not kill" has found no place in the lexicon of commercial avarice. The "government of the people, by the people, and for the people" has become the government of trusts and corporations, and citizenship without property has no protection under the constitution of State or nation. . . .

A civilization that demands the implements of war to protect it is doomed, and the great mass whom plutocracy has destined to bear the blunt of conflict will not be carried off its feet by a patriotism that establishes commercial supremacy at the expense of human life. That nation is only strong whose yeomanry bask in the sunlight of a liberty that is free from the noxious effluvia of an atmosphere that breeds in the human heart the germs of murder. Wrong was never righted by the bullet or the sword. The savage and the barbarian who use the club and spear have as high a conception of justice as so-called civilized society that slakes its thirst in blood through the polished steel of Gatling gun and cannon.

Wrong maintained and perpetuated by all the modern machinery of war may have a temporary triumph, and right may be put in prison, but the spirit of justice that will be as eternal as humanity itself shall repeat its demands until the thundering voice of the mighty millions shall shake the pillars of a system that has molded and invented the machines of blood and carnage. The poverty of the world born in greed shall weld together the links of a chain that shall circle the globe, and the plebeian disinherited mass shall come together in a fraternity whose brotherhood will sweep from the face of our planet the last vestige of that tinseled pageantry that marked the era of war.

WESTERN FEDERATION OF MINERS.
CHARLES MOYER, *President.*
WM. D. HAYWOOD, *Secretary-Treasurer.*

22. A Muckraker Charts
a Middle Course

*Ray Stannard Baker was one of the best known of the "muckrakers" (a term sup-
posedly coined by President Theodore Roosevelt), who were the investigative journalists of their day. Through their essays and stories in popular national magazines
and in novels, the muckrakers went after big business interests. Sometimes they attacked corporations for unfair or noncompetitive business practices; sometimes they
tried to expose dangerous working conditions. At the height of their influence, in
the early decades of this century, the muckrakers exercised a great deal of political
influence. This article for a popular national magazine takes a middle-of-the-road
approach to events in the western mining regions by using Colorado as a case study.
Baker points out that the strife between workers, management, and the vigilante
Citizen's Alliance had been exacerbated by violent lawlessness on all sides. What
prescriptions does Baker offer for solving industrial unrest? How does he establish a
neutral position as someone able to make an objective assessment of affairs in the
mining camps? Does it work?*

RAY STANNARD BAKER
"The Reign of Lawlessness: Anarchy
and Despotism in Colorado"
1904

During much of the past year, and continuing until the present moment,
certain parts of the state of Colorado have been governed by military law. Governor Peabody, a banker himself, closely identified with the conservative business
interests of the state, and therefore unlikely to make exaggerated statements, has
proclaimed the existence of a condition of "insurrection and rebellion."

And martial law has been neither gentle nor forbearing; when accused of vi-
olating the Constitution, Judge Advocate McClelland remarked:

"To hell with the Constitution; we are not following the Constitution."

Colonel Verdeckberg, commanding officer in the Cripple Creek district,
declared:

"We are under orders only from God and Governor Peabody."

But, if military rule has been despotic, many citizens have been lawless, and
civil government ineffective. The miners' union has broken the law, there have
been dynamiting and assassination; the corporations have broken the law, there

McClure's Magazine 23 (May 1904): 43–47.

have been bribery and corruption; the citizens' organizations, representing in some degree the great third party — the public — have broken the law; even the Legislature itself, wherein the law is made, has been lawless. We have to-day, indeed, in certain parts of Colorado, a breakdown of democracy and, through anarchy, a reversion to military despotism.

What are the causes of these appalling conditions?

Insurrection and Rebellion Proclaimed

Martial law was declared in the Cripple Creek district on December 4th, and a month later in Telluride. The Cripple Creek proclamation was read in the city of Victor by a cavalry major guarded by fifty troopers, the citizens of the town gathered about, silent. After proclaiming that a condition of anarchy there existed, that civil government had become abortive, that life was in peril, and property unsafe, the Governor pronounced judgment upon this commonwealth:

> Now, therefore, I, James H. Peabody, Governor of the State of Colorado, by virtue of the authority in me vested, do hereby proclaim and declare the said County of Teller, in the State of Colorado, to be in a state of insurrection and rebellion.

Rebellion, then, must be stamped out! The silent citizens return to their homes. The Major, well backed by his troopers, seizes for military headquarters a building owned by a private citizen. He marches to the seat of government and informs the mayor and the chief of police that unless they obey military orders he, the Major, will seize the City Hall. He visits the office of the Victor *Record* and establishes a military censorship. The editor is forbidden to print an editorial concerning these military doings, and the next morning, or maybe the morning after, the paper appears with a black-bordered column, significantly blank, as it happens in Russia.

Having violated the rights of private property, overturned the people's government, suppressed free speech and a free press, the Major left armed men to patrol the city streets, and clattered away up the hill with his troop.

But the Proclamation of the Fourth of December was only the formal dramatic declaration on the part of the Governor of a condition long existent. For some two months prior to this time the military forces had been practically in control. And it had not been pleasant — martial rule. Soldiers are not that way.

Character of Cripple Creek Miners

Cripple Creek and Victor are American towns. Most of the citizens are miners, long resident in Colorado. They have played no unimportant part in making this district, among the tops of the Rocky Mountains, the greatest gold producing camp in the world. In 1902 they dug $25,000,000 from the hills. This is their home; they have here bought land and built houses; have here raised their children. . . .

Arrests without Warrants

Well, some of these men were arrested by the military forces, arrested without warrants and without charges, locked up in an unsavory place called the Bull-Pen, and kept *incommunicado*, often for weeks. Just at this place I am not discussing the reasons for these arrests, nor asserting that the men were not guilty; the point is: every right of the individual citizen was here trodden upon and disregarded.

Friends of the men arrested had immediate recourse to the civil courts. They began habeas corpus proceedings before District Judge Seeds, of Cripple Creek.

As every one knows, the writ of habeas corpus is one of the most precious rights of the Anglo-Saxon, called by Blackstone the "second Magna Charta." It has for its object the protection of the precious personal liberty of the free citizen — it provides that he shall not be held a prisoner without due process of law. Judge Seeds ordered that the Bull-Pen prisoners be brought into court, that an orderly inquiry might be made as to whether any innocent man was deprived of his liberty. General Chase and General Bell, then in command, obeyed the writ in their own significant way. They surrounded the court house with armed men; they planted sharpshooters on the roofs of the buildings roundabout; they set a gatling gun in the street outside, and then they marched into court with an overawing force of troopers which they planted squarely in front of the judge's bench. When the judge approached his own court he was halted with a bayonet brought to his breast, and kept waiting the pleasure of an officer from Denver! After the bailiff rapped for order, Eugene Engley, former attorney-general of the state of Colorado, one of the attorneys for the prisoners, declaring that no real justice could be administered in a court intimidated by armed men, left the room. "The constitutional guarantee that courts shall be open and free has been invaded and overthrown," he said. But the judge finally decided that the prisoners, whatever their offense, must not be deprived of their liberty without charges, and ordered that they be surrendered to the civil court.

Writ of Habeas Corpus Suspended

The generals deliberately violated the court order, and marched the prisoners back to the Bull-Pen, with the sharpshooters and the gatling gun. They were subsequently released by special order of the Governor, but others were arrested repeatedly and held for considerable periods. And finally the Governor himself took the gravest step which any executive officer in this country can take, a step forbidden, except under the most stringent safeguards, by the constitution of practically every state in the Union, including that of Colorado — suspended the writ of habeas corpus in the case of one Victor Poole, keeping him locked up without due process of law, for weeks.

Censorship of the Press

Nor was this all. I have already spoken of the censorship of the Victor *Record*. Some weeks before this occurred, a company of cavalry, under the command of General Chase himself, appeared one night after eleven o'clock, surrounded the *Record* office, arrested the entire force, and marched them off to the Bull-Pen, without warrant and without charges, although it was understood that Mr. Kyner, the editor, had criticized the methods of the soldiery. Here they were kept without proper food for twenty-four hours. It so happened that the plucky wife of one of the linotype operators, herself an operator, Mrs. Emma F. Langdon, hurried to the office after the force was arrested, and she and the office boy and the business manager, aroused from his bed, barricaded the doors, refused to admit a military guard which demanded entrance, and at three o'clock in the morning got out the paper. At the head of the first page there was this line: "Somewhat Disfigured, but Still in the Ring."

And in the gray of the next morning she stuffed her sleeves with damp copies of the paper, and climbed the hill to the Bull-Pen, there to be halted by the guard and not allowed to see the editor and his force, among whom was her own husband.

Small boys, and even women, one the wife of a merchant, were actually arrested for speaking disparagingly of the soldiers and sent to the Bull-Pen. Private homes, the castles of the citizens, were entered and searched without warrant. A squad of soldiers visited the home of Sherman Parker in the night, while Parker himself was away, aroused his wife from bed, forced her, in her night-clothes, in the presence of these men, to hold the lamp while they searched the house — and found no arms.

In Cripple Creek, on December 28th, John M. Glover, former United States Congressman from Missouri, who stood upon his constitutional right to own and keep arms (with undue truculency, it may be, though this does not alter the facts of the case), was attacked in his law office by a squad of soldiers. He barricaded the door, and, when the troops attempted to force an entrance, he opened fire through the panels. The soldiers replied with a volley through the door and walls. Glover, shot through the arm, finally surrendered. His revolvers were seized and he himself detained a prisoner.

Doings not dissimilar to these also took place at Telluride. Citizens, some of whom owned property and had been long residents of the town, were arrested for *vagrancy*. Most of them were strikers; strikers by right, if they wished to strike, neither beggars nor vagrants, and having no specific charges of crime against them. Some of them were put to work like criminals in a chain gang on the streets. . . .

Democracy and Despotism

And, finally, as a result of all this long-continued brazen law-breaking, we see the privileges of free government taken from the people and placed in the hands of an outside despot who rules by powder and shot. In the long run, the law gets itself executed, inevitably, mercilessly; if not by the ordinary machinery of the civil officials, then by the extraordinary machinery of martial rule.

Getting down at last to fundamental principles, this is the condition in Colorado: the people have broken the law and they are being punished. Not part of the people, but every person in Colorado; not only he who bludgeoned or bribed, but he who, greedily, in the pursuit of his private business, has forgotten his civic duties, who has not, himself obedient to the law, *demanded* the election of men who will enforce the law, not union men, nor corporation men, but Americans.

There is no better evidence of the responsibility of every voter in Colorado than that every voter has suffered — if not directly in the strike, then in loss of business, in increased cost of coal and other commodities, in rising taxes. Colorado will long bend under the burden of paying for its troops, now for many months in the field, and for the endless lawsuits arising out of these disturbances. It is not cheap — lawlessness.

Perhaps just this appalling punishment was necessary to shake the people of Colorado — and of the country — from their indolent indifference. The white-hot anger of the people of Colorado, though it may be directed at the wrong thing — at the union, at the citizens' alliance, at the trust, when it should be directed at lawlessness — is a sign of hope: through the passion of this anger changes may be wrought.

23. PROTESTING CONDITIONS IN COLORADO

Mary Harris Jones, known throughout the nation as "Mother Jones," was for decades an active and provocative friend of the industrial laborer. At the time she wrote this letter from southern Colorado, where she had been jailed by military authorities, Mother Jones was probably in her late seventies (or perhaps as old as she claims to be in the letter). Regardless of her age, she was without doubt an important American labor leader; her activities on behalf of miners, from West Virginia to the Rocky Mountains, earned her the enmity of mine owners as well as police and the military. Here she casts herself as a victim of the heavy-handed power of men like John D. Rockefeller. How does Mother Jones link events of the period to a greater struggle? What claims does she make about the legitimacy of the miners' actions in Colorado?

MOTHER JONES
"To My Friends and the Public Generally"
1914

Walsenburg, Colo.
Military Bastile
March 31, 1914.

To My Friends and the Public Generally:

I am being held a prisoner incommunicado in a damp, underground cell, in the basement of a military bullpen[1] at Walsenburg, Colorado. Have been here since 5:30 a.m. of the 23rd of March, when I was taken from the train by armed soldiers as I was passing through Walsenburg. I have discovered what appears to be an opportunity to smuggle a letter out of prison, and shall attempt to get this communication by the armed guards which day and night surround me (me, a white-haired old woman eighty-two years of age).

I want to say to the public that I am an American citizen. I have never broken a law in my life, and I claim the right of an American citizen to go where I please so long as I do not violate the law. The courts of Las Animas and Huerfano are open and unobstructed in the transaction of business, yet Governor Ammons and his Peabody appointee, General Chase, refuse to carry me before any court, and refuse to make any charge against me. I ask the press to let the nation know of my treatment, and to say to my friends, whom, thank God, I number by the thousands, throughout the United States and Mexico, that not even my incarceration in a damp, underground dungeon will make me give up the fight in which I am engaged for liberty and for the rights of the working people. Of course, I long to be out of prison. To be shut from the sunlight is not pleasant, but John Bunyan, John Brown and others were kept in jail quite a while, and I shall stand firm. To be in prison is no disgrace. In all my strike experiences I have seen no horrors equal to those perpetrated by General Chase and his corps of Baldwin-Feltz detectives that are now enlisted in the militia. My God — when is it to stop? I have only to close my eyes to see the hot tears of the orphans and widows of working men, and hear the mourning of the broken hearts and the wailing of the funeral dirge, while the cringing politicians whose sworn duty it is to protect the lives and liberty of the people crawl subserviently before the national burglars of Wall Street who are today plundering and devastating the State of Colorado economically, financially, politically and morally.

Let the nation know, and especially let my friend General Francisco Villa[2] know, that the great United States of America, which is demanding of him that

---

[1] **bullpen:** Stockade or jail patrolled by military authorities (see Document 22 for further description).
[2] **General Francisco Villa:** Francisco "Pancho" Villa, Mexican revolutionary.

Edward M. Steel, ed., *The Correspondence of Mother Jones* (Pittsburgh: University of Pittsburgh Press, 1985), 125–26.

he release the traitors he has placed under arrest, is now holding Mother Jones incommunicado in an underground cell surrounded with sewer rats, tinhorn soldiers and other vermin.

Mother Jones

24. Support for Mine Owners

No single family symbolized mine ownership in the American West more than the Rockefellers. At the turn of the century, the Anaconda Mine in Montana, controlled by the Rockefellers' Standard Oil Company, employed an astonishing 75 percent of the wage earners in the whole state. This made Montana, for all intents and purposes, a "company state." The Rockefellers' Colorado Fuel and Iron (CF & I) was no small operation either; the largest industrial enterprise in Colorado, it employed more than ten thousand workers to pump out Rocky Mountain coal and steel. The following address to company officials and worker representatives highlights a perspective common to mine owners like Rockefeller: if everyone just understood his place at the "table" of labor relations, all would be fine. In the spring of 1914, CF & I's coal fields became the site of a disastrous encounter between national guardsmen and striking members of the United Mine Workers of America. The guardsmen and strikebreakers set fires that ignited the tents where people had sought protection from gunfire. The resulting conflagration — the "Ludlow Massacre" — killed dozens of strikers and many women and children. The shadow of this event hovers over Rockefeller's October 2, 1915, address. How would you characterize Rockefeller's position toward industrial labor? What major points does he make before the group? How would Jack London (see Document 20 on p. 93) have responded to Rockefeller's assumptions?

John D. Rockefeller Jr.
Address to Colorado Fuel and Iron Officials
and Employee Representatives
1915

Mr. President, and Fellow Members of The Colorado Fuel & Iron Company: This is a red-letter day in my life. It is the first time I have ever had the good fortune to meet the representatives of the employees of this great company, its

Address by John D. Rockefeller Jr. Delivered at Pueblo Colorado (Denver: W. H. Kistler Stationery Co., 1915), 3–6, 9–11.

officers and mine superintendents, together, and I can assure you that I am proud to be here, and that I shall remember this gathering as long as I live. Had this meeting been held two weeks ago, I should have stood here as a stranger to many of you, recognizing few faces. Having had the opportunity last week of visiting all of the camps in the southern coal fields and of talking individually with practically all of the representatives, except those who were away; having visited in your homes, met many of your wives and children, we meet here not as strangers but as friends, and it is in that spirit of mutual friendship that I am glad to have this opportunity to discuss with you men our common interests. Since this is a meeting of the officers of the Company and the representatives of the employees, it is only by your courtesy that I am here, for I am not so fortunate as to be either one or the other; and yet I feel that I am intimately associated with you men, for in a sense I represent both the stockholders and the directors. Before speaking of the plan of industrial cooperation to which our President has referred, I want to say just a few words outlining my view as to what different interests constitute a company or corporation.

Every corporation is composed of four parties. First, there are the stockholders; they put up the money which pays the wages, builds the plants, operates the business, and they appoint the directors to represent their interests in the corporation. We have, secondly, the directors, whose business it is to see that the chief executive officers of the Company are carefully and wisely selected, to plan out its larger and more important policies, particularly its financial policies, and generally to see to it that the company is wisely administered. And, thirdly, we have the officers of the company, whose duty it is to conduct the current operation of the business. While last, but by no means least — for I might just as well have started at the other end — we come to the employees, who contribute their skill and their work.

Now the interest of these four parties is a common one. An effort to advance one interest at the expense of any other, means loss to all, and when any one of the four parties in this corporation selfishly considers his own interest alone, and is disregardful of the interests of the other three parties, sooner or later disaster must follow. This little table [*exhibiting a square table with four legs*] illustrates my conception of a corporation; and there are several points in regard to the table to which I want to call your attention. First, you see that it would not be complete unless it had all four sides. Each side is necessary; each side has its own part to play. Now, if you imagine this table cut into quarters, and each quarter separated from the others, what would happen? All of them would fall down, for no one could stand alone, and you would have no table. But when you put the four sides together, you have a useful piece of furniture; you have a table.

Then, secondly, I call your attention to the fact that these four sides are all perfectly joined together; that is why we have a perfect table. Likewise, if the parties interested in a corporation are not perfectly joined together, harmoniously working together, you have a discordant and unsuccessful corporation. . . .

When you have a level table, or a corporation that is on the level, you can pile up earnings on it [*piling coins on the table*]. Now, who gets the first crack at the earnings? You know that we in New York don't. Here come along the employees, and first of all they get their wages [*removing some of the coins*], every two weeks like clock-work, just what has been agreed on; they get the first chance at the pile. You men come ahead of the President, the officers, the stockholders and directors. You are the first to put a hand into the pile and take out what is agreed shall belong to you. You don't have to wait for your share; you don't have to take any chances about getting it. You know that there has never been a two-weeks period that you have worked when you have not been able to get your pay from this company; whatever happens, so long as the company is running, you get your pay.

And then the officers and superintendents come along, and they get theirs, they don't get it until after you have gotten yours [*removing more coins*].

Then come the directors, and they get their directors' fees [*removing the balance of the coins*] for doing their work in the company.

And, Hello! There is nothing left! This must be the Colorado Fuel & Iron Company! For never, men, since my father and I became interested in this company as stockholders, some twelve or fourteen years ago — never has there been one cent for the common stock. For fourteen years the common stockholder has seen your wages paid to you workers; has seen your salaries paid to you officers; has seen the directors draw their fees, and has not had one cent of return for the money that he has put into this company in order that you men might work and get your wages and salaries. How many men in this room ever heard that fact stated before? Is there a man among you? Well, there are mighty few among the workers who have heard it. What you have been told, what has been heralded from the Atlantic to the Pacific, is that those Rockefeller men in New York, the biggest scoundrels that ever lived, have taken millions of dollars out of this company on account of their stock ownership, have oppressed you men, have cheated you out of your wages, and "done" you in every way they could. That is the kind of "dope" you have been getting, and that is what has been spread all over this country. And when that kind of talk was going on, and there were disturbances in this part of the country because the four sides of this table were not square and the table was not level, there were those who in the streets of New York and in public gatherings, were inciting the crowd to "shoot John D. Rockefeller, Jr., down like a dog." That is the way they talked. . . .

This meeting has been called today for the purpose of seeing whether we can work out and agree upon, among ourselves here, some plan which will accomplish what I feel sure we all want to accomplish. I have been asked to explain the plan which is up for our consideration. I may say, men, that for years this great problem of labor and capital and of corporate relationships has engaged my earnest attention and study, while for the last eighteen months I have spent more of my time on the particular problems which confront this company than I have put on any other one interest with which I am related. I have talked with all of the men whom I could get in touch with who have had experience with or have studied these vital questions. I have conferred with experts, and I have tried in every way to get the best information I could looking toward the working out of some plan which would accomplish the result we are all striving to attain. Nearly a year ago the officers of the company, after having studied this question with us in New York, introduced, as you know, the beginning of such a plan, namely, the selection by the men at each camp of duly chosen representatives, to confer with the officers of the company in regard to matters of common interest. . . . I have visited every camp, with the exception of those on the western slope, and lack of time alone has prevented my getting over there to see you men. I have gone, as you know, to every camp in the southern fields, have talked privately with every superintendent, except one who was away, and with all of the representatives at each camp with the exception of some two or three who were not available at the time; I have gone into scores of your homes and met your wives and children, and have seen how you live; I have looked at your gardens, and in camps where fences were only recently built have seen how eagerly you have planted gardens the moment opportunity was afforded, and how quickly you have gotten the grass to grow, also flowers and vegetables, and how the interest in your homes has thereby been increased. I inquired specifically about the water supply at each camp; I went down into several of the mines and talked with hundreds of the miners; I looked into the schools, talked with the teachers, inquired what educational advantages your children were getting. I asked what opportunities you men, my partners, had for getting together socially, and I visited some of your club-houses and saw plans for others. I went into your wash-houses and talked with the men before and after bathing. As you know, we have pretty nearly slept together — it has been reported that I slept in one of your nightshirts — I would have been proud had the report been true. If any man could have gone more carefully, more thoroughly, into the working and living conditions that affect you, my partners, I should be glad to have had him make me suggestions as to what further I might have done. . . .

I want to stay in Colorado until we have worked out some plan that we all agree is the best thing for us all, because there is just one thing that no man in this company can ever afford to have happen again, be he stockholder, officer, or employee, or whatever his position, and that is, another strike. I know we are all agreed about that, every last man of us, and I propose to stay here if it takes a year, until we have worked out among ourselves, right in our own family, some plan that we all believe is going to prevent any more disturbances, any more interruption of the successful operation of this great company in which we are all interested. . . .

Suggestions for Further Reading

Byrkit, James. *Forging the Copper Collar: Arizona's Labor-Management War of 1901–1921.* Tucson: University of Arizona Press, 1982.

Dubofsky, Melvyn. *We Shall Be All: A History of the Industrial Workers of the World.* Chicago: Quadrangle Books, 1969.

Lingenfelter, Richard E. *The Hardrock Miners: A History of the Mining Labor Movement in the American West, 1863–1893.* Berkeley: University of California Press, 1974.

Lukas, J. Anthony. *Big Trouble: A Murder in a Small Western Town Sets Off a Struggle for the Soul of America.* New York: Simon and Schuster, 1997.

Montgomery, David. *The Fall of the House of Labor: The Workplace, the State, and American Labor Activism, 1865–1925.* Cambridge: Cambridge University Press, 1987.

Peterson, Richard. *The Bonanza Kings: The Social Origins and Business Behavior of Western Mining Entrepreneurs, 1870–1900.* Lincoln: University of Nebraska Press, 1977.

Schwantes, Carlos. *Radical Heritage: Labor, Socialism, and Reform in Washington and British Columbia, 1885–1917.* Seattle: University of Washington Press, 1979.

Wyman, Mark. *Hard Rock Epic: Western Miners and the Industrial Revolution, 1860–1910.* Berkeley: University of California Press, 1979.

California Campaign Edition

THE WESTERN WOMAN VOTER

VOL. I   SEATTLE, WASHINGTON, SEPTEMBER, 1911   NO. 9

COLLEGE GIRLS PUTTING UP SUFFRAGE POSTERS

WASHINGTON, last November, gave women the ballot by 20,000 majority---the largest majority ever given a suffrage amendment in the history of the world. Here's to a bigger majority in California on October 10!

California Next ! !

The Woman Suffrage Movement, 1911

This front page of *The Western Woman Voter*, a suffragist newspaper in Seattle, rallies Californians with a photograph of young women plastering a wall with posters. Women toiled over many decades to achieve the right to vote, and they succeeded first in Wyoming in 1869. Other western states soon followed suit, thus paving the way for the rest of the nation. As their posters indicate, these Washington women promoted suffrage by allying their 1910 campaign to such public figures as Theodore Roosevelt, Abraham Lincoln, and even Mark Twain. Why do you think they invoked these famous men in support of their cause?

Courtesy of the Huntington Library, San Marino, California.

CHAPTER SIX

THE PROGRESSIVE ERA

Expanding Democracy

T
he reform efforts that characterized the first two decades of the twentieth
century have led historians to dub these years the Progressive Era. It was
a time of marked public activity on the part of Progressives, a loose collection of people trying to find solutions to social and political problems. Imbued
with optimism and an unwavering faith in technology and efficiency, Progressives
believed — somewhat naively — that they could make the nation better, often by
harnessing the power of government in their favor.

Despite its all-encompassing label, however, Progressivism was not a united
movement. It consisted of many, sometimes contradictory, perspectives. Progressives were members of both the Democratic and the Republican political parties,
and they championed causes at the national and the local levels. The plight
of the nation's poor, for example, especially in the cities, became a popular focus
among grass-roots activists. Progressives gravitated to politics because they believed that an active government could be an effective problem solver.

The Progressive Era witnessed critical changes in the American political and
economic system, from President Theodore Roosevelt's legislative and public relations attempts to limit corporate power to the passage in 1920 of the Nineteenth
Amendment granting women the vote. Countless other political developments
occurred at the local and state levels, usually as a result of Progressives' attempts
to rein in the power of the special interests — the powerful railroad monopoly, for
example, or the political boss — which they believed corrupted politics and made
it harder for democracy to function. Progressive innovations included important
changes in the ways voters could express their wishes (or their anger) and new
methods of organizing municipal political leadership within cities and towns:
it was during the Progressive period that a number of American cities opted to
abolish the office of elected mayor in favor of the more "efficient" appointed city
manager.

In the West, progressive reform-mindedness had a long tradition. Reformers
tackled the political and social problems of western cities and tried to curtail the

reach of railroads and similar giant corporations. Other issues were more obviously grounded in the western context. The legal and political movement to protect the environment had western roots. The first national parks, including Yellowstone and Yosemite, were established in the nineteenth century. By the Progressive Era, conservation was a national issue, and westerners, including the naturalist John Muir (founder of the Sierra Club), played a critical role in publicizing the plight of American nature.

Sometimes, however, reformist fervor went too far. For all their claims about expanding democracy, progressives also had a hand in limiting the political rights of ethnic and racial minorities. In the West, as elsewhere, they embraced "Americanization" efforts designed to turn immigrant minorities into model citizens. Often well intentioned, these programs — after-school language classes, cooking classes, playground and recreation programs for children, public health efforts in tenements — were evidence of a deeper desire that immigrants remake themselves into white, middle-class, Christian Americans. Recalling previous efforts at "civilizing" Native Americans, the progressive approach to newcomers could be as clumsy and ethnocentric in practice as it was humanitarian and reform-minded in purpose.

During the Progressive Era, the nation began to see technology and science as a source of positive change. Many progressives believed that where politics had failed, science and technology could succeed. This is not to say that progressives uniformly embraced technological innovation; some wanted technology kept in check. This was particularly true if it meant keeping big business out of government. One of the period's most successful politicians, Hiram Johnson of California, won the governorship in 1910 by demanding that disinterested governmental bodies more tightly regulate the Southern Pacific Railroad Corporation, which had engaged in monopoly pricing and political bullying. The time had come, Johnson said, to kick the railroad out of California politics.

Successful progressives like Johnson knew they had to enlarge their voter bases, but such efforts faced limitations. Many western politicians, like their counterparts elsewhere, did not believe in racial equality. In fact, they sometimes used racist issues to win votes. Hiram Johnson was only too happy to support anti-Asian legislation, which added further restrictions to those already placed on Asians and Asian Americans by the Chinese Exclusion Act of 1882.

Ultimately, Progressives were only partially successful. The outbreak of the First World War, and America's eventual involvement in the conflict, dampened the fire of many progressive efforts. The legacy of the Progressive Era is mixed.

The selections in this chapter address different forms of Progressivism in the West. Not everyone was in favor of woman suffrage, as the essay by George Patton illustrates, but activists for women's wider participation in the rights and privileges of citizenship, like Charlotte Whitney, believed fervently in their work. The account of Oregon's recall legislation attests to the ability of voters to affect local or state politics. Finally, the selection on Americanization serves as a reminder that although access to voting might have increased during the Progressive Era, age-old tensions about the "right kind" of voter continued to arise.

As you read the following selections, consider the ways in which progressive reforms focused on issues of citizenship and government. According to the authors of these documents, who gets to vote and what do they get to vote for? Why did these issues become so prominent in the early twentieth century? Why was the West a pioneer in the arena of woman suffrage?

---

25. A Californian Argues against Woman Suffrage

The father of the famed World War II general of the same name, George Patton was a Virginian who moved to Southern California in the latter years of the nineteenth century. A political mover and shaker in and around Los Angeles (he served as a kind of right hand to the railroad magnate Henry Huntington), Patton vehemently opposed woman suffrage. This excerpt from an essay originally published in The West Coast Magazine, *a monthly literary and political journal from Los Angeles, is a strongly worded statement of his ideas — ideas that appealed to many Americans (men and women alike) who believed that equal suffrage was a mistake. Their traditional views generally put them at odds with many progressive reforms. Patton reveals his assumptions about the role of women in society as well as his fears about the racial future of the Pacific Coast. Why does Patton oppose suffrage? How would women like those in the photograph on page 112 respond to Patton's arguments? What evidence does he marshall to show that equal suffrage has been a mistake?*

George S. Patton
"Why Women Should Not Be Given the Vote"
1911

. . . You will observe that I do not state the problem as the suffragists do. I do not state that the question is whether or not women shall enjoy a right now de-

The West Coast Magazine [Los Angeles] (September 1911): 3–16.

nied them, or whether we shall confer upon women a privilege not now enjoyed by them, — but shall we or shall we not impose upon them a burden, a duty, an obligation, from which they are at present free. . . .

I submit . . . that the electoral franchise, by which men in our modern civilization, . . . carry on the functions of such government, is . . . a duty and an obligation, and not a privilege at all; that politics, through and by means of which the electoral franchise is utilized as an effectual means of human government, is in its final analysis, a struggle, a contest, a combat; is, in fact, merely modified war, — and that it necessarily follows that its carrying out rests upon that half of the human race, upon which from its very birth, through all its evolution, has rested the warlike and combative obligation, to the exclusion of the other half of the race. That the electoral obligation now rests, as it should rest, exclusively upon men.

. . . In the prolongation of the human period of infancy some have seen the direct hand of an overruling Providence, thereby compelling a division and specialization of the duties of the man and of the woman. Thus prior to the birth of the human young, and for a long period thereafter, and repeated over and over again during the whole period of child-bearing, the mother was not only helplessly unfitted to the man's task, but her special duties and obligations were so heavy, and of such an absorbing nature that she could not if she would, perform, or share in, his special duties. . . . There was no question here between the primeval pair, of superiority or inferiority. Each was superior in his exclusive sphere, and between them there was perfect equality, perfect unity of purpose. . . .

. . . In these communities, the men necessarily continued to be the physical defenders and providers.

In these primitive communities it necessarily early became essential that some means should be devised by which, from time to time, questions of tribal or community policy should be settled. These we now call questions of public policy. Such questions then, as now, gave occasion for radical differences of opinion, or a selfish and powerful individual or group of individuals attempted, then as now, to seize and enjoy some special privilege or immunity.

Such controversies could only be settled by an appeal to arms, to force. . . .

As tribes grew into peoples, and nations, by the orderly process of evolution, stable governments were evolved, based upon the rule of the majority of the force and power of the nation. Today, in every civilized government it is in its last analysis, force and force only, fighting physical brute force, if you will, that stands behind and gives efficacy to the verdict of the majority cast at the polls. . . .

From all participation in this ultimate appeal to force women are necessarily excluded, and the reasons for such exclusion are as compelling and immutable in this day as they were in that earlier day when she relied for protection from stalking dangers in forest shadows, upon the strong arm of her mate. . . .

Between the nations of the world there exists an armed truce. Never since the creation of man has he so feverishly and madly prepared for war.

Here in California we occupy the position of the vanguard of Aryan civilization, and before our very eyes the Asiatic Titan stretches his giant limbs after the sleep of centuries.

Every great invasion in times past, when the hordes overran Europe, came when some prolific people were pressed for land to live upon. Such a condition now confronts such a people beyond the Pacific. The men of our race, as if by some instinct, are preparing to hold by force the vantage ground we have gained. Hence the Panama canal, the fortifications at Guam and Pearl Harbor, and new Dreadnaughts[1] and guns.

The possibilities that led to the recent mobilization of army and navy are patent and known to all men; and yet in the face of all these things suffragists vaguely tell us, "When women vote there will be no more war — we will not allow it."

When asked the direct question, "How will you accomplish this laudable result?" they become both dumb and indignant. . . .

The argument of those suffragists who claim and declaim that women have a "right" to the ballot, and that this "right" is denied them by men, is wholly fallacious. The truth is, the voting function is not a "right" and cannot become a right until it has been granted by law.

. . . Another fallacious "argument," often heard from suffragist women, is that man and man-made laws treat women as though they were inferior beings. Nothing could be further from the truth. Men do not treat women as inferior beings — rather they treat them as superior beings — and it is only from women's lips that we hear of woman's inferiority to man. . . .

Another argument frequently heard — that withholding the franchise from women is a similar case to that of Great Britain in the levying of the stamp tax, and is "taxation without representation" — will not bear a moment's analysis and betrays an ignorance both of logic and of the plain facts of history. The cry of "taxation without representation" arose in the Revolutionary period of our history and was founded upon substantial reason. Between England and the American colonies, it was practically the case of a foreign tyrant imposing laws upon the subject colonies which were not imposed upon the home people. . . . If men, therefore, should impose upon women or their property, a tax which men and their property did not bear, there would be just and grievous cause of complaint. But certainly it is not tyrannous if men say "my property" as well as "your property," shall be subject to the same uniform law. . . .

. . . What worthy cause is now being injured or jeopardized by delay? What are women going to do when they get the ballot? Do they know themselves? Have they, or has a single one of them outlined a policy in government and its origin and evolution, that indicates real thought or study of our governmental structure, or pointed out where woman suffrage will advance a single reform, not now as readily or more readily attainable? . . . Then why this clamorous demand for

[1] **Dreadnaughts:** Battleships.

change? Does it not really spring from the misconception of the nature of the voting function, the erroneous idea that it is a privilege and therefore something to be desired, which is denied and forbidden to women?

. . . I most solemnly warn all women against entertaining the belief that the ballot in their hands will have the slightest effect upon ameliorating their economical conditions. Such amelioration and betterment, and no woman desires it more than men do, can never come through statute laws, but can and must come only from the education and enlightenment of public sentiment, coupled with the organization of labor, working for its own betterment. . . .

In other respects and wherever the law thinks it wise so to do, an absolute equality is established, not only between the sexes, but between husband and wife. Thus, the husband has absolutely no control over his wife's property, and the wife is as free as the husband to contract with him or with anybody else, not only as to property but as to any other matter which is the subject of contract. . . . An unmarried woman may as freely engage in business or trade as may a man and under no restrictions. Even a married woman may engage in trade entirely apart from her husband's control. . . . Could women armed with the ballot and divided as they say they will be into hostile and contending political factions — as men are, — have secured these or any of these valuable privileges and immunities which men have freely accorded them upon their own motion or upon the request of women — as women — without the ballot?

In all of those great rights of modern life, the right to own, control and dispose of property and the right to contract, it will be seen that in this state, women not only stand upon an equality with men, but, if anything, are favored over men by laws designed for their protection. There is but one class of property over which a husband exercises a dominion superior to that of a wife. That class of property is known to the law as community property. Over this class of property the husband is given the dominion and control within certain limitations, and this must be so because in our modern civilization, wherever the married state exists, it is usually the husband that is the bread winner; it is usually the husband who transacts what we call business. . . . But even upon his right of control and notwithstanding the fact that this property has been acquired wholly by his own endeavor . . . he may not give it away nor part with it except for value. If he proposes to make any gift, it cannot be done unless the wife assents thereto and joins therein, and upon the husband's death she takes, beyond his power to dispose of it by will, one-half of all the community property so accumulated during their married life. . . .

What are the great advantages which it may be said men take to themselves under their laws? They grow almost entirely out of the obligations which men take upon themselves to the state by the exercise of the franchise. Men alone vote and men alone, with certain limitations not necessary here to consider, fill the offices of state. Women or rather the suffragist minority of women are seeking to enter upon this domain upon terms of equality with men. I have before pointed out that it can never in the nature of things be that they enter upon these duties upon terms of equality. You cannot have an army of women. You cannot have the city of Los Angeles policed by women. You cannot have any law which may be placed upon the statute books by women enforced, unless it meets the approbation of men, because, as I have said, in the last analysis it is the physical force of men which executes the law.

Ask yourselves, therefore, my suffragist friends, what laws you would put upon the books, if you had the suffrage, which men have not put upon the books, and whenever you can think of such a law I will make answer that if it be a reasonable law, one for the betterment of women, the men themselves will be swift, not only to put it upon the books but to see that it is enforced. "This means, of course," you answer, "that the law must appear to be reasonable to the men or it will not be placed upon the books." But to this I reply, that if it does not appear reasonable to the men, even if the women placed it upon the books, it would never be executed. . . .

And here let me repeat that few things are more destructive of the well-being of the state than indifference to or disrespect for the law. . . . Disrespect and disregard for the law mean the swift destruction of any form of government. . . .

But I now propose to speak briefly of what I conceive to be the threatened evils of woman suffrage — evils to women themselves, evils to the state; particular and specific dangers, as against the vague general expressions that the ballot in the hands of women will do so much good.

Women, even the highly intelligent ones, are prone to compare themselves with men of much inferior education and ability. They say: "You give the ballot to this ignorant day laborer, do I not know more than he?" They say: "My coachman or chauffeur whom I pay can vote. Does he know more than the woman who pays his wages?" But this is not the true consideration. One answer to it is that the same chauffeur and the same day laborer can bear arms and may be called upon to bear arms in defense of the laws which they have made. But when women discuss the question of universal suffrage they must not select individuals of their sex. They must treat their sex as a mass. They must bear in mind that the ballot to them does not mean the ballot to the most intelligent of them, but it means the ballot to the day laborer's wife, who, if anything, is more ignorant of public affairs than is her husband — who, by the way, is actually frequently one of the most intelligent of voters. . . .

The very best that can be said upon this topic is that suffrage for women means a doubling of the present vote without in any material sense changing the character of that vote for the better. . . .

. . . Women now have full suffrage in five states; the State of Washington having recently joined Colorado, Utah, Wyoming and Idaho in the experiment.

In the four last named states it has been in operation for a number of years.

If a tithe of the great benefits which suffragists declare will follow the granting of the franchise to women are to be realized — some indication must surely by this time have been given toward that result in these states.

Instead, the history of legislation in the states named without exception indicates the very reverse, and demonstrates a pitiable failure to achieve any of the benefits so freely predicted. Recently the editor of the Ladies Home Journal sent Mr. Richard Barry as a special commissioner to investigate the workings of suffrage in the then four suffrage states. The Journal published his report, which now, in pamphlet form, is being distributed by the Woman's League opposed to suffrage.

It is a most complete and damning arraignment of suffrage, a most amazing demonstration of failure and folly.

It is too long to reproduce here — but a few extracts will prove enlightening. Says Mr. Barry, speaking of Colorado:

> . . . The chief of police of Denver told me that juvenile crime is on an alarming increase in that city. . . .
>
> The chief of police of Denver joins with the chief of police of Salt Lake City (the only two towns of any size in the woman-suffrage country) as my authority for the statement that prostitution is largely on the increase both in Colorado and in Utah. Idaho and Wyoming, being rural communities, can show a better record, but still no better than similar communities elsewhere. . . .

> . . . Supplementing Mr. Barry's report, here is what a prominent Colorado woman, Mrs. Francis W. Goddard, President of the Colonial Dames of Colorado, has to say as recently as December last:

> . . . For years I believed in woman suffrage and have worked day in and day out for it. I now see my mistake and would abolish it tomorrow if I could.
>
> No law has been put on the statute book of Colorado for the benefit of women and children that has been put there by the women. The child labor law went through independently of the women's vote. The hours of working women have not been shortened; the wages of schoolteachers have not been raised; the type of men that got into office has not improved a bit.
>
> Frankly, the experiment is a failure. It has done Colorado no good. It has done woman no good. The best thing for both would be if tomorrow the ballot for women could be abolished.

> . . . In view of all these objections theoretical and practical, I say with deep earnestness that the men of California whose votes will determine the question on October 10, have never had presented to them a political question more fraught with potency of evil to the cause of good government, or government by responsible voters, enacting wise and enforcible laws. . . . The dictates of simple prudence should impel the thoughtful men of the state to smother under an overwhelming adverse verdict the attempt of a handful of mistaken enthusiasts to place upon the unwilling shoulders of our good women a responsibility and a burden which they are constitutionally unable to assume.

26. Suffragist Strategy in California

This document was written by the president of the College Equal Suffrage League of Northern California, Charlotte Anita Whitney, in 1911, just after California voted in favor of woman suffrage. In this foreword to a book published by the league, Whitney discusses various strategies for keeping the suffrage juggernaut moving across the nation's political landscape. The movement demands strong organizational leadership, she declares, as well as clear-cut goals and aims so that others will join the cause. Whitney's insistence that the suffrage movement is an educational, even a spiritual, endeavor is very much at odds with the perspective of an opponent like George Patton. In terms of political strategies, what suggestions look familiar, even these many years later? How would Whitney respond to Patton's declaration that equality between men and women already existed in many areas? How do Whitney's strategies for cooperative organization contrast with Patton's notions of "rule by force"?

Charlotte Anita Whitney
"Suggestions for Successful Organization"
1911

In making an active campaign for equal suffrage, no matter how vital other reforms may appear, let equal suffrage and equal suffrage alone be the issue of your organization. If your association allows itself to become identified with Socialism, Women's Christian Temperance work, Prohibition, reforms for working women, or any other measure, it will be at the expense of alienating the interest of some of the friends of your own cause. . . .

The planning of a campaign is the first work of a president and her board, but as the actual work must be carried out in committee a president should put her best effort into building up strong committees and in discovering fit chairmen. In this the president should insist on the advice and coöperation of her board. A committee once formed should be held responsible for the work for which it was created, and though the presiding officer may have to spend much time in keeping the committee up to its business, it is far more advantageous, on all accounts, that she should do this than that she should perform any part of its work, since the assumption of a committee's duties destroys its interest and usefulness. A committee may be reorganized and should be strengthened and refreshed by new members, as its work unfolds.

College Equal Suffrage League of Northern California, *Winning Equal Suffrage in California* (San Francisco: National College Equal Suffrage League, 1913), 13–16.

ˊ Whenever it is possible, volunteers should be placed at once upon some committee, because real work should be supplied for everyone. Experience in our campaign convinced us that when a woman was set actively to work her interest kindled and her neutrality warmed into partisanship. Sometimes a single errand to the printer's or a trip to arrange for a permit from the Chief of Police, was enough to draw in a new enthusiast, who, from that hour, felt that the work of the League was her own intimate concern. The vigor of a league may be measured by the number of its healthy and well-sustained enterprises, and this demands a body of ardent and intelligent workers, constantly reinforced by new members. . . .

One of the gravest puzzles of organizations is involved in the effort to attain a thorough coöperation between all the different suffrage societies of a State or city. How much time and effort can be wisely expended in harmonizing the work and plans of all? In an effort to attain such coöperation we had an Interleague Conference, formed of representatives from all of the societies for equal suffrage in San Francisco, and we found that this body of eighteen was much too large for swift decisions, on a variety of complex activities. It is inevitable that the most conservative, or the most obstructive, members of such a group must either be converted, or swept along protesting, by the more enterprising majority. A small body of strong representatives should gain much by a short weekly conference, and if the chairman insists that no new plan can be submitted, except in writing, and that no member may speak more than once to a motion — until all have spoken — it is possible to control the waste of time to some extent. Perhaps the best plan is to coöperate on matters that show an unmistakable gain from large concerted action, such a plan as election day work at the polls, and to leave separate plans to be handled by each group, reporting upon them, in a very general way, at the weekly conference, to prevent any unfortunate interference of dates or engagements. With frankness and forethought there need not be the least rivalry between people who are all working for one end, and something is certainly gained by the experience of special groups in planning for the sort of people whose needs and interests they know best.

In all of the work, it should be borne in mind that a suffrage campaign is an educational campaign and must be kept clear-cut, clean and open. Invite interested members of the society, from time to time, to the meetings of your board, or executive committee. Every campaign will develop workers of good judgment and enthusiasm who will be invaluable assets in the work, and though such a worker may not become a voting member of the directorate, she should be made so welcome a guest at your councils that you can avail yourself of her experience and suggestions. No chairman of an important committee should ever be excluded from the board. Unity of aim and method, harmonious progress of plan and development can be attained only in this way. An intelligent visitor, who is present during the discussion of an important policy, who hears the pros and cons as they are advanced, gains a comprehension of a situation which is apt to bring both herself, and, eventually, the group to which she belongs, into harmony with the board's carefully worked out policy. Full and accurate information about any of the plans of the organization should be easily accessible to all members, and they should be encouraged to get a working knowledge of the progress of the work.

The president should remember that she is, first of all, presiding officer of the board, and that her chief duty is to see that the business of the board is conducted as quickly and efficiently as possible. She should not hesitate to use her gavel, nor to hold members of the board to business methods of debate and procedure. But she will weaken her board as a whole, and, therefore, her organization, if she assumes duties and responsibilities and makes decisions that rightfully devolve upon the board. She should never be drawn into any conference or correspondence that is not known to her directors, and that may not be freely told to any member. In this way, only, can she command the respect and confidence of her fellow-workers, and upon this depends the position of her organization in the outside world. She must remember that no one person can develop a strong organization, and that her function is to bring out in her board and in her membership the spirit of good team-work. She must bring as many members as possible to the front — giving them as far as possible opportunities to carry out plans that enlist their special capabilities, and accord to them due credit for all such work. Let her not be afraid to put responsibility on others.

The president may well consider herself an understudy to every committee chairman and should stand ready to fill in gaps and avert failures in any work that has been undertaken, always bearing in mind that the committee should, when it is possible, be made to do its own work. It is more essential that a president sees that no piece of work, to which her league has put its hand or its name, fails, than that she inaugurate many new enterprises.

Above all, every worker for equal suffrage must believe in equal suffrage as a great, world-wide movement — an essential part of a moral and spiritual awakening; believe in it so firmly that faith begets courage and enthusiasm; and never forget that because it is a great, educational movement the foundation of work must be laid with all sincerity and truth.

27. LEGISLATIVE REFORM IN OREGON

Woman suffrage doubled the number of voters in one stroke, but additional electoral reforms, such as the recall, the ballot initiative, and the referendum, were necessary to enable voters to take action more quickly and (at least theoretically) efficiently. As tools for expressing voter preference and voter frustration, these innovations began popping up in states like Oregon and California not long after the turn of the century. Along with equal suffrage, these laws changed American voting. These excerpts from a volume addressing the Oregon reforms explain the basic tenets of direct government and give readers examples of how they operate. The recall, for instance, allowed voters to gather signatures on a petition declaring their dissatisfaction with an elected official. If they gathered enough signatures, a special election would be held to determine whether the official could continue in office. The initiative and the referendum allowed voters to take similar action over specific laws. It is interesting to note, as this document attests, that Oregon's recall law came about through an initiative movement of the state's voters. How would George Patton respond to these innovations? Would he be likely to claim that women would use innovations like the initiative or the recall differently from men? How does the Klamath County judge challenge the recall petition aimed at removing him from office?

GILBERT L. HEDGES
From *Where the People Rule*
1914

Enactment. The recall amendment to the Constitution was submitted by initiative petition to the vote of the electors at the regular election held in the State of Oregon on June 1, 1908. There were 58,381 votes cast for the amendment and 31,002 votes cast against it. By virtue of the proclamation of the Governor, the amendment became effective June 23, 1908. . . .

The Recall in Klamath County. The recall was invoked against William S. Worden, county judge of Klamath County. The petitions containing the required number of names were regularly filed and the county clerk called the election for June 2, 1913. Two candidates were placed in the field against the judge. One of these polled few votes and his part in the campaign was negligible. The principal reason for resorting to the recall was the court's decision to build a new court house upon a site some distance from the old building in the town of Klamath Falls, the county seat. Some of the older residents who were opposed to the change were instrumental in instituting and promoting the recall. Other charges were made and the campaign against the recall was conducted by Judge Worden with vigor and energy. He stumped the county and everywhere awakened the people to a full realization of the meaning of the election. The charges brought against the judge as set forth in the petition and on the sample ballot are as follows:

> Unlawful, unwise and inefficient management of county finances; the incurring of a large amount of unlawful indebtedness; unnecessarily increased taxation; waste of money in county expenses; favoritism in contracting with and

Gilbert L. Hedges, *Where the People Rule, or, The Initiative and Referendum, Direct Primary Law and the Recall in Use in the State of Oregon* (San Francisco: Bender-Moss Company, 1914), 93, 97–99, 107–10.

employing relatives of members of the county court and certain firms and corporations at a financial loss to the county; unlawful issuing and selling warrants of the county at a discount; carelessness and inefficiency in auditing bills against the county; accepting employment from corporations whose interests are opposed to the public interests and at far greater salaries than that paid by the county; inefficient and unsatisfactory service as a county judge; failure to get value received for money spent for roads, though petitioners are not opposed to good roads; lack of ability, as shown in the past, to expend future levies for roads; inability to construct a new courthouse with economy and a due regard for cost, though petitioners are not opposed to the new courthouse and are indifferent as to its location, but only insist that it shall be built economically and that the cost shall not be excessive, which the past actions of said officer indicate that he will not be able to do.

To these charges, the judge replied on the sample ballot as follows:

This is not a regular election. It is an attempt to remove me from office in the middle of my term.

Two years ago you elected me on a basis of Good Roads and the building of a new courthouse on the Hot Springs site. I have kept my promises. The work has been done well and as cheaply as consistent with permanency. What has been done will not have to be done over again.

The new courthouse has been built economically and well. We have saved money for you in our plan.

I deny the accusations of the opposition on the ground that they are gross misrepresentations and intended to cloud the issue and fool the voter. No other county in the state has accomplished so much in the way of good roads. The men who are behind this recall have threatened me ever since my term of office began unless I would submit to their dictation.

The Grand Jury report was not correct and has been so proven relative to culvert, harness and other matters. If wrong in some, wrong in others. All I want is a square deal. The opposition will not give it.

With the exception of one paper, the press of the county was against the recall. This one paper was acquired by friends of Judge Worden before the campaign closed. The election was held pursuant to notice on June 2, 1913. The vote stood as follows: J. R. Ritter 56, Frank Ira Wade 974, and Wm. S. Worden 2286. By their votes, the people sustained the county judge and registered an emphatic protest against the recall movement. . . .

The Recall in the City of Medford.   Medford is a thriving town of about 9,000 inhabitants, situated in the southern part of the State of Oregon. The progress made by this city during the past decade has been remarkable. The temper of the people is essentially progressive. The official acts of two of the city's councilmen were strongly disapproved by many of the leading citizens. This feeling against the two councilmen increased until it crystallized into a recall movement against them. The regular city election was held January 13, 1914, and prior to this date recall petitions had been circulated, signed and filed, and a recall election called for the date of the city election. The councilmen whose official acts were condemned were: G. H. Millar, councilman from the Third Ward, and J. E. Stewart, councilman from the Second Ward. To oppose G. H. Millar, the organization carrying on the recall campaign nominated Dr. H. P. Hargrave. To run against Councilman J. E. Stewart, the organization nominated Mr. V. J. Emerick.

Of all the recall elections held in the State of Oregon, this one in the city of Medford was probably the most exciting. Every voter within the corporate limits of the city was thoroughly alive to the issues involved. The newly enfranchised women played a prominent part in this election and the result may be ascribed, in great part, to their participation in the election.

The reason for demanding the recall of G. H. Millar as set forth on the sample ballot was:

> That the said G. H. Millar does not truly represent the residents of said (Third) Ward and because of his general incompetence and extravagance in office.

To this charge, Councilman Millar replied upon the sample ballot as follows:

> The recall charges of general incompetence, extravagance and not truly representing the residents of the Third ward, are both untrue and ridiculous, as a just investigation of the city records will prove.

The charge of general incompetence and extravagance in office was also made against Councilman J. E. Stewart and given as the reason for demanding his recall. To this charge J. E. Stewart replied as follows upon the sample ballot:

> One year ago the electors of my ward elected me to the office of councilman and I assumed the duties of that office in entire good faith and with a purpose on my part to perform those duties to the best of my ability and with a due regard to the welfare of my City. This purpose, I have performed; many accusations have been made as to misconduct in my official position, but no official act of mine has been pointed to as being a violation of my duties, or of my oath of office.
>
> If I have erred, it is an error of judgment; no person is infallible. If I should be recalled by the citizens of my ward, there can be no certainty of perfection of official conduct in my successor. He, too, may be fallible as myself.
>
> Should a man be recalled from an official position he occupies because somebody is piqued by his conduct or differs in judgment from him? Such a result is substantially a conviction, without trial, and a judgment without a preferred charge.
>
> I ask the suffrages [1] of my fellow citizens in my behalf.

---

[1] **Suffrages:** Votes.

The recall was successful and both councilmen were recalled. The vote by which Mr. Millar was deposed stood as follows: Millar 244, Hargrave 283. Councilman Stewart received 300 and his opponent 368 votes.

The Recall Generally. In the preceding paragraphs specific instances of the use of the recall have been set forth. It will be noted that the highest office involved in these various elections has been that of county judge. . . . It is a difficult position to fill without making enemies. The county judges, who have run the gauntlet of the recall, have been attacked for their acts performed while sitting as a member of the board of county commissioners.

The recall has been used at times without sufficient reason. Since its enactment it has been used frequently, and with the lapse of time it will be invoked more often. Different officials have been threatened with the recall. A circuit judge was threatened with the recall because of his charge in a murder trial; a sheriff was threatened with the recall because of his vigorous suppression of a street speaking nuisance; an assessor has been threatened with the recall because he dared to do his duty and list property for taxation which many thought exempt.

The recall can not take the place of impeachment trials. Charges are preferred against an official under the recall amendment, but the campaign is a general campaign to defeat the incumbent by the use of any political device or charge. Quite often the charges preferred are ignored and title to office is tried with the people as judges by the introduction of any evidence which might be urged in an unrestricted political campaign.

To give those against whom the recall is invoked a fair trial, all of the people should be compelled to vote. A man's right to hold office should not be determined by a minority. It is not enough that the opportunity to pass upon a man's official acts should be given. He is entitled to have his right to hold office passed upon by the entire jury of qualified voters.

28. New Voters and the Americanization Movement

Progressives expressed qualms about the ability of immigrants to participate in American politics, and this was true in the West no less than in other regions of the country. Progressives often latched onto "Americanization" as a way of allaying their own concerns about the effect of immigrants on American culture and American institutions. At heart, the effort was motivated by humanitarianism, but Americanization also imposed a set of ideas about citizenship determined by mainstream values on class, religion, and other concerns. In other words, while progressive reforms were broadening the voting base of the American polity, progressive reformers were working to Americanize new voters or the parents of American-born citizens along acceptable lines of behavior and culture. This selection illustrates some of the organizational strategies of the California Americanization effort spearheaded by the state's Commission of Immigration and Housing. How would you define "true democracy" as used in this selection? How would George Patton define the term? Charlotte A. Whitney? Why do you think Americanization is seen as a problem?

CALIFORNIA COMMISSION OF IMMIGRATION AND HOUSING
From *Americanization*
1918

Out of an actual experience in the field of Americanization extending over five years, the Commission of Immigration and Housing of California has evolved certain lessons which it has the honor of presenting to the attention of those interested in the subject.

First, the commission has come to a realization of the seriousness of the situation. . . . A nation made up, as is America, of diverse elements must be unified to be safe.

Then the commission's experience has brought out the fact that Americanization should take within its scope the native born as well as the immigrant. Not all antipatriots are foreign born. Furthermore, the attitude of the alien toward this country, in great part, is a reflection of the attitude of our own citizens towards him. Americanization should undertake to teach the duty of the host, not less than the duty of the guest.

Again, the commission has discovered that Americanization means infinitely more than teaching English to foreigners. That is of great importance, for many reasons, but there is much which can not wait for a new language, and which it is vitally important, both to the foreigner and to the country, that he should know. It must never be forgotten that these people are being transplanted, and "in transplanting it is fatal to destroy the roots." If while the roots are fresh and vital they are to find the subsoil of American ideals, of an intelligent conception of liberty, and of a new loyalty, the foreigner must be reached in a language which he understands, and through media with which he is familiar.

Further, the commission has learned very definitely that to succeed in this task of Americanization, an organization must be thoroughly and sincerely democratic. All committees should carry representation of the foreign born and of labor. . . .

State Commission of Immigration and Housing, *Americanization: The California Program* (Sacramento: California State Printing Office, 1918), 5, 7–8, 13.

As the result of its own successful pioneering efforts, the commission presents the following outline of a working program of Americanization, and offers its very hearty service to any and all counties of the state.

True democracy is the goal of Americanization.

Upon true democracy, then, must the Americanization movement itself be based and the spirit of that democracy must direct every aspect of the organization of such a movement.

The program of Americanization of the Commission of Immigration and Housing of California is built on this conviction. On this conviction also is built its method of procedure in organizing the state for this work.

The rapid awakening of our foreign-born element to the desirability of Americanization justifies our seeking their large co-operation. No program, however excellent, can have its best success when handed down ready-made from above. Only when it is built on the needs of the people, which they themselves best understand, and when they themselves have had a hand in its making, can it be a living and working thing.

And it is right that the foreign born and native born should share the responsibility of choice as to what is for the good of all.

Experience is showing that leaders in the foreign-born groups are ready and eager to enter upon this work, and to co-operate cordially with their American neighbors.

There is, in the working out of a program such as this, the greatest possible amount of unity and good feeling. There is, from the start, a sense of co-operation and friendliness. The pride of organization and the feeling of responsibility go far toward adjusting any possibility of disagreement at any point in the program, for that program must be recognized as an elastic thing, subject to modification by advancing experience. New problems will arise at every step and the greatest care will have to be given to each one of these. And only if throughout we are governed by the spirit of true democracy can we hope to keep our way.

The Commission of Immigration and Housing has been given charge of the entire subject of immigration in California. Upon the commission, therefore, rests the responsibility of definite plans for the solution of the problem of Americanization. . . .

In each county the commission is appointing a chairman of Americanization — an American-born man or woman, who can attract a more general following than a member of any foreign group.

The county chairman will seek out the leaders of various foreign groups, and invite them, with well informed representatives of the native born, to a meeting for organization, where these Americans, born here and abroad, will determine their plans. At this time the committees and subcommittees should be chosen, including men and women representing —

(*a*) Foreign born.
(*b*) Labor.

(c) Employers.
(d) Americanization organizations.
(e) Education authorities.

The county chairman should use the organized machinery of all existing agencies in carrying out the program. . . .

The county committee, including men and women representing the foreign born, labor, employers, Americanization organizations and educational authorities, should first *determine upon the exact task to be undertaken.*

To reach this determination definite information as to the foreign population must be gathered swiftly, by temporary committees, which may be appointed throughout the county, on

Nationality.
Education.
Social agencies.

The Committee on Nationality should secure careful estimates on

The number,
The nationality,
The location,

of the foreign-born people of the country. It should find whether these people live in groups or scattered throughout the community; whether they speak English, read foreign newspapers, attend foreign-speaking churches, have American standards of living and have contact with wholesome American living. . . .

Suggestions for Further Reading

Atkinson, Diane. *Votes for Women.* Cambridge: Cambridge University Press, 1988.

Beeton, Beverly. *Women Vote in the West: The Woman Suffrage Movement, 1869–1896.* New York: Garland, 1986.

Cherny, Robert W. *Populism, Progressivism, and the Transformation of Nebraska Politics, 1885–1915.* Lincoln: University of Nebraska Press, 1981.

Deverell, William, and Tom Sitton. *California Progressivism Revisited.* Berkeley: University of California Press, 1994.

Fitzpatrick, Ellen. *Endless Crusade: Women Social Scientists and Progressive Reform.* New York: Oxford University Press, 1990.

Gould, Lewis. *Reform and Regulation: American Politics, 1900–1916.* New York: Wiley, 1978.

Hays, Samuel P. *The Gospel of Efficiency: The Progressive Conservation Movement, 1890–1920.* Cambridge: Harvard University Press, 1959.

Hofstadter, Richard. *The Age of Reform.* New York: Vintage, 1955.

CHAPTER SEVEN

WORLD WAR I

Western Mobilization for Global Conflict

W orld War I jolted America out of its Progressive Era optimism. When hostilities first broke out in 1914, Americans felt little need or urgency to become involved in what to many was a European affair. Many Progressive leaders urged neutrality, and they were joined by a broad coalition of pacifists, labor leaders, and other political figures, including President Woodrow Wilson.

Yet America remained closely attached to Europe. Americans with family ties to Europe felt the war deeply. Some of German and Eastern European ancestry rallied in support of the Central Powers and found allies among Irish Americans who harbored a deep mistrust of England. Others who traced their roots to Great Britain, Russia, and France generally supported those nations in the war against the Central Powers.

Loyalties such as these drew the nation closer to war. More important, however, was the escalation of German submarine attacks in the Atlantic. When a

---

Soldiers Boarding a Train in Southern California, 1917 (left)

This image of World War I soldiers leaving for training camp is in many ways familiar: young American men have gone off to fight many times in the last eighty years. But the First World War, the "Great War," was not a war that America went into willingly. On the contrary, the nation stayed out of the conflict until it was nearly over. Yet to say that the United States was not affected by the war would be wrong. Even before the Congressional declaration of war against Germany and its allies in 1917, the war touched the lives of Americans everywhere. After all, millions of Americans traced their roots to those very European nations caught up in the crisis. Wartime troop mobilization changed the lives of those who suddenly found themselves fighting in the trenches of Europe. Wartime fears and national prejudices erupted in towns large and small. How do you think the experiences of soldiers like these mirrored those of other soldiers in other wars? What might their thoughts be at this moment?

Seaver Center for Western History Research, Natural History Museum of Los Angeles County.

German U-boat torpedoed and sank the British ocean liner *Lusitania* in the spring of 1915, many Americans were convinced that the time had come for the United States to enter the war. Woodrow Wilson withstood these pressures, however, and kept the nation neutral.

But American neutrality did not last. Germany stepped up submarine warfare against British and American ships. Shortly thereafter, Great Britain intercepted a coded telegram sent by Germany's foreign secretary, Arthur Zimmermann, to the German ambassador in Mexico City. The message urged Mexico to join the Central Powers in the war. In exchange, Germany would help Mexico regain Texas, New Mexico, and Arizona, territory it ceded to the United States in 1848, after the Mexican War. Outraged by the telegram and by Germany's continued submarine attacks on U.S. ships, President Wilson went before Congress in April to seek a declaration of war. Before long, American soldiers were shipping out from U.S. training fields to the trenches of Europe.

Military and diplomatic relations with Mexico played a key role in the nation's involvement in the war. The Zimmermann telegram, with its threat of a German and Mexican–led invasion of the Southwest, was one of many border provocations preceding the U.S. declaration of war against Germany and its allies. In fact, parts of the American West were first to mobilize for the war.

Woodrow Wilson had strong views about Mexico's future. Beginning in 1911, the year dictator Porfirio Diaz was overthrown, Mexico experienced recurrent cycles of political revolution. Wilson felt increasingly obliged to involve the United States in its affairs, believing that American democracy could be exported, even if by force, to other regions of the world. This perspective would also color Wilson's view of American involvement in World War I, as he put it, to make the world "safe for democracy."

In 1914, following the assassination of the Mexican leader Francisco Madera, Wilson ordered U.S. troops to occupy the Mexican port of Veracruz. The situation only got worse. When the revolutionary Francisco "Pancho" Villa destroyed the little town of Columbus, New Mexico, in 1916, Wilson dispatched General John J. Pershing on a punitive expedition into Mexico to capture Villa. Mexican authorities angrily demanded that Pershing and his thousands of soldiers pull back to the U.S. side of the border, which they did, but only after a fruitless chase of many months. For a time, another U.S.–Mexican war seemed inevitable. The Zimmermann telegram only reignited tensions in the Southwest. Eventually, General Pershing went east to become the commander of the American expeditionary force to Europe in 1917.

Western support for the war varied. Across the Great Plains and further west in cities like San Francisco, groups of Irish and German Americans believed that the United States ought to stay out of the war — or that Woodrow Wilson had picked the wrong side. Some of these people were attacked as anti-American in the wave of anti-German sentiment that rolled across the country. Labor organizations like the Western Federation of Miners (WFM) and the Industrial Workers of the World (IWW), which took a hard line against U.S. policy, were hit with heavy-handed government reprisals. Representative Jeannette Rankin of Montana, the first woman elected to Congress, voted against the declaration of war, and the western Populist and Democrat William Jennings Bryan resigned as secretary of state because he disagreed so strongly with the administration's policies. But once the United States was committed to the war, the West mobilized rapidly.

The selections in this chapter illuminate the region's response to war. From the firestorm of anger provoked by the Zimmermann telegram to newspaper editorializing, from patriotic, German-bashing speechmaking in Wyoming to a young soldier's reactions to training camp in Texas, these documents provide a glimpse of the impact of wartime preparations and wartime fever on everyday life.

As you read through these selections, consider why the United States's preparation for, and eventual involvement in, the First World War may have taken different forms across the country. What special circumstances in the West would induce the editors of the *Los Angeles Times* to make such bold claims about preparedness and wartime patriotism? Why did events in Mexico provoke particular responses among people in the West?

---

29. Mexico Invited to Join the Central Powers

Intercepted by the British in early 1917, the Zimmermann telegram immediately prompted a rallying call for American preparedness. By suggesting a possible Mexican reconquest of the Southwest with German help — the details of which were conveniently left vague — the document incited a strong response in the border states. Army troops and tens of thousands of National Guardsmen were soon patrolling the border, as politicians and military leaders organized in anticipation of German or Mexican attacks on American soil. Would a German alliance with Mexico have produced a wartime front in, for instance, Arizona or New Mexico? Why would German officials expect Mexican authorities to give the Zimmermann telegram any attention?

The Zimmermann Telegram
1917

We intend to begin on the first of February unrestricted submarine warfare. We shall endeavor in spite of this to keep the United States of America neutral. In the event of this not succeeding, we make Mexico a proposal of alliance on the following basis: make war together, generous financial support and an understanding on our part that Mexico is to reconquer the lost territory in Texas, New Mexico, and Arizona. The settlement in detail is left to you. You will inform the President [of Mexico] of the above most secretly as soon as the outbreak of war with the United States of America is certain and add the suggestion that he should, on his own initiative, invite Japan to immediate adherence and at the same time mediate between Japan and ourselves. Please call the President's attention to the fact that the ruthless employment of our submarines now offers the prospect of compelling England in a few months to make peace.

ZIMMERMANN.

30. PREPARING FOR WAR

The following sharply worded editorial appeared in response to the disclosure of the captured Zimmermann telegram. In it the editors of the Los Angeles Times *declare that there "is no longer any doubt of the desire of Germany to make war upon us" and suggest that Germany's alliance with Japan and Mexico is a foregone conclusion. "Get together and get ready," the paper urges Californians, for the war is coming. The* Times *suggests, however, that "the greatest danger" is not from foreign nations but from "treason and sedition within our own gates." Sentiments such as these encouraged hostility toward Americans of German heritage. The excesses of patriotic fervor also led to repression of groups considered un-American; members of political and labor organizations found their patriotism and loyalty to the nation in question. If you compared this editorial with those in other American newspapers of the period, would you expect the response to be the same? How would you compare the language in this editorial to that in the Wyoming speech reprinted on pages 138–42?*

Samuel Spencer Jr., ed., *Decision for War, 1917* (Rindge, N.H.: Richard R. Smith, 1953), 61–62.

LOS ANGELES TIMES
Editorial
1917

Get Together and Get Ready!

The people of no American city have shown more patriotic zeal for military preparedness than the citizens of Los Angeles. The need of this government has met with a response from Los Angeles that has rung with enthusiasm and sturdy eagerness to serve. On every hand patriotic societies are springing up, pledged to the furtherance of our belated military activity. . . .

Out of their zeal, these societies and movements have created one complication; the danger is that these activities may not follow the same path — that they may scatter their strength.

Working in concert, these patriotic organizations might be able to do a great deal of good. Working along their scattered lines, they may still do much good, but they will always be in danger of crossing one another's paths.

It would appear to be the practical thing to first ascertain just what the government wants from its citizens in the way of practical help. The War College and the General Staff have very definite plans. In working along the lines of our own enthusiastic efforts, it is most important that we should do nothing to embarrass these plans in any remote way.

There surely is a way, however, for us to get behind these war plans and to do what we can toward forcing them through to completion in a way that seems best to the army officers who have made a special study of these matters.

The first step toward this end would seem to be the formation of a sort of central Los Angeles war board made up of representatives from the different movements. They could take stock of their various resources and see that a complete co-operation existed between the different bodies and patriotic movements.

It would then be possible to bring the entire patriotic movement into close communication with the War College and General Staff in order to help these army officers bring about the necessary legislation.

Let us find out how we can help the army; then get together in one big organized movement to do the work.

We must bestir ourselves — for the sky is full of portents. There is no longer any doubt of the desire of Germany to make war upon us — and the proposed alliance with Mexico and Japan is no dream. The thing long dreaded has come. We are virtually at war today. AND THE GREATEST DANGER IS FROM TREASON AND SEDITION WITHIN OUR OWN GATES!

Los Angeles Times (1 March 1917): 4.

31. Support for the War in Wyoming

Harrison Dale, a political science professor at the University of Wyoming, delivered this address before the Laramie One Hundred Per Cent American Club on Lincoln's birthday in 1918. Like other exhortations of its kind, the speech distinguishes between good Americans and bad, between "one hundred per cent Americans" and those whose loyalties could be called into question. Dale's discussion of those he calls "hyphenated" Americans is typical of this period of hyperpatriotism. According-ing to this line of thought, America had no place for people who hyphenated their origins and thus, it was thought, their loyalties. The war years proved especially in-tolerant of ethnic diversity in the American population. How would Professor Dale identify a "one hundred per cent American"? How do the sentiments in this speech compare with those in the newspaper editorial of a year earlier?

Harrison Clifford Dale
"What We Are Fighting For"
1918

It is altogether fitting that, on the anniversary of the birth of the man whom I think we can safely describe as the most American American that ever lived, we should consider, as he considered in the masterful language of the Gettysburg Address, the things for which we are fighting. President Wilson has sketched these objects, these principles, in his historic message to Congress before the out-break of the war, later in his reply to the Pope's peace proposals, more recently in his address before the opening session of the present Congress, and finally in his remarks of yesterday. In looking over these statements of principles and of policy one might be inclined to think that our objects are manifold. So they are. But in last analysis it strikes me that they boil down to three main purposes: (1) an Amer-ican America, not a German-America or a hyphenated America of any sort or description, but an American America; (2) the preservation of the Monroe Doc-trine,[1] or, to put it more generally, the preservation of all America north and south for Americans; and (3) the attainment through democracy of the peace of the world, so that just as death overcame death so war may overcome war and not only the world be made safe for democracy, but the world made SAFE by making it democratic!

---

[1] **Monroe Doctrine:** In 1823, President James Monroe warned European nations not to meddle in political affairs of the Western Hemisphere. This aggressive diplomatic stance became known as the Monroe Doctrine.

Harrison Clifford Dale, *What We Are Fighting For: An Address Given Before the Laramie One Hun-dred Per Cent American Club* (Laramie, Wyo.: n.p., 1918), 1–4.

First, then, to make of this splendid country of ours an American America. I put this object first because, it seems to me, it is one of the aims, one of the purposes in which we here in Laramie, we the members of the One Hundred Per Cent American Club, can most surely and most helpfully assist. We are not ninety-nine and nine-tenths per cent Americans; we are one hundred per cent Americans. Now did you ever realize what it means to be an American citizen? "A Frenchman may reside for years in England, or Germany, or Russia, but he will always remain a foreigner, no matter how many papers of citizenship he may secure. An Englishman may spend a lifetime in Italy, and catch, as Browning[2] caught, the poetry of her soul; but he will die an alien. A Russian may rear his family in Holland, but they will never become Dutch. But let this same Frenchman or Englishman or Russian come and dwell on our shores, and this great moving force of Americanism transforms him into a true American. A nation so composed cannot stand upon a narrow platform of provincial patriotism. Its fundamentals of citizenship must transcend race, and its ideals must be so high that ancient animosities and hereditary loyalties cannot compete with them, or divide the allegiance which they demand. Had our President called for a rally 'round the banner of the Anglo-Saxon, millions would have answered: 'We are not ready to die for Anglo-Saxon traditions.' Had he raised the cry of Teutonic loyalty, other millions would have answered: 'We do not acknowledge the divine right of the Hohenzollerns.'"[3] The only call which can command the support of the American nation is the call of America.

Now it is undeniably true, it is regrettably true, alas! the evidence is all too overwhelming, that the hyphen has been cultivated in this country for the benefit of that natural foe to liberty, the Imperial German Government. I say regrettably true because, thank God, not all Americans of German antecedents have allied themselves with this effort to create in our midst a separate nationality, and a separate culture, whose allegiance lay not here, but across the seas in the realm of the Hohenzollerns. Certainly it is a gratifying thing that we can count as members of this One Hundred Per Cent American Club, as loyal and true members, a number of Americans of more or less remote German origin. Not all Germans in this country are hyphenated Americans. Isn't it a heartening thing, ladies and gentlemen, that practically all of those who breathe our pure mountain air — and somehow all through history mountain air has been called the air of freedom — isn't it a splendid and a heartening thing, I say, that practically all those of German or Austrian origin who live in our county, and our city, are able in their heart of hearts to sign our constitution and by-laws as one hundred per cent Americans!

But, alas! this has not been the case in all parts of the United States. There has been a concerted effort to keep alive German culture, German traditions,

---

[2] **Browning:** Elizabeth Barrett Browning (1806–1861), English poet of the Victorian era.
[3] **Hohenzollerns:** Members of the German royal family.

and the spirit of German nationality in the United States, not with real object of enriching AMERICAN life, but with the aim and purpose of fostering the ambitions of a foreign and at present an enemy state.

For example, there are a great number of German organizations in this country which are bound together for a common purpose in the German-American National Alliance. One of the aims of this Alliance has been, so it is stated, to promote friendly political relations between the United States and the German Empire. That those societies which make up the German-American National Alliance have done much to promote friendly political relations between Germany and the United States is doubtless correct. But, true to the hopes and expectations of their leaders here and in Germany, they have acted in this work as members of the German nationality and not as Americans. "They have sought to keep the peace by trying to force the United States during the past three years to endure such a series of insults, affronts, and injuries at the hands of Germany as were never before inflicted by one nation on another with which it was at peace." The statement that the German-Americans could give complete devotion to their adopted country and yet cultivate the German language would be accepted by most Americans as harmless and as true, were it not for the assertion of Dr. Julius Goebel, a German-American college professor, that the German language and German culture are the best means of preserving German nationality and that "the possession of them alone is sufficient to prevent the process of Americanization." This same Professor Goebel urges "that all the teachers of the German language and literature in American Universities, the teachers of German in the lower schools, the German clergy of all confessions, and all educated Germans in America should co-operate in spreading the German language and German ideas, for these will prevent citizens of German descent from becoming Americans in spirit." Thank Heaven, this is not true to the degree that Professor Goebel and others of his ilk believe.

After declaring that the Alliance will always be loyal to its adopted country and promote its welfare, the constitution continues: "The Alliance has no particularistic interests in view, it does not intend to found a state within a state, but sees in the centralization of people of German origin the shortest way and the best security for the ends laid down in this constitution." "The statement that the Alliance does not intend to found a state within a state is doubtless true, because such an enterprise is obviously impossible to carry out in the United States. It does aim, however, to assist in founding a NATION WITHIN A NATION, to establish amidst the American nation another national unit whose members shall be bound together by the ties of a common race, a common language, a common spirit, a common civilization, in a word, by all those bonds which consolidate nationalities everywhere." The members of the German nationality resident in the United States are, according to the repeated asservations of its creators both here and in Germany, to be distinct in all these fundamental characteristics from the American nationality. And more than that, they are to feel a special attachment for an alien and at present an enemy state. "Of all the outrages which Germany has inflicted on the United States, none is more infamous than this subtle and insidious effort to undermine the national life of the American people. For if the effort is successful, and there are numberless proofs that it has succeeded all too well, it will destroy the unity of national sentiment in this country. What greater danger could the nation face?"

"What will be the results in the United States if the comprehensive and energetic effort is successful to weld the German-Americans into a separate national unit? The greatest result of all can be stated with certainty, because it is already upon us. This effort has produced a schism in the AMERICAN NATION along the line of race cleavage. Many thousands of people of German blood have acted on the doctrine, long inculcated, that they belong together and apart from the rest of the American people. If this German principle were followed by the members of other nationalities here, it would result in disaster for America. For its population would disintegrate into racial groups, each with its program of a separatist and particularistic aims, as the German group now has. There would be a Russian, a Hungarian, an Italian, a Swedish, a Greek, and a south Slav group. The United States would find itself in a racial and political condition resembling in some important particulars that of the Austro-Hungarian Empire or the Balkan peninsula. The racial division throughout the nation would be reflected in Congress and questions of national policy would become race issues." They have already become such in part, for, before we entered the war, there was a German party acting in the interests of Germany both in the Senate and the House of Representatives of the United States of America.

"GERMANISM IN THE UNITED STATES IS A DESTRUCTIVE AND DISINTEGRATING FORCE. In just so far as it grows strong, the United States grows weak, nationally and internationally. Its unity of national sentiment is destroyed and its patriotism undermined. Its power to act as a unified nation is crippled. Internationally it grows weak because the members of an alien nation within its borders make impossible freedom of action in dealing with foreign states."

What can the people of the United States do about it? They can at least exert against the nationalistic German societies here the force of a justly angered public opinion. For these societies are a detriment to America. Our national life will be stronger, sounder, and healthier without them. "There is no place in any state for a press and for organizations which aim to consolidate a foreign nationality, to propagate a foreign civilization and to serve a foreign state. What would the German government do under similar circumstances?"

One of the results of this war, one of the results of the work of this One Hundred Per Cent American Club, must be to create a newer, a more vigorous sense of American nationality. We are a nation; we must think, feel, and act as a nation, as ONE nation, one and indivisible.

And then, in the second place, we are fighting for the Monroe Doctrine, and Cuba, and Panama, and Brazil are fighting with us for the Monroe Doctrine. This is no selfish motive. We are not fighting to grab the trade of Latin America under the guise of the Monroe Doctrine. In the noble words of President Wilson,

"We have no selfish ends to serve. We desire no conquest, no dominion. We seek no indemnities for ourselves, no material compensation for the sacrifices we shall freely make." For the last ten years we have been enjoying increasingly friendly relations with our Latin neighbors in the other American continent. At times it has been pretty up-hill work to convince them of the sincerity of our friendship. Do you know why this is so? It is because German propaganda in Latin America has sedulously endeavored to prevent those democracies from becoming friends with our own great republic of the north. The Zimmermann note with its slimy scheme of stirring up Mexico against us is only one effort of this kind. . . .

32. CAMP LIFE IN TEXAS

This selection from a soldier's description of his World War I experience details life in one of the wartime camps designed to turn young American men into soldiers. Camp Bowie, outside the town of Fort Worth, Texas, became an important military training camp for U.S. soldiers and civilians called up by the wartime draft. Private Harlow's account of the drills, the routines, and the military tedium of camp life stands in stark contrast to the horrors of trench warfare some of these young men would soon face in Europe. How did the surrounding community respond to the soldiers stationed at Camp Bowie? Why were the draftees treated so differently from the others? What role did the experiences of some soldiers on the Mexican border play in their preparation for war?

REX F. HARLOW
"Camp Bowie"
1919

. . . All of the organizations that were used in the development of the 61st were made up of National Guard troops, who were gathered from all parts of Texas and Oklahoma and sent to Camp Bowie, Fort Worth. Upon arriving at Fort Worth they detrained and proceeded immediately to the Clark farm,

Rex F. Harlow, *Trail of the 61st: A History of the 61st Field Artillery Brigade during the World War, 1917–1919* (Oklahoma City: Barlow Publishing Company, 1919), 13–17, 19–20, 22–25.

so called because it was owned by Mrs. Clark. It was covered by Johnson grass about knee high and showed nothing of the great camp that was later built, except that a few piles of lumber lay scattered at random over the place. The men put up tents the first afternoon, immediately after their arrival, but slept that night on Johnson grass, which bed, in fact, served them for several nights thereafter.

The first duty of the newly arrived troops was that of acting as camp guards, for each day brought in vast amounts of government property, especially building material. Not all of the men were used as guards, however, and just as rapidly as time permitted and men could be spared for the purpose, the camp was put into shape. Grass was cut, troop streets were laid out and graded, ditches were dug and a thousand and one things incident to the building of a new camp were done by the men. There were no quiet hours, for the soldiers realized that they were engaging in the biggest piece of work of their lives and that they must enter into this work with energy and spirit if they were to become properly trained for overseas. Moreover, most of them believed that their stay in Camp Bowie would be short and that they would rapidly be trained to the point where they could leave for France; and this belief caused them to lose no time in putting themselves into condition.

As the cavalry troops were the first soldiers to occupy Camp Bowie, they were forced not only to do guard duty over government stores, but also to furnish military police for Fort Worth, where troops were coming and going and over-patriotic citizens were being imposed upon. Work of this kind occupied about three months of time, after which other troops arrived and the cavalry units were transferred to the artillery service.

But most of the work during the early months of their stay in Camp Bowie was pleasing to the men because of the generous manner in which the towns-people of Fort Worth proved their appreciation of the soldiers and gave of their bounteous hospitality. Nothing was too good for the newly arrived soldiers; no opportunity was overlooked to give them automobile rides or to treat them to candy, ice cream and cold drinks; and it early became an established policy on the part of families of Fort Worth to invite soldiers to their homes for Sunday dinners and for other forms of entertainment. No city could have shown a warmer attitude of helpfulness and kindly interest toward its soldiers than Fort Worth did during the first few months after Camp Bowie was opened.

So many people called at the camp to take the boys for automobile rides that the soldiers soon learned to accept this kindness as a matter of course and thought nothing more of it than they did of receiving food free of charge from the government. It is a sad fact that this attitude grew to such proportions that carelessness in their treatment of the citizens of Fort Worth became common among the soldiers, and the city in self-protection, practically shut its doors to the camp. . . .

To the majority of soldiers who first came to Bowie, camp life was not new, for they had passed several months on the Mexican border and had grown accustomed to soldier life. They felt with reason that since they had served their apprenticeship on the border they would not be compelled to remain long in an American camp, but would soon be developed into efficient fighting men competent to meet the best troops of the German army and to successfully cope with them. . . .

Shortly after the various units of the National Guard had gotten properly settled in camp a training schedule was established by the Commanding General and the men were soon engaged in executing such squad movements as were required on the parade grounds or in the field. This training was made difficult by the fact that the drills were held over ground which was badly broken and cut by ravines and literally covered with rocks, which had to be removed with hands or shovels. Camp Bowie is located on seven hills to the west of Fort Worth and these hills are separated by small valleys over which the men had to work in their maneuvering and training. . . .

The Y. M. C. A. provided interesting and educative entertainments practically every evening and these entertainments were usually attended by large audiences, the soldiers eagerly accepting an opportunity to get away from their quarters for a while. Any number of first-class moving pictures were offered at the "Y.". . .

Likewise, the entertainments furnished by the Liberty Theater, were welcome to the majority of the soldiers, for at nominal expense good bills could be seen there practically any evening. Thousands of soldiers were entertained at the Liberty Theater by Theda Bara, Douglas Fairbanks and other noted movie stars. . . .

Other amusements supported freely and enjoyed greatly, were boxing and wrestling matches. Frequent bouts were held and the men were given the opportunity of seeing the country's best fighters and wrestlers in action. . . .

Moreover, many of the national singers and entertainers found their way to Camp Bowie during the time the 61st was in training there and it was largely the fault of the soldiers themselves if they didn't have pleasant times. . . .

On October 15, 1917, the 61st Field Artillery Brigade was formed from the Oklahoma and Texas Guards, but as these organizations did not contain a sufficient number of men to fill the brigade to full war strength a large number of drafted men from the first national army draft were secured on October 22, 1917, from the 165th Depot Brigade at Camp Travis; and the first week in June, 1918, a second contingent of draft men were brought to Camp Bowie from Texas and Oklahoma, though chiefly from Camp Travis. The life of these newly drafted soldiers was entirely different from that of the National Guardsmen at the time the latter entered camp. The drafted men were taken to detention camp immediately upon arrival, where they were given bed-clothing and cots and were assigned to tents. The detention camp, which was constructed to accommodate about 5,000 troops, was surrounded by ten-foot woven wire, at the top of which were stretched several strands of barbed-wire. The entrances were kept heavily guarded and it was seen that none of the new men were allowed to leave detention camp during their stay there.

The theory upon which the detention camp was established was that men coming from all parts of the country were likely to carry diseases with them. . . . It was here that the authorities carefully examined every man, vaccinated him for small-pox and typhoid, and saw to it that he was made into a perfectly sanitary being before being allowed in the camp proper.

The tents, occupied by the new-comers, accommodated from six to eight men and were practically a replica of the tents in the main camp. The men were taught to prepare their bunks, to answer reveille, and to police their quarters each day — experiences entirely novel to them. They were arranged into companies, having their own company streets, latrines and messhalls, and were placed under the immediate command of sergeants who had been selected for this purpose from the trained units in the main camp.

To these civilians, life in the detention camp was "one damn thing right after another." They were rudely awakened each morning by the shrill whistle of the "Top Cutter" and, in case they didn't fall out promptly, were more rudely ousted from their bunks by some unsympathetic, curt orderly who was sent to their tents with the gruff admonition to "get those rookies to hell up in line; what do they think this is — their birthday?". . .

After having "fallen in" and dressed their lines they were given orders for the day and were likely divided into groups to take exercises. This exercise business proved to be quite an interesting affair to these soft men, who had come to camp from offices and indoor work. Some fat fellows, especially, found it difficult to execute all of the movements, their grunts and pantings often keeping time to the commands of their leaders. With the perspiration bursting forth from their round cheeks and their flesh forming in great remonstrating rolls, the only indication they gave of ever becoming soldiers was the earnest manner in which they entered into their work. . . .

The morning meal was usually followed by general policing of quarters and preparations for the day's drill. The men were placed in groups of from eight to fifty, according to the number of men available to train them and usually each group contained several men who had had some previous military training, these men being always in demand by the sergeants in charge. . . .

The vaccinations were the most unpopular experiences in the detention camp, for not only did sore arms develop from the small-pox vaccinations, but fever and racking headaches also resulted from the injection of anti-typhoid serum. Sometimes as many as half of the men in a company of three or four hundred were too sick to drill or to go on hikes and marches. The men dreaded each trip to the infirmary, for they never knew when they were going to be examined or made to take some kind of medicine. Salts, especially, seemed to be quite popular with the medical officers, the men being lined up quite often to "pass in review" before a large tub of strong salts, each man receiving from a half pint to a pint of this pleasant drink. The results of such kindly attention on the part of the medical officers always resulted in great camp activity, the men often living up to the reputation of sprinters while engaged in the proper execution of their pressing military duties. . . .

An order in detention camp which will long live in the memory of the men who were affected by it was that calling for the cutting of all hair to a shortness of one-half inch. When this order was read to the troops it created much consternation, many lads fondly passing their fingers through their endangered locks, with the prayer that they might escape. But the ruthless mule clippers found their way to the heads of even the most beautiful hair and each man was turned out a freshly sheared sacrifice to the god of military efficiency, bearing witness that lice and Uncle Sam had declared war on each other. Many of the Indians refused to credit the order when it was first read to them and, upon being approached about having their braids of hair removed, were emphatic in their refusals to be subjected to such indignity. But the sergeants, firm in their duty, marched forth with a host of assistants to impress upon these wayward nephews of Uncle Sam that all individual religious customs and rights must be waived when Uncle Sam issued orders. The Indians were seized by enough men to hold them securely and rough hands applied the mule shears to the quivering indignant heads of these embryonic war chiefs, leaving them in a badly shorn condition. In several instances they bellowed and roared, threatening to subject all sergeants and "Uncles" to the deepest and hottest depths of perdition, but their vitriolic upheavals always subsided into stoic moroseness, from which they were again aroused with difficulty.

Most of the men enjoyed the opportunity of going on hikes, even though the weather was tremendously hot and the marches were several miles in length and over rough roads. . . . The trips to Lake Komo were especially pleasing to them because they were allowed to take swims there on numerous occasions. The change from the stuffy hot camp to the freedom of this nice cool lake was a Godsend and they enjoyed it accordingly. . . .

Suggestions for Further Reading

Bristow, Nancy K. *Making Men Moral: Social Engineering during the Great War.* New York: New York University Press, 1996.

Hall, Linda B. *Revolution on the Border: The United States and Mexico, 1910–1920.* Albuquerque: University of New Mexico Press, 1988.

Katz, Friedrich. *The Life and Times of Pancho Villa.* Stanford: Stanford University Press, 1998.

Kennedy, David. *Over Here: The First World War and American Society.* New York: Oxford University Press, 1982.

Lotchin, Roger. *Fortress California, 1910–1961: From Warfare to Welfare.* New York: Oxford University Press, 1992.

Luebke, Frederick. *Bonds of Loyalty: German-Americans and World War I.* Dekalb, Ill.: Northern Illinois University Press, 1974.

Tuchman, Barbara Wertheim. *The Zimmermann Telegram.* New York: Macmillan, 1966.

Speakeasy in Oakland, California, 1929

The Eighteenth Amendment to the United States Constitution outlawing "the manufacture, sale, or transportation" of alcoholic beverages went into effect in January 1920. Prohibition, long an issue of fierce debate in American politics and society, had become federal law. This police photograph of a speakeasy in Oakland, California, captures the obvious discomfort of the illegal bar's patrons. Notice that the people in the photograph do not want their faces seen. Some try to stay out of the picture altogether, but the mirror catches their reflection. Their reaction hints at the social and legal complexity of the era. These people might be ashamed of breaking the law, or they might be ashamed of their drinking. What does the photograph suggest about how western saloons changed after Prohibition became law?

Bancroft Library, University of California at Berkeley.

CHAPTER EIGHT

THE 1920s

PROHIBITION

The 1920s stand out as one of the most contradictory periods in American history. The decade was characterized by creativity and economic exuberance on the one hand, and conservative repression on the other. A strong national economy led Americans to spend money on a vast array of consumer goods: cars, household appliances, radios, and thousands of other things. The 1920s also ushered in greater freedoms for women, marked most notably by the passage of the Nineteenth Amendment in 1920, which granted women the right to vote. Popular culture grew as radio and motion picture entertainment reached greater audiences, and Americans began listening to jazz, an innovative new form of music. African American artists, musicians, and writers came together in New York City in the renowned artistic movement known as the Harlem Renaissance. The energy of these times inspired the decade's nickname: the Roaring Twenties.

But not everything was so rosy. Throughout the decade individuals and groups squared off against one another in ferocious cultural battles all across the nation. Americans disagreed, often vehemently, over such issues as the role of science in the schools, the place of immigrants in the country's future, and the morality (or immorality) promoted by urban culture. These clashes often pitted the modern values of city dwellers against the traditional values of country folk.

These tensions were mirrored in the Prohibition movement's efforts to outlaw the consumption of alcohol. Opposition to alcohol was inextricably intertwined with deeply held cultural traditions and religious beliefs. The Prohibition effort of the 1920s was only the latest stage in America's long-standing temperance crusade.

More than any other region, the American West propelled the Prohibition issue toward its final destination in 1919: the ratification of the Eighteenth Amendment forbidding the manufacture, distribution, and sale of alcoholic beverages. For years prior to this victory, the West promoted the issue, sometimes quietly but occasionally with considerable fanfare. Carry Nation, a reformer of fearless religious conviction, became famous for her antisaloon exploits in Kansas. She barged into saloons swinging a club or a hatchet, smashing everything that got in her way.

On the less explosive side of the issue, the West acted as a proving ground for national legislation, much as it did for woman suffrage. Town after town "went dry" in the nineteenth century. In many cases they had started out that way when they were founded as Protestant, Mormon, or other alcohol-free communities. Local measures rapidly grew into statewide laws prohibiting liquor sales. Kansas outlawed the sale of liquor in 1878, North Dakota and South Dakota by the end of the nineteenth century; Oklahoma entered the union as a dry state in 1907. Arizona, Colorado, Washington, and Oregon also adopted antiliquor laws. During World War I anti-German sentiment helped push the Prohibition impulse forward: breweries came under attack because the industry was dominated by German Americans, and many argued that a nation at war needed to turn its grain into bread, not beer. By the time the Eighteenth Amendment went into effect, more than thirty states had already embraced Prohibition, the bulk of them in the West and the South.

Woman suffrage, an issue that, as we have seen, also had powerful western roots, likewise influenced Prohibition. Through the 1910s, women campaigned for both suffrage and Prohibition, especially through such groups as the Women's Christian Temperance Union. Historians recognize a connection between those western states that offered women the vote and those that embraced temperance legislation ahead of the rest of the nation. Even as far back as the 1850s, women helped raise temperance before the eyes of the nation, and their activism in the West made the region, in the words of historian Richard White, "a bastion of prohibition."

Prohibition laid bare the tensions in American society. In the West as elsewhere, support and opposition were likely to break along religious and class lines, with Protestants, Mormons, and the middle class more likely to be in favor of the ban on alcohol, and Catholics and the working class more likely opposed. Prohibitionists called the liquor interest a conspiracy against moral reform. Prohibition opponents fought the measure every bit as energetically as proponents pushed it. Brewery workers opposed Prohibition because it cost them their jobs. Catholics fought Prohibition because they felt the measure, supported by Protestants and anti-Catholic groups like the Ku Klux Klan, unfairly attacked their religion and culture. Others simply resented the measure as an intrusion into private life. In many ways, the Prohibition movement reflected other Progressive Era efforts such as Americanization, with its moralistic overtones. The arrival of millions of eastern Europeans, the bulk of them Catholic and working class, exacerbated the conflict over Prohibition in the 1920s. The revival of the white-supremacist Ku

Klux Klan can in part be explained by the Klan's support for Prohibition and "traditional American values." The Klan also gained popularity by championing other supposedly "old-fashioned" values, such as anti-Catholicism and immigration restriction. In the mid-1920s the Klan briefly dominated the state governments of Colorado and Oregon. The West also added a further dimension to Prohibition squabbles with its long-standing history of liquor laws aimed at Native Americans.

Despite the passage of the Eighteenth Amendment and its enforcement legislation, the Volstead Act, Americans did not stop drinking (though statistics from the early 1920s suggest that they cut back). By the middle of the decade, however, rampant drinking and the rise of violent organized crime syndicates to control alcohol sales indicated that Prohibition had gone awry. Secret drinking establishments called speakeasies flourished. By the early 1930s, as the nation became preoccupied by the disaster of the Great Depression, Prohibition looked like a large-scale blunder. The Eighteenth Amendment was finally repealed in 1933.

The 1920s showed the growing pains of America's headlong rush into modernity. This chapter's selections provide a glimpse of America's struggle with modernity as it was played out in the West. Pre-Prohibition subtleties from the legal code of Montana reveal the West as the vanguard of the nationwide move toward banning alcohol. Accounts of public opinion and Prohibition enforcement — one focused on the Northwest and another on the Rockies — offer insight into the difficulties of making Prohibition stick. In the final selection, a physician offers reasons why Prohibition should be enforced.

As you read these selections, think of the ways in which the American West led the nation in the Prohibition movement. Why do you think it played this role? If, as historians argue, Prohibition was a reaction of the rural against the urban, of the native-born against the immigrant, of traditional America against modernism, how do these themes play out in the American West?

---

33. Montana Takes a Stand on Alcohol

Laws about the consumption of liquor reveal a great deal about social attitudes. This is true even in the years preceding national Prohibition, as states and territories in the West experimented with various forms of legal temperance and outright

Prohibition. This selection of the Montana legal code covering liquor laws prior to the Eighteenth Amendment is no exception. Note the special prohibitions aimed at women selling liquor and the sale of liquor to the state's Native American population, the latter a common feature of western liquor laws. It is curious, though, that the compiler of the pamphlet Liquor Laws of Montana *was one C. N. Kessler, a brewery owner and beer distributor. Can you construct a list of the events, issues, and people these laws are designed to control? In other words, what is at stake here besides the sale, purchase, or consumption of alcohol? What attitudes are being described and promoted by this kind of legislation? Why would someone in the alcohol business compile liquor statutes? What would he achieve by doing so?*

C. N. KESSLER
From *Liquor Laws of Montana*
1915

Sales to Drunkards, Minors and Indians Prohibited. . . .

Section 8380.   Every person who sells or gives intoxicating liquors to persons who are in the habit of getting drunk or intoxicated, or of drinking intoxicated liquors to excess, *after being notified in writing of such habit,* or who sells or gives intoxicating liquors to persons at the time in a state of intoxication, or visibly affected by intoxicating liquors, or who sells or gives intoxicating liquors to a minor or to an Indian, is liable in damage to any person who is injured thereby in money, property or means of support. In a suit for recovering damages named in this section, a married woman may sue in her own name and a minor by guardian.

Section 8380 (a).   A violation of any of the provisions of this act shall be deemed a misdemeanor, and upon conviction the offender shall be punished by a fine of not less than Fifty Dollars and not exceeding Two Hundred and Fifty Dollars, and persons acting as servants, employees or agents shall be liable in the same manner as their employers or principals.

Section 8380 (b).   Any person convicted a second time for a violation of the provisions of this act, in addition to the penalty above named, if he be engaged in the business of selling intoxicating liquors, shall be prohibited from the conduct of such business for a period of three months from the date of such conviction, and any such person convicted a third time for a violation of the provisions of this act shall, in addition to the penalty prescribed in Section 8380 (a) hereof, be

C. N. Kessler, comp., *Liquor Laws of Montana* (Helena: Montana State Brewer's Association, 1915), 16–19.

barred from obtaining a retail liquor license for a period of six months to three years within said county.

Section 2. Any minor who shall misstate his age shall be guilty of a misdemeanor, and any person who shall send a minor to any person to purchase any such intoxicating liquors shall be equally guilty with the person who shall give or sell such intoxicating liquor as provided in Section 1 of this act.

Section 8373. Sale of Liquors and Employing Women to Sell Liquors. Every person who sells or furnishes any malt, vinous or spirituous liquor to any person in the auditorium, boxes or lobbies of any theater, melodeon, variety show, museum, circus or caravan, or any place where any farce, comedy, tragedy, ballet, opera or play is being performed, or any exhibition of dancing, juggling, wax-work figures and the like is being given for public amusement, and every person who employs or procures or causes to be employed or procured any female to sell or furnish any malt, vinous or spirituous liquors at such place is guilty of a misdemeanor.

Section 8374. Selling Liquors at Camp Meeting. Every person who erects or keeps a booth, tent, stall or other contrivance for the purpose of selling or otherwise disposing of any wine, spirituous or intoxicating liquors or any drink of which wines, spirituous or intoxicating liquors form a part, or for selling or otherwise disposing of any article of merchandise, or who peddles or hawks about any such drink or article within one mile of any camp or field meeting for religious worship during the time of holding such meeting is punishable by a fine of not less than five nor more than five hundred dollars. . . .

Section 8376. Females Exhibited in Public Places. Every person who causes, procures or employs any female for hire, drink or gain to play upon any musical instrument or to dance, wait, promenade or otherwise exhibit herself in any drinking saloon, dance-cellar, ball-room, public garden, public highway, common park or street, or in any steamboat or railroad car, or in any place whatsoever, if in such place there is connected therewith the sale or use as a beverage of any intoxicating, spirituous, vinous or malt liquors, or who shall allow the same in any premises under his control where intoxicating, spirituous, vinous or malt liquors are sold or used, when two or more persons are present, is punishable by a fine of not less than fifty nor more than five hundred dollars or by imprisonment in the county jail not exceeding three months, or both; and every female so playing upon any musical instrument or dancing, waiting, promenading or exhibiting herself, as herein aforesaid, is punishable by a fine not exceeding one hundred dollars or by imprisonment in the county jail not exceeding one month, or both.

Section 8382. Prohibition Against Use of Screens and Other Obstructions in Saloons. During the time or hours when, by the provisions of any statute of the State of Montana saloons must close, all curtains, screens, movable blinds, shutters, paint, frost, dirt, or other things that obstruct the view from the outside of the bar or place in any saloon where liquors are sold, or kept for sale, shall be removed. It shall be the duty of every owner, licensee, proprietor or employee in charge of any saloon to remove any and all movable obstruction or obstructions at the hour that the saloon is by law required to close, or within fifteen minutes after said hour.

Section 8383.   Wine Rooms or Private Apartments in Saloon Must Be Kept Open to Public View.   It shall be unlawful to erect or maintain, or allow to remain in existence in, or in connection with any saloon, either as a part thereof, or as an adjunct thereto, or on any floor, or in any basement of any saloon, any wine room, or private apartment, with any door, curtain or screen of any kind, or any room or private apartment unless the interior thereof is left open to public view, and unless there be an opening from such rooms or apartments of at least three feet in width and six feet in height, without any curtains or screens whatsoever in, or in front of, or inside of such opening or in any passageway connected therewith or adjacent thereto. And every day during which any such prohibited apartment or room is maintained or allowed to remain in existence shall be deemed a separate offense.

Section 8384.   Prohibition Against Female Persons Entering Saloons.   It shall be unlawful for any owner, licensee, proprietor or manager of any saloon, or his clerk, agent, servant or bar tender, to have with, or as a part of, any saloon any room or apartment, with or without door or doors, curtain or curtains, or screen of any kind, in which any female persons shall be permitted to enter from the outside or from such saloon.

Section 8385.   Same (as above).   It shall be unlawful for any owner, licensee, manager, clerk, agent, bar tender, or other employee, having for the time being charge or control of any saloon, or any place connected therewith, either by doors or otherwise, to suffer or permit any female person to be or remain in such saloon, or place connected therewith, for the purpose of being there supplied with any kind of liquor whatsoever. Provided, that when a bar-room is maintained in any hotel, this act shall not be construed to apply to the parts of the building where the other business of the hotel is transacted.

Section 8386.   Prohibiting Display of Certain Signs.   It shall be unlawful for any owner, proprietor, licensee, manager or other person owning, running or conducting any saloon, to put up, maintain or allow to remain in place over or near any door, or in or near any passageway, opening or leading into such saloon, the words "ladies' entrance," or "women's entrance," or "private entrance," or any words of like import on any wall, door, sign board or otherwise.

Section 8387.   Loitering of Female Around Saloon Prima Facie Evidence of Guilt.   If it shall appear that any female shall at any time be allowed to loiter in any saloon, or to be or remain in any room, apartment or place in or connected with such saloon, such fact shall be prima facie evidence or presumptive evidence that such female was permitted to be or remain in said saloon or place connected therewith for the purpose of being supplied with liquor, and shall be prima facie or presumptive evidence in favor of the guilt of the accused party or parties. *Provided,* that when a bar-room is maintained in any hotel, this act shall not be construed to apply to the parts of the building where the other business of the hotel is transacted. . . .

34. WET AND DRY IN THE FAR WEST

The historian George Fort Milton traveled through the West in 1926 trying to track the region's sentiments on Prohibition for the important national journal Century Magazine. *He found that while western "wets," those who favored repeal of Prohibition, appeared to have great influence, the dry forces could count on getting more people to vote to keep Prohibition going. His descriptions here, especially those of the Pacific Coast and Montana, hint at the complexity of the issue. What western groups would you expect to be vociferous wets? Which would you expect to be dry? Why do you think the wets were unable to muster strength at the ballot box, despite their outspokenness? How does Milton's account of Prohibition support and enforcement in the West compare with the findings of Martha Bensley Bruere or August Kuhlmann in the selections that follow?*

GEORGE FORT MILTON
"The Wets and the West"
1926

Not even the most ardent dry will contend that Rudyard Kipling had prohibition in mind when he made his famous assertion regarding East and West and the improbability of their ever meeting.[1] Yet despite the modification demands of the Eastern wets, the facts are that the "heart of America" — to use Woodrow Wilson's characterization of the country west of the Mississippi — is becoming more and more convinced of the value and necessity of prohibition.

. . . From my observations, conversations, and experiences, I should say, speaking broadly, that the wet drive has failed in the West. . . .

Several well intentioned newspaper gentlemen recently devised the idea of a series of nation-wide polls that they might ascertain the general feeling

---

[1] **meeting:** This reference is to a line in "The Ballad of East and West," a poem by the English author and poet Rudyard Kipling (1865–1936), that reads "Oh, East is East, and West is West, and never the twain shall meet."

Century Magazine 112 (July 1926): 344–47.

toward prohibition. The result of these polls was received by the dripping wets, the moists, and even the merely humids as evidence of a vast overturn of public sentiment, and as foreshadowing the doom of the Volstead Act.

Such a poll was stirring up the citizens of the hospitable city of Seattle during the week of my visit there. Pretty constantly it ran about seven wet to one dry. The totals were rather amazing. Not only were polls conducted, but one of the city's newspapers, not in the poll-conducting group, was so conscious of its lack that it opened a letter-writing contest offering large cash prizes for the best arguments for and against prohibition. The wets proved to be the readier letter-writers, although the difference was not nearly so great as in the coupon-clipping polls of the other papers.

At the same time Seattle was quarreling her way through a city election campaign, and as usual there was a variety of alleged issues. One of the candidates was Mayor Edwin J. Brown, an ex-socialist, dentist, lawyer, and would-be successor to himself. He had gained considerable national reputation by forceful handling of some I.W.W.[2] disturbances in Seattle; he had a powerful political organization; and even his enemies conceded him an eccentric and appealing career, as well as a strong and vote-getting personality.

Now Dr. Brown had been mayor of Seattle for a number of years. He had all the prestige and the power that the office always gives. Incidentally — no, not incidentally, but by intention and most vigorously — Dr. Brown was wet. One of his pungent campaign phrases was, "You can't run a seaport town like a church bazaar."

His opponent was a woman, Mrs. Bertha K. Landes, the wife of a professor at the University of Washington. She was not unknown in Seattle's public life, as she had once been president of the city council and had clashed with the mayor a number of times. . . .

Mrs. Landes is a dry. She believes in the enforcement of the prohibition law, both State and national. One of her campaign planks was for cleaning up and drying up Seattle. Of course there were other issues on which the candidates were divided; as, for example, Mrs. Landes favored the city manager form of government, while Brown frowned on it. Both were supposed to be friendly to continued municipal ownership and operation of Seattle's amazing power project. But the dominant issue between them was defined by most local observers as "wide open" against law enforcement.

Mrs. Landes won. The total votes were: Landes, 48,700; Brown, 42,802. Out of 91,502 votes, she had a majority of 5898.

So there can be seen, side by side, the seven-to-one wet straw vote in Seattle newspapers, and the eight-to-seven prohibition enforcement vote in Seattle ballot-boxes. . . .

---

[2] **I.W.W.**: Industrial Workers of the World, a radical labor organization, prominent in the timber belt of the Northwest in the early twentieth century.

A San Franciscan's pithy comment on the situation in California perhaps indicates the general Western trend:

"Never depend on the wet vote. It talks big and votes little. The straw polls are a joke. The wets vote in the newspapers. The drys vote in the elections."

A wet himself, he was disgusted with the people on whose support he felt he should have been able to count in a recent election.

"California to-day would go a hundred and fifty thousand or more dry," he went on. . . .

"Why, look at it! When the country and the State were wet, we had all the wet influences organized and active to keep us wet: the brewers, and the distillers — organized, financed, and politically powerful; the property-owners who rented to saloons; the saloons themselves — the 'poor man's club'; the dives and speak-easies; the men who loved to drink and who wanted to be able to keep on drinking. And then last, but not least, the theoretical wet who believed in 'personal liberty.' And don't forget the grape and hop growers, the brewery unions, and all of their ties and connections.

"And still the country went dry, and the State voted for the enforcement act. Where can the wets get to-day? They had it then and couldn't keep it. Anybody that tells you California is wet is stringing you."

The California grape-grower was generally conceded to be on friendly terms with the wine-cup. But he is so no longer. For curiously enough, he is making more money under Volstead than he did in the good old days.

Before prohibition the wine-grape grower often was paid as low as $8 a ton and seldom higher than $30 a ton for his grapes. Since prohibition he has been getting from $60 to $140 a ton. Perhaps many of his grapes go into home-made wine. But a limited quantity of home-made wine for home consumption is not a violation of the Volstead Act. Raisins have had a tremendously increased sale, while grape-juice is in demand where its existence was not even recognized before. . . .

Montana is to have another test of strength this fall. Having easily secured the small percentage of registered voters necessary to a referendum, the wets have put on the November ballot a drink or dry query. They are conducting a well financed and highly organized campaign.

But during my trip through Montana Governor John Erickson and ex-Governor Sam V. Stewart assured me that in their opinion the referendum would show Montana quite as dry as ever. Butte and Helena, they thought, might go wet, as both have a large foreign mining element. But the dry farmers of the State are expected to overwhelm these wet city ballots.

As against this opinion, a prominent Butte lawyer believes that the reverse will happen, that the Butte-Helena vote will overcome the farmer. Only the election will tell.

In none of the Western States could I learn of any definite tendency toward modification. In Nebraska some of the associates of former Senator Gilbert M.

Hitchcock, who has been an anti-prohibition champion, privately admitted that they thought Nebraska drier than ever. Nowhere could I find a friend of the swinging door and the brass rail, the unsung and unhonored American saloon.

The States in which prohibition sentiment seemed to be gaining, chiefly because of economic conditions, are, I should say, California, Wisconsin, Iowa, and Nebraska. The States in which the increasing support is due to moral convictions would include the two Dakotas, Montana, Idaho, Washington, Oregon, Utah, Colorado, and the other intermountain States. . . .

The Western drys did not seem to understand that the Eastern wets are as resolute in their wetness as they themselves are determined in their dryness. . . . As the sides line up it really begins to look — and unfortunately — as if the East is East and the West is West.

35. Prohibition in the Mountain West

From the very moment that it became law, Prohibition came under intense scrutiny. Did it work? In this selection, Martha Bensley Bruere, a social worker and writer, examines Prohibition in the mountain states of the West. Working with a small team, she distributed a detailed questionnaire on Prohibition to social workers. They asked respondents about local declines in alcoholism, any rise in crime and delinquency rates, and such things as "the political significance of the present disregard of the amendment." Her findings about Prohibition and the legacies of earlier antiliquor legislation, published as Does Prohibition Work?, *reveal the differences in opinion in places like Colorado compared to Nevada. What specific social or political realities in the mountain West made enforcement or support of Prohibition so complex? How would you compare the findings of Bruere with those of George Fort Milton in the Northwest and C. N. Kessler in Montana? How would you explain regional differences?*

Martha Bensley Bruere
From *Does Prohibition Work?*
1927

South of the Inland Empire the high Sierras cross and crisscross. They divide populations from one another, interests and occupations. Mountains, deserts,

Martha Bensley Bruere, *Does Prohibition Work?* (New York: Harper and Brothers, 1927), 31–37.

and tablelands know both solitary prospectors and city populations. Here lies a wilderness tamed by religious devotion; there is a wilderness not yet tracked except by wild creatures. Here is a man's world and men's work. Can prohibition be enforced under these physical and psychological conditions?

Colorado, in a revolt against the saloon, went dry in 1914. The dry votes came largely from the small towns and cities with a Nordic population, from the agricultural districts and financial centers. Labor generally and the mining camps of southern Colorado were wet. Here are populations from the south and east of Europe and from Mexico. It was believed by many that the elimination of the saloon would diminish labor troubles, which at times, in the Colorado Fuel and Iron mines, had developed into veritable warfare.

Today, reports from the social workers show the old lines of cleavage. The press of the cities and rural districts is dry and for enforcement. The mining camps are relatively wet and the rank and file of labor is for modification. Labor's leaders tend to copy the bosses — to speak "dry." Denver's local enforcement problem is complicated by the fact that the city is a Mecca for conventions, for great hordes of summer vacationists, for a transient population which brings in a personal interpretation of the law. There is further complication by the winter hibernation of hundreds of Mexican beet-field workers in the city. To them bootlegging is not a serious crime.

"We believe," writes Mrs. Anna G. Williams of the Denver Social Service Bureau, "that while rum was a great disturber of domestic peace, it was but a minor cause of poverty. Prisoners in making application for parole used to state that they were intoxicated at the time they committed their crimes. Among the poorer families statistics show greater savings and a higher standard of living."

The report from a social worker of Boulder is enthusiastic. Here is the state college and here there has always been local option.[1]

"In a recent election, Colorado overwhelmingly defeated the attempt to change the Volstead Act. Colorado may not be entirely satisfied with prohibition enforcement, but it is not entirely satisfied with the divorce laws, either. Burglary still goes on, but we do not repeal the laws against it because they do not operate. Boulder has no recent comparisons to make, for it refused to consider saloons for years, but the surrounding towns, particularly mining camps, were hotbeds of drinking and vice. Boulder escaped the delirium tremens, poverty, crime, undernourished children, and dirt of the surrounding mining camps where saloons flourished."

"The only noticeable effect of state prohibition, which come in 1914, was the decrease in the number of homeless men," writes Mr. Justin L. Hills of the Colorado Springs Associated Charities. "And we felt that in all probability this was because the men who were making their transcontinental tours[2] followed the northern route through Wyoming, which had remained wet, or the southern route through wet New Mexico."

---

[1] **local option:** When voters declare a particular jurisdiction — a town or a county — dry.
[2] **transcontinental tours:** Often by stowing away on railroad cars.

Colorado Springs, since its founding in 1871, has always had a clause in all deeds that no intoxicating liquors shall be manufactured, sold, or otherwise disposed of in any public place or upon any premises within the city of Colorado Springs. An infraction of this law causes the property to revert to the original owner.

"Therefore," Mr. Hills writes, "with the enactment of national prohibition there was no noticeable change in the family problem. Probably the amendment has had no effect one way or the other in the amount and nature of crime and disorder in this distinctly American town, where public conviction is wholly on the side of law enforcement."

Just as Colorado is made sectional by its geography, so is it made sectional by religion, by industry, by race. It is natural that the enforcement of prohibition should also show sectional differences. The Klan, Protestant and dry, has fought the Catholics, fought "wets," fought "foreigners." Issues have become confused by the injection of extraneous factors. A "dry" foreign miner is driven into the camp of the "wets" to protect himself from junker Americanism.[3] An American with sentiments for a modification of the Volstead Act is driven into the camp of the "drys" because of the attack on his religion. This confusing of interests, this blending of hatreds, has divided the state in factional allegiances and complicated considerably law enforcement.

In southern Colorado, among the coal and metal miners, and in the beet fields among the Mexicans, there is widespread feeling that prohibition was imposed upon the workingman by the mine-owning class and large employers who thought thereby the better to control and further to exploit him. They see the law unequally applied; the homes of the workingmen unlawfully entered, judges holding that if liquor is found the entry was justified. They know the homes of the financially powerful are safe against such raiding. With the knowledge that the interests which they have so long fought in their struggle for wages and protection are publicly dry and often privately wet, labor has always been antagonistic to dry laws, and officers without the backing of public sentiment find enforcement in mining camps extremely difficult. Lonely gulches and isolated ravines furnish places, as in the mountains of Kentucky, for the manufacture of "moonshine," and people used to hard liquor as well as to drudging labor are resistant to the Eighteenth Amendment.

Enforcement officers in Colorado have geographical barriers on their side. Colorado is as isolated as an island from the mainland of bootleggers. North of the state are mountains and barren plains; east of it are driest Kansas and sparsely settled Oklahoma; south is New Mexico with its deserts and sandstorms; west is Utah, dry Mormon territory. With the militant Klan, with newspapers, with great financial interests, with a large Nordic-American population, with an arid boundary, all on the side of the Eighteenth Amendment, Colorado's enforcement problem should not be so difficult as that of other mountain states. . . .

What of Nevada's attitude toward the Eighteenth Amendment? In Novem-

---

[3]**junker Americanism:** A reference to the charged anti-German patriotism of the World War I era.

ber, 1926, Nevada, in a vote of 12,500 as opposed to 3,290, demanded that a constitutional convention be called for amending the Volstead Act. Nevada further said, in a vote of 11,840 as against 3,350, that "experience has demonstrated that the attempt to abolish recognized abuses of the liquor traffic by the radical means of constitutional prohibition has generally failed of its purpose."

This is the conclusion of the desert state with a surplus male population after eight years of national prohibition.

According to Mrs. F. E. Humphrey of Reno, a former social worker, the net gain of prohibition is that the saloon is done away and with it the treating habit. Alcohol was only a minor cause of poverty and many of the social and economic troubles of other states "are not real troubles here."

As regards youth, Mrs. Humphrey says that "the situation is much worse than before prohibition. It is now the smart thing to carry a flask. Nobody respects a law that cannot be enforced. The danger of blindness is a menace. There are 'rings' everywhere and anybody can get liquor." Mrs. Humphrey, herself a club woman, says that many mothers' clubs feel a grave mistake has been made and the majority of people who voted "dry" want the law amended to governmental control. . . .

Other social workers give a different picture. Mrs. M. L. Macauley, executive secretary of the American Red Cross, says: "I do know that many families who knew no comfort under the saloon conditions, whose earners spent every dollar obtainable drinking and left their dependents to be fed, clothed, and cared for by charitable organizations or kind neighbors, now are independent. They buy food, clothing, and small luxuries, enjoy the movies, go into the higher grades in school, and are generally progressive.

"While we hear of the cases of bootlegging all too often to suit law-abiding people, they are really not numerous when compared with the great bulk of our people who are going along, without a thought of stepping backward after the big move forward.

"The poverty we are meeting in our work here in Reno is largely due to the restless spirit bred by unemployment. Many unsuccessful people, believing that another locality will afford better opportunity, buy cheap cars and start out. Result: greater poverty and need for help elsewhere. Drink does not enter into our cases. Of old it was the great trouble. All of the causes contributing to poverty cannot begin to furnish the trouble that was due of old to drink alone."

The principal of the Reno high school, Mr. E. Otis Vaughn, says: "I know from my experience, dating back to 1907, that there is very much less habit-forming drinking. I believe that prohibition has been very successful, when we consider the slight hold that the liquor habit has on our young people today."

With this conclusion, Mr. J. A. Fulton, director of the Mackay School of Mines, connected with the University of Nevada, agrees: "At our meeting of deans of the different departments here in the University last Monday, I asked the assembled deans what their opinion was as regards the beneficial results of prohibition here in the University among the student body. The replies were all of a uniform nature, namely that the student body was much more orderly, that there was much less evidence of drinking at dances and at other gatherings, and that the opinion of the deans was that there was no question that the Eighteenth Amendment had been very beneficial to this student body."

Nevada, in the orderly way provided by democratic government, in a vote of over three to one, says prohibition has failed — Colorado by the same test says it is a success.

36. A Physician Supports Prohibition

Both before and after it became law, Prohibition kept printers busy as each side of the debate hustled out pamphlets and booklets to support or protest the ban on alcohol. In this typical Prohibitionist tract, August Kuhlmann, a physician, suggests that Prohibition is good for both the human body and the body politic. He traces the impact of Prohibition legislation by studying the groups and individuals who operated in violation of the law. Prohibition's supporters, in the West as well as elsewhere, sought the endorsement of physicians like Kuhlmann, believing that publicity on the health benefits of an alcohol-free society would only help their cause. In this passage, however, the writer makes much of Prohibition's tendency to create a criminal underclass, which would be quick to take advantage of the situation. How could an experiment often couched in tones of moral reform possibly countenance the high levels of law-breaking — from illegal cocktail parties to large-scale rum running — that immediately followed adoption of the Eighteenth Amendment? What are the major points in Kuhlmann's essay? How does he characterize the impact of Prohibition? What comparisons does he make between the health of individuals and the health of the nation? Why does Kuhlmann argue that Prohibition ought to be obeyed?

August Kuhlmann
From *Prohibition as It Is*
in Some Parts of the West
1928

. . . Liquor in a moderate form in the proper quantity would hardly hurt anybody. It is a mild stimulant and appetizer, and creates a little pep, but, most all of us who do some observing realize it sometimes creates an awful undesirable habit.

August Kuhlmann, M.D., *Prohibition as It Is in Some Parts of the West* (n.p., 1928).

Some of the most sincere arguments that prohibition reduces crime, empties our jails and changes the people to a more noble and higher level have all been (apparently) shattered so far; because there evidently is more crime now, than there was before prohibition.

In spite of all the above arguments we can live just as happy without booze as with booze. It is a luxury and sometimes worse than that. In fact if a young man would ask me about certain points, for success in life, one point I would emphasize in my advice would be, "keep away from booze." If we all would do that, it would settle the whole prohibition problem at once. But we know people think differently. We have to abide by the happy majority, otherwise we would live in a state of continuous warfare. To conquer ourselves is the greatest victory. Let us enjoy liberty, but we must not infringe upon the liberty of others. These are all wise sayings which means we should always consider our neighbor. If the money involved in the liquor traffic would be taken out, it would quickly die a natural death.

That there is too much brewing in some parts of the country is unquestionably true, and it is a big factor to destroy the morale of our youth and land. Since moon-shining is here and is a big business, so let us discuss it as follows: There are four main types or classes involved in order of their importance.

1. Hijackers.
2. Active distillers, cookers, bootleggers, and dispensaries.
3. The army of soaks — or losers.
4. The irreconcilables and defenders of personal liberty.

The hi-jackers are the real brains of the moonshine business. They are a class of people of the intelligent type. They are in the business only and solely for making easy money quickly. They are working in the dark. They are fully conscious of the penalty attached. Therefore hire their underlings to do the active work. They furnish the money for the equipment, stills, etc., and take over the finished product. They like to shine in society and make propaganda for their business. They organize and facilitate transportation and attend to the wholesale work. They see to it that something is furnished at parties, dances, etc. They sometimes out-wit the clergy at church parties.

You see them often sitting at special tables at church parties, gambling or playing for money in a conspicuous place. They have the moon in a coal bin or an automobile attended to by an underling. They like to have prominent people with them to advertise through them to make an impression. In smaller towns or villages they like to get a mayor or president elected who is under obligation to them and who is willing to hire an extra policeman to look out for the federal agents.

They are a very clever bunch and have a conscience like a rubber bag, that will stretch as long as a dollar is in sight. They like to pose and have their tools sitting on a wagon box or grandstand on public occasions for public adoration in order to make an impression. They are smooth-tongued artists and inspire their force under them as if they were heroes.

They work on the ignorant and superstitious — trying to make them believe it is all right to make moon because Christ made wine and that Eve ate from the forbidden apple. They try to make people believe that moon is a cure for many ills. They usually have a roll of cash with them that staggers almost some federal agents and paralyzes them. Some like to act as a double — a law-breaker and a law-enforcer. If you are siding with them they are jake, but if you do not pull with them, then they are dirty fighters — fabricate false stories and slander for punishment. They try to get a person mixed up with them in order to stick.

They enjoy holding high offices in lodges where the ritual is against booze in order to make it look absurd and hypocritical. They are a polished class trying to brush everything aside that is not working with them in order to make clear sailing for their underlings. So you see they are a dirty set and hypocrites destroying the public morale and decency. In this class we find the pistol shooters, safe-crackers and love artists.

The second class includes the active distiller, cooker, the bootlegger and dispenser. They are not so hard and rotten as class number one — the hi-jackers. They are also mainly in the business because it is easy money, and for other reasons. Some say, "I am in this business because it is easy money to make a living. It means bread and butter for me and my family." Some say, "I want to make a few thousand in order to get a start in something else then I'll get out." Some are out of a job and class number one offers them a great inducement. Some young fellows want to shine and get a car because they are furnished by class number one. Some have lost money in banks, etc., and think it is all right to get it back in some way or another.

Of late many farmers have fallen victims and have been induced by the hi-jackers, because it has been told them, that it is an easy way to pay off their mortgage and make money. In fact they are outwitted by class number one because they want to have a place where they can put their stills, get their raw supply easily and feel secure. It is surprising to find some good farmers where you least expect it.

It has been a very good winter for the cookers on account of the abundance of snow. Many of the roads were impassable and they felt secure. There are thousands and thousands of gallons hidden and stored up. There is such a supply on hand by the subs, who are not in with class number one, that a gallon of liquor has gone down to three dollars. A sign of over-production — an index of trade, of supply and demand. Some of these moonshiners drive fine cars, thereby creating the admiration of the youth and the envy of some ladies. Some think a person cannot be sociable unless you dish out some booze to their friends. They look upon you with scorn and disdain if you refuse a drink. Most of these farmers who dabbled in this business have lost more by not attending to their farms than they have made. Some are making soaks out of themselves and their children and spoiling the neighbor's children.

What they call a good bootlegger, is usually a bold and a confirmed liar. They seem to have a certain admiration or fear of class number one — the hi-jackers.

The third class includes the "army of soaks" — because they like the stuff. It seems they are not happy unless they have a few under their belts. They sacrifice everything in order to get booze. One of their most fervent prayers seems to be: "I and my stomach — my stomach and myself — have mercy on me, amen." This class are always the losers; but they do not seem to have the moral and physical stamina to hang on to themselves. Some claim they have to take a shot before they go to church and think they can pray better and take another afterwards so it soaks in. Some claim they can work better. Some get drunk when they have a quarrel with their wife and seek consolation in a saloon, because a good saloon-keeper never contradicts his patrons.

The fourth class constitute the irreconcilables and defenders of personal liberty. These are otherwise a well-balanced crowd. They can afford to take a drink and know how to handle themselves. They have been accustomed to take a drink before and stay within the psychological limit.

They insist that prohibition is an infringement of their personal liberty. They take a drink and make nothing of it. They are indifferent until it strikes home, until their sons or daughters are meshed in what they know is not very honorable.

Now what is the solution for a right-minded citizen, hearing all these pros and cons; some say, "it almost makes a person crazy." Some think "the world is coming to an end," etc. Nothing to it! The solution is a simple one. Since it is the law of the land we as citizens have to obey the law for the sake of our country, until we change the law to a different form in an election. Those who think they can defy the United States government are sadly mistaken.

Suggestions for Further Reading

Bader, Robert S. *Prohibition in Kansas.* Lawrence: University Press of Kansas, 1986.

Blocker, Jack S. *Retreat from Reform: The Prohibition Movement in the United States, 1890–1913.* Westport, Conn.: Greenwood, 1976.

Clark, Norman H. *The Dry Year: Prohibition and Social Change in Washington.* Seattle: University of Washington Press, 1965.

Dumenil, Lynn. *The Modern Temper: American Culture and Society in the 1920s.* New York: Hill and Wang, 1995.

Goldberg, Robert. *Hooded Empire: The Ku Klux Klan in Colorado.* Urbana: University of Illinois Press, 1981.

Gould, Lewis L. *Progressives and Prohibitionists: Texas Democrats in the Wilson Era.* Austin: University of Texas Press, 1973.

Kerr, K. Austin. *Organized for Prohibition: A New History of the Anti-Saloon League.* New Haven: Yale University Press, 1985.

Noel, Thomas J. *The City and the Saloon: Denver, 1858–1916.* Lincoln: University of Nebraska Press, 1982.

CCC Workers in Coeur d'Alene National Forest, 1934

This photograph depicts young men planting trees in an Idaho forest following a forest fire. These men were members of the Civilian Conservation Corps (CCC), one of dozens of federal programs created by the Roosevelt administration to put people to work during the Great Depression. CCC workers, mostly young and male, spread out across the West, planting trees, fighting fires, and building trails. Their projects, many of which are still in use or visible today, helped refashion and reshape vast stretches of the western landscape. The CCC owed much of its organizational ethos to the United States military. What clues about the agency's military orientation can you identify in this photograph? Are you aware of any CCC projects near where you live?

Courtesy of the U.S. Forest Service.

CHAPTER NINE

THE GREAT DEPRESSION

The New Deal and the Western Landscape

ew periods in American history have demonstrated the transformative power of the Great Depression. The years 1930 to 1941 were punctuated by dramatic national and global events: the stock market crash in October 1929, the introduction of President Franklin D. Roosevelt's New Deal, and the Japanese attack on Pearl Harbor in December 1941. The Depression itself was as much a world crisis as World War II. Yet regional circumstances in the United States made a difference in how the Depression looked, how it felt, and what it meant on the domestic front.

The roots of the Great Depression stretch back into the 1920s and can be traced in part to overconfidence. As world markets for natural resources (many of them, such as timber, coal, oil, and farm products, from the West) began to dry up, Americans were slow to recognize signs of trouble. They continued to do business as usual and to speculate in an overheated stock market.

Like millions of his fellow Americans, the president of the United States also failed to see the coming disaster. A mining engineer born poor on an Iowa farm, raised in Oregon, and educated at Stanford University, Herbert Hoover had risen to worldwide acclaim during World War I through his relief work in war-savaged Europe. In 1928 he became the first U.S. president to be elected from the American West. Nine months later, the stock market crashed, ushering in the Great Depression.

President Hoover was convinced that America could weather the storm and blamed collapsing European economies for the Depression. It was only a matter of time, he believed, before the American economy would right itself. Federal intervention was unnecessary. But Hoover was wrong, and his inability to grasp the magnitude of the economic crisis doomed him politically. By the early 1930s, homeless Americans — many of whom had never before faced such privation — mocked the president by building shantytowns named "Hoovervilles" or "Hoovertowns." They were not alone. Unemployment continued to increase;

at least 25 percent of the workforce was without a job. Private charities, as well as local, regional, and state relief agencies across the country, buckled under the strain. Families tried to make do with less; they grew more of their own food and moved in with one another to wait out the crisis.

But by 1932, political discontent, much of it in the West, was rising as people struggled to deal with the effects of the collapse. In some areas people threatened to take violent action unless the government stepped in to alleviate their misery. In the summer of 1932 thousands of World War I veterans, many from the West, marched on Washington in an attempt to pressure Congress to authorize early payment of their military pensions. Farmers throughout the West, fearful of losing their homes and farms, banded together to demand that government find some way to raise farm prices, which had fallen through the floor. When Hoover ran for re-election in 1932, even with powerful and important western supporters, he could not succeed. He had far too little to show to a nation in trouble, and on election day, he didn't carry a single western state. Voters instead pinned their hopes on Franklin D. Roosevelt.

Roosevelt, or FDR as he was known to millions, immediately set to work answering the nation's call to action. Within months of taking office, he launched a dizzying number of federal programs, known collectively as the New Deal, designed to combat the worst effects of the Depression: to alleviate suffering, to get people back to work, and to make prices rise.

The New Deal operated mostly through programs often referred to (for good reason) the "alphabet" agencies. In short order, the president or Congress created the Federal Emergency Relief Administration (FERA), the Agricultural Adjustment Administration (AAA), the Home Owners Loan Corporation (HOLC), the Works Progress Administration (WPA), the Civil Works Administration (CWA), and the National Recovery Administration (NRA). These and other federal programs offered employment and brought in federal funding to relieve depressed areas, especially in the West. Federal dollars came to the rescue of hundreds of thousands of young men who found work in the Civilian Conservation Corps (CCC). CCC workers fought fires, worked on flood control projects, and built thousands of miles of hiking trails in the West, making the environment a safer, more accessible recreational outlet. The Roosevelt administration's dam-building projects reshaped western rivers to supply the West's hydroelectric, freshwater, and irrigation systems. The WPA also carried out projects across the West: agency construction workers built federal buildings, roads, schools, and bridges, while its artists and historians labored on a vast array of artistic and cultural endeavors. Through the Agriculture Department, New Deal workers also aided cattle ranchers devastated by the horrendous dust storms that turned huge sections of the Southern Plains into a Dust Bowl.

The New Deal's many programs were felt everywhere in the West, and its ef-

fects can still be seen, from the Rocky Mountain hiking trails to the huge aqueducts of California and the giant dams in the Pacific Northwest. Its canals and
aqueducts still carry water through the Far West, and cars still travel on roadways
built by New Deal dollars and engineers.

The selections in this chapter illustrate the impact of the New Deal on western lives and landscapes by focusing on one site, Boulder Dam, and on one important federal program, the Civilian Conservation Corps. The first selection
explores the social history of the Boulder Dam (later renamed Hoover Dam) project in the words and memories of those who helped build it. The dangers of working on this project are illustrated in the compilation of Boulder Dam fatalities in
the second selection. President Roosevelt's dedicatory address at the opening of
Boulder Dam in the third selection offers insight into how he thought about such
huge New Deal undertakings as damming western rivers. Last, a question-and-
answer document from the Civilian Conservation Corps provides a glimpse into
one of the New Deal's most well known and important employment programs.

AS YOU READ, think about some of the ways in which the federal government's policies and programs affected the West. What similarities do you find between what people experienced working on the Boulder Dam project, for instance, and working for the CCC? How well did the work experience of the dam
builders match the conception of the project offered by President Roosevelt?

---

37. WORKERS ON BOULDER DAM

Although it was begun during the administration of President Herbert Hoover,
Boulder Dam, on the Colorado River, represents the quintessential New Deal proj-
ect. The dam was built with government funds at a site just outside Las Vegas,
Nevada, by a consortium of engineering and construction firms called the Six
Companies. It was the first giant project completed during the New Deal, fittingly
in the American West. Like other New Deal projects of similar magnitude, Boulder
Dam accomplished a number of things at once. It completely changed the natural
landscape, in this case the Colorado River and large swaths of the Southwest. It em-
boldened and empowered federal agencies, especially the Bureau of Reclamation,
which would become the West's most active dam-building entity. It enriched those
private companies large enough to benefit from New Deal partnerships with the
federal government (the Six Companies made millions of dollars on the project).
It also put people to work, employing over five thousand men. Boulder City, the

*project headquarters, was built from scratch to house the workers. The following
oral histories, collected in the 1970s, describe the labor involved in an undertaking
of this kind and some of the social realities workers, especially minority workers,
faced in the overnight communities that housed and entertained them in their off
hours. How would you describe working conditions on this New Deal project? How
would you describe the racial climate? Did the project help change these attitudes
in any way? How would you compare the actual work described here with the comments made by President Roosevelt at the dam's dedication in 1935 (p. 178)?*

Oral Histories of the Boulder Dam Project
1931–1935

Joe Kine

. . . They was hiring men, and I was working down there. They just had to
have men. They just took you over, and you was a high scaler if you wanted it or
not. I had worked in the mines, but I had never done any high scaling. It was all
brand-new to me. Then it wasn't all that bad of a job once you got it going, got
on to it.

My first job high scaling was over the Nevada valve house, cutting down to
put the valve house in. That was the steepest canyon wall of all. We had a crew
of men, and they came and went together all the time. I'd have a buddy that
worked with me, and we'd be together all the time unless he took a day off or
something. We tied our rope to a steel in the ground at the top of the canyon wall.
We tied our safety belts and our bos'n chair on that. We had inch ropes. We had
good ropes. They didn't break. That was never any worry. And then as they got
frayed and unraveled out, they'd drop them down on the ground and burn them.
We had an extra rope to tie the jackhammer on, and we tied our steel on, too.

We dropped ourselves over. Then we slid down to where we wanted to work,
whether it was close or way down. We could move back and forth pretty good with
our ropes. Then if you had to go up a little bit, you put a twist around your foot
with the rope and slid up. We could sneak up pretty slow with that, but we very
seldom had to go up. We used to climb out before the cableways were put up.
Once the cableways got up, they'd go back and forth, and they could pick us up
and move up and down and all ways. Then we had a big cable ladder too that we
could go out on.

We didn't have expert powdermen. We done the whole business ourselves:
drilled, loaded the holes and shot, barred down. Whatever was loose, we'd stick a

Andrew J. Dunar and Dennis McBride, *Building Hoover Dam: An Oral History of the Great Depression* (New York: Twayne Publishers, 1993), 145, 147–50, 159, 184, 140, 142, 144.

bar behind it and pry it off and let it drop down. The engineers would mark it how far back we wanted to go. They'd take their transits and shoot and check it and tell you whether you had enough off or didn't have enough off. They had that all figured out. They'd mark it. Then we'd drill some more and go ahead.

There was never a dull moment on that high-scaling job. Something was going on all the time. . . .

Jake Dieleman

They hired anyone who didn't have brains enough to be scared. You was 900 feet up in the air. It took a lot of guts.

Tommy Nelson

We had some Marion electric shovels down there. When I think about it today, guys dragging that 2,300-volt cable around in that water and the foreman saying, "It won't hurt you" — oh boy. It would just scare you to death.

I was assigned to the excavation of the riverbed as a flagman. The purpose of this flagman was to . . . keep the trucks busy, and the shovels busy.

There was quite a number of dump trucks down there during this excavation, hauling this debris, this rock out of there: the International, the Mack, the Boreman, the White, and the GMC. The workhorse was the old International, the corn binder. As she went up the hill with a load, she'd belch fire up the river. Many of these trucks that we had down there were hard tails. I better explain what a hard tail is, because the younger generation wouldn't know. A hard-tail truck was a truck that had hard rubber [tires] on the back, solid rubber. We had quite a few of those down there on the job. Now, a person had to be very careful where he set that truck, because if you got him back in there where he was going to get mired down, you were in for a chewin'. You might have quite a job to get him out. Now this driver who piloted that truck, he was in reverse about as much as he was forward. There was a little canopy built right over the steering wheel. That would keep the rocks from falling on him.

Curley Francis

After my dad died in 1933, I rustled around and got a job up at the high mix. I was the extra man there, running the gas locomotives and flatbed trucks. My job was to haul concrete to the cableways. I ran locomotives from the high mix mostly.

When you went into the high mix, you'd come out the outside track and come to a spring switch. Then you'd come underneath the mix, get your load.

Then you'd start out, and you'd have a red light. I worked graveyard shift. It was kind of challenging, because you'd run into a red light on the track, by golly, and you'd sit there and you'd get two or three minutes' sleep. You always kept a water bag outside the window. Whenever you didn't wake up good, you'd just put it on top of your head and shake it around.

If it was green, of course, you went around the turn. You might go on the inside; you might go on the outside. You didn't know where you was going, except when you got your assignment with the train, they'd say, "You're on Number 8 Cableway." Or Number 10 Cableway. You didn't care where they was pouring; it was just the fact that you had to go to that cableway with the bucket.

Oh, I'll tell you, that was a complicated system. . . .

Tommy Nelson

I was running a jackhammer at the side of the cliff. This was during the dam construction, after the concrete had started being poured. I was running a jackhammer in there to put an anchor bolt in. It was just shaking the daylights out of me. An old construction stiff came by, and he said, "Hey, kid. Why don't you get a Mexican to hold up that hammer?" I looked up at him, and I said, "We haven't got any Mexicans around here." "Oh," he said, "you don't know what I mean." He grabbed a piece of reinforcement steel and he came over with it, stood it up alongside the jackhammer, put a little haywire around it. "There, let it hold you up, kid." And it did. So that was a little trick, you know. You learned a lot of them. That was kind of humorous, when I think about it.

Agnes Lockette

The people that I know usually think of Boulder as a town — it's an all-white community, most of them think it is. This is based on the fact that many [black] people have relatives who came to Boulder to seek employment in the time that the dam was being built and were turned away. Historically they think of Boulder as being an all-white community.

Bud Bodell

Right at the beginning there wasn't [any blacks], but by the time I'd been there a month, there were Negroes, 13 or 14. One was killed. I went down to the funeral, and I found out there were 14, including him, down there. All laborers.

Erma Godbey

There weren't hardly any Negroes in this area anyhow until they started Basic Magnesium.[1] Then they brought a lot of Negroes to work at Basic Magnesium. There were a few over in West Las Vegas, but not many. And, of course, we

---

[1] **Basic Magnesium:** Industrial firm that processed magnesium, a silvery metal that burns with an intense white light.

hadn't started all the hotels and all those things, so there wasn't any reason for them to be here.

Bob Parker

There were a lot of them that worked on the dam. I say a lot; I'd say a maximum probably of 50 or 100. But they all lived in Las Vegas.

Claude Dumas was a big black man. In the old days they thought that any scale or rust on reinforcing steel or concrete wouldn't cause the concrete to bond to it. So they brushed all the scale off the steel they took down there, and any rust. They had it all there in the steelyard over where the Park Service Building [warehouse] is, down through there and over below Lakeview now. They unloaded all that steel over in there. These black men, several of them, were out there brushing this steel. Black people do everything with a rhythm. Brushing steel, they'd be going this way, and the rear end would be going the other, back and forth. They developed a rhythm brushing steel, [and] they were singing hymns.

Charlie Rose had the colored crew down at the dam, the colored crew that built the parapet walls along the highway there and around the spillways, around the canyon wall there, all that rockwork. That's as beautiful a piece of rockwork as you'll see anywhere in the country. He was a white man, Charlie was. When Charlie would take a day off, they'd put someone else down there to run the colored crew, and the colored crew wouldn't work. Most of them [would] take the day off too. Charlie Rose knew how to treat them. They would work for him. Anybody else they wouldn't work for.

But there was another deal down there. We had a [Bureau of Reclamation] regional director here. I'm not going to mention any names, because I don't know whether they're all gone or not. I know that the man that put the winged figures in, and the safety island down there and all of that terrazzo work, outlined the center of the flagpole — I know that Hansen, Oskar J. W. Hansen, was the sculptor on that. He was out there one day, and one or two of the colored men asked him something about that terrazzo work there. He was explaining it to them. This project manager, he was actually — was over there and heard it. He went over there, and he really chewed Oskar Hansen out about associating with those colored men out there in the public. Of course, the tourists and everybody else heard him. Old Oskar flipped his lid. He really told that project manager off. He told him he wasn't fit to have those men working for him. He really read him off. Two weeks later that project manager was running an engineering chain gang in Redding, California, at Shasta Dam. He wasn't here a month after that happened down on top of the dam. . . .

Madeline Knighten

I remember one time [at the Green Hut]. It could have developed into a free-for-all. In those days, you know, the Negroes weren't welcomed into any café. The Green Hut did have a very wonderful Negro cook. He was a very fine man, and he was a marvelous cook. But so far as serving was concerned, back in those days it was not common.

I was back in the kitchen visiting with my husband one of these dance evenings when we were expecting a dance crowd in any moment. The waiter rushed back to the window just all in a tizzy. He said, "There's a great big Negro out here." The waiter was a southern boy, Johnny Whittingham. He rushed back all in a tizzy and said, "There's a big Negro out here wanting to eat. What will I do with him?"

Howard, my husband, looked out and saw him. Fortunately, we had lived on the Apache reservation in Arizona and we knew the Apache people. Instantly he knew that he wasn't a Negro; he was an Apache Indian. He thought he probably was one of the high scalers. He said, "I want to talk to him anyhow." So he went out and talked to him, and he was one of the high scalers. They had at least two Apaches high scaling.

It was all eventually diverted. He ordered what he wanted to eat. They prepared it back in the kitchen, the other cooks back there. The waiter brought it out to him. My husband talked to him for a few minutes about things we knew. So he ate and left. But if he had realized that they were not ready to serve him, no telling what he might have done. He might have had a rage right there. He could have. But he didn't.

38. Death on Boulder Dam

Construction of Boulder Dam lasted for four years. At completion, it was easily the biggest dam in the world, and its sheer massiveness overwhelms the modest engineering description of it as "a storage reservoir." But success came at a high human price. This tabulation, drawn from government records and those of the Six Companies consortium, records the deaths that occurred on the project. First and last killed were a father and son: J. G. Tierney worked for the U.S. Bureau of Reclamation, the agency that superintended the dam and oversaw federal water projects across the West. His son, killed not long after Franklin Roosevelt dedicated the dam, also worked for the Bureau of Reclamation. The consortium of construction and engineering firms that made up the Six Companies had a huge workforce, but it also had the highest casualty rate during dam construction. This tabulation contains some fascinating information about the human costs of massive engineering projects. What can you deduce from these statistics and from the oral accounts in the last selection about the kinds of danger workers encountered on the project? How did these dangers change over the duration of the project?

Boulder Canyon Project Fatalities
1922–1935

1922

12/20	J. G. Tierney, U.S. Bureau of Reclamation (USBR)	Drowned

1931

5/17	Harry Large, Six Co.	Rock Slide
5/17	Andrew Lane, Six Co.	Rock Slide
5/18	Fred Olsen, Lewis Const. Co.	Premature Explosion
6/20	William Bryant, Six Co.	Explosion
6/20	J. P. Sweezy, Six Co.	Explosion
6/26	Ray Hapland, Six Co.	Heat Prostration
6/27	Pat Shannon, Six Co.	Heat Prostration
6/28	Mike Madzia, Six Co.	Heat Prostration
7/5	Joe Rolland, Six Co.	Drowned
7/5	Martin Puluski, visitor	Drowned
7/8	Robert Core, Newberry Elec.	Heat Prostration
7/10	A. E. Meridith, Lewis Const.	Heat Prostration
7/11	Joe Lyons, Anderson Bros.	Heat Prostration
7/13	Earl Parker, Six Co.	Heat Prostration
7/15	John Swenson, Six Co.	Heat Prostration
7/20	Chase Allen, Six Co.	Heat Prostration
7/22	A. A. McClurg, Int'l. Truck Co.	Heat Prostration
7/23	Tom Noonal, Six Co.	Heat Prostration
7/24	Joe Ganz, Anderson Bros.	Heat Prostration
7/26	Lew Starnes, Anderson Bros.	Heat Prostration
9/11	H. H. Kidd, Six Co.	Falling Rock
9/29	Jack Seitz, Six Co.	Fell 400 feet
10/2	Lauri Lehto, Six Co.	Falling Rock
10/17	Ralph Henderson, Six Co.	Falling Rock
10/17	M. C. Stuckey, Six Co.	Falling Rock
11/7	D. R. Elston, Six Co.	Struck by Truck
12/15	M. J. Sidmore, Six Co.	Premature Explosion
12/15	Frank Manning, Six Co.	Premature Explosion

Andrew J. Dunar and Dennis McBride, *Building Hoover Dam: An Oral History of the Great Depression* (New York: Twayne Publishers, 1993), 317–20.

1932

1/7	S. A. McDaniel, Six Co.	Fell
2/11	Joe Talbert, Six Co.	Power Shovel
2/25	Ben Johnson, Six Co.	Drowned in Tank
3/11	O. A. George, Six Co.	Crushed — Trucks
3/30	Frank Brady, Six Co.	Falling Rock
4/14	Carl Bennett, Six Co.	Explosion
4/21	H. H. Nightingale, Six Co.	Shovel — Crushed
4/26	L. N. McBride, Six Co.	Struck by Skip Line
4/27	Bert Lynch, Six Co.	Falling Rock
4/28	V. R. Moore, Six Co.	Struck — Concrete Skip
5/11	John Abercrombie, Six Co.	Transport Collision
5/20	B. S. Joyce, Six Co.	Falling Rock
5/30	H. A. Willis, Six Co.	Electrocuted
6/17	H. L. Scothern, Six Co.	Struck by Cable
7/25	Walter Hardesty, Six Co.	Struck by Crane
7/27	E. A. Bishop, Six Co.	Truck Went Overboard
7/29	Alexander Girardi, Six Co.	Fell from Wall
8/24	A. E. Wooden, Six Co.	Crushed by Form
8/31	E. H. Gammill, Six Co.	Premature Explosion
9/24	V. I. Kemnitz, Six Co.	Rock Fall
9/25	P. B. Hicks, Six Co.	Fell from Wall
9/28	James C. Roberts, Six Co.	Falling Rock
11/9	Louie Goss, Six Co.	Fell from Wall
11/16	Carl Soderstrom, Six Co.	Drowned
12/12	Dan Shovlin, Six Co.	Struck by Truck
12/23	Walter Hamer, Six Co.	Fell from Valve House

1933

1/1	F. C. Palmer, Six Co.	Fell from Valve House
1/10	Gus Enberg, Six Co.	Explosion
1/11	Howard Cornelius, Six Co.	Explosion
2/1	V. H. Blair, Six Co.	Fell from Truck
2/7	J. H. Powers, Six Co.	Truck Fell on Him
2/7	M. H. Kaighn, Six Co.	Rock Slide
3/12	Tome Markey, Six Co.	Fell
3/16	William Koontz, Six Co.	Run Over by Truck
4/8	Dan Kalal, Six Co.	Gravel Slide
5/20	H. D. Bluhm, Six Co.	Struck by Shovel
5/22	Pete Savoff, Six Co.	Fell
6/23	Mike Landers, Six Co.	Falling Rock
6/26	L. W. Steele, Six Co.	Run Over by Truck

7/1	F. B. Kassell, Six Co.	Premature Explosion
7/13	George Falkner, Six Co.	Falling Timber
7/19	J. M. Nelson, Six Co.	Fell from Form
9/15	V. O. Lee, Six Co.	Electrocuted
10/1	James Jackman, Six Co.	Falling Concrete Bucket
11/8	W. A. Jameson, Six Co.	Concrete Slide
11/8	James Tocci, Six Co.	Run Over by Truck
12/6	L. E. Roach, Six Co.	Fell from Jumbo
12/29	P. A. Malan, Six Co.	Fell from Form

1934

1/22	George Good, Six Co.	Falling Material
2/1	Rosyn Grant, Six Co.	Fell
2/6	Kenneth Walden, Six Co.	Crushed by Concrete Bucket
2/26	Eugene Buckner, Six Co.	Falling Timber
3/10	George R. Robinson, Six Co.	Elevator Accident
3/23	Harry Morgan, Six Co.	Fell
4/14	Allen Jackson, Six Co.	Fell
5/16	G. D. McIsaac, Six Co.	Electrocuted
5/20	Howard Bently, Six Co.	Falling Rock
5/26	Samuel L. Carter, Six Co.	Hit by Concrete Dinky
5/26	Fred Deckmann, Babcock & Wilcox (B&W)	Fell
6/11	Grant Miles, Six Co.	Fell 60 feet walking thru drain. Not considered industrial by Six Co. as he did not accept furnished mode of transportation
6/24	Victor K. Auchard, Six Co.	Crushed under Jumbo
8/27	Harris Lange, B&W	Objects from Broken Sling
9/16	Frank A. Fritz, Six Co.	Electrocuted
9/26	John W. Rawls, Six Co.	Fell from Form
11/1	Paul L. Jordan, B&W	Fell from 30 Foot Pipe
11/1	Richard M. Whelan, B&W	Penstock Car Ran Wild
11/1	Martin L. Hempel, B&W	Penstock Car Ran Wild
11/4	Alfred E. Foreman, B&W	Penstock Car Ran Wild
11/14	K. H. Rankin, USBR	Struck by Concrete Bucket

1935

1/3	J. W. Pitts, Six Co.	Struck by Concrete Bucket
2/19	Kenneth L. Wilson, Six Co.	Line Broke — Fell 200 Feet
2/21	B. R. Reaves, Six Co.	Fell into Tunnel; Drown
5/15	David C. Nixon, Six Co.	Crushed: Concrete Bucket
5/17	Verne Matson, B&W	Falling Pipe
6/21	Harold Koile, B&W	Falling Casting
8/14	William R. Skaloud, B&W	Fell
11/17	Albert G. Loper, Six Co.	Fell
11/24	Roy Stevens, Six Co.	Struck by Flying Object
12/20	Patrick W. Tierney, USBR	Fell: Intake Tower, Lake

Summary

Company Name	Total Fatalities
Anderson Brothers	4
Newberry Electric	1
International Truck Co.	1
Babcock & Wilcox	9
Lewis Construction Company	2
Six Companies	91
U.S. Bureau of Reclamation	3
Visitors	1
Total Deaths	**112**

39. THE DEDICATION OF A NEW DEAL PROJECT

It may seem ironic that a project paid for and completed during the Roosevelt administration is now named after Roosevelt's predecessor. But the Hoover administration had initiated the Boulder Dam project in the 1920s, and through accidents of timing as much as anything else, it became a New Deal challenge. To get the dam built in just four years, the U.S. government joined with the Six Com-

panies consortium of construction firms, the Morrison-Knudson Corporation of Boise, MacDonald & Kahn and Bechtel & Kaiser of San Francisco, the Pacific Bridge Corporation and J. F. Shea Company of Portland, and the Utah Construction Company in Salt Lake City. Following Boulder Dam, these firms went on to build other giant projects throughout the American West, the nation, and the world. Boulder Dam embodied the New Deal approach to the western landscape: through partnerships with firms like the Six Companies, the government would employ people hard hit by the Depression and, at the same time, sponsor projects producing huge environmental changes. This is the text of President Franklin D. Roosevelt's dedication of the dam in the fall of 1935. He praises the project as a triumph of engineering and of the New Deal itself. He also characterizes the dam as a victory over nature. Does the president view the dam as a political opportunity? What does he mean by an "unregulated river"? How does Roosevelt characterize the work of building Boulder Dam? In what ways does he claim the project for the New Deal? How does he characterize the dam's workers?

FRANKLIN D. ROOSEVELT
Address at Boulder Dam
1935

. . . Ten years ago the place where we are gathered was an unpeopled, forbidding desert. In the bottom of a gloomy canyon, whose precipitous walls rose to a height of more than a thousand feet, flowed a turbulent, dangerous river. The mountains on either side of the canyon were difficult of access with neither road nor trail, and their rocks were protected by neither trees nor grass from the blazing heat of the sun. The site of Boulder City was a cactus-covered waste. The transformation wrought here in these years is a twentieth-century marvel.

We are here to celebrate the completion of the greatest dam in the world, rising 726 feet above the bed-rock of the river and altering the geography of a whole region; we are here to see the creation of the largest artificial lake in the world — 115 miles long, holding enough water, for example, to cover the State of Connecticut to a depth of ten feet; and we are here to see nearing completion a power house which will contain the largest generators and turbines yet installed in this

Andrew J. Dunar and Dennis McBride, *Building Hoover Dam: An Oral History of the Great Depression* (New York: Twayne Publishers, 1993), 311–15.

country, machinery that can continuously supply nearly two million horsepower of electric energy.

All these dimensions are superlative. They represent and embody the accumulated engineering knowledge and experience of centuries; and when we behold them it is fitting that we pay tribute to the genius of their designers. We recognize also the energy, resourcefulness and zeal of the builders, who, under the greatest physical obstacles, have pushed this work forward to completion two years in advance of the contract requirements. But especially, we express our gratitude to the thousands of workers who gave brain and brawn to this great work of construction.

Beautiful and great as this structure is, it must also be considered in its relationship to the agricultural and industrial development and in its contribution to the health and comfort of the people of America who live in the Southwest.

To divert and distribute the waters of an arid region, so that there shall be security of rights and efficiency in service, is one of the greatest problems of law and of administration to be found in any Government. The farms, the cities, the people who live along the many thousands of miles of this river and its tributaries — all of them depend upon the conservation, the regulation, and the equitable division of its ever-changing water supply.

What has been accomplished on the Colorado in working out such a scheme of distribution is inspiring to the whole country. Through the cooperation of the States whose people depend upon this river, and of the Federal Government which is concerned in the general welfare, there is being constructed a system of distributive works and of laws and practices which will insure to the millions of people who now dwell in this basin, and the millions of others who will come to dwell here in future generations, a just, safe and permanent system of water rights. In devising these policies and the means for putting them into practice the Bureau of Reclamation of the Federal Government has taken, and is destined to take in the future, a leading and helpful part. The Bureau has been the instrument which gave effect to the legislation introduced in Congress by Senator Hiram Johnson and Congressman Phil Swing.

As an unregulated river, the Colorado added little of value to the region this dam serves. When in flood the river was a threatening torrent. In the dry months of the year it shrank to a trickling stream. For a generation the people of the Imperial Valley had lived in the shadow of disaster from this river which provided their livelihood, and which is the foundation of their hopes for themselves and their children. Every spring they awaited with dread the coming of a flood, and at the end of nearly every summer they feared a shortage of water would destroy their crops.

The gates of these great diversion tunnels were closed here at Boulder Dam last February. In June a great flood came down the river. It came roaring down the canyons of the Colorado, was caught and safely held behind Boulder Dam.

Last year a drought of unprecedented severity was visited upon the West. The watershed of this Colorado River did not escape. In July the canals of the Imperial Valley went dry. Crop losses in that Valley alone totaled $10,000,000 that summer. Had Boulder Dam been completed one year earlier, this loss would have been prevented, because the spring flood would have been stored to furnish a steady water supply for the long dry summer and fall.

Across the San Jacinto Mountains southwest of Boulder Dam, the cities of Southern California are constructing an aqueduct to cost $220,000,000, which they have raised, for the purpose of carrying the regulated waters of the Colorado River to the Pacific Coast 259 miles away.

Across the desert and mountains to the west and south run great electric transmission lines by which factory motors, street and household lights and irrigation pumps will be operated in Southern Arizona and California. Part of this power will be used in pumping the water through the aqueduct to supplement the domestic supplies of Los Angeles and surrounding cities.

Navigation of the river from Boulder Dam to the Grand Canyon has been made possible, a 115-mile stretch that has been traversed less than half a dozen times in history. An immense new park has been created for the enjoyment of all our people.

At what cost was this done? Boulder Dam and the power houses together cost a total of $108,000,000, all of which will be repaid with interest in fifty years under the contracts for sale of the power. Under these contracts, already completed, not only will the cost be repaid, but the way is opened for the provision of needed light and power to the consumer at reduced rates. In the expenditure of the price of Boulder Dam during the depression years work was provided for 4,000 men, most of them heads of families, and many thousands more were enabled to earn a livelihood through manufacture of materials and machinery.

And this is true in regard to the thousands of projects undertaken by the Federal Government, by the States and by the counties and municipalities in recent years. The overwhelming majority of them are of definite and permanent usefulness.

Throughout our national history we have had a great program of public improvements, and in these past two years all that we have done has been to accelerate that program. We know, too, that the reason for this speeding up was the need of giving relief to several million men and women whose earning capacity had been destroyed by the complexities and lack of thought of the economic system of the past generation.

No sensible person is foolish enough to draw hard and fast classifications as to usefulness or need. Obviously, for instance, this great Boulder Dam warrants universal approval because it will prevent floods and flood damage, because it will irrigate thousands of acres of tillable land and because it will generate electricity to turn the wheels of many factories and illuminate countless homes.

But can we say that a five-foot brushwood dam across the head waters of an arroyo, and costing only a millionth part of Boulder Dam, is an undesirable project or a waste of money? Can we say that the great brick high school, costing $2,000,000, is a useful expenditure but that a little wooden school house project, costing five or ten thousand dollars, is a wasteful extravagance? Is it fair to approve a huge city boulevard and, at the same time, disapprove the improvement of a muddy farm-to-market road?

While we do all of this, we give actual work to the unemployed and at the same time we add to the wealth of the Nation. These efforts meet with the approval of the people of the Nation.

In a little over two years this work has accomplished much. We have helped mankind by the works themselves and, at the same time, we have created the necessary purchasing power to throw in the clutch to start the wheels of what we call private industry. Such expenditures on all of these works, great and small, flow out to many beneficiaries. They revive other and more remote industries and businesses. Money is put in circulation. Credit is expanded and the financial and industrial mechanism of America is stimulated to more and more activity.

Labor makes wealth. The use of materials makes wealth. To employ workers and materials when private employment has failed is to translate into great national possessions the energy that otherwise would be wasted. Boulder Dam is a splendid symbol of that principle. The mighty waters of the Colorado were running unused to the sea. Today we translate them into a great national possession.

I might go further and suggest to you that use begets use. Such works as this serve as a means of making useful other national possessions. Vast deposits of precious metals are scattered within a short distance of where we stand today. They await the development of cheap power.

These great Government power projects will affect not only the development of agriculture and industry and mining in the sections that they serve, but they will also prove useful yardsticks to measure the cost of power throughout the United States. It is my belief that the Government should proceed to lay down the first yardstick from this great power plant in the form of a State power line, assisted in its financing by the Government, and tapping the wonderful natural resources of Southern Nevada. Doubtless the same policy of financial assistance to State authorities can be followed in the development of Nevada's sister State, Arizona, on the other side of the River.

With it all, with work proceeding in every one of the more than three thousand counties in the United States, and of a vastly greater number of local divisions of Government, the actual credit of Government agencies is on a stronger and safer basis than at any time in the past six years. Many States have actually improved their financial position in the past two years. Municipal tax receipts are being paid when the taxes fall due, and tax arrearages are steadily declining.

It is a simple fact that Government spending is already beginning to show definite signs of its effect on consumer spending; that the putting of people to work by the Government has put other people to work through private employment, and that in two years and a half we have come to the point today where private industry must bear the principal responsibility of keeping the processes of greater employment moving forward with accelerated speed.

The people of the United States are proud of Boulder Dam. With the exception of the few who are narrow visioned, people everywhere on the Atlantic Seaboard, people in the Middle West and the Northwest, people in the South, must surely recognize that the national benefits which will be derived from the completion of this project will make themselves felt in every one of the forty-eight States. They know that poverty or distress in a community two thousand miles away may affect them, and equally that prosperity and higher standards of living across a whole continent will help them back home. . . .

That is why I have the right once more to congratulate you who have built Boulder Dam and on behalf of the Nation to say to you, "Well done."

40. WHAT TO EXPECT
IN THE CIVILIAN CONSERVATION CORPS

Franklin Roosevelt established the Civilian Conservation Corps in the first months of his presidency. Immensely popular and successful, the CCC put nearly three million young men, often from the cities, to work outdoors on flood control, forestry, and soil conservation projects throughout the United States. Because the CCC was a federal agency, such entities as the National Park Service, the Forest Service, the Department of Agriculture, and the Soil Conservation Service directed various CCC projects. The CCC concentrated its efforts on federal land, and the U.S. government owned more land in the West than in any other region of the country. One CCC contingent employed tens of thousands of Native Americans to work on the West's Indian reservations. Although the impact was not nearly as dramatic as Boulder Dam, we can argue that it was as lasting and certainly as important. The agency's work can still be seen all over the West. CCC laborers were young men, often teenagers. This document is a mock question-and-answer pamphlet designed to inform the parents of CCC workers in California about the work their sons would be doing for the agency. What questions or responses strike you as specific to this period? Which are more timeless? How would you compare CCC work to the Boulder Dam project? What parallels can you find between the CCC and the U.S. military?

CALIFORNIA STATE RELIEF ADMINISTRATION
"Typical Questions and Answers"
c. 1936

Q[uestion]. Can my son be assigned to a camp near here so that he can come home now and then?

A[nswer]. The Army recruiting units and those in charge of the acceptance stations assign the boys to the camps where they are needed. We do not know the camp to which your son will be assigned and can give you no assurance that he will be sent to any particular camp.

Q. Will my son have to fight forest fire[s]?

A. Yes, if a fire breaks out in the vicinity of the camp to which he is assigned. However, it may ease your mind to know that with the modern, efficient methods of combating fires there is very little danger. The camp officers and forestry officials directing a forest fire are cognizant of the inexperience of the average youth in fighting forest fires and do not allow them to get into difficulties. In addition the fire loss in California has been reduced since the advent of CCC to just about 20% of the average annual loss suffered in years before 1933.

Q. In the event of war, will my son be subject to immediate draft by the Army?

A. No more so than he would be if he remains at home. The Civilian Conservation Corps is not a military organization. There is neither military training nor discipline. The clothing issued is not a military uniform. The fact should be known that because he goes to an Army acceptance station for enrollment, it does not mean that he joins the Army. He remains a civilian from beginning to end. The Army is in the picture because they have trained officers, equipment and systems available to handle the examinations, enrollments and transportation in the most efficient manner possible. However, the training received by young men in the CCC from a standpoint of learning to carry out orders properly and efficiently would stand them in good stead and greatly increase their chances of survival in the event of foreign conflict at any time, but they are in no way any more subject to military draft in a CCC camp than they would be right at home.

Q. Do the men have adequate medical attention?

A. Yes, there is a doctor, usually an Army Reserve Officer, on duty in each camp to whom the youth can apply at any time for medical treatment. In addition, a periodical, compulsory examination is given that insures your son being well cared for. In cases of serious illness the ailing youth is removed to the nearest Government hospital, such as Letterman Hospital in San Francisco, where

California State Relief Administration, Civilian Conservation Corps, "Typical Questions and Answers" [Sacramento: State Relief Administration, c. 1936], 1–4.

some of the finest physicians and surgeons in the country are on duty and if the youth is too ill to travel, or requires an immediate operation, he is taken to the nearest local hospital and his care paid for out of Government funds.

Q. Do the men have adequate supervision in camp and on leave?

A. The youths are, in most instances, under far more rigid and close supervision in camp and on leave than they would receive in their home town. An officer or responsible man is placed in a supervisory capacity covering each group that goes on leave in an adjacent town or city and the enrollee's actions, if not of the best, are reported to his Commanding Officer. . . .

Q. How is the food in camps? I have heard contradictory stories about it — some good and some — not so good.

A. The food must pass Government inspection and measure up to standards prescribed by the War Department. It is of good wholesome quality and your son may have all of it he can eat. The food is not fancy, but it is solid, substantial food, fresh and clean and provided in a balanced diet. There is a proper ratio of salads, entrees, vegetables, desserts and beverages. The fact that recent statistics show an average gain per man of ten pounds during a six-month's enrollment is more eloquent than words in proof of the quality and abundance of the food served in camp.

Q. How will my son attend church?

A. Regular, non-sectarian services are held in camp. In addition, enrollees are granted liberty regularly to attend the church of their own denomination if they so desire where the camp is adjacent to a town or city.

Q. If a better position for the youth than the one in camp develops is there any difficulty in obtaining his immediate discharge?

A. None whatsoever. Upon submission to the camp commander of proof of an available position the youth will be immediately honorably discharged and furnished transportation home, or to the point of selection, at the discretion of the Army.

Q. Is it permissible for me to return to my son part of the allotment check?

A. Return of all or part of the allotment check[1] to the enrollee is against the basic principles of this program and is cause for immediate discharge of the enrollee receiving it.

Q. My son overstayed his leave and has been discharged for desertion. How may he be reinstated?

A. He cannot be reinstated except on the filing of an appeal to the Corps Area Commander through his Commanding Officer, stating the circumstances. If the enrollee can prove illness to himself, member of his family, or transportation delays, etc. beyond his control, the Corps Area Commander would be inclined to look favorably upon his appeal. Otherwise, the enrollee could not be reinstated.

---

[1] **allotment check:** In this program, the family of the CCC worker received a check from the government. Workers drew an allowance while in camp.

Q. What opportunity does a youth have for improving himself while in camp other than the out-door life he naturally spends at work and play?

A. Each camp has an Educational Advisor. Regular classes are conducted in camp covering many subjects. Over 100 valuable correspondence courses are available and a certificate awarded to those satisfactorily completing any course or courses. In addition, a very complete library of proper and acceptable books and current magazines of intelligent selection is maintained in each camp.

Q. What opportunities are there for promotion?

A. There are a limited number of promotions available in each camp for youths who show marked ability and application. These ratings are known as "Leaders" and "Assistant Leaders." A leader receives an additional $15 per month allowance and an assistant leader an additional allowance of $6.00 per month over the basic $30. The basic allotment of leaders and assistant leaders may be increased but it is not mandatory.

Q. What opportunities are available in camp for private employment?

A. The President authorized, some time ago, that the Technical Services (that is, the Forestry units supervising the work projects) should select from the ranks of their youths in camp a certain percentage of the foreman and supervisory personnel. During the past year over 100 young California Juniors have been given positions as Camp Foremen, Fire Lookouts and Assistant Wardens at salaries ranging from $80 to $120 per month.

Q. What insurance does an enrollee have while in the CCC?

A. The enrollee is protected under the Federal compensation laws which provide compensation for injury or illness sustained while in the CCC and only excepts cases where the injury or illness is contracted by wilful misconduct or intent to bring injury upon himself or others. . . .

Suggestions for Further Reading

Dunar, Andrew J., and Dennis McBride. *Building Hoover Dam: An Oral History of the Great Depression.* New York: Twayne Publishers, 1993.

Hill, Edwin G. *In the Shadow of the Mountain: The Spirit of the CCC.* Pullman, Wash.: Washington State University Press, 1990.

Gregory, James. *American Exodus: The Dust Bowl Migration and Okie Culture in California.* New York: Oxford University Press, 1989.

Kennedy, David. *Freedom from Fear: The American People in Depression and War, 1929–1945.* New York: Oxford University Press, 1999.

Lowitt, Richard. *The New Deal and the West.* Bloomington: Indiana University Press, 1984.

Mullins, William H. *The Depression and the Urban West Coast, 1929–1933: Los Angeles, San Francisco, Seattle, and Portland.* Bloomington: Indiana University Press, 1991.

Nash, Gerald D. *The Federal Landscape: An Economic History of the Twentieth-Century West.* Tucson: University of Arizona Press, 1999.

Terkel, Studs. *Hard Times: An Oral History of the Great Depression.* New York: Avon Books, 1971.

Internees Gathered at a Rail Depot in Los Angeles, 1942

This photograph shows Japanese and Japanese American families at a rail station in Los Angeles preparing to be sent off to an internment camp in eastern California in the aftermath of the Japanese attack on Pearl Harbor and U.S. entry into World War II. Note the presence of Army personnel in the crowd and along the railroad tracks. What do people's facial expressions and body language tell you about this scene? Why might you assume that the internment process has uprooted the lives of these people unexpectedly?

Library of Congress.

CHAPTER TEN

WORLD WAR II

Japanese Internment

It would be difficult to overestimate the shock Americans felt on December 7, 1941, when a Japanese air attack came close to wiping out the United States fleet at Pearl Harbor in Hawaii. Americans everywhere knew that there was a war on and that the Roosevelt administration was playing a critical role, mostly through the lifeline of supplies sent to Allied forces in Europe. But the mayhem, destruction, and death at Pearl Harbor were a new experience. It became clear that the United States could not stand idly by while the conflict threatened to engulf the whole world. The Japanese attack on Pearl Harbor provoked the United States to declare war.

Like the Great Depression, World War II transformed the West in remarkable ways. People still came West, and for many of the same reasons, such as work, but now the wartime economy promised a better chance of finding a job. African Americans migrated from the South to take jobs in the labor-starved defense industry. In California, many of the same Dust Bowl migrants who had poured into the rural flats of the huge Central Valley now found work in the defense plants or shipyards of the Bay Area and southern California. And many came west during the war years because they were newly enlisted or drafted into the armed forces. The military presence in the West, increasing through the late 1930s by presidential order, grew at blinding speed in the months following Pearl Harbor. Millions of young men and women in uniform found themselves at the airfields and shipyards that seemed to pop up almost overnight.

But movement in the West during World War II was not only due to opportunity or wartime military service. The forced internment of Japanese aliens and Japanese Americans in camps in the West and South was an outgrowth of the wartime paranoia and hysteria that followed the attack on Pearl Harbor. Not long after, President Roosevelt signed Executive Order 9066, which allowed the rounding up of all those who were of Japanese descent, whether citizen or noncitizen, along the entire Pacific Coast, from the Canadian border south to San

Diego. Over one hundred thousand people (most of them American-born) were evacuated from their homes, their jobs, and their communities, ostensibly because they constituted a potential threat to the internal security of the United States. Once the order to evacuate was given, people had two days to arrange their affairs, pack a few belongings, and say good-bye. Most believed that wartime hysteria would soon subside and they would be allowed to resume their normal lives. And while some Americans bravely spoke out against internment, public opinion supported the president's action.

The government moved internees away from the Pacific coast, believing that the coastline was vulnerable to enemy attack. German and Italian aliens living in or near San Francisco also found their civil liberties curtailed, if only briefly, but it was the Japanese community that bore the brunt of this policy. Many viewed the presence of so many of Japanese descent as an invitation to treachery and treason, although no Japanese American was ever charged with wartime espionage. A special government agency called the War Relocation Authority was set up to deal with the problem of imprisoning tens of thousands who had broken no laws. Internees first faced processing and paperwork, their introduction to a dehumanizing process. Then they were sent to one of the internment camps that dotted the deserts and interior of the West (and locations as far away as Arkansas). Internees were housed in these isolated outposts for an average of two-and-a-half years.

The internment camps were usually hastily constructed barracks enclosed by barbed wire. The movements of internees were heavily restricted. Because of the fear of espionage, they were not allowed to own or use camera equipment (at least at first), and their access to the outside world was limited. Like prisons, the camps were communities within communities, with separate facilities, schools, and social activities. Certain people could come in — schoolteachers, government officials, and journalists — but internees could not leave except under tightly controlled and temporary circumstances. Serving in the U.S. armed forces was the only means to avoid incarceration. The federal government evidently trusted young Japanese American men to fight for their country, but it did not trust the families that had raised those same loyal soldiers. This irony was not lost on internees or their extended families. While Japanese American military units served with distinction — the 100th Battalion and the 442nd Regimental Combat Team remain the most-decorated units in U.S. history — many in the community resisted wartime service precisely because they recognized the stark inconsistency in the government's stance. Most internees struggled through the humiliating years of confinement without overt protest, however, believing that resistance to the government's policies would only make things worse.

As if troubled by a nagging conscience, the War Relocation Authority gradually relaxed its supervision of the camps during the later stages of the war. Some student internees were allowed to leave to attend college and then, gradually, all were set free to try to pick up the pieces of their lives. Most had very little to return to when they were released. Many of the internment victims had lost their homes and their businesses when ordered to the camps in early 1942. Some estimate that the interned Americans sold off, often at ridiculously low prices, upwards of $500 million worth of farmland, homes, and other property. The U.S. Supreme Court upheld internment in 1944, though one member of the Court declared the government's actions the "legalization of racism." Only recently did the United States government recognize the moral and constitutional lapses of internment; in 1988, Congress voted to pay reparations and apologize to those the federal government had robbed of their freedom.

The selections in this chapter cover various facets of the internment issue. Two eyewitness accounts of the internment process, one an excerpt from a memoir, the other a series of captioned drawings, capture the fear of those considered so dangerous, they had to be removed from their homes and jobs. The Presidential Executive Order authorizing internment attempts to justify it on the grounds of internal security. In the final selection, the government director of internment argues that somehow, in the midst of the wholesale violation of the civil liberties of tens of thousands of Americans, democracy might be preserved.

AS YOU READ these selections, think of the social and racial situation in the wartime West that made internment possible. What do these documents reveal about the West's role in the federal internment effort? What fears and biases are reflected in these documents? From what you know, do you see any similarities between internment and the Native American reservation system in the West?

---

41. INTERNMENT IN WASHINGTON

This passage from her memoir describes the impact of Pearl Harbor and the internment order on the lives of Monica Sone and her family, friends, and neighbors in Seattle. Wrenched from a peaceful life in the Pacific Northwest, where her father ran a small hotel, Sone and her family spent several years in an internment camp in Puyallup, Washington. Her description of how rumor and hearsay played into local fears of espionage and treason are particularly revealing. She also records local racism directed at Japanese people, which only increased in the wake of the Pearl Harbor attack. How do Monica Sone and her family react to Executive Order 9066? How do her responses compare to those of Miné Okubo (p. 195)? How would you describe Sone's fears as the internment rumors become a reality? Would things have been any different if Sone and her family had lived in the Midwest or the South?

MONICA SONE
From *Nisei Daughter*
1953

On a peaceful Sunday morning, December 7, 1941, Henry, Sumi and I were at choir rehearsal singing ourselves hoarse in preparation for the annual Christmas recital of Handel's "Messiah." Suddenly Chuck Mizuno, a young University of Washington student, burst into the chapel, gasping as if he had sprinted all the way up the stairs.

"Listen, everybody!" he shouted. "Japan just bombed Pearl Harbor . . . in Hawaii! It's war!"

The terrible words hit like a blockbuster, paralyzing us . . . I knew instinctively that the fact that I was an American by birthright was not going to help me escape the consequences of this unhappy war.

One girl mumbled over and over again, "It can't be, God, it can't be!" Someone else was saying, "What a spot to be in! Do you think we'll be considered Japanese or Americans?"

A boy replied quietly, "We'll be Japs, same as always. But our parents are enemy aliens[1] now, you know." . . .

The pressure of war moved in on our little community. The Chinese consul announced that all the Chinese would carry identification cards and wear "China" badges to distinguish them from the Japanese. Then I really felt left standing out in the cold. The government ordered the bank funds of all Japanese nationals frozen. . . .

In the afternoon President Roosevelt's formal declaration of war against Japan was broadcast throughout the nation. In grave, measured words, he described the attack on Pearl Harbor as shameful, infamous. I writhed involuntarily. I could no more have escaped the stab of self-consciousness than I could have changed my Oriental features. . . .

We had a family conference to discuss the possibility of Father and Mother's internment. Henry was in graduate school and I was beginning my second year at the university. We agreed to drop out should they be taken and we would manage the hotel during our parents' absence. Every week end Henry and I accompanied Father to the hotel and learned how to keep the hotel books, how to open the office safe, and what kind of linen, paper towels, and soap to order.

---

[1] **enemy aliens:** *Issei* refers to those Japanese in America who were born in Japan and thus not U.S. citizens. *Nisei* are the American-born children, and thus U.S. citizens, of *issei* parents.

Monica Sone, *Nisei Daughter* (Boston: Little, Brown and Company, 1953), 145–46, 149–50, 157–61.

Then a new menace appeared on the scene. Cries began to sound up and down the coast that everyone of Japanese ancestry should be taken into custody. For years the professional guardians of the Golden West had wanted to rid their land of the Yellow Peril, and the war provided an opportunity for them to push their program through. As the chain of Pacific islands fell to the Japanese, patriots shrieked for protection from us. A Californian sounded the alarm: "The Japanese are dangerous and they must leave. Remember the destruction and the sabotage perpetrated at Pearl Harbor. Notice how they have infiltrated into the harbor towns and taken our best land." . . .

In February, Executive Order No. 9066 came out, authorizing the War Department to remove the Japanese from such military areas as it saw fit, aliens and citizens alike. Even if a person had a fraction of Japanese blood in him, he must leave on demand.

A pall of gloom settled upon our home. We couldn't believe that the government meant that the Japanese-Americans must go, too. We had heard the clamoring of superpatriots who insisted loudly, "Throw the whole kaboodle out. A Jap's a Jap, no matter how you slice him. You can't make an American out of little Jap Junior just by handing him an American birth certificate." But we had dismissed these remarks as just hot blasts of air from an overheated patriot. We were quite sure that our rights as American citizens would not be violated, and we would not be marched out of our homes on the same basis as enemy aliens. . . .

Once more I felt like a despised, pathetic two-headed freak, a Japanese and an American, neither of which seemed to be doing me any good. . . .

Events moved rapidly. General DeWitt[2] marked off Western Washington, Oregon, and all of California, and the southern half of Arizona as Military Area No. 1, hallowed ground from which we must remove ourselves as rapidly as possible. Unfortunately we could not simply vanish into thin air, and we had no place to go. We had no relatives in the east we could move in on. All our relatives were sitting with us in the forbidden area, themselves wondering where to go. The neighboring states in the line of exit for the Japanese protested violently at the prospect of any mass invasion. They said, very sensibly, that if the Coast didn't want the Japanese hanging around, they didn't either. . . .

The orders were simple:

> Dispose of your homes and property. Wind up your business. Register the family. One seabag of bedding, two suitcases of clothing allowed per person. People in District #1 must report at 8th and Lane Street, 8 p.m. on April 28.

. . . We were advised to pack warm, durable clothes. In my mind, I saw our permanent camp sprawled out somewhere deep in a snow-bound forest, an American Siberia. I saw myself plunging chest deep in the snow, hunting for small game to keep us alive. I decided that one of my suitcases was going to hold nothing but vitamins from A to Z. I thought of sewing fur-lined hoods and parkas for the family. I was certain this was going to be a case of sheer animal survival. . . .

---

[2]**General DeWitt:** General J. L. DeWitt of the U.S. Army Western Defense Command, who convinced President Roosevelt to issue Executive Order 9066 authorizing internment.

42. INTERNMENT ORDERS
FROM THE PRESIDENT

In his executive order, issued shortly after the December 1941 attack on Pearl Harbor, President Franklin D. Roosevelt outlines the distribution of authority to those military bodies charged with interning people deemed dangerous to the U.S. war effort. Roosevelt had been persuaded by the U.S. Army that the presence of so many people of Japanese descent along the Pacific Coast could lead to possible foreign attack or sabotage. More than one hundred thousand people were immediately transferred to one of ten internment camps scattered throughout the West or to one of two camps in Arkansas. Note that the document does not specifically mention people of Japanese descent. How does the Executive Order describe the threat posed by the Japanese and Japanese Americans? How are the various military commanders supposed to recognize such threats? What provisions does the Executive Order make for returning to peacetime existence?

FRANKLIN D. ROOSEVELT
Executive Order 9066
1942

Whereas the successful prosecution of the war requires every possible protection against espionage and against sabotage to national-defense material, national-defense premises, and national-defense utilities as defined in Section 4, Act of April 20, 1918, 40 Stat. 533, as amended by the Act of November 30, 1940, 54 Stat. 1220, and the Act of August 21, 1941, 55 Stat. 655 (U.S.C., Title 50, Sec. 104):

Now, therefore, by virtue of the authority vested in me as President of the United States, and Commander in Chief of the Army and Navy, I hereby authorize and direct the Secretary of War, and the Military Commanders whom he may from time to time designate, whenever he or any designated Commander deems such action necessary or desirable, to prescribe military areas in such places and of such extent as he or the appropriate Military Commander may determine, from which any or all persons may be excluded, and with respect to which, the right of any person to enter, remain in, or leave shall be subject to whatever restrictions the Secretary of War or the appropriate Military Commander may impose in his discretion. The Secretary of War is hereby authorized to provide for residents of any such area who are excluded therefrom, such transportation, food, shelter, and other accommodations as may be necessary, in the judgment of the Secretary of War or the said Military Commander, and until other arrangements are made, to accomplish the purpose of this order. The designation of military areas in any region or locality shall supersede designations of

Office of the Federal Register, National Archives and Records Service, *Code of Federal Regulations, Title 3 — The President 1938–1943 Compilation* (Washington, D.C.: General Services Administration), 1092–93.

prohibited and restricted areas by the Attorney General under the Proclamations of December 7 and 8, 1941, and shall supersede the responsibility and authority of the Attorney General under the said Proclamations in respect of such prohibited and restricted areas.

I hereby further authorize and direct the Secretary of War and the said Military Commanders to take such other steps as he or the appropriate Military Commander may deem advisable to enforce compliance with the restrictions applicable to each Military area hereinabove authorized to be designated, including the use of Federal troops and other Federal Agencies, with authority to accept assistance of state and local agencies.

I hereby further authorize and direct all Executive Departments, independent establishments and other Federal Agencies, to assist the Secretary of War or the said Military Commanders in carrying out this Executive Order, including the furnishing of medical aid, hospitalization, food, clothing, transportation, use of land, shelter, and other supplies, equipment, utilities, facilities, and services.

This order shall not be construed as modifying or limiting in any way the authority heretofore granted under Executive Order No. 8972, dated December 12, 1941, nor shall it be construed as limiting or modifying the duty and responsibility of the Federal Bureau of Investigation, with respect to the investigation of alleged acts of sabotage or the duty and responsibility of the Attorney General and the Department of Justice under the Proclamations of December 7 and 8, 1941, prescribing regulations for the conduct and control of alien enemies, except as such duty and responsibility is superseded by the designation of military areas hereunder.

FRANKLIN D. ROOSEVELT

THE WHITE HOUSE,
February 19, 1942.

43. PICTURES OF INTERNMENT

These captioned sketches are from a book written by Miné Okubo, a young Japanese American woman from Southern California who was a promising art student at the University of California in Berkeley when the internment order was issued. First sent to the Tanforan Assembly Center, a racetrack near San Francisco, for processing and incarceration, Okubo was then sent to the Central Utah Relocation Camp known as Topaz. Her sketches and captions capture the surreal quality of the entire internment process: everyday life went on. People in the camps went to school, held community meetings and elections, and maintained social and religious rituals. These sketches portray the early stages of internment at the Tanforan racetrack. What attitudes toward the internment process can you discern from Okubo's sketches and captions? What parallels can you draw between this account and that of Monica Sone (p. 191)? How do these drawings compare with the statements of the internment director, Dillon S. Myer, in the following selection?

Miné Okubo
From *Citizen 13660*
1946

Civil Control Stations were established by the Wartime Civil Control Administration in each of the designated areas. One member of each family was asked to register for the family; people without families registered individually. On Sunday, April 26, 1942, I reported to Pilgrim Hall of the First Congregational Church in Berkeley to register for my brother and myself — a family unit of two. Soldiers were standing guard at the entrance and around the buildings.

Miné Okubo, *Citizen 13660* (New York: Columbia University Press, 1946), 18–21, 35.

A woman seated near the entrance gave me a card with No. 7 printed on it and told me to go inside and wait. I read the "funnies" until my number was called and I was interviewed. The woman in charge asked me many questions and filled in several printed forms as I answered. As a result of the interview, my family name was reduced to No. 13660. I was given several tags bearing the family number, and was then dismissed. At another desk I made the necessary arrangements to have my household property stored by the government.

On Tuesday when I returned to the Civil Control Station, I found our names posted on the board along with the family number. My family unit of two was scheduled to leave with the next to the last group at 11:30 A.M. on Friday, May 1, 1942. Our destination was Tanforan Assembly Center, which was at the Tanforan Race Track in San Bruno, a few miles south of San Francisco.

We had three days and three nights to pack and get ready. My brother was excused from the University with a promise that he would receive his B.A. degree in June.

Our friends came to cheer us up and to wish us luck. It was like old home week but we were exhausted from work and worry. On the last morning the main part of the packing was finished but there was still plenty to be done. I asked different friends to take care of some of my cherished possessions. In the last hour I dashed to the bank to get some money, picked up my laundry, and paid my household bills.

[At Tanforan, a] guide left us at the door of Stall 50. We walked in and dropped our things inside the entrance. The place was in semidarkness; light barely came through the dirty window on either side of the entrance. A swinging half-door divided the 20 by 9 ft. stall into two rooms. The roof sloped down from a height of twelve feet in the rear room to seven feet in the front room; below the rafters an open space extended the full length of the stable. The rear room had housed the horse and the front room the fodder. Both rooms showed signs of a hurried whitewashing. Spider webs, horse hair, and hay had been whitewashed with the walls. Huge spikes and nails stuck out all over the walls. A two-inch layer of dust covered the floor, but on removing it we discovered that linoleum the color of redwood had been placed over the rough manure-covered boards.

44. The Director of Relocation Addresses Internment

When he was tapped to head up the internment camps in June 1942, Dillon S. Myer had been a longtime federal and civil service employee. In this fascinating essay, published in a well-known civil rights journal, Myer did not exactly attempt to justify internment. Instead, he tried to show how democratic principles might be preserved in the internment program, suggesting that the internment process was a referendum on the American commitment to democratic ideals. If he believed that internment of Japanese Americans was an indictment of the nation's democratic claims, he wished that the careful way in which the program was run might mitigate the worst of the offenses. In many ways, as this essay makes clear, Myer wished the internment camps to be miniature versions of small-town American life. While this might be partly true — internees worked hard to maintain some semblance of normal routine — the fact was that they spent each day behind barbed wire. How would you characterize Myer's view of internment? How did Myer attempt to envision democracy within internment? How might Monica Sone or Miné Okubo react to his views? What do you think motivated Myer to write this essay? Could democracy exist within internment?

Dillon S. Myer
"Democracy in Relocation"
1943

The greatest involuntary migration in the history of the United States has been completed. Within the space of a few months, some 110,000 men, women, and children of Japanese ancestry, about two-thirds of them American citizens, have been moved from their homes in the western portions of the country. After temporary residence in assembly centers, they now are living in ten relocation centers between the Mississippi River and the high Sierras.

This mass evacuation shatters all precedent so far as this nation is concerned.

But evacuation was a step which seemed necessary to help insure the safety of our western shore against an enemy who looked like these people and who had taken advantage of the situation to infiltrate the Japanese population of our West Coast with his agents. Even the people of Japanese ancestry who were loyal to the United States could not always detect the enemy agents in their midst. . . .

The exclusion order, which called for all persons of Japanese ancestry to leave the western portions of Washington, Oregon, California, and the southern

Common Ground 3.2 (Winter 1943): 43–48.

part of Arizona (later all of California was included in the area to be evacuated), was issued on March second of this year. The evacuated persons might leave when they liked and go to any place outside the area to be evacuated. As might have been anticipated, they were slow to move. Most of the Japanese and their American-born children and grandchildren always had lived in the coastal states and were at a loss to know where to go. It took time to make arrangements for disposing of businesses, farms, and homes. Many made no effort to move. So it became apparent that voluntary evacuation within a short period of time was doomed to failure, not only because of reluctance to go but because the movement of more than 100,000 people into new communities was bound to cause trouble. . . .

On March 29, just twenty-seven days after evacuation was begun, voluntary evacuation was halted, and planned and systematic evacuation began. Area by area, evacuees left their homes when they were ordered by authorities to do so. Temporary quarters were provided hurriedly by the military, while a search was made for other places where evacuees might live and work until such time as they might be reabsorbed into society. The temporary quarters, provided by the Wartime Civil Control Administration, were called assembly centers, fourteen in number, all located in the area to be evacuated. In a few weeks 10 other sites were chosen for relocation centers into which the evacuated persons would be moved as soon as accommodations could be provided. These are in eastern California, Arizona, Utah, Idaho, Wyoming, Colorado, and Arkansas, for the most part on publicly owned land which has possibilities of development for agriculture and other enterprises.

The War Relocation Authority has responsibility for the welfare of the evacuees after they have been removed from the assembly centers to these relocation centers. This is a responsibility not to be taken lightly, for on the conduct of the relocation program as a whole rest the future attitudes of some 110,000 persons, including about 70,000 American citizens.

If the evacuees are permitted to live in a manner as nearly normal as possible, with responsibility for the management of the communities in which they live, with educational opportunities, with a chance to develop initiative, and with reason to look forward to a better day, then there is a probability that they may be retained as contributing members of a democratic society.

II

. . . In certain respects, life in relocation centers is not unlike life in any other community. In other respects, for reasons of economy and efficiency of administration and because of the temporary nature of the centers, conditions are necessarily different.

Housing is on the pattern of Army "Theatre of Operations" type of construction: barrack-type buildings, 100 feet long by 20 feet wide, usually divided into four compartments, 20 by 25 feet. Some of the single men live in barracks without the compartment divisions. The buildings are arranged in blocks, with a dining hall, bath house, and recreation hall to each block, to serve the needs of 275 to 300 people. The feeding problem, purchasing, distribution, and preparation of food is handled much like Army mess. Everyone eats in dining halls, and the menus are planned as a compromise between the tastes of the aliens, who have a preference for Oriental dishes, and their American-born children and grandchildren who prefer American-type foods. Families live together, but it is not feasible at present to provide for individual family feeding.

Almost all the families, of course, had household goods. Put in storage at government expense at the time of evacuation, it is now being sent to the owners at relocation centers as rapidly as possible, so that each family may have its own furniture.

Clothing is provided within certain maximum limits. It is up to each family to determine what clothing will be bought within the limits of the allowance.

The community stores are to be operated as co-operative enterprises, by an association to which any evacuee resident of the community may belong. The co-operative association chooses its own officers who determine what kinds of shops, stores, and other enterprises will be undertaken, and how the profits will be distributed, in accordance with the laws of the state in which it is incorporated. The staff of the War Relocation Authority audits the books at intervals, but the management is entirely in the hands of the evacuees themselves, and of course there is an abundance of merchandising experience and skills upon which they may draw. In most centers, whose population ranges from 7,000 to 18,000, the co-operative association elects to establish one or more "general stores" which sell soft drinks, ice cream, usually a few items of groceries, clothing, shoes, tobacco, candy, toilet articles, and other items not supplied to the evacuees by the administration of the center, and a shoe repair shop, barber shop, and beauty parlor. A newspaper is also a standard enterprise to meet the needs of the community.

The newspaper stands as one of the notable evidences of democracy in the center. Once the paper has been established as a community enterprise under evacuee management and control, the editorial staff has complete freedom of expression except for the restrictions against libel and personal attack which limit the activities of the press anywhere.

Organizations of many kinds are permitted. Since the Issei, or Japanese-born people, usually do not speak English well, their meetings are held in the Japanese tongue, if they desire.

There is freedom of worship. Services are conducted regularly by members of Buddhist, Catholic, and most of the Protestant faiths. Many of the ministers are evacuees, though Caucasian ministers come in from outside, representing their national church organizations.

In each relocation center schools have been established, with curricula which meet the standards of the state in which the center is located. The regular school system within the community covers the range from kindergarten through high school; other educational activities go beyond the usual school age limits, with day nurseries for the tiny ones, and an extensive program of adult education for persons beyond ordinary school age. Evacuee teachers are used to the fullest available extent, but approximately two-thirds of the teachers are Caucasians. The one major respect in which the curriculum in a relocation center school varies from other schools in the state is that more opportunity is provided for vocational education. The work activities provide laboratories for youngsters, particularly in high school, so they may obtain more than the usual amount of supervised experience in agriculture, carpentry, sewing, and other vocational activities.

The extent to which democracy is practiced in the relocation centers is represented best, perhaps, by the community government. While the administrative staff of necessity must have responsibility for such things as food, housing, employment, and agricultural production, the supervision of life in the community is left largely up to the evacuees themselves. The legislative body is a Council, with representatives chosen from each block. All residents of the center eighteen years of age and above may vote, but only American citizens twenty-one and older may hold elective office. Anyone of voting age, however, may serve on committees or in appointive positions.

The regulations and laws of the community are established by the Community Council, and the "court" is a Judicial Commission, usually consisting of three persons, which sits in judgment on cases of violation of the community laws. Major offenses, such as felonies, are turned over to officials and courts outside.

Each relocation center has its own fire department and its own police, or "wardens" as the evacuees prefer to call them. The wardens are not armed, and their job for the most part is one of helping, rather than restricting, the residents of the community.

III

With the nation fighting for its life and needing the productive effort of every man and woman, it is unthinkable that the available manpower in the relocation centers should not be employed in productive effort of some kind. True, the Geneva Convention, governing treatment of enemy aliens, prevents the use of citizens of Japan in direct war work, but there are other ways in which their skills may be used. A fundamental objective of the administration of the relocation centers is to see that work opportunities are provided for everyone. During the early days of each center, this was rather difficult, but as time passes, more and more things are developed which mean jobs for more people.

One of the basic considerations in selecting sites for the relocation centers was the possibility of agricultural production. In some instances, part of the available land already was in production; other land had to be cleared, or leveled; water had to be brought onto the land, or drained off. But with potentially productive soil, and with about half the population composed of farm people, agriculture is one of the great possibilities. About 2,700 acres of crops were planted and harvested in 1942 and several hundred acres of winter vegetables now are growing. Before the close of the production season in 1943, it seems likely that the relocation centers will produce all their own vegetables, all their eggs and poultry, and about half their meat requirements, largely in the form of pork and pork products. This, of course, will help reduce the public expense of operating the relocation centers. In addition to subsistence production, there are some agricultural commodities which can be produced to meet the needs of the nation as a whole: one of the centers is in the heart of the long-staple cotton area of Arizona; others are well suited to the production of sugar beet seed and vegetable seed, and some of the evacuated farmers are skilled in seed production.

Opportunities for the establishment of industries in which evacuees may work are being explored, and hold considerable promise. It is planned to establish some types of industries to manufacture goods needed by the evacuees themselves. Clothing and school furniture are two things which appear to be likely objects of manufacture at the present time. Early in the evacuation program, American citizens among the evacuees went to work weaving colored burlap into nets, to make camouflage screens for the Army. The long lists of materials needed by the Army and the Navy suggest other items which might be manufactured in relocation centers.

As this is written, one manufacturer who has a war contract is breaking ground for a factory building at one of the relocation centers. At first, about 120 evacuees will be employed and trained in a trade completely new to all of them. If the experiment is successful, the factory may be expanded to employ several times as many persons.

All evacuees at relocation centers are provided with food, lodging, and medical care. In addition, those who perform services for the community as a whole, such as the cooks, stenographers, farm workers, truck drivers, and timekeepers, receive nominal wages, or "cash advances" from the War Relocation Authority and clothing allowances for themselves and their dependents. The cash advances are $12 for beginning workers, $16 monthly for the majority of the workers, and $19 monthly for those performing difficult, responsible, or professional tasks.

Those employed in enterprises run by the co-operative association receive wages and clothing allowances on the same scale, paid out of funds of the co-operative association. However, industries under private management established at or near the relocation centers to employ evacuee workers will pay the wages prevailing in the industry. Workers in these industries will reimburse the administration for the cost of subsistence for themselves and their families. It will be left to the evacuee community to determine whether those workers will keep all the remaining money, or whether everything above $16 or $19 monthly will be put into a general fund to be divided among all workers, those employed in community services as well as those who earn the higher wages. Thus far, there has been no opportunity for an evacuee community to cast a vote on the matter, but the first decision of this sort will be watched with a great deal of interest.

During the summer months, there was a serious shortage of labor in many parts of the country, and sugar beet growers asked that groups of evacuees be permitted to leave the assembly and relocation centers to care for the growing beet crop. About 1,700 workers left the centers to work in the sugar beet fields. The locations in which they worked all were outside the evacuated area and, within limits, they traveled, lived, and worked without guard, just as any other group might have done. About 1,200 stayed outside the centers through the harvest season. When harvest time for sugar beets came, the demand for labor was even greater, and several thousand were permitted to leave the centers for this work. At the close of the season, they will return to the relocation centers. Several hundred other evacuees picked long-staple cotton in Arizona, living in the relocation center and going to and from the cotton fields daily. The total employment of evacuees in the harvesting of farm crops at this writing is over 7,600.

Before the workers went out of the centers to the sugar beet fields, there were certain conditions which had to be met: the employer agreed to provide satisfactory housing; and an official of the state or county agreed to be responsible for law and order. There were no serious incidents of any kind, and the workers met with the general approbation of their employers.

The success of this large-scale experiment suggests that as the supply of manpower in the nation grows smaller and the demand grows stronger, employers of many different kinds may request that persons now living in relocation centers be permitted to leave to take jobs. If that should become the case, the policies of the War Relocation Authority will permit such employment of individuals or groups. The evacuees now living in the relocation centers may leave the centers if certain conditions prevail: (a) if they have a definite place to go and means of support, outside of designated military areas; (b) if they agree to report any change of address; (c) if there is reasonable assurance of their acceptability in the community where they plan to go; and (d) if nothing in their records with official investigative agencies indicates they would constitute a danger to the security of the nation. The great majority of the 110,000 residents of the relocation centers will be able to meet these requirements, and so will be available for employment if needed and desired.

The success of this permanent, dispersed phase of relocation will be dependent on the sentiment of the public in general, and the sentiment of the evacuees. If evacuated persons will be accepted by the public, and if the evacuees themselves are willing to try to establish themselves in communities outside the relocation centers, then genuine progress can be made in permanent relocation. The principles underlying public acceptance of the evacuees as individuals would seem to be closely allied to the things we are fighting for.

Suggestions for Further Reading

Crost, Lyn. *Honor by Fire: Japanese Americans at War in Europe and the Pacific.* Novato, Cal.: Presidio Press, 1994.

Houston, Jeanne Wakatsuki. *Farewell to Manzanar: A True Story of Japanese American Experience During and After World War II Internment.* New York: Bantam Books, 1995.

Johnson, Marilynn S. *The Second Gold Rush: Oakland and the East Bay in World War II.* Berkeley: University of California Press, 1993.

Lotchin, Roger. *Fortress California, 1910–1961: From Warfare to Welfare.* New York: Oxford University Press, 1992.

Nash, Gerald. *The American West Transformed: The Impact of the Second World War.* Lincoln: University of Nebraska Press, 1990.

Taylor, Sandra C. *Jewel in the Desert: Japanese American Internment at Topaz.* Berkeley: University of California Press, 1993.

The View from Within: Japanese American Art from the Internment Camps, 1942–1945. Los Angeles and Seattle: Japanese American National Museum and the University of Washington Press, 1994.

Observing an Atomic Blast, 1958

This photograph shows reporters on "News Knob," where the press gathered to cover experiments at the Nevada desert proving grounds. Ten miles away, a mushroom cloud forms over ground zero. The intimate contact with atomic explosions illustrated here was not uncommon in the 1950s West: soldiers, journalists, government officials, and even local residents often joined scientists at test sites to observe atomic "bursts." Many eyewitnesses described the explosion and the resulting cloud as beautiful. How do you think the American public of the late 1950s reacted to images like this? How might that reaction compare to those of Americans today?

CORBIS/Bettmann.

CHAPTER ELEVEN

THE COLD WAR

THE NUCLEAR WEST

T he Cold War helped create the modern American West. The nation's weapons industry grew rapidly as a result of heightening tension between the United States and the Soviet Union after World War II. In 1953, the United States exploded its first hydrogen bomb, thus upping the ante in the arms race. When the Soviet Union launched Sputnik, the world's first satellite, in the fall of 1957, America responded by supporting what President Dwight D. Eisenhower would call the "military-industrial complex." During the 1950s and 1960s, this arms buildup contributed to the speedy expansion of western cities, infused with federal dollars, federal workers, and wartime veterans wanting to start life anew in the Sun Belt. Across the West, cities such as Los Angeles, Denver, Tucson, Colorado Springs, Albuquerque, and Seattle all benefited from the strong postwar economy and increased defense spending.

Despite this economic growth, the Cold War cast a shadow over the West, and the rest of the nation, during these years. The antagonism between the United States and the Soviet Union provoked widespread fear of nuclear attack. The government felt compelled to respond to make the nation feel more secure. Schoolchildren participated in civil defense drills during which they were instructed to drop to the ground and seek shelter under their desks. Families in the West and across the nation were told they could survive a nuclear attack in well-stocked homemade backyard bomb shelters. These and other similar exercises may seem naive today, but they show that the fear of nuclear war touched everyone.

The coming of the Cold War transformed the American West into an environmental guinea pig for a new form of partnership between science and warfare. Atomic weapons were tested there, both above and below ground, throughout the 1950s and 1960s, and it is still not clear how extensive the long-term damages to the environment or to the human population might be. No one really knew the effects of living in proximity to atomic explosions — or, if they did, they weren't telling. Even after the bombing of Hiroshima and Nagasaki, testing continued.

President Harry Truman ordered the establishment of a permanent testing site north of Las Vegas called the Nevada Test Site. There, government scientists developed newer, more powerful hydrogen bombs, and the Atomic Energy Commission, working with the U.S. military, tested them. Throughout the 1950s and early 1960s, at the height of the Cold War, the United States performed over one thousand atomic bomb tests at this site. Soldiers were ordered to watch the atomic and hydrogen bomb detonations and to engage in mock atomic warfare battles. Entire imitation villages, called "doom towns," were constructed in the Nevada desert and populated with mannequins so scientists could examine the potential effects of nuclear war. Journalists, answering a public need for more information, flocked to the site to write stories about these new weapons of mass destruction.

People living near the Nevada Test Site (later called "downwinders") grew accustomed to the frequent explosions in their own backyard. One couple recalled being startled awake by a ferocious "boom" in the early morning hours. "Oh, go back to sleep," said the wife to her husband. "It's only an atomic bomb." These people, who included small-town folks in Utah and Nevada as well as Navajo and other Native Americans in New Mexico, often had no idea these tests were harmful. No one bothered to tell them that atomic testing might be dangerous, that it might poison the land or the water or the sheep — or their own bodies.

The 1950s were a scary time for many Americans. The documents brought together in this chapter help us understand the level of fear and the ways in which Americans still went about trying to live normal lives in the shadow of "the bomb." An eyewitness account of an atomic test reveals the era's sheer excitement, if naiveté, over nuclear technology. Next, civil defense instructions and pronouncements demonstrate Cold War realities in everyday life in places like North Dakota. Finally, a newsmagazine story about Nevada's testing ground reveals the strange life of people living near the "Earth's most A-bombed area."

AS YOU READ, think about what it was like to live in the Cold War West. How does the description of the observer at the Nevada Test Site compare with the description of the lives of nearby residents? Which civil defense cautions strike you as dated or naive? How does the eyewitness account of the nuclear blast compare with the warnings in civil defense manuals?

---

45. WITNESSING AN ATOMIC TEST

This eyewitness report was prepared by Frank P. Zeidler, the mayor of Milwaukee. Along with Atomic Energy Commission officials, Department of Defense employees, and others, he watched an atomic test in the spring of 1952 at the Nevada Test

Site, *a federal facility outside Las Vegas that became the nation's major atomic test-*
ing site for more than a decade. In his account, Zeidler describes the use of troops
in the exercise: the soldiers not only watched the blast, they were ordered into mock
battle shortly after the bomb was detonated. Only in recent years, with the release
of formerly secret Atomic Energy Commission documents, has the full extent of
radiation testing on individuals during the 1940s and 1950s come to light. What
does this eyewitness account suggest about the era's faith in science? Why do you
think the mayor of a city like Milwaukee would make the journey to Nevada to wit-
ness this test?

FRANK P. ZEIDLER
"Observer's Report of Atomic Test"
1952

Proving Grounds.   . . . For a city dweller accustomed to narrowly constricted
views, it is important to remember the large distances of the proving grounds.
When one sees the floor of a desert ten miles across boiling from the force of a
single burst, it becomes easier to translate this effect on a center of population.

An elaborate system of security is maintained. Forty-two miles from Las Vegas
is Indian Springs Air Force Base which gives the air support to atomic experiments; 17 miles farther is Camp Desert Rock, the army support base; and 3 miles
up a special road is Mercury, Nevada, a construction camp where construction
companies engaged in numerous works for the Atomic Energy Commission have
their field offices. Nineteen miles farther are the main control buildings for
Frenchmen Flat and Yucca Flat experiments. It is here, near these two flats, that
observations are made. . . .

Inspection Tour.   On April 20th, a caravan of invitees inspected Indian
Springs Air Force Base, Camp Desert Rock, and the proving grounds.

At Indian Springs, Brigadier General John Mills described the support work
of his planes including transport devices, atomic cloud gathering devices, atomic
cloud tracing planes, "drop" planes and helicopter services.

At Camp Desert Rock, General Stork described the use of soldiers in this exercise. The bomb was to be dropped from an airplane on a target, theoretically
an enemy strong point, surrounded by two hills, back of which were masses of
material.

Troops would advance from the front and cross ground zero to take the objective while the airborne troops would drop at the rear of the objective and cross
to the front to join forces.

Frank P. Zeidler, "Observer's Report of Atomic Test at Nevada Proving Ground, April 2, 1952," type-
script (Milwaukee, Wisc.: Milwaukee Public Library).

From Camp Desert Rock, the inspection party proceeded to Mercury, Nevada, construction camp for a respite. Upon another security check, the caravan then drove past Frenchmen Flat to the main observation point of A.E.C.[1]

At this point, the party was shown a broad view across the desert to the approximate location of ground zero in Yucca Flat which lay below at a much lower elevation. The party also got a brief review of the control room with its intricate timing devices and recording devices.

Some of the staff described the location. Many of the staff members were young persons in their early twenties and thirties. These are among the "atomic scientists." I was told by Gordon Dean, head of the Atomic Energy Commission, that the average age of persons at the Los Alamos project was 33 years. These young persons with their ingenuity and powers of reasoning, invented and designed many of the devices to create the ultimate effects of a massive explosion of nuclear energy.

From the control house, the inspection party was taken to Yucca Flat where it saw certain installations. These included two towers for further explosions, one bunker for housing recording devices one-half mile from one of the towers, and other installations which were not identified. . . .

Beneath the towers where future explosions were to take place were instruments and cables to collect data and to transmit it in millionths of a second before the instruments themselves were vaporized.

The bunkers were of massive construction with lead doors, baffled entrances, thick concrete walls and roofs, mounded with earth. Whether such a shelter could withstand a direct burst overhead of say 2000 feet, I do not know.

The inspection party was then taken to the point where it was expected to observe the burst, 10 miles or 11 miles on a large rock outcropping in the desert near the main A.E.C. observation point.

After inspecting the site, the party returned to Las Vegas.

The effect of this inspection tour was to tend to ease uncertainties about hazards which might be encountered in the actual test.

Second Briefing. On Monday, April 21st, before the test the group was briefed both in the morning and afternoon. Speakers included Gordon Dean of the Atomic Energy Commission who pointed out that the explosion was the largest anticipated for continental United States. Dean stressed the necessity of carrying out these experiments because of the tremendous growth in the nature and diversity of present weapons.

Governor Millard Caldwell, Director of Federal Civil Defense Administration, pointed out the vital nature of this program for civil defense and the millions of lives that would be lost if atomic warfare started. He cited statistics showing the enlargement of civil defense functions in Europe and Russia and the actual construction of shelters in Scandinavian countries. . . .

---

[1]**A.E.C.**: The United States Atomic Energy Commission.

Burst Day.　Photographers left Las Vegas on April 22, 1952, at 4:00 A.M. The main party followed at 5 A.M. A general tension gripped everyone, even those with extensive front line experience in World War II and Korea.

Just before reaching Camp Desert Rock, the troops who were to participate in the exercise pulled out in convoy and proceeded ahead. At the main observation point the troops proceeded in their trucks to the trenches about six miles ahead of the main party of observers on the rocky outledge called "News Knob."

It had been announced in the briefing that the bomb drop would occur at 9:30 A.M. on April 22nd if the weather permitted, and if the wind was blowing right. The forecast made the night before indicated the program would proceed.

Announcements from the loud speakers kept the observers posted. A half million dollars worth of cameras and radio and television equipment had been assembled. A TV expert named Klaus Landsberg made television possible by finding an unnamed peak near Charleston Peak from which he could transmit a beam to another peak in California and then by various stages to Los Angeles.

Observers were given "4.1" goggles to allow them to look at the burst which was a hundred times brighter than that of the bright desert sun. The sun through these goggles appeared merely as a glowing orb.

H hour–2 was announced. At about H–1 the drop plane from Kirtland, New Mexico airbase appeared. High above, the observers saw vapor trails of the various planes. At H–1 a ton of high explosive was detonated to get blast characteristics and other data.

H hour–30 minutes and H hour–15 minutes were announced. Repeated warnings were given not to look at burst except through goggles, not to take goggles off until after the count of three, not to look at burst through binoculars and to brace oneself for any massive shock.

It was announced that the bomb would be dropped from a height near 33,000 feet to explode at a height of between 3,000 to 3,500 feet. The bomb would drop in 42 seconds. A great tenseness held the audience.

The minutes were counted. At H–1 goggles were put on. An announcement was made that the bomb was away. The seconds were counted and the explosion occurred with a few seconds of scheduled time within 200 feet of ground zero.

The Explosion.　An indescribably brilliant flash occurred. Those without glasses who turned away saw the desert become blinding with light. After a few seconds goggles were removed, and an expanding ball of fire, turning over and over was seen. The ball rose rapidly and turned to pink and white and other colors.

Almost simultaneously with the burst came the blast of heat. Many seconds later came a hard crack of the burst followed by the blast wave.

The ground boiled with dust for miles across the desert.

So many phenomena occurred in so short a time that no one could see all of them. Some persons observing the rising ball, missed the stem of the mushroom, enormous as it is, until completely formed. Others failed to see the boiling dust. Still others failed to see the changes going on in the cap of the mushroom itself.

People were gripped by the awe of the tremendous spectacle, fascinated by a sort of hypnotism. Constant exclamations were heard that "This is the most beautiful thing I have ever seen." The colors are not readily described since they range through the spectrum.

Some persons, including myself, heard two distinct bursts, although others heard only the one. The blast wave itself was not as strong as anticipated since it was not focussed where the observers were.

No one, who has not seen this phenomenon, can appreciate its beauty and its horrifying power.

Military Exercise.   Planes circled the atomic cloud at a respectful distance. After some time a helicopter went into the dust cloud and came out. Far away on the desert, trucks to convey troops started to move to ground zero. Planes flew in and out of the area on tests. Finally paratroopers, picked up by planes on the far end of Yucca Flat, flew to the site and the paratroopers jumped.

After about an hour, a commanding general of the 6th Army flew into the dust zone to talk to the men in the trenches and shortly after three men, a captain, a sergeant, and a private, were flown out of the area in a helicopter to describe what the first radiological team did in the area.

The captain was a school teacher, called up as a reservist; one of the privates was a Ph.D. in nuclear physics. The men described their apprehension at the announcement that the bomb was dropped. They were ordered to crouch in their trenches and look down. After the burst, a loud speaker system ordered them to look up and see the ball of fire. The ball, however, was quickly obscured by the dust wave and blast which slapped them back against the trench and then forward.

The men were four miles from the burst. Fires were burning at what I judged to be two and one-half miles away from the burst. After twenty minutes, the men came out of the trenches. After an hour they walked to their objective which took another hour. The dust however had not completely settled at the time the main party left three hours later.

Observations on the Bomb.   Discussion between observers and officials of the Army and the Atomic Energy Commission brought out interesting effects.

1. The bomb itself was close to the largest, if not the largest exploded in the United States. Data taken will later reveal what rank this explosion holds.

2. The flash was seen 400 miles away in Idaho on the ground. The blast was felt at St. George, Utah, 120 miles away, although observers close at hand said the blast effect was somewhat disappointing. However, this probably was due to focusing of blast waves.

3. There have been larger balls of fire than in this blast.

4. The bomb was bigger than the Hiroshima, Nagasaki, and Bikini bombs, but much larger ones have been exploded at Eniwetok. I guess that this bomb might be described as a "$1\frac{1}{2}$x" or 30,000 kiloton bomb.

5. Fires were started by bomb. Several shacks burnt, and troops reported fire damage $2\frac{1}{2}$ miles out.

6. The same target was used 6 times before.

7. Troops could have gone into ground zero much sooner than they did.

8. The radioactive cloud dispersed after several hours and by six o'clock P.M. search planes could not find it.

9. AEC personnel went into ground zero and found only $\frac{1}{10}$ roentgens[2] per hour. Since 3 roentgens per hour are permissible for a time, the area was considered safe for a man to stay for about 30 hours.

10. Atomic clouds did go higher than this one.

11. Army observers said trenches fairly close up were destroyed if not well revetted. Sandbags were burnt or scorched. Bunkers of army type probably would have been squashed flat.

12. The atomic bomb is not yet considered an artillery weapon.

13. Anesthetized pigs and conscious mice were in the zone. . . .

14. Soldiers were apprehensive at the distance of 4 miles. The psychological effect of the bomb is going to be studied. Practically all observers were impressed by the beauty of the spectacle and those close up expressed a desire to see it again. . . .

[2] **roentgens:** A unit of radiation measurement.

46. CIVIL DEFENSE IN THE NUCLEAR AGE

This excerpt from a booklet prepared by the North Dakota Civil Defense Agency discusses how to respond to the threat of nuclear attack. During the 1950s and 1960s, across the West and the nation as a whole, civil defense operations published literature instructing Americans on what to do in case of nuclear war. This booklet may seem naive or silly to us today, but the outdated ideas and instructions should not obscure people's real fear of a possible attack. What aspects of this booklet strike you as particularly dated? What specific fears does it address? Do you think this civil defense information would have allayed the anxieties of North Dakotans?

NORTH DAKOTA CIVIL DEFENSE AGENCY
"How You Will Survive"
c. 1960

Yes, We Can Be Attacked

Long range jet bombers are presently in the hands of many nations, friendly and hostile. The intercontinental missile that can be sent almost anywhere in the

North Dakota Civil Defense Agency, *The North Dakota Plan: How You Will Survive* (Bismarck, N.D., c. 1960).

world is being rapidly developed. Both the jet bombers and the missiles will be able to bring deadly weapons down on the United States. Military planners admit that even the best defense system will not be able to stop all enemy planes or missiles.

The weapon most likely to be used in an all out war is the hydrogen bomb which now has 1000 times the explosive force of the atomic bombs dropped on Japan in World War II. The North Dakota Survival Plan anticipates the use of bacteriological and chemical mixtures to further cripple the nation.

Heat.   Since the hydrogen bomb is expected to be the most dangerous weapon, we must know what this bomb can do. Its explosion will generate heat that comes close to that actually on the sun. With an expected temperature of several million degrees Fahrenheit at the point of the blast, the heat will melt metal and destroy all life within the immediate area.

Blast.   The concussion created by the explosion will turn skyscrapers into shambles. Humans or animals caught in the immediate area will die from rupture of lungs and blood vessels due to the sudden changes in pressure.

Radioactivity.   The explosion of a hydrogen bomb will create deadly rays which can pass through flesh and destroy it. The radiation intensity from residual fallout will be so great near the target area that people won't be able to live there for days, weeks, months, and possibly years. As the bomb bursts, it will throw radioactive particles into the air where the winds will pick them up and spread them throughout the country. As a result, the effects of hydrogen warfare can reach several hundred miles from the target.

Targets.   North Dakota is presumed to have four possible targets which the enemy may strike. They are the air force bases at Minot and Grand Forks, Hector Airport at Fargo and the State Capitol in Bismarck.

The largest hydrogen bomb presently anticipated in our plans is equal to 20 million tons of TNT. This would create damage 20 miles from the point of explosion, creating a damage area 40 miles across. Destruction would be absolute at the burst site but would gradually diminish outward.

What Will Happen

Four Major Cities May Be Destroyed
Communications Will Be Gone
Evacuation of Endangered Areas
Radioactivity Will Be a Hazard
Government Will Have to Be Reorganized
Volunteers Will Be Needed
Families Will Be Separated
Economy Must Be Rebuilt
Everyone Must Plan for Survival

The Plan of Defense

Interception.   The major portion of the American defense system is military. This includes the mobilization of the armed forces for repelling an attack and proceeding to defeat the enemy. We can expect rapid interception of enemy planes but even the best of the military planners concede that some enemy planes are bound to get through.

Warning.   As soon as enemy planes are sighted or enemy action is definite, the national warning point at Colorado Springs, Colorado will relay the warning to four points in North Dakota. All four points are the police station at Bismarck, Minot, Fargo and Grand Forks where there is a 24-hour watch.

Warning Point.   As soon as the warning point receives the alert, it will send the alert to the entire State Civil Defense organization through the police radio system. On this system are the highway patrolmen, the state game wardens, all sheriffs and city police departments. The state points as well as the local points will immediately warn the Civil Defense organizations, the governing officials and civilians.

You Will Be Alerted!   Every city and county will have a warning system to reach the public, according to the North Dakota Survival Plan. The system must be finely developed in the four target areas as evacuation or shelter are the only practical defenses against hydrogen weapons. Alert systems are necessary outside of the target areas since radioactivity may endanger lives and the Civil Defense forces must be mobilized to help meet the demands for housing and supplies. In target areas, a steady siren blast will mean evacuate; a wailing sound will mean to take cover. Battery radios will be important for receiving the official Civil Defense broadcasts on CONELRAD, which will be on 1240 and 640 only.

Evacuation

Government.   One of the most critical responsibilities during an attack is the preservation of our government — and law and order. Since we know that destruction of democracy is one of the objectives of communism, we can be assured that they shall seek to destroy our organized society. All officials of government in each target area must evacuate as a group and re-establish themselves at a new site.

Civil Defense.   Local Civil Defense organizations will have the responsibility of supervising the evacuation of equipment and supplies from the target areas. This will include rescue trucks, fire trucks, radio equipment, foodstuffs, heavy equipment and a mass of usable items that will be needed for recovery.

Civilians.   The people must be prepared to leave the target areas as well as stand by for possible movement out of fallout patterns. Civilians must take all supplies possible so they can maintain themselves until they can be taken care of outside of the target areas.

You Must Follow Traffic

We can expect congested traffic in a full-scale evacuation of the target areas. Everyone must be prepared to follow the emergency traffic rules:

1. Know your evacuation plan. Each city has one.
2. Outbound highways will be for one direction only — OUT.
3. Follow directions given by police and auxiliary police.
4. Do not try to travel into a possible target area when an alert has been given.

You Will Be Assigned Shelter

Evacuees coming from the target areas will be cared for in the outlying areas, with Civil Defense organizations in the "support" area being responsible for housing and feeding. In most cases, housing will be in private homes and farms. Evacuees will remain in private dwellings until the alert is over or the economy can be rebuilt.

You Must Be Self-Reliant

Provide Your Own Travel. Every family should arrange for its own travel. Vehicles should always be kept in good running condition. The tank should always be half full of gasoline. A reserve supply should be kept in the trunk for emergencies. Every family should make arrangements for travel under all circumstance[s]. In addition to providing its own transportation, families should pick up others who may be stranded.

Provide Your Own Needs for Seven Days. In the initial attack, you will be unable to depend on others. So be prepared to survive by yourself for one week.

1. Stock basic foods for immediate packing.
2. Take a good supply of fresh, clean water.
3. Take blankets and clothing for cold weather.

Shelter in Target Area. If you are caught in the target area when the "Take Cover" signal (a wailing signal on the siren) is given, you must get into the deepest possible location. Perhaps the handiest will be your house basement. Shut off all power, gas and water lines leading into your house.

Shelter Yourself from Fallout. Once in the reception area, your main concern will be radiation from fallout. Fallout is the radioactive particles falling from the sky which can be fatal if you are exposed over [a] period of time. Fallout will be carried by the wind in an oval pattern away from the target. The Civil Defense organization will attempt to constantly monitor the fallout intensity so you can be alerted when it becomes critical.

Root Cellars. In the rural parts of North Dakota, farmers and residents of smaller communities have built root cellars to store foodstuff and as shelter from tornadoes. Whether constructed of concrete or sod, these root cellars are excellent protection against heavy radioactivity. The ideal covering is two or three feet of sod or concrete. Such a shelter should be equipped for living for two weeks and should have carefully controlled ventilation.

Basements and Interiors. If a root cellar is not available, the next best shelter is the home itself, and more particularly the basement, if you have one. An ordinary house without [a] basement probably would cut the radiation in half, if you stay on the first floor near the center of the house. Staying in a house basement will reduce your exposure to about $\frac{1}{10}$ the outside exposure rate. If you should elect to build a shelter in a corner of your basement, you may reduce the exposure to $\frac{1}{500}$ or more. The State Civil Defense Office in Bismarck has plans and specifications for several types of fallout shelters. These plans are designed to aid the homeowner who desires to build his own shelter at a minimum cost and graduate in scale to a more expensive shelter located underground adjacent to the home.

Shelter Supplies. Whether you evacuate or take shelter in an emergency, one of the basic necessities is an adequate food supply for your family. You should assemble a two-week food supply in your home shelter area, and a three-day evacuation survival kit in your family automobile. The North Dakota Civil Defense Office in Bismarck has a suggested list of these supplies available in pamphlet form, or you may obtain this information from your local Civil Defense Director.

Shelter Livestock. If you have livestock of any kind, you should get it under cover. A barn or cattleshed will prevent material damage to your animals. If you have no enclosed area for them, even a roof shelter will help prevent the particles from settling on their bodies. You should also get their feed under cover.

Cleaning the Contaminated. As soon as possible, the people who have been in radioactive areas must wash thoroughly in purified water to wash off any particles that may have fallen on them. Everything exposed should also be washed in clean water, such as clothing, blankets, and household goods. Radioactivity cannot be cleansed but it can be washed away with the particles emitting it. . . .

47. Conditions in Bombed Areas

This magazine article describes the sections of Nevada most affected by atomic testing, which by the time this story appeared had already been going on for several years. Many Americans had probably never heard of the places mentioned in this article. But nuclear testing and the effects of radiation were big news stories in the era. What makes this story unusual is that it put atomic testing and Cold War fears together with the grassroots interviews done with people near (sometimes very near) the test sites. In this way, people would be reminded that the Cold War was both an international and a very local phenomenon. In what ways is this account similar to or different from Frank Zeidler's eyewitness account? Are there any hints in this article about the long-term environmental costs of such testing? Does the article suggest any area of government concern about the effects of radiation?

U.S. NEWS & WORLD REPORT
"What It's Like to Live in Earth's Most A-Bombed Area"
1957

Out of sixty-eight atomic explosions set off by the United States, forty-nine have taken place at the Nevada test site near here. More A-bombs have been exploded in Nevada than in any other part of the world.

What has been the result? Are people living near the test area panicked? Have cattle in nearby ranching areas become radioactive? Is the food supply contaminated?

If anybody in the world, outside of Hiroshima and Nagasaki, should be alarmed by fall-out and other effects of bomb tests, the people in this region should be. A sampling of sentiment, however, fails to uncover general alarm — or any convincing evidence that things are much different than they were before tests began.

Margin of Safety.   Scientists making regular checks for the Atomic Energy Commission report officially that radiation has not reached danger levels anywhere in this test-site region that includes parts of Nevada, Utah and Arizona.

The maximum recorded for any one community, during the entire six-year period since nuclear tests began in Nevada, is 4.3 roentgens. . . . That compares with the AEC's recommendation that 23.4 roentgens could safely be permitted for the period.

In one freak case, near Bunkerville, Nevada, a cloud dumped an extra-heavy dose of fall-out on a motel occupied by fifteen people, who might have accumulated up to 13 roentgens if they had continued to live there. The motel has since been deserted.

And yet, here and there in this desert region surrounding the test site, you do find people wondering — and, in some cases, worrying — over possible effects of the atom tests. This is clear in soundings made throughout this three-State area by a Regional Editor of "U.S. News & World Report."

Local Events.   Several local happenings in recent years are blamed by some people on fall-out or bomb shock. For example, there are the cases of Mrs. Gerald Sharp, of Nyala, Nevada, 80 miles north of the test area, and Dewey A. Hortt, of Mesquite, 110 miles to the west. Both have lost all the hair on their heads.

Martin Bardoli, a seven-year-old, has died of leukemia, as has Robert Howe, four and a half. Some cattle belonging to the Fallini Ranch, near Warm Springs, have developed "cancer eye." Sheep have died after tests, as have ducks and chickens in their eggs.

The people affected admit that all this is nothing new, nor is it limited to the area surrounding the major tests. Hereford cattle had "cancer eye" long before the atomic age began. People in other places, at other times, have died of leukemia or suddenly lost their hair.

Another man admits that "the thing is you don't know, so you begin to wonder, when you have aches and pains, if the tests could be to blame." Dr. D. D. Carr, Clark County's health director, explains, "There's a psychological effect on people to find reasons for what they have."

Claims for Damage. The AEC investigates all claims made against it. These claims for alleged damage, injury or illness caused by nuclear tests have reached a total of 640 since 1951. So far, payments totaling $53,624 have been made for 384 claims — for damage only, and mostly blast damage.

The AEC, in reviewing its investigations into these claims, says this:

"No claim has ever been settled on the basis of alleged biological injury to humans, although the AEC compensated the owners of some horses which were grazing very near the test site."

General Acceptance. By and large, despite claims and complaints, most people in this desert region seem to agree that living here appears to be just about as safe as living anywhere else. This feeling is summed up by J. C. Adams, a retired ranch hand at Glendale Junction, Nevada.

Mr. Adams says:

"Those AEC people are pretty accurate about how much has fallen and how much it takes to do you harm. We don't pay any attention any more."

R. L. Hickman, sales manager for the Arden Meadowgold Dairy in Cedar City, Utah, declares: "I think people are more concerned about smog in California than about fall-out in Cedar City."

Just about the only outward reminder that people here are living close to the world's main atomic test site is the badges that some of them wear, each containing a test strip of film to record exposure to fall-out.

These badges permit local AEC offices in seventeen different zones to check up regularly on the levels of radiation — in towns, on ranches and in different occupations. The badges are not compulsory for ordinary citizens, but some two thousand people wear them.

Lingering Fears. While there are no signs of general alarm over fall-out, you do find some people wondering more than others about how the unseen and largely unknown cumulative hazards of radiation might affect them.

One worry that some hold is expressed by Robert A. Crandall, editor of the *Times-Bonanza* in Tonopah, Nevada, some 100 miles north of the test site. In an editorial, Mr. Crandall puts it this way: "Tests have been delayed because of the possibility of 'light but unacceptable fall-out' over Las Vegas, says the AEC. But we're in the 'virtually uninhabited area,' so we get it."

That is denied by AEC, and refuted also by an AEC map showing the amounts of radiation recorded in various places around the test site. This shows that there is no set pattern of fall-out favoring certain areas over others. Towns lying side by side vary greatly in the amount of radiation received.

Extra Precautions.   The AEC has stepped up its safety measures for the current series of nuclear tests. Some bombs are being detonated from balloons and even underground to cut the danger of local fall-out caused by the metal used in the steel towers.

Then there is the weather to reckon with. If clouds are too low or conditions otherwise might unduly concentrate what fall-out there is in local areas, a nuclear test is postponed. So far this year, more than 80 such postponements have been caused by weather.

Local health authorities are running their own checks all the time to safeguard against food or water contamination. Marvin T. Skodje, public-health-service monitor at Mesquite, says: "There's more danger to Mesquite's water supply from natural causes than from fall-out."

Short-Lived Jitters.   Six years of living practically side by side with the A-bomb has made little change in the lives of most people. A young mother in Hurricane, Utah, shrugs and says: "It kinda gives you the jitters when it goes off, but then you forget." Most everyone seems to be agreed that it would be nice if further tests did not have to be held — but there's no sign of any public protest against them.

Instead, most people here seem to agree with Morris Dannelly, a tractor driver who works near Cedar City.

As Mr. Dannelly puts it:

"It might be dangerous — this fall-out and all — but I'd rather have us find out all about this atomic business so the Russians won't be the only ones."

What the Folks Say in "Fall-Out City"

[These remarks originally appeared in a photo essay next to each resident's picture.]

Jeter C. Snow, mayor and manager of a chain store, recalls that, during the 1955 tests, "some people came to us to see if they couldn't stop them." Uranium prospectors said the tests "messed up" the Geiger counter readings. A farmer blamed tests for the death of a new-born calf. Nowadays, however, Mayor Snow says: "I've not noticed any real concern," though "people here wish it could be some other way."

Dr. M. K. McGregor, who assists his father at the McGregor private clinic, finds that some people are inclined to put the blame on atom tests — wrongly — for all sorts of ills and mishaps. The young doctor says: "There's a lot of spotty baldness, but it's all due to anxiety — not to any fall-out I know of." He recalls hearing that one man, just back from a trip, claimed that marks on his arm were caused by fall-out. The marks turned out to be fingernail scratches. Dr. McGregor concludes: "It's important to know more about fall-out."

Mrs. Kate Empey, secretary of the town information office, once was dead set against the atom tests. Last year she visited an AEC exhibit, heard that radiation can affect the body, came back to town ready to circulate a petition to stop the tests. But she never did. She says she is still concerned with the health hazard, but "I've never felt any ill effects."

Wayne Whitehead, of Whitehead's Dairy, says: "The tests don't worry me. I think that the guys who are doing it are competent. If they weren't, they wouldn't be doing it."

Rex Frei, cattleman who helps work some thousand head on a public range, says: "I don't see how that little flash down at Vegas could affect us. I had my wife operated on for cancer and they gave her tremendous doses [of radiation] over months. She's still alive, so this can't be too bad."

Mrs. Margie Bowler, waitress and cashier at Dick's Cafe, confesses that she once had been "quite alarmed" about atom tests — but no more. She says: "We've got pretty used to the tests; this year they are pretty small. Our relations back East have asked us about living so close, but we told them we were not concerned."

Ellis Everett, instructor in physics and mathematics at Dixie College, says he knows of some people who have written to their Congressmen to try to get the tests stopped. As for him, "I take the AEC's word on how much people can stand. I'm not worried about it. Our big problem here is finding a physics teacher."

Suggestions for Further Reading

Boyer, Paul. *By the Bomb's Early Light: American Thought and Culture at the Dawn of the Atomic Age.* Chapel Hill: University of North Carolina Press, 1994.

Fernlund, Kevin, ed. *The Cold War American West, 1945–1989.* Albuquerque: University of New Mexico Press, 1998.

Fuller, John Grant. *The Day We Bombed Utah: America's Most Lethal Secret.* New York: New American Library, 1985.

Hevly, Bruce, and John Findlay, eds. *The Atomic West.* Seattle: University of Washington Press, 1998.

May, Elaine Tyler. *Homeward Bound: American Families in the Cold War Era.* New York: Basic Books, 1988.

Misrach, Richard. *Bravo 20: The Bombing of the American West.* Baltimore: Johns Hopkins University Press, 1990.

Titus, A. Constandina. *Bombs in the Backyard: Atomic Testing and American Politics.* Reno and Las Vegas: University of Nevada Press, 1986.

Szasz, Ferenc Morton. *The Day the Sun Rose Twice: The Story of the Trinity Site Nuclear Explosion, July 16, 1945.* Albuquerque: University of New Mexico Press, 1995.

United States Congress, Senate Committee on Labor and Human Resources. *Health Effects of Radiation Exposure.* Washington: Government Printing Office, 1990.

Free Speech Movement, University of California at Berkeley, c. 1965

In the autumn of 1964, officials at the Berkeley campus of the University of California banned political activity at a popular campus spot. Before long, students organized to protest the action. Banding together in what they called the Free Speech Movement, or FSM, these students helped inaugurate an era of student civil rights activism on campuses across the nation. Many of them, at Berkeley and elsewhere, had been active in the civil rights movement in the South. Returning North after working on issues such as voting rights for African Americans, they brought with them the techniques and organizing practices that they had learned in places like Mississippi. With the rise of civil rights activism across the nation in the 1960s, American students, like Berkeley's FSM participants pictured here, joined with others working toward greater civil rights for millions of Americans. How would you describe the scene pictured here? Why do you think the FSM protestors are dressed the way they are?

Bancroft Library, University of California at Berkeley.

CHAPTER TWELVE

THE 1960s

CIVIL RIGHTS AND PROTEST IN THE WEST

Although efforts toward greater civil rights and better social conditions can be traced to earlier political struggles, it was in the 1960s that the civil rights movement peaked in the West. Energized by the increasing militancy of the civil rights movement in the South in the 1950s and 1960s, westerners embarked on their own forms of activism.

As in the South, civil rights activism in the West traces its roots to previous decades. In the anti-Communist hysteria that followed World War II, many westerners took a stand defending their rights of free speech and free association. The infamous "Hollywood Ten" episode, in which the careers of screenwriters and directors working in the film industry were ruined because of their alleged Communist Party connections, is one such case. Some refused to cooperate with government committees trying to ferret out Communist screenwriters and directors and were vocal and public in their opposition. This defense of civil rights also spread to western college campuses. At the University of California, for instance, students and faculty members protested against the anti-Communist loyalty oaths that professors were required to take before they could begin a career in public education. In the spring of 1960, a small group of college students marched on San Francisco's City Hall to protest hearings held by the House Un-American Activities Committee (HUAC). Denied entrance, the students sat on the steps of City Hall and sang civil rights songs. In a surprisingly brutal response, the local police turned high-pressure water hoses on the peaceful assembly. The next day, some five thousand Bay Area students showed up to protest police tactics. This spontaneous demonstration occurred only a few months before the lunch counter sit-ins in the South protesting the segregation of public places. Although the focus was different, the West was at the forefront of civil rights activism.

By the fall of 1964, student interest in free speech and the free expression of ideas had developed into the famous Free Speech Movement at the University of California at Berkeley. The magnitude of their effort surprised the nation, and probably the students themselves, and marked the beginning of an association between western college campuses and the era's civil rights struggles.

By the 1960s the fight for civil rights for African Americans had turned to radical protest across the nation. In 1966, two young men from Oakland, California, Huey Newton and Bobby Seale, founded the militant Black Panthers. The Panthers, who carried weapons and dressed in military uniforms, espoused the violent defense of the rights of African Americans. Although this stance frightened white America, these militants expressed the concerns of many African Americans who had not joined their movement. Thousands of African Americans believed, and with good reason, that prosperity had passed them by and that they had carried much of the burden of combat in the expanding Vietnam War.

Mexican Americans, a potent political force throughout the West, also took part in the civil rights struggles of the 1960s. In earlier decades, Mexican Americans had organized politically with notable success. In the late 1940s, Mexican American Edward Roybal was elected to the Los Angeles city council. By the 1960s, Mexican Americans had tapped the radicalizing possibilities of ethnic unity. Using a single ethnic identifier — that of Chicano — people of diverse Latino descent forged a collective identity they could use to leverage power in the dominant society. Chicano activists were most evident on the college campuses and in the cities of the Southwest. At the same time, Mexican American farm workers used their political unity to rally around the civil rights efforts of César Chávez, a founder of the United Farm Workers, which organized strikes against the giant fruit and vegetable growers of the far West.

Of course, civil rights activism on behalf of minorities and others did not go unchallenged. On the contrary, the civil rights protests of the 1960s helped trigger social unrest and violence, and some of the first, and worst, of these episodes took place in the West. A tense confrontation between white police officers and community members from the largely African American neighborhood of Watts in Los Angeles erupted into several days of rioting in the summer of 1965. Similar incidents, all too common at the time, occurred in urban areas across the country following the Watts riots. As racial tensions flared into violence and destructive upheaval, the nation woke up to the tremendous challenges it faced in addressing the troubled state of race relations.

Indians in the West also continued their active campaign for greater civil rights in the 1960s: the Indian Civil Rights Act of 1968 was passed in response to Native American activism. But violence and frustration also overtook this movement. For two years starting in 1969, radical Native American activists occupied the island prison of Alcatraz in San Francisco Bay as a statement of their dissatisfaction with the state of affairs existing between the federal government and Indian tribes. This kind of dramatic activism continued into the 1970s with the takeover of Wounded Knee, South Dakota, by the American Indian Movement

(AIM) in a dramatic two-month siege that turned into a deadly confrontation with the government.

The 1960s were filled with protest and unrest among a wide cross section of Americans. The selections in this chapter touch upon some of these movements, along with their ideas and ideals. A famous speech given at the height of the Free Speech Movement provides insights into students' concern about their freedom to express their ideas. Martin Luther King's telegram in support of striking California farm workers reveals the ways in which civil rights activists in different parts of the nation sought common ground. The writer Peter Matthiessen records his impressions of César Chávez of the United Farm Workers at a critical point in the union's rise to influence. Oral histories of the Black Panthers offer insider accounts of that group's founding and operations. A document from a citizens' group in Watts shows people in that community working to protect their civil rights after the 1965 Watts riots. Finally, a manifesto from the Native American activists who seized Alcatraz justifies their actions by referring to patterns of Native American history.

As you read these selections, think of the ways in which different groups of people viewed civil rights. How did they define the civil rights they wished to gain or protect? How do the aims and goals of a group like AIM compare with those of the citizens' committee in Watts, for instance? How are the tactics of the various groups similar? Do you see connections between the history of the West and the protests that arose there in the 1960s?

---

48. Student Mobilization for Free Speech

The Free Speech Movement (FSM) proved to be a turning point for student activism in the West in the early 1960s. It galvanized student leaders who would play prominent roles in protest movements in later years; it reminded the West, and the nation, that students in places like northern California might have something important to say about civil rights; and it helped make Berkeley a national symbol for civil rights protests. In the following impromptu exhortation, graduate student Mario Savio urges his fellow students to fight for civil rights. Savio cautions his audience against the impersonal politics and institutions that he fears are gaining power over the hearts and minds of the American people. Before long, the FSM had inspired thousands of students at Berkeley. They performed acts of civil disobedience, seized a number of campus buildings, and held large rallies in support of free political expression. FSM activists infuriated the administration and may have horrified their parents, but in the end the university relented and allowed the free distribution of political literature on university property. Do you think that there are particular reasons why the Free Speech Movement began at a place like the University of California? How would you describe Savio's impression of the modern university? What words or phrases mark the speech as a product of the 1960s?

MARIO SAVIO
Address to the Free Speech Movement
1964

Well. This started out as a completely spontaneous response of students at this University against arbitrary action taken by the dean's office here against certain students who thought they had the right to free expression at this University. Well, free expression, for the University, means that you can talk about lots of things, but as we just heard in the statement from Chancellor Strong, those things you can't do are the taking of action on various ideas that you discuss. Now, I'd like to connect that, right here, very, very clearly, with statements that have been made by President Kerr in his book on the multiversity. President Kerr has referred to the University as a factory; a knowledge factory — that's his words — engaged in the knowledge industry. And just like any factory, in any industry — again his words — you have a certain product. The product is you. Well, not really you. And not really me. The products are those people who wouldn't join in our protest. They go in one side, as kind of rough-cut adolescents, and they come out the other side pretty smooth. When they enter the University, they're dependent upon their parents. That kind of dependency is the sort of thing that characterizes childhood and adolescence. When they're in school, before they enter the University, part of that dependency is shifted to the various schools that they're in. Then they come to the University. And now, instead of suckling at their mother's or at the breast of their schools, they suckle at the breast of Holy Mother University. So here they are. Now, they're dependent upon the University. They're product. And they're prepared to leave the University, to go out and become members of other organizations — various businesses, usually — and I hope I'm not offending anyone in this, but I'm speaking *my* mind — which they are then dependent upon in the same way. And never, at any point, is provision made for their taking their places as free men! Never at any point is provision made — you know, someplace in society, some things you can do which in some ways can be

David Lance Goines, *The Free Speech Movement: Coming of Age in the 1960s* (Berkeley: Ten Speed Press, 1993), 151–53.

expressive of your individuality. You just can't do that unless you have no intention of making it in this society. You can be poor and have dignity, but if you have any intention of making it in any way, you're out of it, you're just completely out of it! You've gotta be a part; part of a machine. Now, every now and then, the machine doesn't work. One of the parts breaks down. And in the case of a normal, regular machine, you throw that part out; throw it out, and you replace it. Well, this machine, this factory here, this multiversity, its parts are human beings. And, sometimes, when *they* go out of commission, they don't simply break down, but they really gum up the whole works! (*Scattered laughter.*) That's what we're all doing here. We've kind of gone out of commission. We won't operate according to the way the parts of this machine should operate, and the machine started to go out of commission. But the remedy is the same! In the case of a regular machine, in the case of *this* machine, you throw the parts out! And that's what they decided to do. That's what the statement says. They're an indefinite suspension — I presume that's close to the words he used — of those students who went out of commission; those students who weren't good enough parts, who didn't function well enough. For one brief moment, there were lots of people, lots of students, whose imaginations were fired. Maybe we would not have to likewise be parts. Maybe somehow we could take our place as free men also! So those students said, "We're with you! We stand right with you! Not behind you. We're next to you! We're brothers!" They signed that sheet! That sheet said, "We want you to treat us *all the same way.*" Now, you know it was an unreasonable demand. It was unreasonable in this regard: it's not a demand the University could have met without completely dropping any kind of disciplinary action against anyone. And they knew it! And . . . we knew it.

Well, they've decided, instead, to disregard your protest, and to assume that you had never come in here, nothing like that had happened, that instead what it is — the eight students, they refused to speak with the proper authorities, and they've been axed.

We can do various things. I suppose that's really what we want to talk about. We can do various things. We can — and this is what I would hope the group here would want to do — we can make as the issue of our continued protest three things: First, whatever action has been taken against these particular individuals singled out by the administration, this action be dropped, completely! (*Thunderous applause and cheers.*)

Are there any abstentions? (*Laughter.*)

The second thing is that we here, all of us, the committee of the whole, we demand those particular demands I read to you from that yellow sheet earlier today concerning freedom of expression on this campus. We are putting our weight behind those demands. (*Applause.*)

In particular, our protest is demanding a meeting with Chancellor Strong — none of these little guys, we're done with that. (*Laughter and applause.*) We're demanding a meeting with Chancellor Strong to discuss those demands!

Third, we demand that, at least until that meeting has taken place, if there are any groups on campus who exercise what they believe to be their rights of free expression, there will be no disciplinary action taken against them, at any time! (*Cheers and applause.*)

I presume that, from the basis of the response, in the name of all the people assembled here, and hopefully in the name of the University of California, we can make these demands public, and make them to the administration; to the chancellor. Is this something we can do? (*"Yes! Yes!" Great applause.*)

49. Support for California Farm Workers

This remarkable telegram ties together two of the nation's greatest civil rights leaders — César Chávez, a leader of Mexican Americans, and Martin Luther King Jr., the critical figure in the African American civil rights movement. Under the leadership of men like Chávez, of the National Farm Workers Association, and Larry Itliong of the Agricultural Workers Organizing Committee, field-workers went on strike in the agricultural region around the small California town of Delano. Chávez and the others were protesting the working conditions imposed upon the multiethnic migratory workforce by the area's growers; they called their struggle for greater civil rights and economic power la Causa, or the Cause. The strike lasted five years and resulted in greater recognition of union labor by the state's large agricultural growers. The Delano strike, out of which grew the United Farm Workers, helped make Chávez into a recognized leader in the civil rights efforts of poor migrant workers of the West, regardless of their race or ethnicity. In this telegram, King expresses his solidarity with Chávez and the striking Mexican, Filipino, and other workers. What does King see as common ground between the African American and Mexican American civil rights movements? Why do you think King expressed his interest and support in a civil rights struggle in the American West?

Martin Luther King Jr.
Telegram to César Chávez Regarding the Delano Strike
1965

As brothers in the fight for equality, I extend the hand of fellowship and good will and wish continuing success to you and your members. The fight for equality must be fought on many fronts — in the urban slums, in the sweat shops of the

Jacques E. Levy, *César Chávez: Autobiography of La Causa* (New York: W.W. Norton, 1975), 246.

factories and fields. Our separate struggles are really one — a struggle for freedom, for dignity, and for humanity. You and your valiant fellow workers have demonstrated your commitment to righting grievous wrongs forced upon exploited people. We are together with you in spirit and in determination that our dreams for a better tomorrow will be realized.

50. THE LEADERSHIP OF CÉSAR CHÁVEZ

The novelist Peter Matthiessen met and visited with César Chávez in the late 1960s, when Chávez had embarked on a fast as part of the continuing Delano strike that had begun in 1965. Here, Matthiessen describes Chávez the man and Chávez the labor organizer. Many of the civil rights protests of the 1960s, in the West and across the nation, were defined by the leaders they produced. For many Americans, the Mexican American civil rights movement was César Chávez. Matthiessen, a strong sympathizer with the farm worker movement and civil rights efforts in general, offers his opinions about the leadership of César Chávez. In Matthiessen's view, Chávez was at the helm of a "new American Revolution." What points about Chávez's character and leadership does Matthiessen emphasize? How might those opposed to Chávez's labor leadership interpret these traits? What aspects of Chávez's character ensured the dedication of his followers? What mistakes did Chávez think the African American civil rights movement made?

PETER MATTHIESSEN
From *Sal Si Puedes*
1969

Before leaving for California I had expected that I would be impressed by Cesar Chavez, but I had not expected to be startled. It was not the "charisma" that is often ascribed to him; most charisma is in the eye of the beholder. The people who have known him longest agree that before the strike, Chavez's presence was so nondescript that he passed unnoticed; he is as unobtrusive as a rabbit, moving quietly wherever he finds himself as if he had always belonged there. The "charisma" is something that has been acquired, an intensification of natural

Peter Matthiessen, *Sal Si Puedes: César Chávez and the New American Revolution* (New York: Random House, 1969), 171–74, 179–80.

grace which he uses, not always unconsciously, as an organizing tool, turning it on like a blowtorch as the job requires. Once somebody whom he had just enlisted expressed surprise that Chavez had spent so little time in proselytizing. "All he did for three whole days was make me laugh," the new convert said, still unaware that he'd been organized.

Since Chavez knows better than anyone else what his appeals to public sentiment have accomplished for *la causa*,[1] I had no doubt that as a writer I would be skillfully organized myself; but warmth and intelligence and courage, even in combination, did not account for what I felt at the end of the four-hour walk on that first Sunday morning.

Talking of leadership during the walk, Chavez said, "It is like taking a road over hills and down into the valley: you must stay with the people. If you go ahead too fast, then they lose sight of you and you lose sight of them." And at the church he was a man among his neighbors, kneeling among them, joining them to receive holy communion, conversing eagerly in the bright morning of the churchyard, by the white stucco wall. What welled out of him was a phenomenon much spoken of in a society afraid of its own hate, but one that I had never seen before — or not, at least, in anyone unswayed by drugs or aching youth: the simple love of man that accompanies some ultimate acceptance of oneself.

It is this love in Chavez that one sees and resists naming, because to name it is to cheapen it; not the addled love that hides self-pity but a love that does not distinguish between oneself and others, a love so clear in its intensity that it is monastic, even mystical. This intensity in Chavez has burned all his defenses away. Taking the workers' hands at church, his face was as fresh as the face of a man reborn. "These workers are really beautiful," he says, and when he says it he is beautiful himself. He is entirely with the people, open to them, one with them, and at the same time that he makes them laugh, his gaze sees beyond them to something else. "Without laying a cross on him," Jim Drake says, "Cesar is, in theological terms, as nearly 'a man for others' as you can find. In spite of all his personal problems — a very bad back, poverty, a large family — he does not allow his own life to get in the way." . . .

For most of us, to quote Dostoevsky, "to love the universal man is to despise and at times to hate the real man standing at your side." This is not true of Chavez. But he is super human, not superhuman. He acknowledges that his reactions are not entirely unaffected by the humiliations and pain of his early life, so that even his commitment to nonviolence is stronger in his head than in his heart. And like many people who are totally dedicated, he is intolerant of those who are less so. I asked him once for the names of the best volunteers no longer with the Union, and he said flatly, "The best ones are still here." I dropped the subject. As his leadership inevitably extends to the more than four million Mexican-Americans in the Southwest, Cesar will necessarily become more lonely, more cut off in a symbolic destiny. Already, sensing this, he puts great emphasis

---

[1] *la causa:* The Cause; the name Chávez and his supporters gave to their effort to obtain greater civil and economic rights for farm workers and other poor people of the Southwest.

on loyalty, as if to allay a nagging fear of being abandoned, and people who are not at the Union's disposal at almost any hour of the day or night do not stay close to him for very long. It has been said that he is suspicious of Anglos, but it would be more accurate to say that he is suspicious of everybody, in the way of people with a tendency to trust too much. He is swift and stubborn in his judgments, yet warm and confiding once he commits his faith, which he is apt to do intuitively, in a few moments. The very completeness of this trust, which makes him vulnerable, may also have made him wary of betrayal.

The closer people are to Chavez, the greater the dedication he expects. If they can't or won't perform effectively, he does their job himself ("It's a lot easier to do that than keep after them"), or if they are going about it the wrong way, he may let them persist in a mistake until failure teaches them a lesson. Some of these lessons seem more expensive to the Union than they are worth, but Chavez is determined that his people be self-sufficient — that they could, if need be, get along without him. . . .

In his speech on February 19, 1968, Chavez discussed the civil rights movement and how its recourse to violence had made black people suffer; black homes, not white, were being burned, and black sons killed. The Union, he said, had raised the hopes of many poor people; it had a responsibility to those people, whose hopes, along with all the Union gains, would be destroyed after the first cheap victories of violence. Finally, he announced the fast. It was not a hunger strike, because its purpose was not strategic; it was an act of prayer and love for the Union members because as their leader he felt responsible for their acts as individuals. There would be no vote on the fast, which would continue for an indefinite period, and had in fact begun the week before. He was not going into seclusion, and would continue his work as best he could; he asked that his hearers keep the news entirely to themselves. Since it was difficult to fast at home, and since the Forty Acres was the spiritual home of the Union, he would walk there as soon as he had finished speaking, and remain there until the fast was done. Throughout the speech Chavez quoted Gandhi and the Epistles of St. Paul. "His act was intensely personal," Leroy recalls, "and the whole theme of his speech was love. In fact, his last words to us before he left the room and started that long walk to the Forty Acres were something like 'I am doing this because I love you.'" . . .

51. THE RISE OF THE BLACK PANTHERS

The oral histories that follow recount the origins of the militant Black Panthers, the African American civil rights organization founded in Oakland, California, in the late 1960s. From Oakland, the Panthers spread outward, but their influence was

*always greater than the group's numbers would suggest until government and po-
lice crackdowns at the end of the decade crushed them. Through their aggressive organizing, public displays of guns and force, and effective propaganda, the Black
Panthers struck a particularly harsh chord in 1960s America. To many, the Panthers
seemed to symbolize everything wrong with the country: lawlessness, racial com-
bativeness, and urban struggle. To others, the Panthers represented hope, or at least
concerted action in the face of crisis in American cities. The selections here reflect
some of these hopes and fears. From these brief excerpts, how would you describe the
program of the Black Panthers? Why do you think the Panthers originated on the
Pacific Coast and not elsewhere? Do these oral histories suggest that the particular
circumstances of a place like Oakland might have contributed to the birth of the
Black Panthers?*

Various Oral Histories
1990

Huey Newton

It was in 1953, I think, that Oakland had its first black policeman, who was
a friend of my father's. His name was Kinner. My father broke friendship with
Kinner because of his membership in the Oakland police. Not because he was a
policeman, but because at the time the policy was that Kinner could only arrest
black people. He could detain a white, but he would have to call a white officer.
And my father thought that this was degrading. It was no change from what was
happening in the South.

The police, not only in the Oakland community but throughout the black
communities in the country, were really the government. We had more contact
with the police than we did the city council. The police were universally disliked.
In Oakland, in October '66, when the party was founded, there was about one
percent blacks on the police department. The police were impolite and they
were very fast to kill a black for minor offenses, such as black youth stealing automobiles. They would shoot them in the back and so forth.

Bobby Seale

In 1966, numerous acts of police brutality had sparked a lot of spontaneous
riots — something that Huey and I were against, these spontaneous riots. And
Huey and I began to try to figure out how could we organize youthful black folks
into some kind of political, electoral, *power* movement. Stokely Carmichael was
on the scene with Black Power.

Henry Hampton and Steve Fayer, *Voices of Freedom: An Oral History of the Civil Rights Movement
from the 1950s through the 1980s* (New York: Bantam Books, 1990), 351–54.

Huey and I had been involved for some time, off and on, studying black history — what Malcolm had done, where Martin Luther King came from. I was highly influenced by Martin Luther King at first and then later by Malcolm X. Largely, the Black Panther party came out of a lot of readings, Huey and I putting scrutiny to everything going on in the United States of America. Like we must have subscribed to twenty-some-odd different periodicals, offbeat periodicals like *The Liberator, Freedomways,* what have you, even some periodicals out of Africa. We had digested Frantz Fanon's *Wretched of the Earth.* We knew Lerone Bennett's *Before the Mayflower.* I knew about the two hundred and fifty slave revolts that included Gabriel Prosser and Nat Turner and Denmark Vesey. I mean, Frederick Douglass, the Nation of Islam, what had happened in the 1930s, what have you and so on. And there we were with all this knowledge about our history, our struggle against racism.

At that time, Huey and I were working with the North Oakland Neighborhood [Anti-Poverty] Center on the advisory board. We got five thousand signatures for them to go to the city council, to get the city council to try to set up a police review board to deal with complaints of police brutality. Well, the city council ignored us. So that phenomenon was that the city council was just a racist structure which could care less about the forty-eight percent black and Chicano people who lived in the city of Oakland. So there we are, trying to figure out what to do. We finally concluded through those months that we had to start a new organization.

Huey Newton

Bobby Seale and I used the North Oakland service center as the original work spot to put together our program. They had all the machinery — mimeograph machines and typewriters. The North Oakland service center was a part of the poverty program. The service centers collected names of people on welfare, elderly people who needed aid. We used those lists to go around and canvass the community in order to find out the desires of the community. So we would go from house to house and explain to people our program. We printed up the first program at the North Oakland service center.

Our program was structured after the Black Muslim program — minus the religion. I was very impressed with Malcolm X, with the program that Malcolm X followed. I think that I became disillusioned with the Muslims after Malcolm X was assassinated. I think that I was following not Elijah Muhammad or the Muslims, but Malcolm X himself.

Bobby Seale

We sat down and began to write out this ten-point platform and program: We want power to determine our own destiny in our own black community. We want organized political electoral power. Full employment. Decent housing. Decent education to tell us about our true selves. Not to have to fight in Vietnam. An immediate end to police brutality and murder of black people. The right to have juries of our peers in the courts.

We summed it up: We wanted land, bread, housing, education, clothing, justice, and peace. Then we flipped a coin to see who would be chairman. I won chairman.

Bobby Seale

We had written the Ten-Point Platform and Program of the organization but yet didn't have a name. A couple of days later, Huey Newton and I was trying to figure out why was it that on a Lowndes County Freedom Organization pamphlet that we had, why they had this charging black panther as the logo. Huey come up with some notion that if you drive a panther into a corner, if he can't go left and he can't go right, then he will tend to come out of that corner to wipe out or stop its aggressor. So I said, "That's just like black people. All the civil rights people are getting brutalized across this country for exercising the First Amendment of the Constitution, which is the law of the land. They can't go left. Other people have tried to control the police with law books and tape recorders and have been brutalized. They can't go right. Even the young whites who were protesting, I saw, who was in support of the black people, can't go left, can't go right. So we just like the black panthers." And in effect Huey Newton and I named the organization the Black Panther party. At first, it was the Black Panther Party for Self-Defense. Later, we dropped the "Self-Defense" because we didn't want to be classified as a paramilitary organization.

52. CITIZENS ORGANIZE AFTER WATTS

After the riots in Watts in the summer of 1965, the attention of the nation was riveted on this community in southwestern Los Angeles. Political and social pundits, journalists, and scholars dissected the riots, trying to figure out what had gone wrong and why. Amid all the attention, the people of Watts picked up their lives and restored the routines of everyday living as best they could. Their efforts included activism in local civil rights circles. This document by community leader Clara James highlights some of the grass-roots activism that emerged after the riots. According to Clara James, in what ways had the recent Watts uprising changed daily life in the community? What are her greatest concerns about her community and her neighbors? Whom does she count as allies? What similarities can you find between this document and the other selections in this chapter?

CLARA JAMES
"The South Side Citizens Defense Committee"
1966

The South Side Citizens Defense Committee was organized as a direct result of the Watts and South side rebellion. When 4,000 persons were rounded up and thrown in jail, including 750 juveniles; 700 hospitalized; and 34 killed; we were determined to ban[d] together for mutual protection and defense against any further onslaughts against our community or our people.

The statistics quoted represent not merely numbers but real . . . live . . . people . . . human beings, mind you, not monkeys as the distinguished Chief of Police William Parker has called them. They are human beings with flesh and bone and blood and soul who have wants, needs, hopes, desires, ambitions and aspirations just like all other human beings.

All men are created equal and are endowed by their Creator with certain inalienable rights that among these are life, liberty and the pursuit of happiness. So states a portion of the "Declaration of Independence" of the United States of America. But this has not applied to the Negro people and for this reason — WE HAVE HAD A WATTS.

Watts is a predominantly Negro community. There are Mexican, Asian and a few Caucasians living there. There are nice homes as well as shacks. There live the educated as well as the uneducated. Good people and bad people. Intelligent and the unintelligent. There are the employed and many unemployed.

Doctors, domestics, lawyers, merchants, students and drop-outs all are to be found there.

But Watts and South Los Angeles has been bypassed by the city administration in terms of servicing this community as it does others. It has needed street lights and parks, schools, banks, nurseries and all the things that other communities have. The unemployment rate is high and the underemployment is almost as serious. The man who is employed can hardly support his family on the low wages he receives and the man who is unemployed gradually succumbs to hopelessness and despair.

These key factors require that both mother and father work which leaves too many of the children unsupervised. Since most of the women are compelled to work as domestics way over on the other side of the city in the Valley or Westside where she tends some other persons children the problems of distance, travel, and long hours, leave her own children unattended.

Do you not think that the Negro mother would like to feed and dress her young child and to see her older child off to school? As it is, the children are left to fare for themselves. Wouldn't she like to be on hand when the family returns in the evening? Certainly . . . how can she? In far too many instances she is the

Los Angeles Committee for the Protection of the Foreign Born, *Defense: Sixteenth Annual Conference Journal* (Los Angeles, 1966): 32–34.

sole breadwinner of the family. And because her child has to eat, she has to leave to earn food.

The husband and father of this same family would also like to be able to provide well for his family . . . but if he is employed, his wages are low and he can't make ends meet. He was the last hired and as the lowest paid he was the first fired.

When he looks for a job, he is told that the job has been filled, and yet, just in line behind him is another man whose skin is different who may be less qualified who is picked for the already "filled" job. When this type of thing happens day after day or week after week how does one expect a man not to become discouraged and disillusioned?

Meanwhile, the wife becomes tired and irritable, overworked and underpaid, feels unappreciated and the children become unruly and unbearable. The children can sense the deprivations they bear while other children have things and cannot be blamed.

The result is a breakdown in family relations, the beginning of juvenile delinquency, infidelity, sickness, broken homes and finally welfare.

Of course not all families end up this way. Sometimes mother, father, and children work. Many times, grandmother, uncle and aunt pile into one house in order to help sustain the family. Added to these family handicaps are the higher prices charged for inferior foods they buy at the markets and higher rents they pay for inferior housing.

Young people in the community face even greater oppression. Like all young men, they face the possibility of the draft — but unlike other young men, they have no desire to fight for a freedom neither they nor their people enjoy. Their desire for an education is negated as they begin to realize how limited their opportunity is to exercise it, once obtained.

They have seen their fathers and mothers before them with college education forced to take menial jobs far below their preparedness and ability. They are a frustrated group of angry young men who see no way out of the dilemma in which they find themselves, and it is not their fault. We must dispel the idea which states, "Pull yourself up by your bootstraps." For where there are no boots, there are no straps by which to pull.

It becomes the duty of all thinking people — not Negroes alone — to erase the sordid conditions that abide in Watts. Some weeks ago, I asked a friend who lives there to give me his picture of Watts. His reply went something like the following:

"You want a picture of Watts . . . well here it is. Every morning, early, the milkman comes around, then the bread man, followed by the guys with rotten food from the stores. Next, the liquor stores open and there is one on almost every corner. About 8 A.M. in come the teachers from other communities and then the children start for school. About 10 A.M., the doctors, lawyers and storekeepers begin to arrive. None of them live in the area. Later come the door to door salesmen and the insurance agents. By this time the cops have begun to cruise the area and Watts is then in full bloom. About 3 P.M. the children get out of school. A little later the teachers all leave, and then about five, the storekeepers, doctors, lawyers get out of the area and the liquor stores are the only thing to remain open. But the boss-man is gone and so is his money. He takes that out to Beverly Hills, you know.

"And then the guys, the kids — with no place to go and nothing to do — start walking the streets, or gathering on corners, and the cops start beating heads."

This goes on day in and day out thruout the year. Add to this lack of decent housing, inferior education, low grade merchandise, police brutality and poverty . . . and you get the Rebellion.

For those who are not yet convinced that there is continuing police brutality, I suggest that you contact our office. We can show you or refer you to those who have documented proof.

The picture tho not a very pretty one is a true one altho I am happy to say that a change seems to be taking place. Many persons outside the Watts community have reacted in a most understanding manner and have been offering to assist the victims and their families. Also, the people within the community have rallied and are responding to suggestions of ways by which to improve conditions.

It became evident to many persons that those arrested during the disorders included large numbers of persons whose only crime was that of their color and the fact that they were present. Understanding this, Mr. Hursel Alexander immediately decided that an organization of defense would be necessary. He appealed to the Los Angeles Committee for Defense of the Bill of Rights and Protection of the Foreign Born who opened their arms and their purse for such a purpose. Had it not been for the Committee's assistance the picture today would be much worse, indeed.

Thus we began the organization of the South Side Citizens Defense Committee . . . And while our immediate efforts were absorbed in assisting those arrested and needing immediate defense, we have been evolving a concrete program, based on the needs of the community that will channel the frustrations and hatred into a collectively constructive fashion rather than individual and oftimes deadend explosive outbursts.

There are a great number of Negroes who are demanding a more militant type of organization than those which are presently in operation thru the churches, labor groups and in the community. They want an organization that is Negro-run that reflects the basic needs and aspirations of the Negro community. No one group can alone fullfill this desire.

Althou we shall concentrate in the area of defense, we call on and urge all organizations fighting for jobs, civil rights, housing and education to unite and work together toward the end that a total program of renewal and rebuilding can be accomplished.

Among the things our Committee hopes to develop in the community is a Co-op program in the form of a Thrift Shop and Employment agency. We appreciate that this, alone, is not the answer, we feel it is a start toward relieving some of the stifling conditions that now beset Watts and the surrounding area.

We sincerely hope that our white friends will support our efforts and appreciate the fact that the best kind of assistance from them to us will be to work in the white community and generate the kind of pressures on the city Administration to assist in our efforts of self-help.

This undertaking requires the help of all. White progressive persons can be more effective at this time among white groups and Negro progressive persons can be more effective among Negro groups. However, I venture to say if we work properly now, the day will come sooner than we think, when all can work hand in hand together.

53. The Liberation of Alcatraz Island

Alcatraz, a small island in San Francisco Bay and site of a former maximum-security prison, may seem an odd target for civil rights activism. But the 1969 seizure and subsequent occupation of the island by a loose confederation of Native American activists was in many ways a master stroke of propaganda. The island was under federal jurisdiction, thus ensuring widespread response to the action. It was also uninhabited, and such a prominent feature of the Bay Area skyline and tourist economy that it might as well have been in the middle of San Francisco itself. This document is a pronouncement released by the activists following their seizure of the island. Echoing the language of countless federal treaties and other documents, the manifesto mocks the supposed commitment of the federal government to the well-being of American Indians. How do the writers of this manifesto use history and past interactions between Native Americans and the U.S. government to make their points? How do you think this manifesto was received by federal authorities? Do you think it might have won over members of the general public in San Francisco or in other parts of the West and the nation?

Indians of All Tribes
"Proclamation to the Great White Father and All His People"
1969

We, the native Americans, re-claim the land known as Alcatraz Island in the name of all American Indians by right of discovery.

We wish to be fair and honorable in our dealings with the Caucasian inhabitants of this land, and hereby offer the following treaty:

Indians of All Tribes, *Alcatraz Is Not an Island*, ed. Peter Blue Cloud (Berkeley: Wingbow Press, 1969), 40–42.

We will purchase said Alcatraz Island for twenty-four dollars (24) in glass beads and red cloth, a precedent set by the white man's purchase of a similar island about 300 years ago. We know that $24 in trade goods for these 16 acres is more than was paid when Manhattan Island was sold, but we know that land values have risen over the years. Our offer of $1.24 per acre is greater than the 47 cents per acre the white men are now paying the California Indians for their land.

We will give to the inhabitants of this island a portion of the land for their own to be held in trust by the American Indian Affairs and by the bureau of Caucasian Affairs to hold in perpetuity — for as long as the sun shall rise and the rivers go down to the sea. We will further guide the inhabitants in the proper way of living. We will offer them our religion, our education, our life-ways, in order to help them achieve our level of civilization and thus raise them and all their white brothers up from their savage and unhappy state. We offer this treaty in good faith and wish to be fair and honorable in our dealings with all white men.

We feel that this so-called Alcatraz Island is more than suitable for an Indian reservation, as determined by the white man's own standards. By this we mean that this place resembles most Indian reservations in that:

1. It is isolated from modern facilities, and without adequate means of transportation.
2. It has no fresh running water.
3. It has inadequate sanitation facilities.
4. There are no oil or mineral rights.
5. There is no industry and so unemployment is very great.
6. There are no health care facilities.
7. The soil is rocky and non-productive; and the land does not support game.
8. There are no educational facilities.
9. The population has always exceeded the land base.
10. The population has always been held as prisoners and kept dependent upon others.

Further, it would be fitting and symbolic that ships from all over the world, entering the Golden Gate, would first see Indian land, and thus be reminded of the true history of this nation. This tiny island would be a symbol of the great lands once ruled by free and noble Indians.

What use will we make of this land?

Since the San Francisco Indian Center burned down, there is no place for Indians to assemble and carry on tribal life here in the white man's city. Therefore, we plan to develop on this island several Indian institutions:

1. A CENTER FOR NATIVE AMERICAN STUDIES will be developed which will educate them to the skills and knowledge relevant to improve the lives and spirits of all Indian peoples. Attached to this center will be traveling universities, managed by Indians, which will go to the Indian Reservations, learning those necessary and relevant materials now about.

2. AN AMERICAN INDIAN SPIRITUAL CENTER which will practice our ancient tribal religious and sacred healing ceremonies. Our cultural arts will be featured and our young people trained in music, dance, and healing rituals.

3. AN INDIAN CENTER OF ECOLOGY which will train and support our young people in scientific research and practice to restore our lands and waters to their pure and natural state. We will work to de-pollute the air and waters of the Bay Area. We will seek to restore fish and animal life to the area and to revitalize sea life which has been threatened by the white man's way. We will set up facilities to desalt sea water for human benefit.

4. A GREAT INDIAN TRAINING SCHOOL will be developed to teach our people how to make a living in the world, improve our standard of living, and to end hunger and unemployment among all our people. This training school will include a center for Indian arts and crafts, and an Indian restaurant serving native foods, which will restore Indian culinary arts. This center will display Indian arts and offer Indian foods to the public, so that all may know of the beauty and spirit of the traditional INDIAN ways.

Some of the present buildings will be taken over to develop an AMERICAN INDIAN MUSEUM which will depict our native food & other cultural contributions we have given to the world. Another part of the museum will present some of the things the white man has given to the Indians in return for the land and life he took: disease, alcohol, poverty and cultural decimation (As symbolized by old tin cans, barbed wire, rubber tires, plastic containers, etc.). Part of the museum will remain a dungeon to symbolize both those Indian captives who were incarcerated for challenging white authority, and those who were imprisoned on reservations. The museum will show the noble and the tragic events of Indian history, including the broken treaties, the documentary of the Trail of Tears, the Massacre of Wounded Knee, as well as the victory over Yellow Hair Custer and his army.

In the name of all Indians, therefore, we reclaim this island for our Indian nations, for all these reasons. We feel this claim is just and proper, and that this land should rightfully be granted to us for as long as the rivers shall run and the sun shall shine.

Suggestions for Further Reading

Cornell, Stephen. *The Return of the Native: American Indian Political Resurgence.* New York: Oxford University Press, 1988.

Griswold del Castillo, Richard. *César Chávez: A Triumph of Spirit.* Norman: University of Oklahoma Press, 1995.

Gutierrez, David. *Walls and Mirrors: Mexican Americans, Mexican Immigrants, and the Politics of Ethnicity.* Berkeley: University of California Press, 1995.

Horne, Gerald. *Fire This Time: The Watts Uprising and the 1960s.* Charlottesville: University Press of Virginia, 1995.

Kushner, Sam. *Long Road to Delano: A Century of Farmworkers' Struggle.* New York: International Publishers, 1975.

Matthiessen, Peter. *In the Spirit of Crazy Horse.* New York: Viking, 1983.

Sonenshein, Raphael. *Politics in Black and White: Race and Power in Los Angeles.* Princeton: Princeton University Press, 1993.

Antiwar Protest in Los Angeles, *1972*

The public furor over United States involvement in the Vietnam War brought together diverse groups of protesters, many of them young and minorities. America's earlier wars had been fought mostly by men in their twenties, but a lower draft age meant that the Vietnam War was fought by much younger men, often still in their teens when they were sent to Southeast Asia. In addition, African Americans and Mexican Americans protested the war because they came to believe that they were being asked to shoulder more of the burden of fighting than white Americans. How does this antiwar march reveal the feelings that prompted people in the West, and the nation as a whole, to protest the Vietnam War?

Photograph by Joe Kennedy, *Los Angeles Times.*

CHAPTER THIRTEEN

THE VIETNAM ERA

A DIVIDED WEST

The Vietnam War shattered America: it divided families, political parties, regions, and communities. The war remains a visible scar on the American body politic that has left many Americans suspicious of government and wary of military intervention abroad.

The sheer speed of deepening American involvement in the war is remarkable. In the early 1960s, President John Kennedy sent more military advisors to Southeast Asia and approved U.S. involvement in the domestic political affairs of South Vietnam. Following Kennedy's assassination, the U.S. commitment to the war accelerated rapidly under President Lyndon Johnson. Johnson made his first bold move while finishing out the remainder of Kennedy's term, ordering retaliatory air strikes on North Vietnamese torpedo bases and oil storage facilities in response to a presumed attack on two U.S. destroyers in the Gulf of Tonkin. The Gulf of Tonkin Resolution, passed by Congress in the summer of 1964 (the only dissenting votes were cast by two western senators, Wayne Morse of Oregon and Ernest Gruening of Alaska), allowed Johnson to operate as he saw fit in Vietnam and amounted to a declaration of war. By the end of his presidency, Johnson had committed more than a half million soldiers to combat in Vietnam, where nearly one in ten would die.

Americans living in the West fought in the war and they fought against it. The Cold War military buildup that had such an impact on the West meant something very different once the United States began to wage war on the Republic of North Vietnam. Personnel at military installations in western states found themselves training for actual combat. Young cadets at the Air Force Academy in Colorado Springs graduated to become combat fighter pilots. Navy and Marine Corps personnel at West Coast installations shipped out to confront an enemy thousands of miles away. Young men in the U.S. Army went from basic training under the big sky of the West to infantry and artillery units in the dense jungles of Southeast Asia.

Through the mid-1960s, American support for the war appeared strong. Americans believed that Communism had to be stopped before it spread, and they seemed willing to send American troops to help do the job. Yet as Lyndon Johnson escalated the U.S. war effort — after promising that he would not — opposition increased, especially among the nation's young people. The antiwar movement, a nationwide phenomenon, had powerful roots in the West. In the autumn of 1967, for example, more than ten thousand students and other demonstrators in Oakland, California, blockaded an army draft center. Many Americans began to protest what they increasingly viewed as an illegitimate war against North Vietnam. College campuses exploded in antiwar demonstrations. With a profusion of peaceful as well as violent protests, California led the nation in opposing the war.

But not everyone opposed it. On the contrary, the West was home to millions of Americans who believed the war just and winnable. In their minds, the problem lay with the antiwar movement, which they saw as sapping the nation's strength. The polarization of views was bitter, and its political reverberations real. In June 1968, Robert Kennedy, campaigning against the war, won the Democratic presidential primary in California. His assassination in Los Angeles soon after, however, ended the hopes of antiwar activists that they might capture the presidency and de-escalate the war. The election of Republican Richard Nixon, a Californian who conveniently claimed he had a plan to end the war once Johnson announced a halt to the bombing of North Vietnam, instead resulted in many more years of U.S. involvement. Nixon's firm stand against mounting protests appealed to westerners and other Americans fed up with the antiwar movement but infuriated those who believed the war immoral.

As president, Nixon, along with his chief advisor, Secretary of State Henry A. Kissinger, furthered the U.S. war effort in an attempt to force North Vietnam to the peace table, going so far as to order a campaign of secret bombings of North Vietnamese troops and supplies in neutral Cambodia. Once the order was made public in revelations published in the *New York Times*, this controversial action galvanized protest movements. Americans, including greater numbers of returning soldiers who had turned against the war, took to the streets to demand that the government find a peaceful way of ending the conflict immediately. Students shut down hundreds of college campuses in mass protest actions, often placing themselves in jeopardy by doing so.

As American servicemen began to return home, the antiwar movement, fractured by internal divisions, lost steam. The United States eventually withdrew from the Vietnam War following the Paris Peace Accords in 1973, but the divisions created by America's longest war would be felt for years to come.

The documents in this chapter illustrate reactions to the Vietnam War from a number of perspectives. A column by an important Mexican American journalist, Ruben Salazar, discusses the divisions within the Mexican American community over continued U.S. involvement in Vietnam. A selection drawn from a student antiwar publication in Denver shows how many young people viewed the war and attempted to make their voices heard. Two popular songs of the era, one against the war and one against the antiwar movement, illustrate the deep social divisions produced by U.S. participation in the war. Last, a 1969 graduation speech by President Richard Nixon at the Air Force Academy in Colorado Springs, Colorado, reveals the Commander in Chief's determination not to be unduly influenced by the antiwar movement.

As YOU READ the documents in this chapter, think of the ways in which both supporters and opponents of the Vietnam War in the West got their respective points across. Whom do you think these groups were trying to convince by their arguments? How did the war introduce divisions in western America that may not have been there previously?

---

54. MEXICAN AMERICAN REACTIONS TO VIETNAM

As the war dragged on through the late 1960s and early 1970s, antiwar protests took on new dimensions. African Americans and Mexican Americans, increasingly angry that they appeared to be shouldering much of the burden of combat, linked the antiwar movement with civil rights activism. Such linkages energized the antiwar movement on the one hand, but they also revealed tensions within the West's ethnic and racial communities.

Ruben Salazar, a journalist for the Los Angeles Times, *began to question the Vietnam War in his columns in the early 1970s. The first Mexican American to have a daily column in an English language newspaper, Salazar had become a well-known and respected figure in the Mexican American community not only in California but across the Southwest. In August 1970, as many as twenty thousand young people, most of Mexican descent, staged a huge rally against the war in Los Angeles. At this protest calling for a moratorium on the war, sheriff's deputies fired rounds of tear gas into the crowds. Ruben Salazar, who was there covering the rally for his newspaper, was killed when he was struck in the head by a tear gas canister fired wildly into the bar where he had sought cover.*

Salazar wrote this column about an antiwar demonstration held six months before his death. It describes how the war was fracturing the Mexican American com-

munity across different generations and points of view. What can you deduce from this article about the rising power of the antiwar movement among Mexican Americans? According to Salazar, what cultural issues divide antiwar Chicanos from more traditional Mexican Americans? From what you have read, how did the gap between differing points of view within the Mexican American community compare with that in other American communities? How does this portrayal of young Chicano activists compare with the perspectives of the antiwar students in Denver? (See Document 56.)

RUBEN SALAZAR
"Chicanos vs. Traditionalists"
1970

Last Saturday's Chicano Moratorium and the activities of the Catolicos por La Raza[1] dramatize the gulf which exists between the traditional-minded Mexican-Americans and the young activists.

Unless this is understood, observers can fall easily into the simplistic conclusions that the traditionalists are Tio Tacos (Uncle Toms) or that the activists are irresponsible punks.

Either conclusion misses the essence of the present Mexican-American condition.

Traditional-minded Mexican-Americans blush at the mention of the word Chicano. They blanch at the thought of being called brown people. The reason for this, outside of personal views, is the psychological makeup of the Mexican in general.

Octavio Paz, the Mexican poet-essayist-diplomat, has tried to explain it this way: "The Mexican, whether young or old, white or brown, general or lawyer, seems to me to be a person who shuts himself away to protect himself . . . He is jealous of his own privacy and that of others . . . He passes through life like a man who has been flayed; everything can hurt him, including words and the very suspicion of words . . ."

The Mexican, says Paz, "builds a wall of indifference and remoteness between reality and himself, a wall that is no less impenetrable for being invisible. The Mexican is always remote, from the world and from other people. And also from himself."

---

[1] **Catolicos por La Raza:** Catholics for The People (or, literally, The Race); a group of liberal and left-leaning Mexican Americans who were questioning the social role of the Catholic Church during this period.

Los Angeles Times (6 March 1970).

Is it any wonder, then, that the more conservative Mexican-Americans — and there are many of them — are embarrassed and angered at Chicanos (suspicious word) who say they don't want to fight the war in Vietnam and Catolicos who are questioning the church and the world about them?

The Mexican, says Paz, wears his face as a mask and believes "that opening oneself up is a weakness or a betrayal."

The Chicano activists are trying to rid themselves of their masks and to open themselves to themselves and to others. It is significant that in doing this they should pick as a means the Vietnam war and the Catholic Church.

That more than three thousand people braved torrential rains last Saturday to participate in the Chicano Moratorium is important not because so many people showed a distaste for the war — Anglos have done this in a bigger way — but because it was Mexican-Americans who did it.

Mexican-Americans, who include a disproportionate number of Medal of Honor winners and who, like the blacks, are suffering a disproportionate number of deaths in Vietnam, had up to now fought our wars without question.

It was part of the "machismo" tradition. When called to war, Mexican-Americans showed everyone how "macho" or manly they were and never questioned the justification for the war.

Mexicans, says Paz, judge manliness according to their "invulnerability to enemy arms or the impacts of the outside world. Stoicism is the most exalted of (Mexicans') military and political attributes."

The Chicano Moratorium strove to end this stoicism, which is hardly a democratic attribute.

"We weren't shedding our machismo," said a young marcher. "We were proving our machismo by asking the establishment the tough question: 'Why are we dying overseas when the real struggle is at home?'"

When the Catolicos por La Raza demonstrated during a midnight Christmas mass last year, they were also breaking with tradition and asking tough questions at the cost of going through the ordeal of being tried for disturbing the peace.

A San Antonio teacher, testifying before the U.S. Commission on Civil Rights last year, said he has noted that the difference between Anglo and Mexican-American students is that when "some situation befalls the Mexican-American," the Mexican-American tends to leave things up to God while the Anglo tries to solve it on his own.

Catolicos por La Raza, who greatly embarrassed the traditional-minded Mexican-Americans by their questioning of the Catholic Church's relevance to present society, were breaking with this concept.

Chicanos and traditional-minded Mexican-Americans are suffering from the ever-present communications gap. Traditionalists, more concerned with the, to them, chafing terms like Chicano, are not really listening to what the activists are saying. And the activists forget that tradition is hard to kill.

55. Students against the War

This excerpt from a Denver, Colorado, newsletter, Stop the War Committee, *hints at the rising influence of the antiwar movement by 1966. The newsletter offers advice on rally chants and proper picketing strategies for antiwar demonstrators, and it keeps the membership up to date on key events and personnel. In the summer of 1966, as the newsletter notes, the war had already taken four thousand American lives. That number rose tenfold by the war's end nearly a decade later. What are some of the tactics that the Stop the War Committee advocates to get its points across? Which tactics do you think were effective and which were not?*

Stop the War Committee Newsletter
1966

. . . Recommendations of Picket Captain Comm.:

1. Don't argue with hecklers.
2. Respond to hecklers with chants. Suggested chants are, "Support our troops, bring them home now," and, "Freedom Now for Lt. Howe."
3. Stay two abreast throughout the march.
4. Notify picket captain immediately in case of violence or any other trouble.
5. Attempts to break up the line should be met by grasping the shoulder of the person in front.
6. Dress comfortably for walking. (High heels didn't work out too well the last time.)
7. On entering the capitol grounds, the march will go immediately to the State Capitol steps on the West side and link arms. (Watch for directions from picket captains on this one; they might change it to fit the circumstances.) . . .

Suggested Slogans for August 6:

1. Johnson cries peace, makes war.
2. 1776 Self Determination USA.
   1966 Self Determination Vietnam.
3. Wipe out poverty, not people.
4. Yankees come home.
5. Support our GI's, bring them home.
6. Stop Johnson's crimes against humanity.
7. 1945 — Hiroshima — A-bomb.
   1966 — Vietnam — napalm.

Denver *Stop the War Committee Newsletter*, no. 13 (23 July 1966).

8. 4,000 US dead, 2,000 wounded.
   400,000 dead Vietnamese.
   End killing now!
9. Stop war profiteering. Bring our troops home.
10. There is no Ky to peaceful settlement.

(More slogans next time!)

56. A CLASSIC ANTIWAR SONG

The singer Country Joe McDonald became an important voice of protest against U.S. intervention in Vietnam. This song, the "I-Feel-Like-I'm-Fixin'-to-Die Rag," which he wrote in 1965 and recorded a few years later, was one of the antiwar movement's most popular anthems. Easy to remember and sing along with, the song was played or shouted at countless antiwar rallies throughout the late 1960s and early 1970s. Its popularity — and its bitter lyrics — helped make Country Joe and his band, The Fish, one of the most important antiwar musical groups. The "Fixin'-to-Die Rag" also helped make Berkeley, California, where Country Joe lived and performed, into a national capital of protest against the war. How would you describe the song's point of view? How would groups supportive of the U.S. war effort have reacted to this song? How does this perspective compare with the point of view expressed by President Richard Nixon at the Air Force Academy in 1969? (See Document 59.)

COUNTRY JOE McDONALD
"I-Feel-Like-I'm-Fixin'-to-Die Rag"
1965

Come on all of you big strong men,
Uncle Sam needs your help again;
He's got himself in a terrible jam,
Way down yonder in Vietnam;
So put down your books and pick up a gun,
We're gonna have a whole lot of fun!

Chorus:

And it's one, two, three,
What are we fighting for?
Don't ask me, I don't give a damn,
Next stop is Vietnam;
And it's five, six, seven,
Open up the pearly gates;
There ain't no time to wonder why,
Whoopie — we're all gonna die.

Come on, generals, let's move fast,
Your big chance has come at last;
Now you can go out and get those Reds,
The only good Commie is one that's dead;
You know that peace can only be won,
When we've blown 'em all to kingdom come!

(*Chorus*)

Come on, Wall Street, don't be slow,
Why, man, this is war Au-go-go;
There's plenty good money to be made,
Supplying the army with tools of the trade;
Just hope and pray if they drop the Bomb,
They drop it on the Viet Cong!

(*Chorus*)

Come on, mothers, throughout the land,
Pack your boys off to Vietnam;
Come on, fathers, don't hesitate,
Send your sons off before it's too late;
You can be the first one on your block
To have your boy come home in a box.

(*Chorus*)

57. THE COUNTER COUNTERCULTURE

"Okie from Muskogee" is the antithesis of the "Fixin'-to-Die Rag" of Country Joe McDonald, and Merle Haggard is, in many ways, the contemporary opposite of a protest singer like Country Joe McDonald, although they share similar western

roots. Born in California's Central Valley, Merle Haggard developed into a musical talent while serving a prison sentence for armed robbery. By the late 1960s, he had become an important country western singer, his songs and ballads often tinged with a patriotic sensibility. In 1969 he wrote "Okie from Muskogee" as a response to the antiwar movement and youthful counterculture. It became a major recording hit and elevated Haggard to a perhaps unwanted role as spokesperson for American tensions over the war. How would you compare Haggard's point of view with that of Country Joe McDonald? Some have suggested that Haggard's song is meant more as irony than as straight political commentary. How would the song be ironic?

MERLE HAGGARD
"Okie from Muskogee"
1969

We don't smoke Marijuana in Muskogee.
We don't take our trips on LSD.
We don't burn our draft cards down on Main Street,
'cause we like living right and being free.

We don't make a party out of loving,
but we like holding hands and pitching woo.
We don't let our hair grow long and shaggy,
like the hippies out in San Francisco do.

And I'm proud to be an Okie from Muskogee,
a place where even squares can have a ball.
We still wave ol' glory down at the courthouse,
and white lightning's still the biggest thrill of all.

Leather boots are still in style for manly footwear.
Beads and roman sandals won't be seen,
'n' football's still the roughest thing on campus,
and the kids there still respect the college dean.

And I'm proud to be an Okie from Muskogee,
a place where even squares can have a ball.
We still wave ol' glory down at the courthouse,
and white lightning's still the biggest thrill of all.

And white lightning's still the biggest thrill of all.
In Muskogee, Oklahoma, U.S.A.

Courtesy of Sony/ATV Music Publishing.

58. THE PRESIDENT'S SUPPORT
FOR THE WAR

Unswayed by the rising antiwar movement, Richard Nixon moved boldly ahead with his plan to win the war in Vietnam. In this important speech before the graduates of the Air Force Academy in Colorado Springs, Colorado, the president argues that the students and other Americans protesting the Vietnam War have no understanding of the nation's defense needs. Nixon countered that the United States had to pursue an aggressive policy of military preparedness abroad while simultaneously attempting to reconcile domestic fissures at home. These sentiments, delivered at the gemstone of Cold War military installations in the West, undoubtedly resonated with the audience assembled to celebrate the new officers in the Air Force as they received their military commissions. How might activists in the antiwar movement respond to Nixon's arguments? How do you think the graduates of the Air Force Academy would react to student protesters at western colleges and universities?

RICHARD NIXON
Speech at the Air Force Academy
1969

For each of you, and for your parents and your countrymen, this is a moment of quiet pride.

After years of study and training, you have earned the right to be saluted.

But the members of the graduating class of the Air Force Academy are beginning their careers at a difficult moment in military life.

On a fighting front, you are asked to be ready to make unlimited sacrifice in a limited war.

On the home front, you are under attack from those who question the need for a strong national defense, and indeed see a danger in the power of the defenders.

You are entering the military service of your country when the nation's potential adversaries abroad were never stronger and your critics at home were never more numerous.

It is open season on the armed forces. Military programs are ridiculed as needless if not deliberate waste. The military profession is derided in some

Congressional Quarterly Inc., *Nixon: The First Year of His Presidency* (Washington, D.C., 1970), 66-A.

of the best circles. Patriotism is considered by some to be a backward, un-fashionable fetish of the uneducated and unsophisticated. Nationalism is hailed and applauded as a panacea for the ills of every nation — except the United States.

This paradox of military power is a symptom of something far deeper that is stirring in our body politic. It goes beyond the dissent about the war in Vietnam. It goes behind the fear of the "military industrial complex."

The underlying questions are really these:

What is America's role in the world? What are the responsibilities of a great nation toward protecting freedom beyond its shores? Can we ever be *left* in peace if we do not actively assume the burden of *keeping* the peace?

When great questions are posed, fundamental differences of opinion come into focus. It serves no purpose to gloss over these differences, or to try to pretend they are mere matters of degree.

One school of thought holds that the road to understanding with the Soviet Union and Communist China lies through a downgrading of our own alliances and what amounts to a unilateral reduction of our arms — as a demonstration of our "good faith."

They believe that we can be conciliatory and accommodating only if we do not have the strength to be otherwise. They believe America will be able to deal with the possibility of peace only when we are unable to cope with the threat of war.

Those who think that way have grown weary of the weight of free world leadership that fell upon us in the wake of World War II, and they argue that we are as much responsible for the tensions in the world as any adversary we face.

They assert that the United States is blocking the road to peace by maintaining its military strength at home and its defense forces abroad. If we would only reduce our forces, they contend, tensions would disappear and the chances for peace brighten.

America's presence on the world scene, they believe, makes peace abroad improbable and peace in our society impossible.

We should never underestimate the appeal of the isolationist school of thought. Their slogans are simplistic and powerful: "Charity begins at home." "Let's first solve our own problems and then we can deal with the problems of the world."

This simple formula touches a responsive chord with many an over-burdened taxpayer. It would be easy to buy some popularity by going along with the new isolationists. But it would be disastrous for our nation and the world.

I hold a totally different view of the world, and I come to a different conclusion about the direction America must take.

Imagine what would happen to this world if the American presence were swept from the scene. As every world leader knows, and as even the most outspoken of America's critics will admit, the rest of the world would be living in terror.

If America were to turn its back on the world, a deadening form of peace would settle over this planet — the kind of peace that suffocated freedom in Czechoslovakia.

The danger to us has changed, but it has not vanished. We must revitalize our alliances, not abandon them.

We must rule out unilateral disarmament. In the real world that simply will not work. If we pursue arms control as an end in itself, we will not achieve our end. The adversaries in the world today are not in conflict because they are armed. They are armed because they are in conflict, and have not yet learned peaceful ways to resolve their conflicting national interests.

The aggressors of this world are not going to give the United States a period of grace in which to put our domestic house in order — just as the crises within our society cannot be put on a back burner until we resolve the problem of Vietnam.

Programs solving our domestic problems will be meaningless if we are not around to enjoy them. Nor can we conduct a successful policy of peace abroad if our society is at war with itself at home.

There is no advancement for Americans at home in a retreat from the problems of the world. America has a vital national interest in world stability, and no other nation can uphold that interest for us.

We stand at a crossroad in our history. We shall reaffirm our aspiration to greatness or we shall choose instead to withdraw into ourselves. The choice will affect far more than our foreign policy; it will determine the quality of our lives. . . .

Suggestions for Further Reading

DeBenedetti, Charles, with Charles Chatfield. *American Ordeal: The Antiwar Movement of the Vietnam Era.* Syracuse: Syracuse University Press, 1990.

Farber, David R. *The Age of Great Dreams: America in the 1960s.* New York: Hill and Wang, 1994.

Franklin, H. Bruce. *The Vietnam War: In American Stories, Songs, and Poems.* Boston: Bedford Books, 1996.

Hillstrom, Kevin. *The Vietnam Experience: A Concise Encyclopedia of American Literature, Songs, and Films.* Westport, CT: Greenwood Press, 1998.

Karnow, Stanley. *Vietnam: A History.* New York: Viking Press, 1983.

Nixon, Richard. *The Memoirs of Richard Nixon.* New York: Grosset and Dunlap, 1978.

Rorabaugh, W. J. *Berkeley at War: The 1960s.* New York: Oxford University Press, 1989.

Useem, Michael. *Conscription, Protest, and Social Conflict: The Life and Death of a Draft Resistance Movement.* New York: Wiley, 1973.

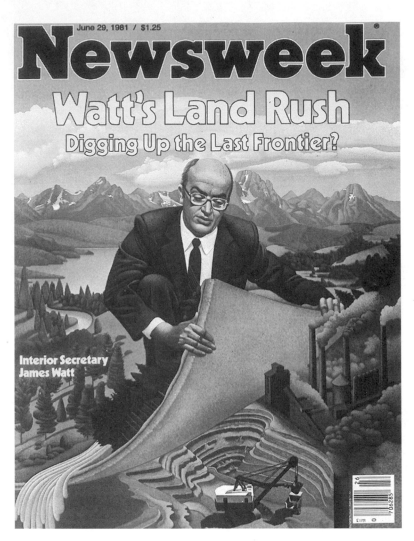

June 29, 1981 / $1.25

Newsweek

Watt's Land Rush
Digging Up the Last Frontier?

Interior Secretary
James Watt

Development vs. Preservation

A westerner, James Watt became secretary of the interior in 1980 under President Ronald Reagan. Watt's tenure in office was controversial and short. Depicted on this 1981 cover of *Newsweek* magazine, Watt became known as a prodevelopment secretary, willing to open federal lands up to industrial and commercial uses that had previously been prohibited. Hugely unpopular with environmentalists of all stripes, from moderates to radicals, Watt nonetheless had many supporters in the West, people who believed that federal authority over the western landscape must be lessened. Watt eventually resigned his post before the end of President Reagan's first term. What does the reference to the "last frontier" mean?

CHAPTER FOURTEEN

THE 1970s AND 1980s

ENVIRONMENTAL DEBATES IN THE WEST

F uture historians will most likely look back on the 1970s and 1980s as a period of environmental awakening in the American West. These years witnessed a great rise in consciousness — and controversy — over environmental issues. The West became the most significant region of the country for the environmental movement and its opponents.

The West has long been an important player in the nation's consciousness about nature. For example, the creation of the national park system, beginning in 1872 with Yellowstone National Park, had everything to do with the awareness of nature inspired by the beauty and resources of the American West. By the early twentieth century, westerners were closely involved in the conservation movement. Even "westerners by adoption" played significant political and other roles. The naturalist John Muir, who founded the Sierra Club in 1892, was one of the earliest environmentalists.

The relationship between environmental thinking and the landscapes of the American West has only become closer in the years since the first Earth Day in 1970. The West has been the birthplace of a variety of environmental groups with different viewpoints. Some have embraced fairly modest goals: the cleanup of local rivers, parks, or public beaches. Others, often with federal help, have attempted to clean up toxic sites or move environmentally dangerous industries out of beleaguered neighborhoods and communities. Still others fight against the suburban sprawl creeping outward from the West's cities and towns.

The West is also home to far more radical environmental groups whose political agendas call for action outside the traditional political arena. Inspired by figures like the writer, naturalist, and activist Edward Abbey, some of these western (and now national and even international) groups believed, and continue to believe, that acts of civil disobedience, including what has been called "eco-terrorism," are legitimate in response to the widespread degradation of western lands. In the West, these groups have been represented since the late 1970s by opponents of western logging, some of them affiliated with the radical Earth

First! movement. In some cases, activists have chosen to chain themselves to trees or perch in treetop structures to keep loggers and logging companies at bay. In a few rare cases, activists have hammered metal spikes into tree trunks in order to disable logging chainsaws.

Another important development in the environmental history of the West during the 1970s and 1980s was the so-called Sagebrush Rebellion. Less an actual rebellion than a modern version of an older struggle between states rights and federal control, the Sagebrush movement claimed that federal control of the West's resources (particularly land) was an outdated and backward approach. Sagebrush rebels, western politicians most prominent among them, wanted federal agencies to loosen their grip on western lands. Western lands ought to be in the hands of western states, they claimed, not under the authority of, for instance, the federal Bureau of Land Management or the Forest Service. But the catch, at least according to the opponents of the Sagebrush Rebellion, was that the most vehement proponents of this loosened control wanted access to federal lands for themselves but did not advocate local or state protection of these lands. On the contrary, the "rebellion" had a real strain of old-fashioned western growth advocacy running through it. If only the federal government would back off, sagebrushers claimed, the West could grow at the pace and to the level that it "should." But the federal government was not interested in stepping aside, and the Sagebrush Rebellion fell apart (though vestiges of it still exist throughout the West in the form of antigovernment sentiment).

If the environmental activists of such groups as Earth First! represent one end of a western spectrum, and the Sagebrush Rebellion the other, what of the great majority in the middle? What did they think? In some ways, we just don't know: historians have only recently begun to examine contemporary attitudes about environmental issues. We do know that people in the West think about the environment and that they worry about it in the face of continued growth, sprawl, pollution, and degradation. But beyond that, it is not clear what impact the environmental awakening of the 1970s and 1980s will have in the years to come.

The documents chosen for this chapter offer a number of perspectives on environmentalism and the environmental movement in the West. The 1970 celebration of Earth Day, an event marked around the world, helped push environmental thinking and environmental consciousness forward, as the brief selection on high-school curriculum in one northern California school attests. Edward Abbey, an important western writer and public figure, helped to spawn environmental "monkey wrenching" with his novel *The Monkey Wrench Gang*, which we have excerpted here. A massive coal operation planned for the sandstone country of southern Utah is examined by a journalist sensitive to the region's environmental splendors as well as the complexities of environmental debates. Last, the controversial Secretary of the Interior, James Watt, comes under scrutiny by a western journalist.

As you read the following selections, think of the different stands that could be taken on environmental issues in the West (or across the nation) during the 1970s and 1980s. How did federal environmental policies change the stakes in western environmental debates? Why did traditional interests — lumber, mining, and cattle — object?

59. Plans for Earth Day

Earth Day, an international celebration of environmental awareness first held on April 22, 1970, helped awaken an environmental sensibility across the nation. Environmental thinking had been stirring for a number of years, thanks in part to the alarm sounded by Rachel Carson in her pivotal book, Silent Spring (1962), *and the increasing political influence of conservation groups like the Sierra Club. But the 1970s saw an expansion of the environmental movement. Young people especially became more environmentally active, seeking redress for such endemic problems as air and water pollution and the destruction of the nation's timber reserves. Students also tried to inculcate an environmental awareness in their parents and peers, as this selection attests. The rising consciousness among young people is illustrated by the following plans of two Palo Alto, California, high-school students for an ecological awareness program on the first Earth Day in 1970. Although their ideas hardly seem revolutionary, it is important to remember that such a perspective was uncommon at the time. A movement was building, but its progress was gradual. What environmental issues are mentioned in this piece? What do the initiators of this curriculum expect to accomplish? Do you think they were able to reach their goals?*

Claire Boissevain and Jim Harding
"Curriculum for Cubberley High School"
1970

Why is it so important to develop environmental awareness in high school students? Because high school reaches all but the most disadvantaged youth, including those who do not go on to college; because the first years in college

Garrett De Bell, ed., *The Environmental Handbook* (New York: Ballantine, 1970), 297–300.

should not be wasted with introductory concepts that can easily be taught in high schools; because eighteen-year-olds will soon have the vote; and because we high school students *want* to know how we can contribute — *now* — to the quality of the world that we shall live in for the rest of our lives.

In response to these motives, we are preparing an "ecology awareness program" to be a workshop aimed at the April 22 Environmental Teach-In — the first national day of environmental concern. We hope that this can be a model for other high schools to consider, because we are calling for the second annual national day of environmental concern in 1971 to be oriented primarily toward the high schools. By including ourselves this year in what is mainly a college effort, perhaps we can show the value of high school participation next year.

Palo Alto High School, another in our city, recently held an antipollution forum, in which speakers representing both sides of several pollution issues presented their cases for student consideration. The organizers of the forum worked extremely hard to present a balanced program. They wanted to introduce their classmates to some of the primary forces that cause pollution, to help them see areas in which solutions can be found, and to motivate them to seek these solutions.

But the Palo Alto High School program was voluntary, and barely 200 out of [a] senior-high student body of 1,500 felt it worth their while to attend. Only those who were already concerned were reached, leaving 1,300 students who were untouched by this excellent program. Further, there was no follow-up to the forum — no continuity to the efforts resulting from the forum.

We chose to make our ecology awareness program mandatory. With a senior high enrollment of 1,200, this challenged us to offer considerable variety. And we wanted to frame our program so that it would be a beginning, leading to efforts that would extend through the rest of our school year, hopefully producing some useful results.

Here is why [a] national environmental day of concern, or an environmental teach-in day, is of such value. Our environmental program, slated for January, becomes a workshop, focused on developing ideas and activities that will grow and carry on, culminating in April on the teach-in day. Instead of just listening to speakers for the educational values of what they have to say, we shall be evaluating what they say, and participating in debates and seminars, in order to define what we can do and what programs and changes we should call for. And the cooperation of our teachers in all of this, certainly to the extent that large portions of the class work after the ecology awareness program are devoted to pursuing ideas introduced during the program, will assure the continuity of our efforts.

Although any program should be developed by the students from their own ideas, let us describe ours as an example. The program will be three days long, from January 26 to 28. Each day there will be a principal speaker to help focus attention on some of the issues. David Brower, president of Friends of the Earth, will open the conference Monday morning. Stephanie Mills will highlight the population discussions in her talk on Tuesday. And Dr. Donald Aitken, Stanford University physicist and a director of Friends of the Earth, will summarize the three-day program in a talk on Wednesday afternoon on "Where do we go from here?" Dr. Aitken's talk will be based on his appraisal of our performance over the three-day program.

These talks will be to assemblies for the entire student body. For the rest of the time there will be forty seminars, field trips, and movies, all repeated on an almost continuous basis for the entire three days. Although attendance during the three days is compulsory, the students will select which seminars they wish to attend, and work out their own time schedules in advance of the program. Each student must think of what he wants to do, or what he might want to learn, ahead of time. For example, does he want to learn all aspects of a single issue, such as the San Francisco Bay, or does he want to learn something of several issues, to see how different ecological problems are related? This is his choice.

Here are some specific examples from our agenda. A population debate will be offered, featuring a woman with thirteen children who opposes population control. A pesticide debate will be offered, featuring a defendant of DDT. Oil companies and electric utility companies will be on hand to defend their policies.

The field trips will include a Bay-walk ecology tour; a trip to Half-Moon Bay to pick up trash from the shore and to analyze the types of containers and other articles that contribute to the greatest amount of litter; and a trip to the DuPont factory in Antioch, to inspect their recent installations of antipollution devices, as well as to ask questions about their general program.

The seminars will cover fields represented by the discussion leaders. Among these will be our own teachers, outside conservationists, and county officials. Subjects covered will include ecology programs for high schools; high-school student participation in local political decision-making and in community conservation activities; technical aspects of certain types of pollution control; legal aspects of environmental defense; and other subjects along these general lines.

The program will be closed by a pantomime presented by the Ecology Action Theater group from the University of California at Berkeley. In pantomime, this group traces the entire cycle of ecological destruction from plants to fish to animals to man. At the end, a human machine is formed which is about to destroy the last life on earth. The students themselves must run from the audience to stop the machine, symbolic of the urgent need for our own participation in the global environmental battle.

Our goal in this program is fivefold: (1) we want to set a precedent for future workshops of this type, especially for the high-school teach-in for 1971; (2) we want to impart an awareness of the dependence of man on his environment to every student in the school; (3) we want to motivate our classmates to involve themselves in the preservation of the environment; (4) we want to make legislative recommendations to our legislators for action; and (5) we want to offer curriculum additions to our own school, to provide a long-term benefit resulting from our first efforts this year.

Material resulting from our studies initiated by the program will be assembled, along with photographs from the program and from the field trips, into a book for action. This book will be released on April 22, when we will send it to all who might be affected by our suggestions.

The only missing ingredient is the assurance that *you*, the high-school student reading this, will join with us this year, on April 22, in calling for the second annual day of environmental concern in 1971 to be directed at an environmental teach-in for high schools, and to join with us next year in developing programs that focus the national attention on what we can do in the high schools to help keep the earth a nice place to live on.

60. Eco-sabotage as Civil Disobedience

One of the West's most ardent environmental defenders in the second half of the twentieth century was Edward Abbey. A prolific and opinionated writer on a variety of environmental issues centered mostly in his beloved West and Southwest, Abbey became a literary and spiritual leader of many radical environmentalists by the late 1970s. This selection from his well-known novel The Monkey Wrench Gang *highlights tactics that would soon become known as "monkey wrenching." Monkey wrenching, which included the destruction of tools or machines, rapidly became a controversial strategy. Proponents, many of whom soon pushed Abbey's examples to further extremes, saw their deeds (such as chaining themselves to trees or spiking tree trunks to prevent logging) as part of an American tradition of civil disobedience stretching at least as far back as the civil rights protests of the 1960s. Opponents of monkey wrenching saw such acts as lawless, violent, and unnecessarily obstructionist. The only clear thing in all of this is that opposing sides continue to disagree. How does the novelist use images of death and resurrection to reveal his, or his characters', feelings about environmental degradation? Does Abbey present Smith and Hayduke as heroes or villains?*

EDWARD ABBEY
From *The Monkey Wrench Gang*
1975

Hayduke and Smith restocked the beer chest and drove on, sunward, downward, riverward, upwind, into the red-rock rimrock country of the Colorado River, heart of the heart of the American West. Where the wind always blows and nothing grows but stunted juniper on the edge of a canyon, scattered blackbrush, scrubby cactus. After the winter rains, if any, and again after the summer rains, if

Edward Abbey, *The Monkey Wrench Gang* (Philadelphia: J. B. Lippincott, 1975), 108–16.

any, there will be a brief flourish of flowers, ephemeral things. The average annual rainfall comes to five inches. It is the kind of land to cause horror and repugnance in the heart of the dirt farmer, stock raiser, land developer. There is no water; there is no soil; there is no grass; there are no trees except a few brave cottonwoods deep in the canyons. Nothing but skeleton rock, the skin of sand and dust, the silence, the space, the mountains beyond.

Hayduke and Smith, jouncing down into the red desert, passed without stopping (for Smith could not bear the memories) the turnoff to the old road which formerly had led to the hamlet of Hite (not to be confused with Hite Marina). Hite, once home for Seldom Seen and still official headquarters of his business, now lies underwater.

They drove on, coming presently to the new bridge that spanned the gorge of White Canyon, the first of the three new bridges in the area. Three bridges to cross one river?

Consult the map. When Glen Canyon Dam plugged the Colorado, the waters backed up over Hite, over the ferry and into thirty miles of canyon upstream from the ferry. The best place to bridge the river (now Lake Powell) was upstream at Narrow Canyon. In order to reach the Narrow Canyon bridge site it was necessary to bridge White Canyon on the east and Dirty Devil Canyon on the west. Thus, three bridges.

Hayduke and Smith stopped to inspect the White Canyon bridge. This, like the other two, was of arch construction and massive proportion, meant to last. The very bolt heads in the cross members were the size of a man's fist.

George Hayduke crawled about for a few minutes underneath the abutments, where nomads already, despite the newness of the bridge, had left their signatures with spray paint on the pale concrete and their dung, dried and shriveled, in the dust. He came up shaking his head.

"Don't know," he says, "don't know. It's one big motherfucker."

"The middle one's bigger," says Smith.

They stared down over the railing at the meandering trickle, two hundred feet below, of White Canyon's intermittent, strictly seasonal stream. Their beer cans sailed light as Dixie cups into the gloom of the gorge. The first flood of the summer would flush them, along with all other such detritus, down to the storage reservoir, Lake Powell, where all upstream garbage found a fitting resting-place.

On to the middle bridge.

They were descending, going down, yet so vast is the scale of things here, so complex the terrain, that neither river nor central canyon become visible until the traveler is almost on the rim of the canyon.

They saw the bridge first, a high lovely twin arch rising in silvery steel well above the level of its roadway. Then they could see the stratified walls of Narrow Canyon. Smith parked his truck; they got out and walked onto the bridge.

The first thing they noticed was that the river was no longer there. Somebody had removed the Colorado River. This was old news to Smith, but to Hayduke, who knew of it only by hearsay, the discovery that the river was indeed gone came as a jolt. Instead of a river he looked down on a motionless body of murky green effluent, dead, stagnant, dull, a scum of oil floating on the surface. On the canyon walls a coating of dried silt and mineral salts, like a bathtub ring, recorded high-water mark. Lake Powell: storage pond, silt trap, evaporation tank and garbage dispose-all, a 180-mile-long incipient sewage lagoon.

They stared down. A few dead fish floated belly up on the oily surface among the orange peels and picnic plates. One waterlogged tree, a hazard to navigation, hung suspended in the static medium. The smell of decay, faint but unmistakable, rose four hundred and fifty feet to their nostrils. Somewhere below that still surface, down where the cloudy silt was settling out, the drowned cottonwoods must yet be standing, their dead branches thick with algae, their ancient knees laden with mud. Somewhere under the heavy burden of water going nowhere, under the silence, the old rocks of the river channel waited for the promised resurrection. Promised by whom? Promised by Capt. Joseph "Seldom Seen" Smith; by Sgt. George Washington Hayduke; by Dr. Sarvis and Ms. Bonnie Abbzug, that's whom.

But how?

Hayduke climbed down the rocks and inspected the foundations of the bridge: very concrete. Abutments sunk deep into the sandstone wall of the canyon, huge I beams bolted together with bolts the size of a man's arm, nuts big as dinner plates. If a man had a wrench with a 14-inch head, thinks Hayduke, and a handle like a 20-foot crowbar, he might get some leverage on those nuts.

They drove on to the third bridge, over the now-submerged mouth of the Dirty Devil River. On the way they passed an unmarked dirt road, the jeep trail leading north toward the Maze, Land of Standing Rocks, the Fins, Lizard Rock and Land's End. No-man's land. Smith knew it well.

The third bridge, like the others, was of arch construction, all steel and concrete, built to bear the weight of forty-ton haulers loaded with carnotite, pitchblende, bentonite, bituminous coal, diatomaceous earth, sulfuric acid, Schlumberger's drill mud, copper ore, oil shale, sand tar, whatever might yet be extracted from the wilderness.

"We're going to need a carload of H.E.," says George Hayduke. "Not like them old wooden truss and trestle bridges over in 'Nam."

"Well, hell, who says we have to blow all three?" Smith says. "If we take out any one it will cut the road."

"Symmetry," says Hayduke. "A nice neat job on all three would be more appreciated. I don't know. Let's think about it. Do you see what I see?"

Leaning on the rail of the Dirty Devil bridge, they looked south to Hite Marina, where a few cabin cruisers floated at their moorings, and at something more interesting closer by, the Hite airstrip, which appeared to be undergoing expansion. They saw a quarter mile of cleared land, a pickup truck, a wheeled loader, a dump truck and, coming to a halt, a Caterpillar D-7 bulldozer. The airstrip was laid out north and south on a flat bench of land below the road, above the reservoir; one edge of the airstrip was no more than fifty feet from the rim of the bench, with a vertical drop-off of 300 feet to the dark green waters of Lake Powell.

"I see it," Smith said at last, reluctantly.

Even as they watched, the dozer operator was getting off the machine, getting into the pickup and driving down to the marina. Lunchtime again.

"Seldom," says Hayduke, "that guy shut off the engine but he sure as hell didn't remove anything."

"No?"

"Absolutely not."

"Well . . ."

"Seldom, I want you to give me a lesson in equipment operation."

"Not here."

"Right here."

"Not in broad daylight."

"Why not?"

Smith seeks an excuse. "Not with them motorboaters hangin' around the marina."

"They couldn't care less. We'll have our hard hats and your pickup truck, and people will think we're construction workers."

"You ain't supposed to make a big wake near the boat docks."

"It'll make one fine helluva splash, won't it?"

"We can't do it."

"It's a matter of honor."

Smith thinking, reflecting, meditating. Finally the deep creases shifted position, his leathery face relaxed into a smile.

"One thing first," he says.

"What's that?"

"We take the license plates off my truck."

Done.

"Let's go," says Smith.

The road wound about the heads of side canyons, rose, descended, rose again to the mesa above the marina. They turned off and drove out on the airstrip. Nobody around. Down at the marina, half a mile away, a few tourists, anglers and boaters lounged in the shade. The Cat operator's pickup stood parked in front of the café. Heat waves shimmered above the walls of red rock. Except for the purr of a motorboat far down the lake, the world was silent, drugged with heat.

Smith drove straight to the side of the bulldozer, a middle-aged dust-covered iron beast. He shut off his engine and stared at Hayduke.

"I'm ready," says Hayduke.

They put on their hard hats and got out.

"First we start the starting engine, right?" Hayduke says. "To warm up the diesel engine, right?"

"Wrong. It's warmed up for us already. First we check the controls to make sure the tractor is in correct starting position."

Smith climbed into the operator's seat, facing an array of levers and pedals. "This," he said, "is the flywheel clutch lever. Disengage." He pushed it forward. "This here is the speed selector lever. Put in neutral."

Hayduke watched closely, memorizing each detail. "That's the throttle," he said.

"That's right. This is the forward and reverse lever. It should be in neutral too. This is the governor control lever. Push forward all the way. Now we apply the right steering brake" — Smith stepped on the right pedal — "and we lock it in position." He flipped forward a small lever on the floorboards. "Now — "

"So everything's in neutral and the brake is locked and it can't go anywhere?"

"That's right. Now" — Smith got out of the seat and moved to the port side of the engine — "now we start the starting engine. The new tractors are a lot simpler, they don't need a starting engine, but you'll find plenty of these old ones still around. These big tractors will last for fifty years if they're taken good care of. Now this here little lever is called the transmission control lever. It goes in HIGH speed position for starting. This is the compression release lever; we put it in START position. Now we disengage the starting-engine clutch with this handle here." He pushed the lever in toward the diesel block.

"Oh, Jesus," mutters Hayduke.

"Yep, it's a little complicated. Now . . . where was I? Now we open the fuel valve by unscrewing this little valve, right . . . here. Now we pull out the choke. Now we set the idling latch in position. Now we turn on the switch."

"That's the ignition switch for the starting engine?"

"Yep." Smith turned on the switch. Sound of a positive click. Nothing else.

"Nothing happened," Hayduke says.

"Oh, I reckon something happened," Smith said. "We closed a circuit. Now if this was a fairly old-model tractor the next thing you'd have to do is get the crank and crank up the engine. But this model has an electric starter. Let's see if she works." Smith put his hand on a lever under the clutch handle and pushed it back. The engine growled, turned over, caught fire. Smith released the starter lever, adjusted the choke; the engine ran smoothly.

"That's only the gasoline engine," Hayduke said. "We still have to get the diesel started, right?"

"That's right, George. Anybody coming?"

Hayduke climbed to the driver's seat. "Nobody in sight."

"All right." The starting engine was warm; Smith closed the choke. The engine throbbed at a comfortable idling speed. "Okay, now we grab these two levers here." Hayduke watching again, all attention. "This upper one is the pinion control and the lower one is the clutch control. Now we push the clutch lever all the way in" — toward the diesel engine block — "and pull the pinion lever all the way out. Now we move the idle latch to let the starting engine run at full speed. Now we engage the starting-engine clutch." He pulled the clutch lever out. The engine slowed, almost stalled, then picked up speed. He moved the compression release lever to RUN position. "Now the starting engine is cranking the diesel engine against compression," Smith said, shouting above the roar of the meshing motors. "It'll start right off."

Hayduke nodded but was no longer sure he followed it all. The tractor was making a great noise; black smoke jetted up, making the hinged lid dance on top of the exhaust stack.

"Now the diesel is running," Smith shouted, looking at the exhaust smoke with approval. He came back to the operator's seat, beside Hayduke. "So now we give it more speed. Pull the governor back to half speed. Now we're about ready to go," he shouted. "So we shut off the starting engine."

He moved forward again and disengaged the starting engine clutch, closed the fuel valve, shut off the ignition switch and returned to Hayduke. They sat side by side on the wide leather-covered operator's seat.

"Now we're ready to drive this thing," he shouted, grinning at Hayduke. "You still interested or would you rather go drink a beer?"

"Let's go," Hayduke shouts back. He scanned the road and marina again for any sign of hostile activity. All seemed to be in order.

"Okay," shouted Smith. He pulled a lever, lifting the hydraulic dozer blade a foot off the ground. "Now we select our operating speed. We have five speeds forward, four in reverse. Since you're kind of a beginner and that cliff is only a hundred yards away we'll stick to the slowest speed for right now." The tractor faced toward the big drop-off. He shifted the speed selector from neutral into first, pulled the forward-and-reverse lever *back* to the *forward* position. Nothing happened.

"Nothing's happening," says Hayduke, nervous again.

"That's right and ain't supposed to neither," says Smith. "Keep your shirt on. Now we rev up the engine a bit." He pulled the throttle back to full speed. "Now we engage the flywheel clutch." He pulled the clutch lever back; the great tractor started to tremble as the transmission gears slid into meshing position. He pulled the clutch lever all the way back and snapped it over center. At once the tractor began to move — thirty-five tons of iron bearing east toward St. Louis, Mo., via Lake Powell and Narrow Canyon.

"I reckon I'll get off now," Smith said, standing up.

"Wait a minute," Hayduke shouts. "How do you steer it?"

"Steering too, huh? Okay, you use these two levers in the middle. These are steering clutch levers, one for each track. Pull back on the right lever and you disengage the clutch on the right side." He did as he said; the tractor began a ponderous turn to the right. "Pull back on the other for a left turn." He released the right lever, pulled back on the left; the tractor began a ponderous turn to the left. "To make a sharper turn you apply the steering clutch brakes." He stepped on first one then the other of the two steel pedals that rose from the floor panels. "You catch on?"

"I get it," shouted Hayduke happily. "Let me do it."

Smith got up, letting Hayduke take over. "You sure you understand the whole thing?" he said.

"Don't bother me, I'm busy," Hayduke shouted, big grin shining through his shaggy beard.

"All right." Smith stepped from the fender to the drawbar of the slow-moving machine and jumped lightly to the ground. "You be careful now," he shouted.

Hayduke didn't hear him. Playing with clutch levers and clutch brakes he wove a crazy course toward the loading machine at the side of the airstrip. At the rate of two miles per hour the bulldozer smashed into the loader, a great mass of metal colliding with a lesser mass. The loader yielded, sliding sideways over the ground. Hayduke steered toward the edge of the runway and the plunge beyond, pushing the loader ahead. He grinned ferociously. Dust clouds billowed above the grind, the crunch, the squeal and groan of steel under stress.

Smith got into his pickup and started the motor, ready to take off at the first hint of danger. Despite the uproar there seemed to be no sign of alarm in any quarter. The yellow pickup remained at the café. Down at the marina a boater refueled his runabout. Two boys fished for channel cat from the end of the dock. Tourists picked over trinkets in the curio shop. A pair of hawks soared high above the radiant cliffs. Peace. . . .

Standing at the controls Hayduke saw, beyond the clouds of dust, the edge of the mesa coming toward him. Beyond that edge, far below, lay the waters of Lake Powell, the surface wrinkled by the wake of a passing boat.

He thought of one final point.

"Hey!" he shouted back at Smith. "How do you stop this thing?"

Smith, leaning against the door of his truck, cupped his ears and shouted back, "What's that?"

"How do you stop this thing?" Hayduke bellowed.

"What?" bellowed Smith.

"HOW DO YOU STOP THIS THING?"

"CAN'T HEAR YOU. . . ."

The loader, pushed by the dozer blade, arrived at the verge, wheeled over, vanished. The bulldozer followed steadily, chuffing black smoke from the burnt metal of the exhaust stack. The steel treads kept firm grip on the sandstone ledge, propelling the machine forward into space. Hayduke jumped off. As the tipover point approached the tractor attempted (so it seemed) to save itself: one tread being more advanced into the air than the other, the tractor made a lurching half-turn to the right, trying to cling to the rim of the mesa and somehow regain solid footing. Useless: there was no remedy; the bulldozer went over, making one somersault, and fell, at minimal trajectory, toward the flat hard metallic-lustered face of the reservoir. As it fell the tracks kept turning, and the engine howled.

Hayduke crawled to the edge in time to see, first, the blurred form of the loading machine sinking into the depths and, second, a few details of the tractor as it crashed into the lake. The thunder of the impact resounded from the canyon walls with shuddering effect, like a sonic boom. The bulldozer sank into the darkness of the cold subsurface waters, its dim shape of Caterpillar yellow obliterated, after a second, by the flare of an underwater explosion. A galaxy of bubbles rose to the surface and popped. Sand and stone trickled for another minute from the cliff. That ceased; there was no further activity but the cautious advance of one motorboat across the dying ripples of the lake: some curious boatman drawn to the scene of calamity.

"Let's get out of here!" Smith called, as he noticed finally, down at the marina, the pickup truck pulling away from the café.

Hayduke stood up dripping dust and jogged toward Smith, a great grim grin on his face.

"Come on!" yelled Smith. Hayduke ran.

They pulled away as the yellow truck ascended the switchbacks leading from marina to road. Smith headed back the way they'd come, across the bridge over the Dirty Devil and on toward the Colorado, but braked hard and turned abruptly before they reached the center bridge, taking the jeep road north around a bend which concealed them from direct view of anyone passing on the highway.

Or did it? Not entirely, for a cloud of dust, like a giant rooster tail hovering in the air, revealed their passage up the dirt road.

Aware of the rising dust, Smith stopped his truck as soon as they were behind the rocks. He left the engine idling in case it became necessary to move on quickly.

They waited.

They heard the whine of the pursuing truck, the vicious hiss of rubber on asphalt as it rushed past on toward the east. They listened to the diminishing noise of its wheels, the gradual return of peace and stillness, harmony and joy.

61. DEBATING LAND USE IN UTAH

The environmental awakening of the 1970s provoked a backlash in the 1980s. The election of Ronald Reagan as president signaled an important shift in federal environmental policies. This was especially evident in the American West, as federal officials, most notably Secretary of the Interior James Watt, increasingly pushed for more development. Whether in natural resource exploitation or support for headlong suburban or urban expansion into surrounding land, this new approach met with approval among many in the West. Others, however, vehemently opposed what they viewed as unbridled and unthinking expansion into the beautiful but fragile ecosystems of the region. Many of these debates focused on energy development, given the West's remarkable supplies of coal, oil, and oil shale. This essay, first published in National Geographic Magazine, *explores the grassroots response to a huge strip-mining and pipeline operation planned for southern Utah, home of one of the nation's most spectacular sandstone landscapes. How would you characterize the different perspectives on this proposed development? How would a sagebrush rebel view the planned mining development?*

How might a monkeywrencher respond? Who would take a position somewhere in the middle, and what might that position be?

FRANÇOIS LEYDET
"Coal vs. Parklands"
1980

Kanab, Utah. Population 4,250. Elevation 4,969 feet. Seat of Kane County. Junction of U.S. Highways 89 and 89-A. If you're looking for a scenic drive, take any road out of town. It's forty-three miles northwest to Zion National Park. Eighty miles north to Bryce Canyon National Park. East seventy-six miles, and you cross the Colorado River at Glen Canyon Dam. South into Arizona, just three miles away, and another seventy-five miles brings you to the Grand Canyon's North Rim.

Motels, restaurants, banks, and shops line the highway. In the center of town stands the Church of Jesus Christ of Latter-day Saints. Tourism is a main business, and this makes some people uneasy: What would gas rationing do to Kanab? There are a few jobs in lumbering across the line in Arizona. There is also ranching — cattle ranged on U.S. Bureau of Land Management (BLM) property, irrigated alfalfa fields.

In fact, there is a good deal of farming right in town. On a balmy spring evening I walk up and down the side streets and note that nearly every house seems to have its vegetable garden, corn patch, and a few fruit trees. Tidy little streets, tidy little houses. Lots of flowers. The scent of lilacs permeates the air. A nice, quiet, safe little Mormon town nestled at the foot of the Vermilion Cliffs, now aglow in the setting sun.

Sleep well tonight, Kanab, I think as I turn back toward my motel. Your days of quiet may be numbered.

During the first half of this year I spent weeks roaming southern Utah. Big things are happening — bigger things may soon happen. They could in the next few years drastically alter the character of this incomparable country of high plateaus and deep canyons, where some of our most splendid national parklands are located. Up to now, its remoteness and tortured topography have largely shielded it from the harsher impacts of industrial civilization.

What I have seen is a concerted drive to open the region to massive exploitation of its wealth of energy-producing coal, uranium, and other minerals. Some of the area's wild beauty, much of its serenity and solitude may be lost in the process. Opponents say that an irreplaceable national heritage is about to be sacrificed for a mess of wattage.

National Geographic Magazine 158 (December 1980): 779–91, 800–03.

Many cite the proposed Allen-Warner Valley Energy System. It calls for a coal strip mine in the Alton hills thirty miles north of Kanab and only five miles, at one point, from Bryce Canyon National Park, and two coal-fired power plants, one of them seventeen miles upwind from Zion National Park.

This controversial project was placed early this year on the administration's proposed Critical Energy Facilities list — energy projects that could reduce our dependence on imported oil and that therefore must receive priority review. It has been the focus of studies by the Department of the Interior's Office of Surface Mining (OSM) and BLM, in cooperation with other agencies, and by the California Public Utilities Commission (CPUC). It has set multibillion-dollar corporations against a coalition of conservation groups. It has posed squarely the question of national priorities.

Shortly after this issue of *National Geographic* comes off the press, the fate of Allen-Warner Valley (AWV) is due to be decided by the CPUC and by Secretary of the Interior Cecil D. Andrus. A decision against AWV would be hailed by environmental groups as a refusal to accept possible degradation of our parklands.

Even more important, in their view, such a decision could indicate recognition that it makes sense, economically as well as ecologically, to veer from the "hard path" of big oil, coal, and nuclear power plants and turn to the "soft path" of renewable energy sources and increased conservation.

Take those magnificent 20,000 square miles of southern Utah bounded on the west by Interstate 15, on the north by I-70, on the east by the Colorado River, on the south by the Arizona state line; they form a rhombus roughly 150 miles to the side. I would be tempted to say that within this one comparatively small area lies more fantastically beautiful — and infinitely varied — country than in any other like-size area on earth.

Here are some of our great national parkland treasures: Zion, Bryce Canyon, Capitol Reef, Arches, and Canyonlands National Parks; Cedar Breaks National Monument; and Glen Canyon National Recreation Area on Lake Powell.

Here also are areas that many believe deserve national park — or at least wilderness area — status. . . .

I have paused, too, in the Robbers' Roost country near Capitol Reef, of which Wallace Stegner wrote: "It is a lovely and terrible wilderness, such a wilderness as Christ and the prophets went out into; harshly and beautifully colored, broken and worn until its bones are exposed, and its great sky without a smudge or taint from Technocracy, and in hidden corners and pockets under its cliffs the sudden poetry of springs."

Stegner wrote that in 1963. The skies, I discovered, are no longer quite so pure. On some days a whitish haze blurs the distant views, causing the colors to be not quite so vibrant and the forms not quite so sharp.

This is not just natural haze from atmospheric moisture, forest fires, or blowing dust. At the Island in the Sky monitoring station in Canyonlands National Park, operated by the Environmental Protection Agency (EPA) and the National Park Service, air-quality scientists told me the haze is composed also of urban smog from as far as Los Angeles, six hundred miles away, and emissions from southwestern coal-fired power plants and copper smelters.

Mines Would Bring Massive Change

But the changes in the offing threaten much more than degradation of ambient air quality. Last August the BLM released the Kaiparowits Coal Development and Transportation Study. It describes scenarios involving the mining of from three to as much as seventy-five million tons of coal a year from beneath the plateau, shipping it by yet unbuilt railroads to destinations in Utah or Arizona, and producing by the year 2000 a population increase of perhaps 95,000 souls in Utah's Garfield and Kane Counties, which boast a total population today of less than 10,000. . . .

One snowy morning in Salt Lake City I called on Dr. Joan Coles, a member of the Sierra Club's Energy Committee and a clinical psychologist for the Salt Lake Community Mental Health Center.

"I've had my life threatened at Escalante for saying the things I'm telling you now," she declared. "But I'm tired of the attitude of so many local people that they have disposition power over national treasures like parks because they have the luck to live nearby.

"The trouble with these little towns," she went on, "is that they lack the ordinary entrepreneurship that would create a reasonable number of jobs. Small industry might be happy to locate in places like Escalante or Kanab. Utah labor is renowned for industriousness and dependability. But Escalante needs a few dozen jobs, and what does it do? It wants to develop Kaiparowits."

Like many others I talked with, Dr. Coles cited Rock Springs and Gillette, Wyoming, as paradigms of what can happen when growth outstrips planning: jerry-built boomtowns with transient populations and increased crime and alcoholism. . . .

If Dr. Coles had expressed these thoughts at the Kane County courthouse in Kanab the day I dropped in to talk with local officials, there might have been an uproar. One young man in particular was fuming.

"Just look at this," he challenged me, dropping a foot-thick pile of papers on the table with a bang. "Wilderness studies, environmental-impact statements, master plans, lease filings. Documents, documents, documents. The feds inundate us at the local level with more data than we can handle.

"Wilderness!" He almost spat out the word. "We don't want one acre of it in Kane County. It's not just what would be locked up in the wilderness areas themselves. If BLM gets a wilderness area, the EPA won't let you do a thing within a hundred miles of it because that might affect the air quality.

"It's the same with the parks. The federal government owns 85 percent of the land in Kane County. We have 16 percent unemployment and no industry. There are thousands of mineral claims — uranium, gold, silver, manganese, copper, lead, gypsum. There are oil, gas, and coal leases. If they'd let us develop some of our resources, we'd be in business. There's enough land here to have beauty *and* development. We don't see that we should be giving everything in the country to preservationists and extremists!"

Here, in one outburst, surfaced some of the antagonisms that rend southern Utah today. Minerals versus parks. Development versus preservation. Us versus Them.

How are "us" and "them" defined in the minds of southern Utahans? More or less as follows, as I gathered from dozens of talks:

"'Us' is we who are born and raised in southern Utah. Brigham Young sent most of our grandparents here to settle the land and make the desert bloom. We are God-fearing, hardworking, patriotic. We want our kids to stay here. We have lots of kids — the Mormon Church encourages large families. But the kids keep leaving. If they want higher education and good jobs, they have to get them elsewhere. If we could develop this country, perhaps they'd stay.

Getting to Know "Them"

"'Them' is all those outsiders who come here and tell us what we can and can't do. The big decisions that affect our lives are made in Washington or Los Angeles or anywhere but here. We've lost control of our own destinies. 'Them' is all the federal government people — the Park Service, Forest Service, the hated BLM that tells us we're overgrazing and cuts our allotments."

"Them" also is those environmentalists.

"The environmentalists have cost the people of this country billions upon billions of dollars," grated a speaker at a hearing in Kanab on Allen-Warner Valley. "They've weakened our nation in every aspect by stopping every power-producing project."

"Them" is the big corporations too.

"We need them just like we need the tourists — they mean jobs — but we don't really trust them." At a Kanab luncheon attended by top Interior Department officials, one young man asked, "What happens if ten years after the mining ends, Kanab and all these ranches find their wells running dry? Where will Utah International be then?" (Utah International Inc., a General Electric affiliate, would operate the Alton mine.) . . .

If you're planning a big energy project, and you hope to have it approved with a minimum of fuss and bother, then you should dream up something other than the Allen-Warner Valley Energy System. So said many of the staff people I talked with in various government agencies.

First, there is the attention-getting energy source itself: 300 million tons of minable, fair-quality coal. Extracting it requires strip-mining 10,000 acres at the base of the Paunsaugunt Plateau, some of them in a nine-mile swath smack under the noses of 300,000 visitors a year who come to admire the spectacular panorama from Yovimpa Point in Bryce Canyon National Park.

To get that coal to destination, you'd probably use a slurry-pipeline system, in which coal is ground and mixed with water pumped from wells drilled deep into the Navajo sandstone aquifer. But that is bound to stir up the local people, who in a dry region are jealous of their water — "It's our life-blood," they'll tell you again and again.

Also, since you plan to pipe the major part of the coal-water slurry out of state, 183 miles to the proposed 2,000-megawatt Harry Allen plant near Las Vegas, Nevada, you've got to provide some beneficial use to Utah for exporting its water. So you have to mollify the town boosters at St. George by offering to divert a good part of the Virgin River into a 55,000-acre-foot reservoir in Warner Valley. (You need 10,000 acre-feet of that water to cool your proposed 500-megawatt Warner Valley plant, terminus of your other slurry pipeline.)

This diversion arouses the Fish and Wildlife Service, since it might eliminate two small fish: the woundfin minnow, an endangered species, and the Virgin River roundtail chub, a candidate for that distinction.

And the power plants. Unless you want a fight, you do not plunk one down in Warner Valley, 17 miles from Zion National Park, when you know there's a good chance — at least, a lot of protesting people are going to claim there is — that the prevailing southwesterly winds will waft the plumes from your stacks in the direction of the park, whose Class I air quality is inviolate under the 1977 Clean Air Act.

And you ponder the wisdom of locating your other plant 25 miles from Las Vegas, when there's a good possibility that its emissions, added to those from the Reid Gardner plant, will at times degrade Las Vegas's air below Class II standards. That will cause the EPA to blow the whistle on you.

Finally, you might just wonder what the local folk would say about using Utah coal and water and polluting Utah and Nevada air, when about 85 percent of the wattage initially will hum away across the Mojave Desert to power hair dryers in Orange County or microwave ovens in Berkeley. . . .

In November 1979 the Environmental Defense Fund, the Sierra Club, and Friends of the Earth petitioned the Office of Surface Mining to declare the Alton coalfields unsuitable for surface mining. This was the first test of Section 522 of the 1977 Surface Mining Act, which provides for such a designation if mining would "adversely affect any publicly owned park" or "result in a substantial loss or reduction of long-range productivity of water supply or of food or fiber products" of renewable resource lands.

In May 1980 I attended the first public hearing on the petition. Some 200 people had gathered in a large windowless basement hall of a Kanab motel to talk about that Alton coalfield north of town. Spokesmen for the environmental groups — and a surprising number of local citizens — stressed the damage they felt the mine would cause to Bryce Canyon National Park.

They claimed that dust from mining would ruin the matchless visibility, that blasting might topple the delicate pinnacles and spires — a fear that tests have since allayed. They decried the sights and sounds of a large strip mine — with its draglines, bulldozers, haul roads, 120-ton coal trucks — and the eventual huge scar if reclamation proved unsuccessful. All these would be incompatible, the speakers insisted, with the experience that visitors to Yovimpa Point had the right to expect.

Another charge in the petition — that the surface disturbance and mining of groundwater from the Navajo aquifer would threaten the area's water supply — worried many local citizens deeply. It was this concern that had caused several ranchers to become copetitioners with the environmental groups, in an alliance that a year or two earlier would have seemed unthinkable. . . .

John [Ferrell, Alton project manager for Utah International] is a personable, thoughtful young Coloradan. . . . He escorted me on a comprehensive three-day tour of UII's Trapper Mine near Craig, Colorado, its huge Navajo Mine near Farmington, New Mexico, and the Alton site.

The scale of the operations left me in awe: the great strips, the gargantuan equipment — especially the walking draglines with 30-cubic-yard buckets at the end of 300-foot booms, operated by one person exerting fingertip pressure on a couple of levers.

I saw that if huge equipment can dig gigantic pits, it can also fill them in. The mined-over strips, once recontoured, had a fairly natural look. Too, there was less noise and rather less dust than I had anticipated. Certainly the mining of coal at Navajo seemed to cause less air pollution than is produced by its burning at the adjacent Four Corners power plant, a smoke-belching mammoth.

Revegetation efforts appeared successful to my untrained eye, although Office of Surface Mining experts had doubts. Cover had been achieved at the Navajo Mine, they said, but it was yet to be proved that the new growth would be self-sustaining. . . .

The big question still begged: Would surface mining, tolerable in the environs of Craig or Farmington, be equally acceptable beside Bryce Canyon National Park? . . .

Agencies Push Soft-Path Alternatives

The BLM's draft environmental-impact statement relies heavily on information supplied by the California Public Utilities Commission and the California Energy Commission. Perhaps more than their counterparts in any other state, these two agencies have been knocking down the utilities' inflated need forecasts and pressing them to implement alternative soft-path strategies.

Much of this year the CPUC has held hearings in San Francisco on the AWV Energy System, preparatory to granting or denying Pacific Gas and Electric and Southern California Edison the "certificate of public convenience and necessity" they must have to invest in an out-of-state power project.

In a sense, the CPUC holds the trump card: If it finds that the utilities do not need the power, or have better ways to develop it, AWV will be dead, no matter the decision on the Alton unsuitability petition and no matter the findings on the impact of Warner Valley on Zion National Park. The CPUC staff position translates into a "yes" on the Harry Allen plant near Las Vegas, fueled by coal trains from central Utah mines, and a "no" on the Warner Valley plant.

"What we're saying," CPUC's AWV project manager Ron Knecht explained to me, "is that if other plants being built come on line, then there is no need for either plant to ensure system reliability — to prevent brownouts, in other words. There *is* a need to displace oil. This is our criterion: Is a given proposal better or worse than continuing to burn oil in generating electricity? We think Harry Allen is better. So are a lot of the conservation and alternative-energy possibilities we are recommending that the commission *mandate* the utilities to develop. It could turn out that Harry Allen would be the last big conventional plant to be built in the Southwest."

"Even that would be too much," according to the Environmental Defense Fund's West coast regional counsel David Roe. He had just handed me EDF's computer-based analysis of AWV Alternative 1 and of EDF's own soft-path scenario. "Harry Allen works economically," he said, "only if *none* of the conservation and other alternative measures are carried out. If Harry Allen is built, and utilities do no more along these lines than the CPUC has *already* ordered them to do, then the energy produced will cost a great deal more than planned over the lifetime of the plant, because it will operate at less than 40 percent capacity. The lesson is that you can't have *both* the plant *and* conservation. And conservation is cheaper." . . .

Hardest Question Still Unanswered

But the coal would still lie in wait at Alton, and there would likely be other plans to dig it. So would it be with the Kaiparowits. . . .

. . . For perhaps a million centuries that coal had lain there. Would it all be dug and burned in the next half century? I thought of all this glorious land I had traveled in southern Utah. I thought of the frantic rush by our unthrifty society to wrest from the earth in a few short decades the stores that nature has guarded for eons. What would we leave to the generations yet unborn?

62. THE SECRETARY OF THE INTERIOR AS SAGEBRUSH REBEL

Secretary of the Interior James Watt became one of the most controversial cabinet members of Ronald Reagan's first term. Though a westerner, Watt was no friend of environmentalists. He presided over sweeping federal legislation that opened up previously closed federal lands to development and resource extraction. Watt had his supporters to be sure, many of them in the West. Westerners, like the so-called Sagebrush Rebels, who wished the federal government out of western resource management, found an ally in Watt. They considered his actions at the Interior Department in line with their own ideology about minimizing federal intervention. In this article, columnist Bill Hornby discusses Watt's enemies and supporters, as well

*as the environmental background to the controversy surrounding him. Embroiled
in one controversy after another, Watt resigned as secretary of the interior in 1983.
Assuming that there were only two sides to the debate over Secretary Watt and his
policies, what side does Hornby come down on? According to Hornby, what was the
conservative philosophy behind federal land use policies? How does this column
reflect the environmental mood of the country in the early 1980s?*

BILL HORNBY
"Jim Watt's Western Exposure"
1981

As Secretary of the Interior Jim Watt treks around the West, he may be demonstrating to regional audiences that he is not the anti-Christ, but it is doubtful that he is improving his image in the Eastern press. He probably doesn't expect and won't receive any better treatment from the *New York Times* or the *Washington Post* when he gets back to Foggy Bottom[1] than he has had so far.

Now as Watt's friends and even the man himself are ready to admit, some of his troubles stem from his own nature. He's a righteous man and one who comes on feisty. Watt would never be on the top of your list for a drinking buddy, an ambassador or maybe even a governor, assuming you think of such types as ones who should try to put on as many Band-Aids as they pick off scabs.

Watt is a true believer used to the advocacy and conflict of the legal process. His trademarks are honesty, candor and bluntness. If he has a dagger for you, it's on his desk, not up his sleeve. Little wonder that the professional Washington environmental lobbyists licked their lips at such a tempting target.

But their real war with Watt stems not from his politically vulnerable personality but from his basic philosophy, which is consistent with the philosophy of the administration which picked him as its lightning rod.

Reagan, Watt, their mutual supporter and confidante Joe Coors of Colorado, and the other Coloradans that Coors has helped to ease into Washington resources management — they all share some fundamental philosophic beliefs, which might be paraphrased as follows:

> Private industry under minimal government regulation can be trusted as much
> as any other sector of the citizenry to do what good citizens should to pro-
> tect the environment under the more enlightened standards of the 1980s.
> The Western resource wealth of the country can be developed without perma-
> nently damaging the environment, and indeed our national interest will re-
> quire that those resources be located and prudently developed over the short
> term of the next few decades.

[1] **Foggy Bottom:** A district of Washington, D.C., and the location of numerous federal office buildings.
Denver Post (16 September 1981).

> Many aspects of resource management would be more economically and
> effectively handled if left to the risks and rewards of the free market system,
> that is to private enterprise, than they are now managed by a government
> system which does not hold its managers accountable as to economics or
> efficiency.

These beliefs are a direct challenge to almost a hundred years of conservation thinking in this country.

It was the thesis of Theodore Roosevelt, Gifford Pinchot[2] and the other fathers of conservation that big business is inherently rapacious and incapable of the arts of good citizenship; that some natural areas are so precious that they can never be available to balanced development but must be sequestered for "future generations," and that a government bureaucracy is inherently more apt to act in the public interest than a market system seeking to maximize economic rewards.

Thus it's no surprise that the conservative establishment of the environmental-conservation movement recognized Watt's dangerous radicalism right from the start. The massive petition and public relations drives of the Sierra Club and the Wilderness Society, mounted when Watt was in office only a few days, dwarf any such protest on their part to past appointments. In Watt they see someone who is a fundamental threat to their beliefs, not just their programs. He has to be obliterated like Carthage.[3]

Probably their vehement opposition has solidified Watt in office. The administration can hardly throw Watt out for saying what the administration thinks, and it can hardly ease him out because he's stage center in a spotlight his enemies have created. So the end result of his Western tour is likely to be that Watt goes back to Washington convinced that a goodly portion of the homefolks are behind him, and discovers that his opposition isn't impressed by that fact one bit.

But more important than the survival of Watt as an individual is the future of his ideas. There is a significant body of opinion in this country, witness the election, that believes that the private business can be a good environmental citizen, that all our resources should be developed, and that government is not by some gift of God the best and only manager of resources "in the public interest."

Watt's enemies might discover they can get rid of him but not his ideas. Their energy might be better spent coming to grips with the ideas than in castigating the individual.

[2]**Gifford Pinchot:** A leading American conservationist, Pinchot (1865–1946) headed the U.S. Forest Service during the Progressive era.
[3]**Carthage:** Great Phoenician city of antiquity in North Africa. The reference here is to the Roman pledge to destroy Carthage in the Punic Wars during the second and third centuries B.C.

Suggestions for Further Reading

Abbey, Edward. *The Journey Home: Some Words in Defense of the American West.* New York: Dutton, 1977.

Brower, David R. *For Earth's Sake: The Life and Times of David Brower.* Salt Lake City: Peregrine Smith Books, 1990.

Cawley, R. McGregor. *Federal Land, Western Anger: The Sagebrush Rebellion and Environmental Politics.* Lawrence: University Press of Kansas, 1993.

Dowie, Mark. *Losing Ground: American Environmentalism at the Close of the Twentieth Century.* Cambridge: MIT Press, 1995.

Foreman, Dave. *Confessions of an Eco-Warrior.* New York: Harmony Books, 1991.

Nash, Roderick F., ed. *American Environmentalism: Readings in Conservation History.* New York: McGraw-Hill, 1990.

Shabecoff, Philip. *A Fierce Green Fire: The American Environmental Movement.* New York: Hill and Wang, 1993.

Worster, Donald. *Rivers of Empire: Water, Aridity, and the Growth of the American West.* New York: Pantheon, 1985.

Immigrant Crossing Sign, Southern California, 1999

Caution signs such as this one began going up along Southern California highways in the 1990s following fatal collisions between automobiles and people. The sign depicts an immigrant family racing across lanes of traffic. Like others warning drivers of deer or school-children or pedestrians, this caution sign reflects a common occurrence — people attempting to cross from Mexico into the United States without proper immigration papers. By the 1980s and 1990s, such border crossings had become a political hot potato in the American West, so much so that westerners voted into law a number of immigration-related propositions. Undocumented immigration into the United States from nations such as Mexico is nothing new in the history of the American Southwest. Do you think the recent appearance of crossing signs signals a different response to the issue or to the people choosing to come to the United States?

California Department of Transportation.

CHAPTER FIFTEEN

CONTEMPORARY AMERICA

IMMIGRATION AND INTEGRATION

Immigration is an American tradition with deep roots in the history of the nation and the American identity. But debates over immigration, which touch on tensions over race, ethnicity, and the ability of national institutions to make Americans out of diverse peoples, are also part of the American psyche. Such tensions continue to be a significant force in contemporary America, particularly so in the West, which stands at the forefront of current controversies over immigration. This complex subject a remains a "hot button" issue in contemporary American society, contested in the electoral arena as well as in the neighborhoods of American western cities and towns.

Some background to the current debate is helpful. Harsh restrictions enacted between 1910 and 1930 halted Asian immigration to the United States and severely curtailed immigration from southern and eastern Europe. The Depression raised new anxieties, particularly in the West, as the nation embarked on a coercive repatriation program that sent tens of thousands of Mexicans, many of whom had migrated to the United States legally (and become U.S. citizens), back across the border. In the 1940s and 1950s, the government reversed course, joining with giant agricultural corporations and Mexico to bring Mexican *braceros*, or "guest workers," across the border on temporary work permits. By the late 1950s, rising concern that Mexicans might be taking jobs away from Americans provoked a new round of immigration restrictions, even though the *bracero* program continued for years in one form or another. Then, in the mid-1960s, the United States changed gears once again: the Immigration Act relaxed the former quotas on immigration for non-Europeans and help create what has come to be known as the "new immigration," especially of people moving to the United States from Asia.

In recent years, immigration to all parts of the nation continues to increase, changing the make-up of American society in dramatic ways. By the mid-1990s, nearly 10 percent of the U.S. population had been born elsewhere. As in the past, immigrants continue to congregate in cities. In the West, Los Angeles and San Francisco act as magnets for immigrants. The greater Los Angeles region in particular is an immigration center for people arriving from Mexico, El Salvador, Guatemala, and Asia. One out of five immigrants in the 1990s settled in Southern California.

The West's larger cities, like Los Angeles and San Francisco, Seattle or San Diego, find that they are often ill-equipped to handle the cultural, social, and other challenges posed by hundreds of thousands of new immigrants. School districts now record as many as eighty languages among enrolled pupils. Many immigrants also arrive poor and in need of help in the form of healthcare or other social services. On top of this, these newcomers discover that they are not always welcome in their new neighborhoods and communities, whether in the cities or in the suburbs or rural areas. The same tensions and fears that accompanied immigration in the past surround the issue today. Anti-immigrant sentiment can be played out in a variety of complicated forms, but it often boils down to a few particular fears about immigrant populations. Some wonder whether new immigrants adopt American customs quickly enough; in the minds of many people, the traditional cultures and languages of immigrants pose a problem. The other major concern is broadly economic. Some question whether immigrants are taking jobs away from Americans and resent their access to social and educational services, especially those who come to the West illegally. On the other side of these debates are those who argue that immigrants add to the West's economic and cultural well-being in significant ways, or that the agricultural and manufacturing industries in the West depend on the labor of immigrant workers.

Recent legislation, especially in the Far West, has recharged the immigration issue by making the debate more public and more vocal. The following documents explore some of these responses. First, a reporter for a western newspaper looks at how the crackdown on undocumented immigration affects life in a famous Rocky Mountain tourist resort. Next, a former official of the Immigration and Naturalization Service offers his views on the immigration issue and characterizes his support of California's Proposition 187 (excerpted on pp. 291–94), a measure designed to prevent undocumented immigrants from receiving a variety of social and educational services. Third, former California governor Pete Wilson, a major supporter of Proposition 187, is lampooned in a newspaper cartoon over his changing rhetoric. Finally, a newspaper columnist explores some of the complexities surrounding another California proposition designed to curtail bilingual education in the public schools.

AS YOU READ these selections, think of the ways in which the American West has become the focal point for the national debate on immigration. How do the issues raised in these selections compare to what you know of earlier periods in the West? From the documents reproduced here, how would you describe the major themes of the immigration debate in the contemporary West? Why is the West different from other parts of the nation on the immigration issue?

63. IMMIGRATION RESTRICTION IN THE ROCKIES

In recent decades, the controversial issue of undocumented immigration has become a truly national one, although it remains particularly germane to the American West. Politicians, political parties, and a variety of citizens' groups have staked out territory on the issue, and many states have passed or proposed one anti-immigrant measure or another. But the issue is far more complex than many people believe, as this article, excerpted from the Rocky Mountain newspaper High Country News, *tries to make clear. This essay discusses the impact of an Immigration and Naturalization Service raid on illegal immigrants in the ski and tourist town of Jackson, Wyoming. As the author suggests, making hard policy choices about immigration and citizenship status is inevitably linked to equally tough decisions about labor. In a world of tighter immigration controls or penalties, who will do the work that immigrants (both legal and illegal) perform? What economic and demographic factors helped bring Mexican workers to western ski towns? According to this article, how does the current situation in a place like northwestern Wyoming mirror the past?*

LISA JONES
"El Nuevo West"
1996

A week before Labor Day, the tourist town of Jackson, Wyoming, lost its labor force.

Teams of federal agents and local police entered hotels and restaurants, asking dark-skinned workers for their immigration papers. Those who couldn't produce them were taken away in police cars. One group was hauled off in a horse trailer.

Within three hours, with more than half of the sixty targeted establishments still unvisited, agents had already netted about four times the number of suspected illegal workers they'd expected. Overwhelmed, they stopped.

High Country News (23 December 1996): 1, 6, 8–11.

The chain-link enclosure outside the Teton County Sheriff's Department contained 151 Mexicans — about one-sixth of the town's Mexican population — and a young pair from England. Numbers were inked on their forearms while their paperwork was processed.

The next day, 120 undocumented Mexicans were on their way back to Mexico by bus and airplane.

It was the biggest immigration bust in Wyoming's history. And, like most busts of undocumented Mexicans, it accomplished virtually nothing. A little over a week after leaving Jackson, all but four of the deportees were reportedly back on the job. One restaurant worker said that after a long bus ride in handcuffs, he spent two hours in the Ciudad Juarez jail. Then he and some friends got into a car, drove six hours west to the Arizona border, and headed back to the Rockies.

"That raid," he said, "it was really stupid."

When the man, whom I'll call Juan Sanchez, tells me this, I am sitting at the kitchen table in his trailer in the town of Driggs, Idaho. Hundreds of Jackson's workers live here, across the pass, where the Teton's famously jagged skyline is obscured by the mild, forested western slope of the range. Only the tallest Teton, the Grand, pokes over the top.

In the trailer, there are enough chairs for me, another reporter, and Juan's wife. The room is crowded. A couple leans against the wall, alternately winding their limbs around each other, kissing and stopping to listen to us. A teenage boy sits with a couple of kids in front of the television. A young man comes to the door, looks in, and leaves.

Everyone is nervous. Juan is nervous because he doesn't know us; we're only there because a local activist he trusts told him she trusted us. Still, he answers our questions as if we're the police. We're nervous because we are talking in Spanish and our tape recorder keeps going dead. If this interview doesn't work, we don't know if we'll find any more undocumented workers who will talk to us. After the raid, even legal Mexicans stayed away from work for a week or more; many families were too frightened to even go to the grocery store. But when we ask Juan if he ever considered staying in Mexico, he looks at us like we're crazy. His wife is here, and his three children.

And there's work. In Jackson's classified ads, hotels and restaurants beg for applicants. There's construction work in Driggs, which is sprouting subdivisions the way its neighbors downvalley sprout potatoes. There's plenty of work, if you're willing to do it.

After finishing the interview and telling Juan that no, we didn't know when the next raid would be, we leave. Up the street we meet a man I'll call José Umaña. He has been in Idaho for about ten years, and has a green card and a full-time job pouring concrete for a construction company in Driggs. Evenings, he cleans the local slaughterhouse. Weekends, he milks cows twice a day. With his earnings, he paid $1,000 to have his wife, Milagro, smuggled from Tijuana into California behind a refrigerator on a moving van. Last summer, he bought the trailer we're sitting in.

"As soon as I have money, I spend it," says the thirty-year-old Umaña while his two children tumble, giggling, from sofa to floor in his warm trailer and Milagro makes piles of fragrant chicken and tortillas to serve the visitors. "But we never go hungry. We have to work hard because these kids are growing. We have to grow them up."

"We make $2 to $3 a day in Mexico. There, people work for beans and tortillas. Not meat, it's too expensive. In Mexico, you have to work for two weeks just for a pair of shoes."

People like Umaña and Sanchez are an employer's dream. The ski industry — no longer able to fill its $6-an-hour jobs with white college kids — is soaking up Latin labor.

The upside of this new relationship is that families like Juan's and José's can prosper in a way they never could in Mexico. The tourists and local merchants benefit, too: Beds are made quickly and well, eggs Florentine is delivered on time. The downside is that an estimated half of the Mexican workers in Jackson and some other resort towns are working illegally, making them and their employers vulnerable to Immigration and Naturalization Service raids, which, if not effective, are at least inconvenient and embarrassing. What's more, employers can be fined thousands of dollars for employing illegal workers.

The hunger of ski towns for cheap, energetic labor and the desire of the INS to uphold immigration law make for moral ambiguities, to put it politely.

After all, the ski industry has cultivated an image that is clean, athletic and non-seedy. We are used to illegal laborers working on farms. Nor do they seem out of place in gambling towns, where the opportunism and survival instincts of the visitors in many ways mirror those of the workers. But unlike a gambling vacation, which sells hope to people who want money, a $15,000 ski vacation sells perfection to those who already have it. Perfection is elusive; its gossamer threads can be strained by one foul look from a maître d'. Just think how the web would rupture if, upon returning from a lobster dinner, the family found the maid with the nice smile up against the wall being frisked by federal agents. The ski industry's use of illegal labor breaks its own logic.

Joseph Greene has thought about this. But he thinks about a lot of things. The holder of two philosophy degrees and the author of a position paper on the inviolability of churches as sanctuaries for refugees, Greene is a regional director for the Immigration and Naturalization Service. He oversees Colorado, Utah and Wyoming from an almost comically bland office complex in Denver. . . .

As far as regional directorships in the INS go, Greene's looks fairly easy at first. Unlike his peers in California, Arizona and Texas, he doesn't have thousands of undocumented Mexicans and Central Americans playing cat-and-mouse with the Border Patrol every night. (Last May, for example, 67,282 Mexicans were arrested in the San Diego area alone.) Of the several million undocumented Latinos in the country, perhaps 38,000 are in this region. On demography maps, much of the area looks like a field of whitest snow.

But the area's number of Mexican workers, both legal and illegal, is expanding fast. The combined effects of stepped-up law enforcement along the border and the decision of California's voters in 1994[1] to make public health care and schooling off-limits to undocumented immigrants and their children have sent Mexicans pouring north and east.

Last winter the Colorado State Patrol found 1,209 undocumented Mexicans within a three-month period. "They'd pull over a U-Haul for weaving," says Greene, "and there would be thirty people in there." The number was twelve, or maybe fourteen, times what they'd found in the past.

Most were passing through to the slaughterhouses of Iowa and the fields of Missouri, but some were headed to join family and friends already holding down two or three jobs in ski country.

Workers in ski towns take the bus from the trailer courts of Glenwood Springs and El Jebel to the glittering streets of Aspen. They drive over Lizard Head Pass to work in the lavender-and-pink mining cabins-turned-restaurants of Telluride; and they make their way from rent-controlled apartment buildings to the brand new Victorian-style hotels of Park City, Utah.

Why are there so many jobs available in ski areas? Myles Rademan, who became town planner in Crested Butte, Colorado, in 1972 and now directs public affairs in Park City, Utah, explains that the industry has experienced dizzying growth. During the same period, most of the ski bums — usually white baby boomers who worked in ski towns — grew up, got serious, and moved to the city.

As for their logical successors, Generation X, they were raised in a less prosperous, more competitive world. For the most part, they'd rather study law or computer programming than hang out in Jackson or Sun Valley for a semester. Even if they wanted to, the rising cost of living in those towns has made it harder to do. In five Colorado ski counties alone, 6,000 tourism jobs reportedly went unfilled in 1994.

"Not many people want to come and work three jobs so they can ski one afternoon a week," says Rademan. "A lot of the Mexicans aren't interested in skiing, they're just making a better wage than where they're coming from. At this point most resorts couldn't live without them."

There's a joke in Park City that goes, "Where can you get Mexican food here?" Answer: "In every restaurant." Indeed, about 700 Mexicans work there. In Jackson, about 1,000 of the town's 7,000 people are Mexican, about half of them working legally. The Roaring Fork Valley below Aspen is home to an estimated 10,000 to 12,000 Latinos, about three-quarters of whom are Mexican. Most of the rest are from Central America.

Although the INS has executed raids all over the region, Jackson's may have been the biggest bust a western ski town has ever seen. Its effects reached far beyond the Mexicans who were deported. . . .

One hotelier actually called Jackson Police Chief David Cameron — whose officers teamed up with the INS, the Teton Sheriff's Department and the Wyo-

---

[1] **voters in 1994:** A reference to California's Proposition 187, passed in 1994, which barred illegal immigrants from receiving a variety of public services in the state. Proposition 187 was subsequently dismantled through a number of legal rulings that determined it to be unconstitutional.

ming Division of Criminal Investigation to pull off the raid — and asked if the police were planning to help him make the beds.

The effects were felt immediately on Jackson's streets. It took twenty minutes to get a burrito at Taco Bell. The Westerner Family Restaurant lost its entire kitchen crew and had to close down. Manager Glenn McAfee told the *Jackson Hole News*, "I'm upset; I'm pissed off. I've hired a total of six (Anglo) people, and I've had two people actually show up for work. That's why we hire Mexicans."

He bristled at the *News'* suggestion that he hire less foreign labor to avoid paperwork pitfalls.

"Excuse the term," he said, "but most Americans are lazy."

Police Chief Cameron figures this is not his problem.

He says the raid's timing, right before one of the biggest tourist weekends of the year, was not a consideration: "We were not in a position, obviously, to say (to the INS), 'That weekend doesn't work for us.'"

But he admits the aftermath of the raid has been stressful.

Furious locals reported seeing a bicyclist being thrown to the ground and police hurling employees up against walls. Both Cameron and INS Regional Director Greene apologized for the fact that fifteen hotel workers were hauled off to the county jail in a horse trailer. Letters to the editor of both local newspapers alternately reviled and supported the raid. . . .

Cameron and other small-town police chiefs aren't just dealing with Latino immigration. They're also dealing with explosive growth which brings problems, regardless of the race of the newcomers.

An infusion of Anglo workers, who would demand better housing and pay than Latinos do, would disrupt mountain towns enormously. Downvalley from Aspen in Glenwood Springs, Police Chief Terry Wilson emphasizes that the first gang in his town was formed six years ago by Anglos who moved in from Reno, Nevada. But Latinos aren't immune from violence; there have been several altercations between Hispanics and Anglos up the road in Carbondale. Last month, a seventeen-year-old Latino, who had been involved in gangs while growing up in Los Angeles, pulled a gun at a party and pointed it at an Anglo teenager's head. He has since been arrested.

"Our juvenile delinquent problems are rising out of local American-born Hispanics and Anglos," says Carbondale Police Chief Fred Williams. "The teenager who was born in Chihuahua, he's not the problem."

Williams has been with his department for twenty years. "I think it's just like twenty-five years ago it was the cowboys and the hippies, and in time we all learned to get along. Right now that's what's happening here . . . People from the city are finding valleys like this, and moving here."

You could argue that Carbondale's restive teenagers are just the latest product of a dynamic that started rolling with the Romantic poets: People like pristine mountain landscapes. As recent history in the West proves, what they like they will pay for. The rarer pristine mountain landscapes become, the more people will pay for access to them.

Over the last fifty years, richer and richer people have moved to the high mountain landscapes of the West. The people who worked in ski areas started to feel the squeeze of rising real estate prices. That squeeze turned into a pinch by the 1980s. But they good-naturedly commuted to work from outlying towns. When the outlying towns got gentrified, they drove for longer and longer distances, until their cheerfulness was expended and they quit.

Into this vacuum came the Latinos, to the horror of many of the people who had driven up the real estate prices. Finding the funky log cabins formerly rented by ski bums occupied by minor movie stars, the new workers moved into trailer courts. They shared their trailers with not only their own family but maybe one or two others. And they worked nonstop. . . .

The police — who know the deportees they're ushering south will probably rebound north as soon as humanly possible — don't share the politicians' unbridled enthusiasm for law enforcement as the solution to illegal immigration.

"From a global perspective," says Jackson Police Chief Cameron, "we don't have a border."

Says Joseph Greene, "We don't take the posture that the immigration service has the mission to arrest every single illegal alien that comes to this country. Practically, that's beyond our ability." Indeed, despite the *Sturm und Drang* surrounding the current immigration bill, the INS won't do more busts like Jackson's in the future, he says.

"We've got to try to be experimental; we've got to try temporary worker permits," he says. For nearly half a century, he explains, immigration law has assumed if a foreigner is in the country for a purpose other than being a student or a tourist, they want to stay here permanently.

"Our world is much more complex than that," he says. "This thing is absolutely huge." . . .

No one can predict how many more immigrants will reach the inland West, but one thing is clear: The world economy has sent a new wave of pioneers in this direction. And history shows that pioneers, with their fear of poverty and limitless energy, change everything.

64. Restricting Undocumented Immigration

Tensions over the presence of undocumented, or illegal, immigrants in California led to legislative action in the 1990s. This is an excerpt from the text of Proposition 187, a 1994 California ballot measure aimed at barring access to a variety of public services then available to illegal immigrants. The sweeping restrictions imposed by Proposition 187 included prohibiting illegal aliens in California from attending public elementary, secondary, or postsecondary schools. The legislation also prohibited access to public health services. A provision of the proposition insisted that public authorities notify the Immigration and Naturalization Service or other authorities of the presence of undocumented immigrants. Despite concerted opposition, Proposition 187 passed easily but was immediately challenged in federal court. Over the next several years, it was dismantled in a number of rulings that determined it to be unconstitutional, in part because individual states cannot make immigration law. What factors do you think motivated California's voters to pass this measure? How do the provisions and restrictions of Proposition 187 compare to earlier actions in the history of the American West? How do you think concerns about the economy affect concerns about immigration?

From California's Proposition 187
1994

SECTION 1. Findings and Declaration.

The People of California find and declare as follows:

That they have suffered and are suffering economic hardship caused by the presence of illegal aliens in this state.

That they have suffered and are suffering personal injury and damage caused by the criminal conduct of illegal aliens in this state.

That they have a right to the protection of their government from any person or persons entering this country unlawfully.

Therefore, the People of California declare their intention to provide for cooperation between their agencies of state and local government with the federal government, and to establish a system of required notification by and between such agencies to prevent illegal aliens in the United States from receiving benefits or public services in the State of California. . . .

SECTION 5. Exclusion of Illegal Aliens from Public Social Services. . . .

Section 10001.5 is added to the Welfare and Institutions Code, to read:

10001.5. (a) In order to carry out the intention of the People of California that only citizens of the United States and aliens lawfully admitted to the United States may receive the benefits of public social services and to ensure that all

California Secretary of State's Office, Web site text of proposed law. http://ca94.election.digital.com/e/prop/187/txt.html.

persons employed in the providing of those services shall diligently protect public funds from misuse, the provisions of this section are adopted.

(b) A person shall not receive any public social services to which he or she may be otherwise entitled until the legal status of that person has been verified as one of the following:

(1) A citizen of the United States.
(2) An alien lawfully admitted as a permanent resident.
(3) An alien lawfully admitted for a temporary period of time.

(c) If any public entity in this state to whom a person has applied for public social services determines or reasonably suspects, based upon the information provided to it, that the person is an alien in the United States in violation of federal law, the following procedures shall be followed by the public entity:

(1) The entity shall not provide the person with benefits or services.
(2) The entity shall, in writing, notify the person of his or her apparent illegal immigration status, and that the person must either obtain legal status or leave the United States.
(3) The entity shall also notify the State Director of Social Services, the Attorney General of California, and the United States Immigration and Naturalization Service of the apparent illegal status, and shall provide any additional information that may be requested by any other public entity.

SECTION 6. Exclusion of Illegal Aliens from Publicly Funded Health Care.

Chapter 1.3 (commencing with Section 130) is added to Part 1 of Division 1 of the Health and Safety Code, to read:

Chapter 1.3. Publicly Funded Health Care Services

130. (a) In order to carry out the intention of the People of California that, excepting emergency medical care as required by federal law, only citizens of the United States and aliens lawfully admitted to the United States may receive the benefits of publicly funded health care, and to ensure that all persons employed in the providing of those services shall diligently protect public funds from misuse, the provisions of this section are adopted.

(b) A person shall not receive any health care services from a publicly funded health care facility, to which he or she is otherwise entitled until the legal status of that person has been verified as one of the following:

(1) A citizen of the United States.
(2) An alien lawfully admitted as a permanent resident.
(3) An alien lawfully admitted for a temporary period of time.

(c) If any publicly funded health care facility in this state from whom a person seeks health care services, other than emergency medical care as required by federal law, determines or reasonably suspects, based upon the information provided to it, that the person is an alien in the United States in violation of federal law, the following procedures shall be followed by the facility:

(1) The facility shall not provide the person with services.
(2) The facility shall, in writing, notify the person of his or her apparent illegal immigration status, and that the person must either obtain legal status or leave the United States.
(3) The facility shall also notify the State Director of Health Services, the Attorney General of California, and the United States Immigration and Naturalization Service of the apparent illegal status, and shall provide any additional information that may be requested by any other public entity.

(d) For purposes of this section "publicly funded health care facility" shall be defined as specified in Sections 1200 and 1250 of this code as of January 1, 1993.

SECTION 7. *Exclusion of Illegal Aliens from Public Elementary and Secondary Schools.*

Section 48215 is added to the Education Code, to read:

48215. (a) No public elementary or secondary school shall admit, or permit the attendance of, any child who is not a citizen of the United States, an alien lawfully admitted as a permanent resident, or a person who is otherwise authorized under federal law to be present in the United States.

(b) Commencing January 1, 1995, each school district shall verify the legal status of each child enrolling in the school district for the first time in order to ensure the enrollment or attendance only of citizens, aliens lawfully admitted as permanent residents, or persons who are otherwise authorized to be present in the United States.

(c) By January 1, 1996, each school district shall have verified the legal status of each child already enrolled and in attendance in the school district in order to ensure the enrollment or attendance only of citizens, aliens lawfully admitted as permanent residents, or persons who are otherwise authorized under federal law to be present in the United States.

(d) By January 1, 1996, each school district shall also have verified the legal status of each parent or guardian of each child referred to in subdivisions (b) and (c), to determine whether such parent or guardian is one of the following:

(1) A citizen of the United States.
(2) An alien lawfully admitted as a permanent resident.
(3) An alien admitted lawfully for a temporary period of time.

(e) Each school district shall provide information to the State Superintendent of Public Instruction, the Attorney General of California, and the United States Immigration and Naturalization Service regarding any enrollee or pupil, or parent or guardian, attending a public elementary or secondary school in the school district determined or reasonably suspected to be in violation of federal immigration laws within forty-five days after becoming aware of an apparent violation. The notice shall also be provided to the parent or legal guardian of the enrollee or pupil, and shall state that an existing pupil may not continue to attend the school after ninety calendar days from the date of the notice, unless legal status is established.

(f) For each child who cannot establish legal status in the United States, each school district shall continue to provide education for a period of ninety days from the date of the notice. Such ninety day period shall be utilized to accomplish an orderly transition to a school in the child's country of origin. Each school district shall fully cooperate in this transition effort to ensure that the educational needs of the child are best served for that period of time. . . .

65. Support for Proposition 187

Harold Ezell served for many years as the western commissioner of the Immigration and Naturalization Service. He also coauthored California's Proposition 187, the ballot measure that sought to deny public health, education, and social service benefits to illegal immigrants. By the mid-1990s, Ezell had become a well-known spokesperson for those who believed that stringent restrictions must be placed upon illegal immigrant access to public facilities and funds across the country. In this essay, Ezell outlines his position and that of other Proposition 187 supporters. How does Ezell seek to blunt the objections of opponents of Proposition 187? How does he use history to bolster his arguments? Compare Ezell's economic arguments to the points raised in Lisa Jones's essay.

Harold Ezell
"Enough Is More than Enough"
1994

The issue of illegal immigration is color-blind; it is not a racial but a legal issue. It is an issue that taxpayers, who have seen our tax dollars squandered on programs that have nothing to do with American citizens or legal aliens, understand.

Los Angeles Times (23 October 1994): M5.

Each of us must ask ourselves: How many illegals can we educate, medicate, compensate and incarcerate before California goes bankrupt? Can we continue business as usual, wasting taxpayer dollars?

The opponents of 187 say it's flawed, poorly written, doesn't really answer the question of illegal immigration and costs too much. They agree that something must be done, but they have no solution. The Democratic Party elder statesman, former Senator Eugene McCarthy, says, "The 'save our state' initiative is a way to let the government know people aren't happy with things as they are."

Proposition 187 is not the total answer, but it is a piece of the puzzle. It will send a message that even the White House will understand. We must do something about our borders. Californians are not going to reward and underwrite those who come here illegally, whether by land, sea or air. Let the White House sue us for not paying for illegals.

The widow of the late Howard Jarvis, founder of the taxpayers' revolt in the 1970s and the father of Proposition 13,[1] told me that she spent many hours gathering signatures for Proposition 187. "If Howard was alive," Estelle Jarvis said, "he would stand shoulder to shoulder with you and see that Proposition 187 becomes a reality."

Proposition 187 is the Proposition 13 of the 1990s. Just as Proposition 13 had its impact on all state and local candidates, so will Proposition 187. Governor Pete Wilson says *yes* on 187. What does your politician say?

We have heard the opponents say that $15 billion, which the federal government pays to California annually, will be taken away if Proposition 187 becomes law. That's baloney; the chances of that happening are as good as that of the Clinton Administration balancing the budget in 1996. Does anyone really believe that the Clinton Administration would take one dime from the most populous state in the nation?

Here's the truth behind the myth of the $15 billion. The federal government pays annually $3 billion for education costs in California. These funds would not be lost. Passage of 187 will require the attorney general to go to the U.S. Supreme Court to test the Plyler vs. Doe decision of 1982. This bad decision allows any five-year-old, here legally or not, to get a free, twelve-year education plus college. We can't afford this. Proposition 187 would force the Supreme Court to revisit the issue.

In addition, $9 billion is spent annually for medical reimbursement to the state of California. California taxpayers alone are paying $400 million per year to provide medical care to approximately 317,000 illegals. The California Medical Assn. wants our dollars without accountability. They say that we cannot ask a person if they are legally in the United States, that it's against federal law. This is not true. The First District Court of Appeals in California said in August that we can ask. The court upheld the 1992 state law requiring all medical applicants to disclose their Social Security numbers.

[1] **Proposition 13:** A 1978 California referendum that cut local property taxes by more than 50 percent.

The additional $3 billion that our opponents say Uncle Sam will "take away" is for Aid to Families with Dependent Children, or welfare. Proposition 187 has nothing to do with children born here, who are citizens whether or not their parents are legal and thus entitled to the federal AFDC.

The Chicken Little opponents, who say the sky is falling if you vote *yes* on 187, are not telling the truth. California taxpayers are spending 10 percent of state general funds to underwrite illegal immigration — $3.4 billion per year. Proposition 187 would cost several million to implement, while saving billions. This is a good investment.

Our opponents ignore the Proposition 187 provisions that require law enforcement cooperation among state and local agencies and the Immigration and Naturalization Service. This initiative requires local law enforcement agencies to cooperate when they come in contact with illegals. Maybe this is why L.A. County Sheriff Sherman Block is a "No on 187" spokesperson. It's hard for me to understand why Block, whose county has the largest population of illegals in the nation and who has sworn to uphold the laws of the land, will not allow his officers to cooperate with the INS.

Another important provision of Proposition 187 is a change in the state penal code that would make it a felony, with a five-year prison term and a $75,000 fine, to manufacture, sell or distribute phony documents. A $25,000 fine and five-year prison term would apply if an individual uses a phony document to get a benefit. This would be a major help in the enforcement of employer sanctions.

Proposition 187 is not enough, but it tells the federal government that California has had enough and we're not going to take it any more.

66. A POLITICAL EVOLUTION

Proposition 187 had strong support from California's governor, Pete Wilson. This cartoon, which first appeared in the San Jose Mercury News, *traces the governor's stance as a case study of reverse evolution. From earlier statements recognizing the economic vitality of undocumented workers, Wilson moved toward a harsher position on the issue. By the time Proposition 187 came before the state's voters in 1994, Wilson had staked out an uncompromising position: those who immigrated to the state without proper documentation must not be granted access to public services. How would you compare this view of Wilson's position with the arguments put forward by Harold Ezell? What significance does the cartoonist place on Wilson's use of the term "illegal immigrants"?*

SCOTT WILLIS
"The Evolution of Pete Wilson"
1994

67. THE ENGLISH-ONLY BANDWAGON

On the heels of California's Proposition 187, Proposition 227, a ballot measure, called for a dramatic pull back in the state's commitment to bilingual education. To many supporters of the English for the Children measure, the continued use of their own languages by immigrants was an affront to American customs. Others believed that the state would be doing immigrants a favor by dismantling bilingual programs in the schools: forced by circumstance to learn English quickly, immigrant children would find their way into the economic mainstream more easily. Oppo-

nents believed the measure a front for anti-immigrant ideas and argued that at-tempting to legislate language use was a bad precedent. This selection from a news-paper column discusses some of the complexities of the ballot measure (which won easily), including support of the measure by Latinos who wished that their children would grow up proficient in English. How would you compare the arguments made in favor of Proposition 227 and those made in favor of Proposition 187? What ar-guments might someone make who was in favor of one but not the other? How do attitudes about education reflect beliefs about immigration and immigrants?

JOANNE JACOBS
"Latino Vote Is Key to Depth of Prop. 227's Victory"
1998

Vote *si* on Proposition 227, say the Mexican-American principal and the Mexican immigrant mother. Vote for *"Ingles para los Niños."* Most of the media dollars for Ron Unz's "English for the Children" initiative are paying for Spanish-language radio ads, which went on the air in Southern California this week. To end bilingual education, Unz is running "the most bilingual campaign" ever, he says, and perhaps the first in which the contents of the Spanish ads are the same as the English ads.

A software millionaire, Unz has spent $640,000 of his own money on the Proposition 227 campaign, more than half the total budget.

Get past the irony, and his logic becomes clear. Proposition 227 is favored by two out of three likely voters in recent polls. Almost certainly, it's going to win. But the way it wins will determine whether this is seen as a vote about educating immigrant children or about bashing immigrants. Unz needs to win with substan-tial Latino support.

In the Field Poll, conducted the last week in April, 73 percent of whites, 74 percent of Asians, 66 percent of blacks and 58 percent of Latinos said they planned to vote "yes." Only 1 percent of Latinos were undecided.

But a poll by the Public Policy Institute of California, done the first week in May, showed Latino voters split 48–48 on Proposition 227, down ten points from PPIC's April survey.

Proposition 227 calls for teaching students English by teaching them "over-whelmingly" in English. They'd start in a special class for students with limited English skills, moving to a mainstream class as soon as they picked up a "working knowledge" of English.

Bilingual education programs, which teach primarily in students' first lan-guage while they're learning English, would survive only if parents of twenty stu-dents in the same grade requested and qualified for a "special needs" waiver. It's likely the initiative will end most bilingual programs statewide.

San Jose Mercury News (13 May 1998).

Without Latino support, a victory for "English for the Children" could be a victory for divisiveness and distrust, nativism and nastiness. The context will be Proposition 187, which tried to bar illegal immigrants' children from public school, and Proposition 209, which ended race-based preferences, leading to a sharp drop in Latino and black admissions at Berkeley and UCLA.

To a remarkable extent, the debate so far has centered mostly on how to teach English, not on all the entangling issues of culture and ethnicity. It's been the education establishment, the ethnic establishment and the political establishment against Ron Unz and two-thirds of the multiethnic electorate.

The "no" campaign has been feeble. Latino politicians haven't been vocal, cowed by early poll numbers that showed overwhelming Latino support for 227. The teachers' unions have been distracted by fighting the anti-union Proposition 226. Only bilingual educators have defended their program with any energy.

On the "yes" side, the anti-immigration groups have stayed out. Anti-immigration activists hate Unz almost as much as they hate bilingual education because of his vocal opposition to Proposition 187. He ensured their opposition to Proposition 227 by including $50 million a year from the General Fund to teach English to adult immigrants who promise to tutor students who aren't fluent in English. (The tutoring pledge keeps the adult English classes within the single-subject rule for initiatives.)

It worked: The immigrant-bashers bashed 227.

It also created a line of attack for no-on-227 ads, which suggest teaching English to immigrants is a "new spending program" that will take money away from the schools and won't help kids learn English.

It's interesting to note that the "no" ads in Spanish don't hit adult English classes; the focus is on letting "parents and teachers decide what is best for us."

Raising the money issue could backfire. Voters think they'll save a bundle by not teaching children in Spanish — more than the cost of teaching English to their parents.

(The Legislative Analyst estimates total state education spending wouldn't change.)

Targeting English classes for adults also gives Unz another chance to stress that immigrants want to learn English, and want their children to learn English. They want to be able to help with homework and talk to the teacher. But those bilingual education zealots won't let them.

There's no doubt many "yes" votes for 227 will be motivated, at least in part, by fear that immigrants aren't assimilating, anger at multiculturalist claims and resentment because Grandpa never got Italian classes and Grandma never got taught in Slovak. Many Californians worry that our society is fracturing because we can't all talk to each other in the same language.

But I think most voters — whatever their family language or ethnicity — really do want the children of Mexican immigrant families to succeed in our schools and in our society. If nothing else, Californians want them to grow up to pay taxes and pay into the Social Security fund. They'll need to be proficient in English. The only question is how?

Foreign-born or native-born, Latino or non-Latino, we are not divided in our goals for our children. All our children. Let's hang on to that thought in the final weeks of the election season.

Suggestions for Further Reading

Daniels, Roger. *Asian America: Chinese and Japanese in the United States Since 1850.* Seattle: University of Washington Press, 1992.

Daniels, Roger. *Coming to America: A History of Immigration and Ethnicity in American Life.* New York: HarperPerennial, 1991.

Eig, Larry M. *California's Proposition 187: A Brief Overview.* Washington, D.C.: Congressional Research Service, 1995.

Gutierrez, David. *Walls and Mirrors: Mexican Americans, Mexican Immigrants, and the Politics of Ethnicity.* Berkeley: University of California Press, 1995.

Rodriguez, Richard. *Days of Obligation: An Argument with My Mexican Father.* New York: Viking, 1992.

Suro, Roberto. *Strangers among Us: Latino Lives in a Changing America.* New York: Vintage Books, 1999.

Takaki, Ronald. *Strangers at the Gates Again: Asian American Immigration after 1965.* New York: Chelsea House, 1995.

[43] Miné Okubo, excerpt from *Citizen 13660*, by Miné Okubo. Copyright © 1946 by Miné Okubo. Reprinted by permission of the author.

[47] "What It's Like to Live in Earth's Most A-Bombed Area," from *U.S. News & World Report*, 28 June 1957, pp. 79–82. Copyright © 1957 U.S. News & World Report. Reprinted by permission. All rights reserved.

[54] Ruben Salazar, "Chicanos vs. Traditionalists," from the *Los Angeles Times*, 6 March 1970. Reprinted by permission of The Los Angeles Times.

[55] Excerpt from the *Denver Stop the War Committee Newsletter* #13, 23 July 1966, P. O. Box 86, Denver, Colorado 80201. Reprinted by permission of the Wisconsin State Historical Society.

[56] Joe McDonald, "I-Feel-Like-I'm-Fixin'-to-Die Rag" (song). © 1965, renewed 1993 Alkatraz Corner Music Company. Words and music by Joe McDonald. Reprinted by permission.

[57] Merle Haggard, "Okie from Muskogee" (song). Courtesy of Sony/ATV Music Publishing.

[59] Claire Boisseau and Jim Harding, "Curriculum for Cubberley High School," from *The Environmental Handbook*, ed. Garrett De Bell. Copyright © 1970 by Garrett De Bell. Reprinted by permission of Ballantine Books, a Division of Random House, Inc.

[60] Edward Abbey, excerpt from *The Monkey Wrench Gang* by Edward Abbey. Copyright © 1975 by Edward Abbey. Reprinted by permission of HarperCollins Publishers.

[61] François Leydet, "Coal vs. Parklands, 1980," from *National Geographic*, vol. 158, pp. 779–803. Reprinted by permission of National Geographic Society.

[62] Bill Hornby, "Jim Watt's Western Exposure," from the *Denver Post*, 16 September 1981. Reprinted by permission of the publisher.

[63] Lisa Jones, "El Nuevo West," excerpted from an article in *High Country News*, 23 December 1996, pp. 1, 6, 8–11, by Lisa Jones. Reprinted by permission of High Country News, Paonia, Colorado (www.hcn.org.).

[65] Harold Ezell, "Enough Is More than Enough," from the *Los Angeles Times*, 23 October 1994, M5. © 1994 The Los Angeles Times. Reprinted by permission.

[66] Scott Willis, "The Evolution of Pete Wilson" (cartoon) from the *San Jose Mercury News*, 1994. © 1994 by Scott Willis. Reprinted by permission.

[67] Joanne Jacobs, "Latino Vote Is Key to Depth of Prop. 227's Victory," from the *San Jose Mercury News*, 13 May 1998. Reprinted by permission.